BENEATH THE CROSS

BENEATH THE CROSS

Catholics and Huguenots in
Sixteenth-Century Paris

BARBARA B. DIEFENDORF

New York   Oxford
OXFORD UNIVERSITY PRESS
1991

Oxford University Press

Oxford   New York   Toronto
Delhi   Bombay   Calcutta   Madras   Karachi
Petaling Jaya   Singapore   Hong Kong   Tokyo
Nairobi   Dar es Salaam   Cape Town
Melbourne   Auckland

and associated companies in
Berlin   Ibadan

Library of Congress Cataloging-in-Publication Data
Diefendorf, Barbara B., 1946–
Beneath the cross : Catholics and Huguenots in sixteenth-century
Paris / Barbara B. Diefendorf.
p.   cm.   Includes bibliographical references and index.
ISBN 0-19-506554-9.
ISBN 0-19-507013-5 (pbk.)
1. Paris (France)—History—16th century.
2. France—History—Wars of the Huguenots, 1562–1598.
3. Paris (France)—Church history—16th century.
4. Fanaticism.   5. Religious tolerance—France—Paris—History—16th century.
I. Title. DC719.D54   1991
944′.361029—dc2
90-20737
Chapters 3, 4, and 5 contain some material previously published
in ''Prologue to a Massacre: Popular Unrest in Paris, 1557–1572,''
American Historical Review 90 (1985): 1067–91. Parts of Chapter 9 were published
in ''Simon Vigor: A Radical Preacher in Sixteenth-Century Paris,''
Sixteenth Century Journal 18 (1987): 399–410. Permission by the editors
of these journals to reproduce that material here
is gratefully acknowledged.

5   7   9   8   6   4

Printed in the United States of America
on acid-free paper

Acknowledgments

It is a pleasure to acknowledge the assistance and encouragement that I have received in writing this book. I am grateful to Denis Richet for the generous spirit with which he welcomed me to the small circle of historians of sixteenth-century Paris and for the many ways in which he encouraged this project over the years. I deeply regret his untimely death. Denis Crouzet and Robert Descimon deserve special mention and thanks both for specific acts of assistance—shared references and critical comments—and for mind-enlarging debates about how to interpet the events in which we share a common interest. Alfred Soman generously shared his unparalleled knowledge of the criminal records of the Parlement of Paris. He offered help with the difficult hand of the *plumitifs* and pointed out a cache of misplaced documents that I would otherwise never have found. On this side of the Atlantic, I would like to thank Katherine Stern Brennan and Mark Edwards for reading and commenting on large parts of the manuscript and Alasdair Drysdale for preparing the maps and charts in Chapter 7. I would also like to thank Nancy Roelker for her unflagging interest and encouragement. I am, as ever, grateful to Natalie Davis, who first opened my eyes to the questions and helped me learn how to go about answering them.

The Marion and Jasper Whiting Foundation, the National Endowment for the Humanities, the Boston University Humanities Foundation, and the American Council of Learned Societies all supported this project through fellowships and grants. They freed up enough time for research and writing to make its completion possible.

At Oxford University Press, Nancy Lane showed an encouraging interest in the project almost from its inception. Paul Schlotthauer guided the manuscript through to publication and influenced its contents as well as its form.

Finally, I would like to thank Jeffry Diefendorf, my first and most exacting reader, in-house computer consultant, and irreplaceable companion.

Boston   B. B. D.
June 1991

Contents

Illustrations

Author's Note

Biblical citations (including the numbering of psalms) are given according to the King James version. All other translations are my own except where noted. I have retained original spellings except for adding an occasional accent or punctuation mark for purposes of clarity and ease of reading. Titles of government offices and bureaus are italicized the first time they appear in the text but not thereafter. In the text, dates have been converted from the old style, with the year beginning at Easter, to the new. In the notes and bibliography, documents dated in the old style are noted with a slash between the original year and the date as we would now calculate it. I have included the name of the publisher for sixteenth-century editions because it is a useful way of showing how much of the polemical literature issued from just a few select presses.

BENEATH THE CROSS

Introduction

> There is nothing so much to fear in a Republic as civil war, nor among civil
> wars, as that which is fought in the name of Religion.
>
> Etienne Pasquier (1562)

The questions that shape this study of the religious conflicts in Paris have their origins in my book on the families of the Paris city councilors in the sixteenth century.[1] Like much of the social history that was written at the time (the late 1970s), that work, in essence a study of the strategies through which the Parisian notability transformed itself into the robe nobility of the old regime, tended to detach itself from the political events of the period in order to concentrate on underlying social processes. Indeed, I deliberately stopped short of the crisis of the arch-Catholic League that divided Paris against itself in the last two decades of the sixteenth century, so as to study the "politics" of social promotion without the added complications of religious factionalism. I did not ignore the religious wars entirely, but I believed that, because Paris was so firmly Catholic a city, the religious conflicts had relatively little effect on the kind of social transformations that I was studying.

As I was finishing the book, I became more and more conscious of the extent of my naiveté. In the first place, I realized that my "solidly Catholic" elite was in fact sorely tainted by heresy. Without even seriously looking for religious dissent, I had compiled a list that showed that nineteen of the ninety city councilors who formed the basis of my study had wives, sons, brothers, or other close relatives who had gone over to the Protestant side.[2] I later found another eleven men who had Protestant relatives, for a total of thirty out of ninety—fully one-third of my group. And so I began to wonder about the real role of Protestantism in this bastion of the Catholic faith. I began to ponder individual cases. Why had Marie Morin, the daughter of a Châtelet officer famous for his persecution of the heretics, converted to the Protestant faith? And what did the religious divisions mean for city councilor Pierre Croquet, who saw his Protestant daughter hanged in effigy and his brother hanged for real on the square in front of the city hall in which he served for twenty years? As time went on, the questions became larger. What part did the notables play in the violence that repeatedly broke out in their city? In particular, what was their role in the infamous events of Saint Bartholomew's Day, 24 August 1572, when an uncontrollable wave of murder left perhaps two thousand Protestants dead in the streets of Paris?

3

Traditional historiography attributes to Paris's municipal officers a sinister role in the massacre of Saint Bartholomew's Day. According to most accounts, King Charles IX, pushed by his mother, Catherine de Medici, and by his arch-Catholic advisers, decided sometime in the afternoon or evening of 23 August to rid himself once and for all of the Huguenot faction that plagued his kingdom by murdering the Protestant leaders, conveniently gathered in Paris for the marriage of the Protestant prince Henri de Navarre to the king's sister, Marguerite de Valois. Someone had already taken a potshot at the Huguenot commander, Gaspard de Coligny, on 22 August, and the anger in the Protestant camp over this outrage meant that war was almost certain to break out once again, for the fourth time in a decade. In order to plan his coup against the Huguenots, Charles IX held a meeting of his closest advisers in the Louvre on the night of 23 August and summoned to his presence two representatives from the city hall. We do not know just what orders he gave these men, except that he commanded them to call out the bourgeois militia. Most historians have assumed that he also gave orders for the militia to take part in the massacre that followed. Contemporary accounts—both by Protestants and by moderate Catholics—describe the city's representatives as coming back to the city hall and delivering a rousing speech to the assembled militiamen. The city's leaders told their men that "it is the king's will that you take up arms to kill the rebels," and not to spare one of them. They added that the signal to begin would be the ringing of the tocsin in the clock tower of the Palais de Justice. According to these same accounts, one of the city's representatives, Claude Marcel, was given additional orders to assemble troops and lead them against the Huguenot nobles who were quartered on the Left Bank, in the faubourg Saint-Germain.[3]

Now, I knew Claude Marcel well; both he and Jean Le Charron, the city's other representative and current *prévôt des marchands*, or mayor, were among the city councilors whose careers and families I had studied. I knew Marcel to have been an ambitious man, a jeweler who rose through the patronage of Catherine de Medici to hold some of the highest financial offices of the crown, and I knew him to have been militantly Catholic. A little ditty had circulated earlier in the religious conflicts that had Marcel, speaking in the name of the city's richest merchants, threatening to pack up and leave if the king did not take steps to drive the heretics out.[4] But there is quite a distance between packing up and leaving and murder, and I had a hard time imagining Marcel having a hand in the killing of women and children or even ordering others to take part in wholesale slaughter. This was an instinctive reaction and not a reasoned judgment, but it made me wonder what my city officers had in fact done on the night of 24 August 1572 and in the days that followed. I remembered reading in the memoirs of Jacques-Auguste de Thou, the son of a city councilor and a moderate Catholic, how he had spent most of the week following Saint Bartholomew's Day shut up in his house, afraid to go out because he was so sickened by his first sight of blood, and I wondered how many of my good bourgeois had likewise spent the week hiding under their beds instead of either taking part in the massacre or helping to restore order in the city.[5]

Neither traditional narrative sources nor more recent historical writings on Saint Bartholomew's Day offered much help in answering these questions. For four hundred years the principal preoccupation of historians writing about Saint Bartholomew's Day has been to determine the respective roles played in these events by the king, the queen mother, and arch-Catholic leaders like the duc de Guise. They have minutely dissected the question of premeditation and discussed at length the relation between the initial attempt on Coligny's life and the orders given for the massacre itself. Some have gone on to ask whether the aim of those responsible was to annihilate all the Huguenots or just to eliminate their leaders, but even those who have concluded that it was in fact just the leadership that was the object of the coup have stopped short of analyzing the mechanisms by which the limited coup became a general massacre.

Janine Garrisson summed up well the reasons for this general avoidance of the popular massacre when she pointed out that until recently most histories of the Wars of Religion have been written in confessional terms, and the popular violence was embarrassing to both sides. The Catholics did not like to admit that Catholic preachers were calling for the extermination of the heretics, and the Protestants preferred for political reasons to show the king, and not the people, as their enemy. For different reasons, Catholic and Protestant historians preferred to "personalize" the crime.[6] But even historians who did not bring a confessional bias to their work have proved themselves uncomfortable with the elements of popular fanaticism and religious hatred in these events, and they have preferred to turn away from the unseemly and brutish elements of popular participation in the murders to focus instead on their more respectable "political" aspects. In doing so, they have reinforced a long historiographical tradition that has tended to see the Wars of Religion—in spite of their name—as having been shaped more by political than by religious motivations.

Even as I began this book, some important attempts had been made to redress this balance. Natalie Zemon Davis's pioneering article, "The Rites of Violence," first published in 1973, and Denis Richet's article on the socio-cultural aspects of the religious conflicts in Paris, published in 1977, in particular offered stimulating new hypotheses about popular and bourgeois involvement in the religious crisis.[7] Philip Benedict's *Rouen during the Wars of Religion*, which appeared in 1980, just as I was beginning to conceptualize this project, presented an admirable model of the integration of political and religious factors in an urban history of the civil wars.[8] There was also a small but growing literature on popular piety, from which each of the works cited above had profited to a greater or lesser degree, but whose potential for contributing to our understanding of the religious conflicts in France had in general been little exploited. In short, the time seemed ripe for a systematic reexamination of the religious quarrels in the key city of Paris during the period prior to Saint Bartholomew's Day, and that is what I set out to do.

In the ten years that it has taken me to write this book, there has been considerable change and growth in the historical literature that deals with this period. If the most recent book by Janine Garrisson and the articles published by Jean-Louis Bourgeon show that interest in the political aspects of Saint Bartholomew's Day is still strong,[9] Denis Crouzet's new book, *Les guerriers de Dieu*, threatens to overturn the traditional understanding of the religious wars.[10] Interpreting the period in terms of an elemental clash between two conflicting faiths whose opposition expressed itself through distinct patterns of violence, each derived from the particular relationship its believers posited between themselves and God, Crouzet has posed a radical challenge to any essentially political interpretation of this period. He has overturned the usual construction of Saint Bartholomew's Day by locating its causes in two sorts of violence, each fundamentally religious: The "royal violence" of the king was motivated by the need to protect the sacrality of the crown from the threat posed by the revolutionary potential of Calvinism, while the popular violence, ultimately a kind of "violence in God," proceeded from the anguished attempt of Parisian Catholics to find union with God by purging their city of the heretics who polluted it.

Crouzet's radical thesis will inevitably cause controversy as historians try to decide just how—or if—it can be reconciled with the more familiar interpretations of the religious wars. Must we go from an overly political interpretation of the period to one that seems to offer very little room for politics, at least as traditionally viewed? I hope that when the dust settles my own work will help demonstrate that there is a middle ground. My interpretation of the religious conflicts has much in common with Crouzet's especially where the essential motives for Catholic violence are concerned, but also more generally in the importance that I attribute to religious factors in explaining the course of events. My work is certainly closer to traditional history in the causative role that it attributes to nonreligious or political factors in explaining these same events—from my perspective, at least, religious and secular motivations were inseparable—although it is far from traditional in the way it evaluates these factors and in the weight it attaches to popular pressures as opposed to the high politics of king and court.

Indeed, in the end my book has a double purpose, which is both to reexamine the religious conflicts in Paris and to reevaluate the role that the Parisian conflicts played in the larger course of the religious wars. I will argue that Paris is important in the wars not only because of its size and economic position but also because of the political leverage that it wielded. When we look closely at the city's role in the wars, we can see that the crown and high noblemen, so often depicted as independent actors in the conflicts, were in fact often constrained in their actions by the force of popular opinion in the capital. This opinion could be expressed as riot and sedition, but it could also be expressed more subtly through the financial pressures that the city's bourgeois leaders were able to exert upon the crown. Long before the rebellion of the League, the king and the queen mother were forced by their "loyal subjects," the citizens of their capital city, into paths they would in all probability not otherwise have taken.

The time frame chosen for this study deserves a few words of explanation. I have deliberately broken with historical tradition that tends to present the events of Saint Bartholomew's Day either in splendid isolation or in the context of the half-century sweep of the civil wars. The first of the standard chronologies is of no use to me because it almost inevitably throws the spotlight onto the short-term causes of the massacre—in other words, back onto the midnight meeting in the Louvre. Besides, it is not the massacre itself that interests me so much as the development of the situation that allowed the massacre to take place. Indeed, the chapter I devote to the events of Saint Bartholomew's Day is one of the shortest in the book. I rejected the second of the traditional chronologies because it seemed to contain an almost inescapable narrative logic by which the first half of the wars, the period that climaxes with Saint Bartholomew's Day, is made to appear as a kind of prelude to the crisis of state that erupts with the League and concludes with Henri IV and the eventual triumph of monarchical absolutism. In other words, it presupposes that the true significance of these events lies in their ultimate political resolution and in the rise of the absolute state. However important these later developments were, they were not what interested me here, and I accordingly chose instead to focus my attention on the earlier part of the conflicts, on the period between 1557, when the first large-scale incidents of religious violence took place in Paris, and 1572, when the massacre of Saint Bartholomew's Day took place.

This period has its own internal logic, as I hope the narrative chapters of the book will make clear. It is, moreover, a particularly important period in the evolution of the religious conflicts and contains the seeds of much that was later to come. We can trace in it a hardening of attitudes and a corresponding reduction in freedom to maneuver for all the parties involved, until, in the shock and horror that followed the massacre, this freedom ceased for a time to exist at all. We can see in these events not only the radicalization of Protestant opinion that led to the renewal of war in the aftermath of Saint Bartholomew's Day but also the radicalization of Catholic opinion that was later to spawn the revolt of the League. At the same time, we can see in these events the seeds of a "politique," or pragmatic, resolution to the conflicts in the realization on the part of at least some Parisian magistrates that a basis for compromise had to be found in order to prevent anarchy and the complete destruction of the social order. It many respects, the paths that led to the final climax of the wars were already set out in 1572.

Because I tried to approach the problem of the religious conflicts from a variety of perspectives, some of the chapters that follow adopt a narrative mode of presentation and others are analytical in character. I begin by describing the socioeconomic situation of the city and its political institutions at mid-century. The fundamental question here is to ask what preexisting social, economic, or political tensions might have contributed to the conflicts as they evolved into open warfare in 1562. Chapter 2 examines the character of Parisian Catholicism as it was practiced at mid-century and underscores two aspects of Catholic piety that were to prove particularly important in shaping popular reaction to the religious divisions. The first is the collective nature of this piety, the belief that society was "one bread and one body"—with all the eucharistic symbolism this phase implies. The second is the interpenetration of Parisian Catholicism with civic and monarchial themes, so that all three identities appeared inextricably intertwined. Chapters 3 through 6 adopt a narrative mode in order to trace a deepening cycle of religious hatred from the first anti-Protestant riots in 1557 up through the massacre of Saint Bartholomew's Day. They argue that the building tensions were such that, by 1572, the slightest spark could prove explosive. It is only in this longer perspective that we can truly understand what occurred on 24 August and in the week that followed.

Chapters 7 and 8 present an analysis of the Protestant subcommunity and the character of the Huguenots' faith. They try to answer a question that, bluntly put, is, "Why would anyone be so foolhardy as to choose to be a Protestant in such a fanatically Catholic city as Paris?" Chapter 9 turns back to the Catholics with an examination of the message from the radical Catholic pulpit. The potential for disaster is evident when we realize that, while Parisian Huguenots were being taught to suffer persecution as proof of their faith, Parisian Catholics were being urged to be avengers in the name of an angry God.

Not all Parisian Catholics, however, responded to the extremists' call. Chapter 10 explores the roots of a moderate reaction among Catholics disturbed by the social disorders occasioned by the wars and fearful of the anarchy that seemed to threaten. The growing division between the radicals in the bourgeois militia and the magistrates responsible for public order in the city serves as the vehicle for this exploration. It reveals incipient splits within the Catholic community and a burden of anguish over the meaning and consequences of the wars.

This book is a historical monograph, closely bound by its chosen limits of time and place. It is nevertheless true that, while writing it, I could not help but be struck by parallels between certain recent displays of popular religious fervor and some of the events that I describe here. The inflammatory rhetoric of Hindu fundamentalists fighting to recover a temple site now occupied by a mosque, the notion of blasphemy encapsulated in the death sentence pronounced against author Salman Rushdie, and the hysterical pitch of the mourning crowds that tore at the shroud of Iran's Ayatollah Khomeni recalled in disturbing ways the rhetoric and logic of my sixteenth-century preachers and the emotional outbursts that they encouraged from their listeners. The use of religion to serve political ends—and vice versa— is by no means a purely historical phenomenon. This book contains neither references to current events nor moralistic condemnations of religious fanaticism. I would nevertheless hope that, somewhere beyond the specific circumstances and events described here, it speaks to the more universal problems that occur when competing faiths stake exclusive claims to absolute truth.

1

The City and Its People

Visitors to Paris were inevitably struck by its size, its animation, and the seemingly endless diversity of its vast population. A young Polish traveler in 1543 thought that the houses of Paris formed not a city but a world and that one might find here all the varieties of humankind.[1] Three years later the more sophisticated Venetian ambassador wrote of the city that it was the "heart of Christendom."[2] These judgments were echoed by a Swiss student in 1599 when he pronounced the French capital "a world unto itself" and "the first city of Europe and Christianity."[3] If we are to understand the effects of the religious conflicts on Paris and the role that the city played in these conflicts, it is necessary first to learn more about the capital and its residents on the eve of the religious wars. To this end, let us explore Paris as it would have appeared to its sixteenth-century visitors.

A few words first about population. The impression Paris made on visitors was such that they tended to give very large estimates of its size. The Venetian ambassador Cavalli estimated the city at 500,000 residents in 1546; his successor, Suriano, ventured the guess of 400,000 to 500,000 for 1561.[4] These evaluations were revised downward to 300,000 to 400,000 by Suriano's successor, Corero, in 1569, after the first round of civil wars, but another Italian, visiting Paris in 1596, reported that, although the city at that time had only 350,000 inhabitants, it had had 600,000 before the wars.[5] Historians have generally dismissed these figures as exaggerated, but they have had difficulty agreeing on just how large the French capital was. In my opinion, the best calculations are those of Jean Jacquart, who, working from the city's annual grain consumption, has estimated that its population reached a maximum of 300,000 in 1565.[6] I would agree with Jean-Pierre Babelon in placing the high point somewhat earlier—before the beginning of the religious wars—but Babelon's recently published estimates of more than 350,000 residents in 1555 and again in 1588 appear to be too high.[7] Somewhat more conservatively, we can surmise that the city grew from about 150,000 to 200,000 persons in the early sixteenth century to a maximum of 250,000 to 300,000 at mid-century. Though its numbers declined with the first wave of religious wars, it regained much of its lost population during the 1580s, only to be hit again by the wars of the League, which reduced it to 200,000 or less by 1591, from which point a new recovery was begun.[8] Even these relatively conservative estimates show the population of Paris to have been tremendously volatile, with periods of rapid growth alternat-

Figure 1–1. Map of Paris known as the "Tapisserie" (approximately 1540). (Phot. Bibl. nat. Paris.)

ing with shocks of sudden loss. Our understanding of the city must take into account the strains produced by these sharp fluctuations in size.

A Traveler's View

The traveler's first sight of Paris was of walls and towers. The part of the city that lay on the Left Bank of the Seine was still enclosed by the twelfth-century wall of Philip Augustus; the Right Bank, which had long since outgrown this old barrier, was rimmed by a wall built in the fourteenth century. These walls did not by the mid-sixteenth century serve very well as defensive fortifications, a fact that caused the Parisians much worry when their security was threatened but one that troubled them little in times of peace.[9] Suburbs sprawled out along the roads that led from the city gates, but the area encircled by the walls was not enormous; one could walk around it in three hours or less.[10] Some open spaces remained within the walls, particularly in the northeast, between the Temple and the Bastille, but most of the city was densely built, with high, narrow houses of three, four, or more stories that took full advantage of the limited space. The young Pole Eustache Knobelsdorf found the tall, narrow buildings with their small entrance ways well adapted to the needs of this crowded city, although an Italian visitor, Francesco Ierni, noted that Parisian dwellings were not nearly as handsome as the urban residences of his own country. He admired their dark slate roofs and glass window-panes but deplored the lack of elegance betrayed by their narrow frontages, exposed half-timbers, and meager proportions.[11] On the other hand, by Ierni's standards, Parisian streets were "handsome, broad, and long," and he commented favorably on the regular, square stones with which they were paved.[12]

Paris was traditionally divided into four parts: the Cité, the Ville, the Université (or Latin Quarter), and the faubourgs—divisions that can serve to guide us in our tour. The oldest part lay on the Ile de la Cité, the site of Notre-Dame cathedral, whose square towers dominated the eastern end of the island as they do today. The Cité was also the heart of the judicial apparatus of state, located in the Palais de Justice at its western extremity. Fifteen parish churches, most of them old and tiny, crowded together on the island, remnants of a smaller scale of urban experience.[13] An important part of the Cité's population—as much as 20 percent—consisted of clerics attached to its parishes and two small priories, the cathedral, and the Hôtel-Dieu, the city's most important charity hospital, which was run by religious even though it was administered after 1505 by lay governors.[14] The Cité was, however, by no means entirely given over to religious and judicial functions. Its streets and bridges teemed with secular—even profane—life; its churches served more than religious purposes. The Swiss student Thomas Platter recorded that pimps and prostitutes commonly solicited customers in the choir of Notre-Dame and that foundlings were regularly left near certain pillars of the cathedral. There was even a special crib in the cathedral where these abandoned infants might be placed on display on warm days, in the hope of inspiring charitable acts. For the most part, however, the mewling infants went unnoticed amid the constant mill of people who came to mass, stopped to gossip, or simply passed through as they went about their business.[15]

In a similar fashion, the Palais de Justice served more than a judicial role. The great hall of the Palais served as a fashionable marketplace, where shops and stalls—224 of them, according to Ierni—sold fine linens, silks, and velvets, precious stones, hats, and other accessories.[16] Sellers of books and paintings catered as well to a luxury trade. Some eighty booksellers had stalls in the Palais.[17] Alongside the boutiques were spacious galleries, where men in the long robes of the legal profession strolled in conversation, paper-stuffed portfolios tucked under their arms. From the galleries one could see the courtyard of the Conciergerie, where men and women imprisoned for nonviolent crimes, such as failure to pay their debts, were allowed to take their exercise during the during the day.[18]

Householders in nearby streets exacted a high price for rooms to let because of their convenience to the Palais. A great many strangers who came to pursue lawsuits sought lodgings in the Cité, which abounded with taverns, inns, and rotisseries to serve this ready clientele.[19] Two bridges joined the island to the university quarter on the Left Bank of the Seine, and three linked it to the mercantile heart of the Right Bank. Because all the bridges were covered with houses, visitors often remarked that one could scarcely tell where the streets ended and the bridges began.[20]

The most impressive bridge was the pont Notre-Dame. Rebuilt on five stone pilings after the old wooden bridge collapsed in 1499, the pont Notre-Dame was lined with sixty-eight narrow but handsome houses, thirty-four on each side. Identical and "absolutely symmetrical," as Thomas Platter wonderingly observed, the houses on the pont Notre-Dame were, nearly a century in advance of the place

Dauphine and the place Royale (now the place des Vosges), the earliest example of the deliberate use of a uniform facade in French urban design.[21] Connecting an important mercantile street of the Right Bank, the rue Saint-Martin, with the Cité, the pont Notre-Dame became a favored location for sellers of hat plumes, decorative trims, and other masculine furnishings and feminine accessories.[22] Some jewelers had their shops on the pont Notre-Dame too, but the traditional location for jewelers was along the crowded pont au Change, which connected the rue Saint-Denis, another principal Right Bank thoroughfare, to the Cité. Not as attractive as the pont Notre-Dame, the wooden pont au Change, was lined with houses described as "low and in need of rebuilding every fifty years." The wares in the shops that lined the bridge, however, were dazzling. "One can scarcely imagine," wrote Platter, "the fortune represented by the articles sold here."[23] Adjoining the pont au Change, but decrepit and in ill repair, was the pont aux Meuniers, which finally collapsed in 1596. Named for the mills that still lined it, the pont aux Meuniers was characterized by a young Dutchman who visited Paris in 1585 as "covered and very dark." It was as a consequence "the refuge for merchants who sell false stones of glass, and earrings, necklaces, and chains of gold-plated copper."[24]

The Petit Pont and the pont Saint-Michel, the two bridges that joined the Cité to the university quarter, were also in ruinous condition until they were rebuilt at mid-century.[25] Although popular locations for merchants in the book trade, neither bridge could rival the pont au Change or the pont Notre-Dame for traffic in luxury items.[26] Until the construction of the Pont Neuf, begun in 1578 but not completed until the reign of Henri IV, no bridge linked the western portions of the Right and Left Banks. Persons wishing to go from the faubourg Saint-Germain to the Louvre had to cross the river by ferry.

The largest part of the city, the area referred to simply as "la Ville," lay on the right bank of the Seine. Within this area, there was extreme diversity. Visitors commented on the handsome townhouses, clearly belonging to gentlemen, in the neighborhood just east of the rue du Temple, in the quarter now known as the Marais.[27] The Marais was particularly fashionable during the reign of Henri II, who made the hôtel des Tournelles, located in this quarter, his favorite Paris residence. When Henri died as a result of injuries suffered during a tournament outside the Tournelles, Catherine de Medici conceived an aversion to this location and moved her family to the Louvre, on the western edge of Paris. The neighborhood that had grown up between the old Temple and the Tournelles retained much of its popularity with both aristocrats and the bourgeois elite, but many courtiers chose to relocate to the vicinity of the Louvre.

What impressed travelers most on the Right Bank, however, was the mercantile heart of the city, which began where the ponts au Change and Notre-Dame touched the river bank and which spread out, fan-shaped, to encompass the markets of the Halles, the wealthy merchants' shops of the rue Saint-Denis, and the mixed commerce around the rue Saint-Martin. The streets in this area were constantly jammed with people—on foot, in carts or litters, and on mule and horseback. The press of the crowd gave a sense of heady excitement to even the most ordinary of occasions and turned easily to agitated disorder when anything untoward occurred.[28] Thomas

Platter recorded that he found the streets so crowded that he often had occasion to wonder if there was anyone left inside the buildings, but when he entered an inn or an eating place, he always found that it too was full.[29]

The central Halles, which had fallen into disrepair with the economic crises of the fourteenth and fifteenth centuries, were rebuilt in the mid-sixteenth century in response to the needs of a city once again in full expansion. In the meantime, however, mercers, drapers, and certain other tradesmen had abandoned the Halles for neighboring streets, where they conducted their business from individual shops.[30] Like the Halles proper, many of these streets were organized by trade. Each type of good might be found in a precise location: hides and skins on the quai de la Mégisserie, poultry in the neighboring Vallée de Misère, meat at the butcher stalls of the the porte de Paris, and at several lesser markets as well. In the rue de la Friperie, one found the sellers of used clothing, who set up a great cry as they tried to draw passers-by into their somber shops, coaxing them to buy some indicated garment or fingering the clothes they were wearing and offering a price for them.

Between the rue Saint-Denis and the Halles, in the thick of this great mercantile quarter, lay the Cemetery of the Innocents, whose soil was said to strip a corpse of its flesh in nine days, clearly an advantage where space was limited.[31] The only large open area in the vicinity, the cemetery attracted strollers, who seemed unaffected in their worldly concerns by the grim bones stacked in open ossuaries along the walls.[32] It also attracted beggars, who, according to Platter, would offer for a few coins to sing "bizarre little hymns for the dead."[33] As one proceeded out the rue Saint-Denis toward the gate that bore the same name, there was an obvious decline in wealth. The rich silks and fine woolens displayed in shop windows gave way to more common fare, and there were an increasing number of inns and taverns to cater to the merchants who entered the city from the north.[34] The traveler who departed from the major thoroughfare to explore the muddy streets just inside the walls would have found himself in one of the city's poorest neighborhoods.[35]

Because raw materials and bulky merchandise were usually brought into Paris by boat, the dock areas were constantly animated, particularly around the place de Grève, which served not only as a port for wood, wine, and other bulky items but also as a hiring ground for casual or day laborers. Workers in the building trades assembled early each morning to learn which foremen were taking on new laborers; porters stood about with their large baskets, waiting for prospective clients with merchandise to carry. The city hall, under construction through most of the sixteenth century, opened onto the place de Grève, which in addition to its other functions served as a gathering place for the militia companies of nearby neighborhoods and as a site for civic ceremonies and public executions.

The fifty or so colleges that made up the University of Paris set the tone of life in the Latin Quarter. Best known for its Faculties of Theology and Arts, the university also offered the study of canon law and medicine. The faculties were the degree-granting units of the university, but teaching was done in the colleges, which also served as student residences. Thomas Platter had no trouble identifying the most prominent colleges as the Sorbonne, "where they debate in a subtle and very eloquent fashion," and the collège de Navarre, "where the children of princes are trained,'' but other colleges, among them Cardinal-Lemoine, Sainte-Barbe, and Montaigu, also had reputations for attracting good teachers—even if Erasmus hated his old collège de Montaigu for the austerities he was made to suffer there.[36]

Not all students boarded at the colleges; many lodged and took their meals with families in the Latin Quarter. High spirited and full of energy, the students made their presence felt. "Anyone who has lived in Paris," wrote Platter, "knows how much noise they make day and night, as well as the pranks they play."[37] Students burned off some of their excess energy on the pré aux Clercs, the open fields along the river outside the porte de Nesle. Eustache Knobelsdorf gave a description of sports and games observed along the Seine that recalls the education of Gargantua: Young men staged races on foot and in carts; they fought mock duels, engaged in calisthenics, high jumping, and wrestling; they threw javelins and heavy stones; they swam in the Seine—on their stomachs, on their backs, and with a great amount of deep diving.[38]

Commerce in the Latin Quarter was also marked by the presence of the university. A great number of printers, booksellers, and bookbinders clustered around the colleges. The center of this trade lay on the rue Saint-Jacques, where the shops of some two hundred printers and booksellers might be found.[39] As far as daily necessities were concerned, the marketing center for the Latin Quarter was the place Maubert. Thomas Platter was impressed by the great number of houses that lined this irregularly shaped square, but the Dutch student, Arnold Van Buchel, was repelled by the stink of the open sewers there.[40]

Van Buchel was not alone in complaining about the stench of the capital, which, he said, so penetrated his nostrils that after three days he lost all sense of smell.[41] One suspects that the Parisians had become similarly desensitized, although some may have adopted Ierni's practice of carrying a bouquet of flowers or a perfumed cloth to ward off the foul odors that arose from the household wastes and garbage dumped in the street, where a constant stream of fetid water ran in a central gutter. The city made repeated attempts to improve the situation by sending around carts at specified hours into which householders might deposit their wastes, but none of these attempts met with much success.[42]

In spite of the fact that it was the ultimate receptacle for the filthy water that ran through the city's streets, the Seine was considered a sweet river, the waters of which were healthy to drink.[43] Some Parisians had wells, and a very few, by special concession, had a small pipe of water run directly to their houses, but the vast majority were dependent upon the seventeen public fountains that served the city.[44] These fountains were all on the Right Bank, as their sources lay to the north, but bourgeois householders could have water brought to their dwellings on a regular schedule by the many water carriers—men and women—who offered this service for a monthly fee.[45]

Outside the city walls, the faubourg Saint-Germain, which had grown up around the old abbey of Saint-Germain-des-Prés, was "as populated as a large city."[46] It was also, by comparison with the other suburbs, as rich and as stable as the city within the walls, for the faubourgs were by and large a sorry lot—a collection of hastily constructed, shabbily built shelters that huddled outside the city gates. Sprawling along the decaying moats and the roads that entered the city, the suburbs had grown rapidly in the 1530s and early 1540s, when the population of Paris was expanding at a rate that made housing within the walls increasingly expensive. In addition, some artisans had settled there to avoid the city's craft regulations. The growth, however, had worried the king, who ordered a part of the suburbs torn down in 1544, when imperial armies threatened the capital. In 1548, Henri II forbade new construction outside the city walls.[47] The prohibition proved unenforceable, but the lack of security and uncertain future of the suburbs meant that, with the exception of the faubourg Saint-Germain, they became largely the refuge of the poor. The typical resident of the northern faubourgs was the market gardener who rented a small patch of land on which to grow vegetables to sell in the city. A few notable families resided in the Left Bank suburbs of Saint-Victor, Saint-Marcel, and Saint-Jacques. The Gobelins, for example, wealthy merchants who had got their start as dyers of woolen cloth, continued to maintain a house at Saint-Marcel, the traditional place of residence for dyers, parchment makers, and papermakers, all of whom employed the waters of the Bièvre River in their industry. Such cases, however, were exceptional. They became more so when, with the outbreak of the religious wars, new armies advanced to threaten the capital.

Economic and Social Structures

In his description of Paris, Thomas Platter remarked upon the number of fine palaces and country retreats in the vicinity of the city. This was not surprising, he said, because for some time Paris had drawn all the riches of France to itself.[48] This observation deserves analysis. Were the city and its inhabitants in fact rich on the eve of the religious wars, and, if so, what were the sources of their wealth? How was it shared? To answer these questions we need to look at the economic functions of the capital—at the nature and extent of its trade, the economics of its administrative and educational roles, the quality of life of the mass of workers, and the provisions that were made for those who did not, by the standards of the day, earn their keep.

The first point to be made in any analysis of the Parisian economy is the close relationship between the city and the surrounding countryside. This may appear a truism, but it is important to recognize that the Parisian population, enormous by comparison with the populations of other northern European cities, could not have been sustained without a large and fertile hinterland from which to draw its food supply. Richard Gascon has calculated that in good years it took the equivalent of twelve or more of today's *départements* just to provide grain for the area around the capital—for the hinterland to feed itself and have enough left over to supply the Parisian market. In bad years grain had to be sought still further afield.[49] Fortunately, Paris lay at the heart of a fertile grain belt, and the network of navigable rivers that laced northern France made transportation of bulky items like wheat, wine, and wood relatively simple. Even so, provisioning the city was a constant worry. As Cavalli recorded in his 1546 report on the French capital, the city could not stock supplies for more than a week, and some items had to be brought in every day. When the Seine iced over for two weeks, scarcity could be felt.[50]

By the mid-sixteenth century, a large and increasing share—as much as 40 percent—of the land in the countryside around Paris belonged to the Parisian bourgeoisie or to royal officers whose principal residence was in the capital.[51] As landowners, these men were well placed to profit from the increasing demand for foodstuffs created by the growing population of the city and the consequent rise in food prices. In cash or in kind, rural rents were increasing.[52] Parisians also profited from their country properties by importing produce grown there for their family's use free of the tax usually charged on agricultural products entering the city. In the case of wine, Parisians could even sell their surplus to local tavernkeepers without being charged an entrance duty.[53]

The surplus of foodstuffs produced in the Paris basin did more, however, than feed the capital. France was an exporter—in good years at least—of the agricultural wealth of her rich soil, and Parisian merchants shared in this export market. They shipped grain from the Oise Valley, the Beauce, and the Chartrain to the Low Countries, Britain, Portugal, and Spain. They forwarded some of the local wine, but also the better wines of Burgundy and the Loire Valley, to northern European markets. They exported locally produced raw materials—plaster of paris and building stone from Brie—and rural manufactures—coarse woolens, paper, and eau-de-vie. In addition, they used their trade connections to share in the profits from the sale of more distantly produced items—the pastel of Toulouse and the salt of the Atlantic seacoast.[54] The luxury items for which Paris was most known—fine woolens, haberdashery, books, jewelry, and bibelots—made up a relatively small, albeit valuable, part of her merchants' trade. For example, fine woolens dyed and finished in the capital made up 20 percent by volume of the woolen cloth imported into Lyons in the sixteenth century but accounted for 50 percent of its value.[55]

The luxury trade went in two directions; Parisians were consumers as well as producers of refined household and personal furnishings, and Parisian merchants bought as well as sold such items as books, jewelry, and works of art.[56] They accounted for one-seventh of all books purchased at the Frankfurt book fair in 1562.[57] They were importers as well of the exotic products of distant lands—furs, spices, and sugar—which found a ready market among the nobility and upper bourgeoisie. The French had begun their own silk industry in Tours and Lyons, but the finest silk fabrics were still imported from Italy. The inexpensive and nondurable silks of Florence and Genoa sold best, Cavalli noted, because the French became bored if they had to wear the same clothing too long.[58]

The scope of the trade conducted by Parisian merchants varied widely. French and foreign merchants came to the city in large numbers; some sales were thus possible without ever leaving home, particularly during the Saint-German fair, held annually during February and March.[59] Parisian merchants, nonetheless, traveled regularly through near and distant towns to sell their wares. Robert Descimon has found, for example, that Parisian cloth merchants dealt directly with traders in the small southern town of Lavaur, rather than operating through the local capital of Toulouse.[60] On the other hand, some Parisian merchants did have agents in Toulouse, Bordeaux, and other cities. Maintaining close relations with trading houses in Rouen and Lyons was particularly important. Rouen served as a funnel through which the Atlantic and Mediterranean trade reached the capital, and Lyons had a key role in the overland trade with Italy and the Levant, as well as dominating an extensive network of markets in southeastern France.[61] Emile Coornaert's study of French trade with Antwerp in the late fifteenth and sixteenth centuries shows that the role of Parisian merchants increased during this period. Especially during the second third of the sixteenth century, Parisian merchants began to go to Antwerp in large numbers and they frequently served there as agents for merchants from other French cities. Moreover, Antwerp was not the ultimate destination for many of these traders but served rather as a staging ground for business elsewhere in the Low Countries, Germany, England, the Baltic, and even southern countries like Portugal, Morocco, and Italy. In Coornaert's opinion, Paris was gradually becoming a commercial center of the first rank.[62]

Paris was not, however, the banking capital of France. That role fell to Lyons. Paris enjoyed only a secondary position here, and the banking that was done in the city remained largely in the hands of the same Italian families that dominated the business in Lyons.[63] From the objections Parisian merchants raised when they assembled on the king's command in 1548 to consider his proposal to establish a privileged bank in the capital, it would seem that their financial thinking was still too conservative to allow them to engage comfortably in the sort of credit transactions at which the Italians excelled.[64]

Paris's role as a commercial center was favored by its geographical position at the intersection of river and road traffic from Burgundy and points south and east to Rouen and points north and west, but it was also furthered by its role as an educational and administrative center. The presence of the university and the judicial and administrative apparatus of state—the Parlement, the Chambre des comptes, and other royal agencies—and the frequent presence as well of the king and his retinue gave Paris the necessary population of cultivated consumers to attract skilled craftsmen and purveyors of luxury goods. Cavalli estimated that the personnel associated with the law courts, from the first president of Parlement on down to the least solicitor, made up "a city of 40,000."[65] These figures are exaggerated—it must be remembered that Cavalli estimated the entire population of Paris at five hundred thousand—but they are suggestive of the evident importance of royal institutions in the makeup of the city's professional classes.

In one respect, the prestigious role accorded to occupations associated with the institutions of state had a negative effect on the city's commercial development, for it tended to foster a social system that placed little value on mercantile enterprise. By the mid-sixteenth century, many successful merchants had diverted the profits of their entrepreneurial activities to investment in lands, annuities, and royal offices for themselves and their sons. The social stratification that resulted from this system of values has been described enough times that I shall not dwell on it here.[66] What is important for our purposes is to realize that although by the mid-sixteenth century this hierarchical social system was firmly in place, movement within it was still possible. The men who held high office in city hall were by this time almost exclusively officers of the king, but many of them came from families in which other branches continued to engage in trade. At the same time, members of the mercantile elite might yet aspire to place their sons in more prestigious careers.[67]

Some historians have suggested that this social evolution represents a sort of "treason of the bourgeoise," a withdrawal of funds from the productive elements of the economy, such as commercial development, in favor of nonproductive forms of wealth such as the ownership of land and office and the loaning of money at interest.[68] There is truth to these accusations, particularly when they are considered in the context of the larger evolution of French society. At the same time, one must remember that the effect these developments had on the Parisian economy was not entirely negative. In their emulation of noble values, the new elite of officeholders spent far more lavishly on their homes, their clothing, and their entertainments than the old mercantile bourgeoisie had done. As consumers, they helped to support a large population of skilled craftsmen, as well as to encourage the formation of new families of merchants and traders.

As in other parts of society, there was a clearly delineated social hierarchy in the crafts and trades. At the top were the famous Six Corps—the mercantile guilds of the drapers, grocers, hosiers, mercers, furriers, and jewelers. Specially consulted on matters involving the city's trade, the wardens of the Six Corps enjoyed the privilege of carrying the ceremonial canopy in civic processions marking the formal entry of French and foreign dignitaries.[69] Along with an occasional bookseller and wine or wood merchant, members of these six corporations were virtually the only merchants elected to civic office in the mid-sixteenth century. They dominated the consular court set up in 1563 to adjudicate commercial disputes and, serving as churchwardens and overseers of poor relief, monopolized the charitable and parish functions to which merchants might be named.[70]

The elite of the Six Corps were inevitably wholesale merchants. They might still keep a shop in which some retail transactions took place, but mercers, grocers, and the like who engaged in a primarily wholesale trade did business on a scale that far exceeded that of the average shopkeeper.[71] A similar division can be found in the book trade, where the typical bookseller operated a small shop in the vicinity of one of the colleges and did a purely local traffic in school books and liturgical works, while a small number of prominent *marchands libraires* kept several publishers busy full time producing books to sell in the larger national and international markets.[72] Wholesale merchants were almost inevitably wealthier than the average retail tradesman, and their higher social position and political standing were in large measure due to their greater wealth. They were also due to the commonly shared opinion that these were men whose horizons extended beyond the limits of their shops and whose skills and experience might be put to good use by the city and the crown.

Among artisans too the prestige of a trade was linked not just to its expected financial returns but also to less tangible matters such as the level of skill and the nature of the work involved.[73] Organized in closed corporations, Parisian artisans were subject to strict rules for admission to and practice of a trade, and the nature and quality of their production were closely supervised by guild wardens. In Paris, as elsewhere in France, the passage from journeyman to master craftsman became more difficult during the sixteenth century. The rules for completing the necessary masterpiece tended to become more complicated; the fees required to solemnize reception as a master escalated and the banquets became more elaborate.[74]

The closing off of opportunities for advancement in one's trade inevitably led to tensions between journeymen and masters, especially during the second half of the century. Journeyman bakers, for example, repeatedly walked off the job to protest the contracts their masters offered. During these strikes, the journeymen are said to have gone about armed with sticks, daggers, and swords, with which they threatened not only owners but also fellow journeymen who did not share their grievances. Journeymen printers, butchers, and shoemakers also earned a reputation for unruly behavior.[75] Labor conflicts were aggravated by the rapid inflation of prices and the lack of a corresponding rise in salaries. In the words of the labor historian Etienne Martin-Saint-Léon, "a petty and jealous aristocracy of shopkeepers was taking shape."[76]

There were several exclusively female guilds in sixteenth-century Paris, such as the *lingères* who made handkerchiefs and linen garments, and the *chapelières de fleurs*, who created the floral crowns for Catholic feast days. There were also some guilds that admitted women as members on the same terms as men and even a few that specifically provided for female wardens.[77] For the most part, however, women remained on the margins of corporate life. They were nevertheless an active part of the Parisian workforce. Francesco Ierni commented that women, more than men, seemed to run the city's shops, and indeed it does seem that women played a particularly active role in retail sales.[78] They served as shopgirls in the fancy boutiques of the Palais, sold fish from stalls along the Seine, and peddled flowers, vegetables, butter, and eggs under the pillars of the Halles. Often a woman's work was an extension of that of her husband or father. Thus we find a number of wives and a few daughters of wood merchants representing their husbands and fathers at a civic assembly held in 1571 to discuss the problems of supplying firewood during an unusually cold winter.[79] Some women, however, had independent trades.[80] Marguerite Bury, for example, a *marchande publique* who engaged in the grain trade, had a husband who was a baker—a related but separate profession.[81]

In many cases, a widow could carry on her husband's business if she did not remarry outside the trade. Certain restrictions sometimes applied. Artisans' widows could not take on new apprentices and in certain trades could not operate without a journeyman in the shop. Nevertheless, women could and did successfully continue their husbands' businesses in wholesale as well as retail trades, and in the provision of services such as innkeeping and transshipment on the Seine.[82] To cite just one example, Charlotte Guillard operated her deceased husband's printing presses under her own imprint for more than twenty years, during which time she produced more than 160 different titles, including four editions of the eleven-volume *Corpus Juris Civilis*. Keeping four or five presses active at a time, Guillard employed a dozen pressmen at a minimum and, counting additional help in the shop, perhaps as many as twenty-five or thirty people in all.[83]

Women were found not just in commerce and the crafts, of course. They did a great deal of menial labor, both as domestic servants and in more public situations. They washed clothes in rented spaces along the river, carried water for bourgeois householders, and worked alongside men and boys on the city's fortifications.[84] The same poor laws applied to women as to men. In times of scarcity, "sturdy beggars" of Parisian origin—male and female alike—were ordered to enroll in charity workshops or assigned to public construction projects. Nonlocals, considered to have no claim to the city's charity, were to be driven from its gates. Women were accorded no special favors here either.[85]

Although laws for the explusion of the "foreign" poor date back at least to the fourteenth century, a series of reforms gave Parisian poor laws a new rigor in the mid-sixteenth century. The laws were first changed in 1536 to outlaw public begging. In order to discourage beggars most effectively, it was declared illegal to give as well as to receive alms in the streets of the city. By 1544, however, it was evident that further steps were needed to deal with the problem of the poor. Traditions of ecclesiastical, confraternal, and private charity had broken down, and the old charitable institutions of the city were no longer able to care for the swelling ranks of the indigent. As a result, a new municipally sponsored agency, the Aumône générale, most often called the Grand bureau des pauvres, was created. Under the direction of a board of governors chosen from among the city's notables, thirty-two commissioners were charged with supervising the distribution of alms in the sixteen quartiers of the city. The parishes were assigned the task of raising the alms money. To qualify for assistance, an indigent had first to apply to the commissioner of his or her quartier and then to submit to a home visit, in order that the commissioner might verify the degree of need and the legitimacy of the claim. Individuals place on the assistance rolls were supposed to wear an identifying badge, a red and yellow cross on their right shoulder, although it is doubtful that this provision was strictly enforced. From time to time, there were to be processions of the poor through the city streets, in order to encourage almsgiving.[86]

In spite of the apparent rigor of these laws, the indigent population continued to grow. In 1551, seven years after the founding of the Grand bureau des pauvres, a parlementary commission estimated that the number of persons on the public assistance rolls had tripled. Ordering a thorough review of the rolls for each parish, the parlementaires insisted that the commissioners for the poor seek out individuals who might be feigning illness or injury and those who had come to Paris just to get public charity. The former were to be punished, the latter expelled. The commissioners of the Aumône générale were to go out daily to the streets where the poor were known to congregate in order to break up the encampments they might find there. Only persons who had lived in Paris for at least five years and who, having earned their living as artisans or workers, had since fallen into poverty through illness or misfortune qualified for aid. And these, if they were able, were to be put to work on public projects and not merely given a weekly dole. These harsh measures reflect a changing attitude toward the poor, a gradual disappearance of medieval notions of "Christian charity." Instead of seeing the poor as especially beloved of God and therefore deserving of alms, officials saw them as slackers and ne'er-do-wells who chose to live at public expense. The change is particularly apparent in a provision of the 1551 poor law forbidding women who sold candles outside of churches to keep their children with them, on the ground that such women were really beggars hoping to appeal to the sympathy of passersby.[87]

The second quarter of the sixteenth century also witnessed the reformation and expansion of the Parisian hospital system. The old Hôtel-Dieu, enlarged in 1535, retained a primary role as the city's central medical facility, but the network of specialized shelters and orphanages was extended to accommodate the larger number of persons in need of assistance.[88] A hospital named the Enfants-Dieu, but known as the Enfants Rouges from the color of the uniforms the children wore, was created to care for orphans of persons who died in the Hôtel-Dieu. The Enfants Rouges soon expanded its role to care for other Parisian-born orphans, because the old orphanage of Saint-Esprit, founded in the fourteenth century, could not take in any more children. In 1547, the Hôpital de la Trinité, founded in the thirteenth century as a shelter for pilgrims, was also converted to an orphanage. The Trinité was given the particular task of caring for foundlings and "the poor little children who beg in the streets," for whom it was to provide lodging and education in a trade.[89]

Private and religious foundations continued to provide specialized services: The hospice of the Quinze-Vingts offered a home for the blind, Sainte-Catherine and the Filles-Dieu gave temporary shelter to women who came to the city seeking work, Saint-Jacques-aux-Pèlerins and Saint-Jacques-du-Haut-Pas sheltered pilgrims and people passing through the city, and Saint-Lazare housed the city's few remaining lepers.[90] None of these hospices, however, took in the local indigents who, aged, crippled, or congenitally ill, could neither be put to work on public projects nor be expelled from the city. In order to solve this problem, Henri II ordered the governors of the Bureau des pauvres to create a new hospital for the "incorrigible poor." Originally intended as almost a prison to lock up individuals for whom no other solution could be found, this hospital, established in a disused leper-house acquired from the abbey of Saint-Germain-des-Prés, eventually assumed the character of an old people's home.[91]

The new laws and newly reformed or newly created institutions did not, however, put an end to the problem of poverty. An unfortunate conjuncture of events—bad harvests in 1551, 1552, 1555, and 1556; plague in 1553; and the threat of invasion in 1552 and 1557, when the Hapsburg-Valois wars were carried to the northeastern plains of France—contributed to the situation, but the underlying problems were structural.[92] Paris had traditionally received a large in-migration of young men and women who left the northern French countryside, where the small holdings were all too frequently divided beyond the point where they could support a family, to come to the capital as servants and apprentices, but by the mid-sixteenth century the city's ability to absorb this surplus population was strained. Rural impoverishment was on the rise: lands were being subdivided at an accelerating rate, indebtedness was growing, and with it the likelihood of losing one's lands altogether.[93] At the same time, conditions of life became more difficult for salaried workers in the city.

The price inflation of the sixteenth century hit hardest at the working classes because the prices that rose first and fastest were those of essential commodities and because wages failed to keep pace with the increasing prices.[94] Indeed, in some fields salaries began to climb only in the second half of the century, long after the price rise began. The disparity between price and wage changes was such that an unskilled laborer (*manouvrier*), who in 1500 would have been able to purchase fifteen kilograms of wheat with the wages he received for a day's work, in 1550 could buy only six. The continued population influx would seem a prime reason for this decline in purchasing power. It increased demand for basic commodities, thereby encouraging the inflation of prices, while it softened the labor market and depressed salaries for those with little training and few skills.[95]

The economic situation of Paris at mid-century thus presents a mixed picture. Trade and commerce were flourishing, the bureaucracy was expanding and its members prospering, but there were signs of stress among workers and the poor. Journeymen artisans saw their opportunities for advancement limited; their salaries failed to keep up with rising prices. Unskilled laborers found it harder to make ends meet; they went more often without work. Indigents had their qualifications scrutinized; a charitable hand was refused to those deemed undeserving, and even the deserving poor had to work for their pittance if they were able.

Still, in the 1550s, the misery was not acute. There was little reason to think that an irreversible cycle of impoverishment had begun. Salaries were beginning to rise; commercial prosperity seemed to promise more jobs. A few good harvests, a few years of peace, and things might level out, . . . or so it must have seemed in 1559. And so it might have been, had the new decade brought peace and prosperity instead of new wars and economic dislocations. As it was, the religious conflicts struck a society already weakened by internal strains.

The Structures of Governmental Authority

Keeping order in the large and tumultuous French capital was a perennial problem and one that became acute with the developing religious conflicts. Because much of this book has to do with precisely this problem of keeping order in Paris, it is important to outline the structures of government and the organization of public security in the city. We will want to consider not only the theoretical distribution of governmental authority but also the human and institutional characteristics that determined the way this authority was exercised.

The first point that needs to be made is that the city was both a royal city, subject to the king's direct command, and a bourgeois city in which a mercantile corporation had long before assumed responsibility for such administrative functions as the collection of taxes, the construction of ports and roads, and the raising of a militia. The king's authority was nominally exercised through his appointed *prévôt* and through the subordinate officers of the *prévôté de Paris*—the *lieutenant civil* and the *lieutenant criminel*—but it was also exercised through direct royal commands to the military governor for Paris, the high court of Parlement, and the municipal government—the *Prévôté de la marchandise*, usually known by the sixteenth century as the *Bureau de la ville*. In addition, Parlement, because of its role as the repository for justice in the state, took a supervisory interest in the maintenance of order in the capital and issued a great many directives to the subordinate officers of the prévôté of Paris and the prévôté de la marchandise. The overlapping of authorities and lack of clearcut lines of jurisdiction could cause problems in times of crisis, when each agency tended to blame the others for any breakdown in order, but it could also lead to fruitful interaction and a sense of participation in an important project of governance on the part of the local elite.

The prévôt of Paris was a high noble from a family that stood close to the king. As such, he was by the sixteenth century usually more occupied with his courtly functions than with his administrative responsibilities. The day-to-day functioning of the prévôté was divided between the lieutenant civil, who had responsibility for all of the functions of police and justice except for criminal cases, and the lieutenant criminel, to whom the latter responsibilities fell. In 1544 a *lieutenant particulier* was added to relieve the lieutenants civil and criminel of some of their growing burdens. The men appointed to these offices came from the Parisian elite. They had close ties to the mercantile bourgeoisie and to the officers of Parlement, and, in spite of occasional attempts to limit the practice, they often simultaneously held municipal office in the Hôtel de Ville. The overlapping of personnel, like the overlapping of jurisdictions, was an important characteristic of Parisian administrative bodies.[96]

The lieutenants of the prévôté made their offices in the old fortress of the Châtelet, and, together with their subordinates, were often referred to by this name. They were assisted in their police functions by the thirty-two *commissaires enquêteurs et examinateurs* of the Châtelet, who investigated reports of criminal activity, took depositions in criminal and civil cases, and otherwise helped keep order and administer justice. The commissaires in turn were assisted by the *sergents à verge*, who served as bailiffs and policemen. In 1570, the Châtelet employed 220 sergents à verge, stationed in makeshift police posts at the principal gates and intersections. Crime in the streets, however, was first and foremost the responsibility of the *lieutenant de robe courte*, who patrolled the city with his troop of twenty archers.[97]

In addition to his civil and criminal responsibilities, the prévôt of Paris had certain military powers, but the primary responsibility for the city's defense was entrusted to a *gouverneur* directly appointed by the king. Always a powerful nobleman and usually in the mid-sixteenth century a member of the Montmorency clan, the gouverneur had the authority to raise troops and to arm and fortify the city as he saw fit and as the king commanded. He also served to transmit the king's wishes to the city and its officers; in particular, he seems often to have been the chosen emissary when the king asked for additional taxes or made other demands to which objection might be raised.[98] In such instances, the personal prestige and might of the gouverneur—who was generally an important military commander quite apart from his role in the capital—lent additional weight to the king's demands. If the gouverneur's other military responsibilities took him from the capital, a *lieutenant général* was appointed in his stead. From 1556 until his death in 1579, François de Montmorency, maréchal de France and the eldest son of the *connétable*, Anne de Montmorency, served as *gouverneur de Paris et de l'Ile-de-France*. A moderate Catholic favored by Catherine de Medici for his attempts to enforce royal policy in an even-handed manner, the maréchal was hated by radical Catholics, who thought him too soft on the Protestant "heretics."[99]

Like the gouverneur, the high court of Parlement could also serve as the vehicle for transmitting the king's commands to the city of Paris. The magistrates of Parlement also intervened on their own initiative where matters of security and welfare were concerned. They kept a close watch on the city's provisioning, ordered sanitary measures during times of plague, and set up commissions to study such problems as poor relief.[100] On rare occasions—during the worst of the religious riots, for example—they sent out their own members to patrol the streets of the city. For the most part, however, Parlement was ill-equipped to deal with the execution of policy and acted instead through the lieutenants civil and criminel of the Châtelet and through the Bureau de la ville.

The official organ of the Parisian bourgeoisie, the Bureau de la ville had its origins in the medieval corporation that controlled shipping on the Seine, the Hansa or Marchandise de l'eau. As in many other European cities, the Hansa had gradually expanded its activities from strictly commercial dealings to assume broader public responsibilities, for which it had been rewarded with special privileges and official recognition.[101] By the sixteenth century, the chief officers of this corporation, the prévôt des marchands and four *échevins*, held positions roughly equivalent to those of mayor and alderman respectively. Along with their subordinates in the Bureau de la ville, they engaged in a wide variety of public services. They secured supplies of grain and firewood in times of scarcity, oversaw the policing of the poor and the expulsion of vagabonds, organized a bourgeois militia and night watch, and collected both regular sales taxes and extraordinary levies demanded by the king. As the century progressed, they also became increasingly involved in the sale of annuities (*rentes*) to raise large amounts of capital for the crown.

The prévôt des marchands and échevins made their offices on the place de Grève, where a new Hôtel de Ville was begun in the 1530s. The design for the Hôtel de Ville, imposed upon the city by François I, reflected the king's infatuation with the new style of the Italian Renaissance. Construction was intermittent, however, and through most of the sixteenth century the building remained incomplete, its classical pillars supporting the gabled roof of a medieval townhouse. A casualty of increasing tax burdens brought on by foreign and domestic wars, the Hôtel de Ville was a vivid reminder of France's aborted Renaissance.[102]

The principal officers of the Bureau de la ville were elected for two-year terms by an elaborate process of co-optation, which ensured that these offices remained in the hands of a relatively narrow local elite. In times of crisis, the kings sometimes intervened to impose their own candidates as prévôts de marchands or échevins, but these men were invariably chosen from the same local elite, indeed from the same pool of candidates as the city's choices. These interventions appear an attempt to ensure continuity and to remind the city of its dependence on the king without going so far as to abolish its traditional privileges.[103]

The prévôt des marchands and échevins were assisted in their deliberations by a council of twenty-four local notables and in their day-to-day administrative tasks by sixteen *quarteniers*, or district officers. Both of these positions were held for life and were in theory elective but in practice co-optative and, increasingly, hereditary and even venal. The city councilors came from the same bourgeois elite as the prévôts des marchands and échevins. Indeed, until the office of city councilor became largely hereditary in the second half of the century, it was the custom to elect an outgoing prévôt des marchands to the first vacancy on the council, if he was not already a member of this body.[104] The quarteniers represented a somewhat broader-based notability, coming most often from families still engaged in commerce. As the century progressed, they stood less and less chance of eventual promotion into the ranks of the *échevinage*. The local officers who reported to the quarteniers, the *dizainiers* and *cinquanteniers*, came from a still lower social stratum, being often craftsmen and other "*gens mécaniques*." After 1554 the dizainiers and cinquanteniers were not allowed to participate in city elections, and they had very little hope of rising further in the city hierarchy.[105] An incipient split is thus perceptible at mid-century between the increasingly oligarchical elite of the Hôtel de Ville and the local officers, who remained closer to the population they served.[106]

Among the responsibilities of the Bureau de la ville was the organization of a militia and a bourgeois night watch for the city's security. All the heads of household and other able-bodied men who could afford to equip themselves with some sort of arms were considered a part of the militia. Called up only in an emergency, the militia was an untrained, unwieldy, and poorly organized assemblage. By tradition, men served in troops organized by trade, each with its captain and banner. The militia made a splendid show of colors in the parade musters that were held in moments of crisis but was not a practical structure for the guard of the city in times of internal unrest.[107] For this reason, professional troops of archers, crossbowmen, and harquebusiers were developed. Until 1566, when the king standardized the three companies at one hundred men each, there were one hundred twenty archers, sixty crossbowmen, and one hundred harquebusiers in the city's service.[108] At the direction of the prévôt des marchands, members of the three companies provided a military escort for civic processions, kept order at public executions, and otherwise helped with local defense and security.[109] In addition, the organizational structures of the bourgeois night watch (*guet bourgeois*), which was organized by administrative district or *quartier*, were adapted to provide troops to guard the city gates and keep order in public squares during moments of crisis.[110] During the religious wars, the guet bourgeois replaced the unwieldy corporate militia as the city's home guard.

The guet bourgeois shared responsibility for keeping the city free from danger at night with a professional patrol, the *guet royal*. Under the direction of a *chevalier du guet*, the royal watch consisted of sixty men who served on alternative nights—ten on horseback and twenty on foot each night—as a roving patrol. By contrast, the guet bourgeois was ordered not to move about the city but rather to maintain a passive, "seated" watch at the city's gates and principal intersections. In theory, all householders were required to serve by turn, forty men each night, in the citizen's watch. In practice, members of many trades—jewelers, barbers, apothecaries, and tanners among them—claimed exemption from the watch, and others often sent servants or hired some poor man to take their place. In 1550 members of the royal watch complained to the king that the bourgeois watch was so ineffective that its men hindered rather than helped in catching criminals and keeping order. Though initially not sympathetic to these complaints, which he thought to be self-serving, Henri II finally agreed that the bourgeois watch was ineffective and in May 1559 abolished it, enlarging the royal watch and substituting a tax on all householders for the old requirement of personal service. The new watch consisted of 240 archers, 32 of them mounted, divided into four companies. The members of these companies were to be recruited among artisans and other residents of the city and paid at the rate of three sous a night for the foot guard and six sous for the horse. The reorganization of the night watch did not, however, solve the city's problems. Crimes continued to occur, and collecting the taxes needed to pay for the watch proved a massive headache for the Bureau de la ville. In 1561 the city asked to return to the old bourgeois watch. Parlement refused the request and confirmed the structures ordered by Henri II in 1559. With the outbreak of religious violence in 1562, however, it became necessary once again to put the bourgeoisie into arms. The old guet bourgeois was resurrected to serve as the city's militia.[111]

The abolition of the citizen's watch by the king in 1559 and the confirmation of this act by Parlement, over the protests of the Bureau de la ville, gives a good lesson in the realities of governmental authority in Paris. Because the scope of their activities was so broad, it is easy to assume that the city officials had a significant degree of independent authority. In fact, a close look at city records shows that the officers of the Bureau de la ville only rarely initiated their public projects but rather virtually always operated in response to directives from higher powers—from Parlement, the gouverneur, the king himself, or members of his council. This is not to say that the Bureau was the helpless tool of these higher authorities. Its officers could and did express their opinions. Not infrequently, they remonstrated with the king or courts about demands that were considered unreasonable, and, particularly where tax levies were concerned, they had some success in moderating the king's demands.[112] They were also often successful at getting their way during moments of crisis—for example in 1562, when the crown had little choice but to allow the city officers to organize a militia for the defense of the threatened capital. Nevertheless, the Bureau de la ville cannot be considered an independent power. A formally sanctioned interest group, the Bureau was endowed with certain rights and privileges but was subject always to the wishes of the king. This was true in general of the corporative bodies—Estates, cities, and guilds—that existed in the old-regime monarchy, but many of the provincial bodies enjoyed a sphere of effective independence that was denied Paris, as the capital, the largest city, and the heart of the realm. As expressed by one writer, playing on the maritime imagery in the city's coat of arms, Paris was a ship and the prévôt des marchands her captain, but the king was the wind that moved her sails.[113]

There were advantages, nonetheless, to being a royal city, and Paris's unique identity as capital was a key element in civic pride. This was best shown in the city's ceremonial life, in which royal entries and events associated with the monarchy—victories or defeats in war or births, deaths, and marriages in the royal family—played an important part. Months of planning went into the formal entry of a newly crowned king into his capital. Staged at great expense by the Hôtel de Ville, the royal entries became ever more elaborate pageants in celebration of the Valois monarchy.[114] The finest poets and artists were hired to decorate the route of the procession from the porte Saint-Denis to Notre-Dame and, ultimately, the Palais de Justice with symbolic statuary and triumphal arches inscribed with verses in praise of the king. Jean Goujon and Philibert de l'Orme were among the artists who worked on the royal entry of Henri II in 1549. Their sculptural program included a Hercules with the features of François I atop a triumphal arch at the porte Saint-Denis. Three Fortunes, in gold, silver, and lead and representing the king, the nobility, and the people, topped the Ponceau fountain in the rue Saint-Denis; a tall obelisk on the back of a rhinocerous, representing France triumphing over the monsters that threatened her, stood before the church of Saint-Sépulcre. At the entry to the pont Notre-Dame, which was garlanded with ivy and entirely covered with a cloth canopy, stood a triumphal arch with the theme of the Argonauts, symbolizing Henri II as the new pilot of the ship that was Paris.

Celebrations of royalty, the entries were also demonstrations of civic pride. The prévôt des marchands presented the king with the key to the city and then served as host for a banquet at the Hôtel de Ville, but participation in the king's entry was not limited to the city hall. The procession for the entry of Henri II included representatives of all of the city's corporations. Fifty pastry chefs, 40 barrel makers, 250 printers, and 200 tailors were among the hordes of artisans who turned out for the parade. They were followed by all of the city's officers, from the least measurer of grain in the Halles to the prévôt des marchands himself, along with "a large number of the richest and most notable merchants and bourgeois of the city," followed in turn by the officers of the Châtelet and then those of Parlement, similarly arrayed from the least solicitor to the highest magistrate.[115] A second procession was held two days later for the entry of the queen. The ritual was very similar to that followed for the entry of the king, but the sculptural program was modified. The martial images that dominated in the decorations created for the king were replaced by more appropriate feminine and maternal emblems.

Except as a cheering audience, the common people or laboring poor of Paris had no part in the royal entry. They did, however, have a part in the celebration of royal victories with speeches, artillery shots, and bonfires on the place de Grève. Triumphs in war were further accompanied by the offering of bread and wine to the people who gathered outside of city hall. This was a charitable offering and not just a celebratory feast, as is made clear in the city's account of the ceremonies for the peace made with the emperor in September 1544, in which it is specified that "a hogshead of wine and twelve dozen loaves of bread were given out to all the poor passers-by, and guards stood ready to make sure that the rich did not drink or carry away any of the wine."[116]

The festivities on the place de Grève were thus not a true communal celebration, an occasion of rejoicing shared by all regardless of social standing, but rather an act of ritual ministration to the city's less fortunate residents by its political elite. We can see here further evidence of the incipient split in the urban social fabric that we observed in our examination of the Parisian economy. At mid-century, however, the split was still latent. There are few signs that the common people overtly resented the dominant elite or wished to challenge its role in the city and the state. They accepted its ministrations as they accepted bread and wine from their parish priests. As Bernard Chevalier has argued in his study of the "*bonnes villes du roi*," urban oligarchies played a mediating role between the urban masses and the state during the later middle ages. From about the mid-fourteenth to the mid-sixteenth centuries, this role and the inequalities it implied were accepted and interiorized by all concerned. The only time that popular anger was directed against the oligarchy was when it failed in its mediating functions.[117] By the mid-sixteenth century, however, the equilibrium on which the urban social system was based was increasingly delicate. The tensions generated by the religious conflicts posed a serious threat to this fragile unity.

2

The Most Catholic Capital

On 5 April 1559 the city of Paris received news of the peace with Spain concluded two days earlier. Celebrated first by city officials and Parlement with a mass of thanksgiving at Notre-Dame, the peace was publicly announced that same afternoon with speeches and ebullient salvos of artillery fire on the place de Grève. The prévôt des marchands ordered kegs of wine opened and a large quantity of bread distributed to the people gathered on the square, after which festive bonfires were lit before the city hall and "in all the streets of the city." As was customary on such occasions, the bells of the Horlogerie rang continuously until midnight.[1] On 8 April, a procession was organized to give thanks for the end of war. Delegations from all the parishes, local monasteries, and city hall converged on Notre-Dame at mid-morning for a massive parade to the Sainte-Chapelle. The mendicant orders led, followed by the parishes, with their banners, crosses, and relics, the chapters of Notre-Dame and the Sainte-Chapelle, and the city officials. An image of the Virgin and a jewel-encrusted reliquary named for Saint Sebastien were brought out from Notre-Dame. On the return procession from the Sainte-Chapelle back to Notre-Dame these hallowed images were joined by the reliquary of the True Cross, carried under an elaborate canopy and surrounded by flaming torches. Scarlet robed, the magistrates of Parlement joined in at the Palais de Justice and marched alongside the city officers as the triumphant parade circled the Ile de la Cité to conclude with high mass at Notre-Dame. Throughout the procession, the bells of the Horlogerie kept up a joyous peal.[2]

Just three months later, on 9 July, there was another procession between Notre-Dame and the Sainte-Chapelle, but this time the mood was different. The city was unusually quiet, its church bells having been silenced on 30 June, when Henri II was injured in a tournament. Now the king lay dying, and a desperate appeal was to be made to the saints that watched over the city to intercede for his life. As was traditional in times of danger or natural catastrophe, the appeal took the form of a procession of the relics of the city's patron, Saint Geneviève. The relics of Saint Marcel, another favorite local saint, were also carried in the procession. In addition, the treasury of the Sainte-Chapelle was emptied of its most precious objects: the relics associated with Christ's Passion—the True Cross, the Crown of Thorns, and the tip of the lance said to have pierced Christ's side—and those associated with kingly rule—the shrines of Saint Louis and "Sainct Charlemaigne." More processions were planned for the next day by the university, the canons of Notre-Dame, and other groups in the city. Some took place, but others were canceled when it was learned that the king had died.[3]

The festivities that marked an end to the Hapsburg-Valois wars and the processions to appeal for the life of the king are but two examples of occasions on which civic pride, monarchical loyalism, and Catholic belief were conjoined in sixteenth-century Parisian life. They are, however, revealing rituals in that they epitomize the way in which Parisians participated in a culture that was simultaneously local, royal, and Catholic. This chapter will use religious processions as a means of exploring the complex interconnections between civic, monarchical, and religious values as they appeared at mid-century, before the foundations of city, state, and church were tested by the religious wars. Before we can begin, however, we need a clearer understanding of the character and intensity of the Catholic faith as practiced by sixteenth-century Parisians.

One Bread and One Body

We can begin, as we began the previous chapter, by observing the scene through the eyes of a stranger. Francesco Ierni, visiting Paris in 1596, remarked upon the great devotion that people showed in church. He thought that the buildings, handsome though they were, needed better maintenance, but he was impressed by the contributions the parishioners had made to their churches. He commented particularly on the large tapestries that decorated the churches on feast days. Saint-Merry, for example, possessed thirty-six scenes from the life of Jesus, each donated by a parishioner and said to be collectively worth fifteen thousands francs. He also noted the rigor with which the Lenten fast was observed and the "beautiful spectacle" of Easter communion, but the custom that interested him most was the ritual distribution of holy bread (*pain bénit*). As Ierni described this "old French custom," every Sunday two or three parishioners would each bring to the church a loaf of bread "as large as a man can carry, and of very fine quality." Presented at the altar during the offertory of the high mass, along with a candle and a large jug of wine, the bread was first cut in the sacristy, with the priests each taking a slice, and then was put out in baskets to be distributed to the congregation. After the offering, the women who provided the bread would go through the church collecting alms for the poor.[4]

Ierni's description, written in the 1590s and not the 1550s, gives the impression that Parisians were pious and observant Catholics whose faith was participatory in spirit and strongly rooted in local tradition. Still, his description raises important questions about the character of Parisian Catholicism. It reminds us that, before we can hope to understand the reaction in Paris to the religious schism produced by the Protestant Reformation, we must understand the fundamental beliefs and practices by which the people's religious views were shaped. As this is a subject too large to allow for comprehensive treatment here, I propose to approach it by looking at several selected aspects of Catholic religious practice at mid-century. Since Ierni's description suggests a need to examine both popular piety and religious sociability, I will look first at the Mass and related forms of eucharistic devotion, including the ritual of the holy bread, which many observers—including Ierni—likened to Holy Communion. I will then briefly examine confraternal and parochial worship as important aspects of religious sociability. Religious processions, which manifested both piety and sociability and demonstrate the arbitrariness of the line between them, will be discussed in the next part of this chapter, within the broader context of the interrelations between Catholic and civic ritual.

We can begin our inquiry into religious practice with the Mass, which all authorities cited as the central and most essential rite of the faith. In one of a series of sermons on the Mass preached in 1558, Pierre Dyvolé, a doctor of the Sorbonne and a popular preacher during the first years of the religious wars, explained the rite in this way:

> Among all the sacraments and sacred mysteries that take place in the church, the first, most singular, and principal is the holy office of the Mass: for the priest consecrates there the precious body of Jesus Christ on the sacred table of the altar, such that the church truly represents to us what is said in the Gospel of Saint Luke about the fatted calf that was killed upon the return and conversion of the prodigal son.[5]

We might wonder what these words meant to Dyvolé's audience. Did his listeners comprehend the notion of the Mass as a "sacrifice," much less understand the reference to forgiving paternal love in the parable of the prodigal son? How did the laity perceive the ceremony that took place at the altar?

In a number Parisian churches, the congregation was separated from the altar by an elaborate rood screen (*jubé*), which reduced visibility and enforced a feeling of separateness from the ritual that was being enacted. The only rood screen that still exists today in Paris is the exquisitely sculpted stone screen at Saint-Etienne-du-Mont, begun in 1530, but such screens were sufficiently popular in the mid-sixteenth century that at least three other important churches—Saint-Germain-l'Auxerrois, Saint-Merry, and the Sainte-Chapelle—commissioned them.[6] Even if a church did not have a rood screen, the congregation lacked a clear view of what took place at the altar. The central part of the Mass, the canon, was executed with the priest's back to the congregation and was not said aloud but rather was chanted in an undertone—not that the common people could have understood the Latin words the priest was using even if they had been able to hear them.[7] These aspects of the Mass earned it the scorn of the Protestant reformers. "Their consecration is nothing but a kind of sorcery," wrote Calvin. "They deem the entire mystery impaired if all is not done and said secretly in a way that no one perceives anything."[8] From the Catholic perspective, however, it was entirely proper that the Mass should have a different meaning for the laity from that which it had for the clergy.

During the later middle ages, lay people were not expected to understand the complex symbolism of the Catholic liturgy or the doctrines on which it was based. The "mysteries of the faith" were best left to God's special servants, his anointed clergy, who reenacted Christ's sacrifice on the altar on behalf of—for the spiritual benefit of—the entire congregation. In a little essay published in 1493, Olivier Maillard, a popular preacher in Paris, explained the Mass in terms of its "conformity and correspondence'' to the stages of Christ's passion. When he came to the consecration and elevation, Maillard said merely that these "mysteries" belonged to the men of God consecrated into the order of the priesthood. For the laity, it sufficed to adopt an attitude of hope and love with which to adore "God the Creator, Redeemer, and Remunerator in the hands of the priest at [the moment of] the elevation, as if we could see him with our eyes in the state in which he was raised onto the tree of the cross.''[9]

Maillard assumed that his readers understood that it was Christ's real body that they were adoring in the Mass, but he did not attempt to explain the act of consecration further, much less hint at the doctrine of transubstantiation. His book, moreover, was directed at lay folk possessing some education and sophistication. "Simple folk" were expected only to attend mass in a regular and seemly fashion and to make some attempt to live in conformity with the faith. Although it was considered desirable for people at least to know the twelve articles of faith, or Apostles' Creed, this was not universally required.[10] Even a humanist like Guillaume Petit, bishop of Senlis until his death in 1536, might concede that "simple people" should not be expected explicitly to know the articles of faith, but needed only to profess their willingness to "live and die in the Catholic church.''[11] In response to the challenge posed by the Protestant Reformation, French church councils began in the 1520s to place more emphasis on the curés' responsibility to teach their parishioners fundamental Christian doctrine. Standards remained lax during the next few decades, however, and the emphasis in religious instruction was still on Christian behavior and not theology.[12]

Even if many French laymen were as yet poorly instructed in Catholic doctrine, we should not assume that they had no role in the Mass or that it had little meaning for them. A gathering of the faithful was pleasing to God, and it was the laity's special role to demonstrate this common union by assembling for worship. To adore God with hope and love, while contemplating the crucified Christ, as Maillard instructed his readers to do, was itself a significant act of piety. In the Catholic interpretation of Christian theology, it was meritorious "work." And if doctrine received little emphasis in religious works written for lay readers before the middle of the sixteenth century, worship and love of God certainly did.

Virginia Reinburg's study of popular prayer during the later middle ages and Reformation makes it clear that, even though lay prayer books did not instruct readers about transubstantiation or explain the ritual of consecration in the Mass, they did stress the adoration that people were to demonstrate in their worship. As Maillard's little book suggests, the high point of this devotion was expected to occur at the moment of the elevation of the consecrated host. The gestures of the priest, as he lifted the host for the congregation to see, and the accompanying sound of bells in the church and from its tower conveyed the message that the elevation was the solemn climax of the Mass even to those who did not understand the liturgical symbolism involved.[13] It was intended, moreover, that those in attendance should acknowledge this climactic moment by beating their breast, raising their arms, crying out, or otherwise expressing the intensity of the emotions they felt. The Mass was thus expected to provide an emotional catharsis for its lay congregation and not simply to be perceived by them as a distant liturgical act.[14]

After the elevation, the most important parts of the Mass from the perspective of the laity were the Pater Noster, the kiss of peace (*pax*), and the distribution of the holy bread. Scarcely mentioned in the clergy's missals, the ceremonial kissing of the "pax board" as it was passed through the congregation and the distribution of the holy bread were for the laity important rituals of Christian unity.[15] The weekly distribution of holy bread was a French custom and not a part of the Roman rite.[16] The Jesuit Emond Auger, in his 1571 treatise on the Mass, explained that the first Christians had taken communion weekly, but as their descendants became less zealous in their faith, this custom declined, and the holy bread came to be substituted for it. The same explanation was customarily given in later works on the Mass, like the seventeenth-century treatise of Pierre Floriot. Citing I Corinthians 10:17 ("For we being many are one bread, and one body, for we are all partakers of that one bread"), Floriot defined the bread as the symbol of the unity that should exist among the faithful, who should "together be one heart and one soul," joined by Christian love (*charité*).[17]

The same symbolism, of course, was associated with the Eucharist. Sixteenth-century guides to worship cite the same passage from I Corinthians 10 in their description of the sacrament of the Eucharist.[18] As John Bossy has explained, the sacrament "completes what the pacifying sacrifice makes possible: the eucharistic eating whereby the Christian participates in communion, common union, the whole-ness of Christ and of his church, the token of his entry into transcendant life."[19] During the sixteenth century people did not partake often of the bread of the Eucharist. The church obliged them to confess and to take Holy Communion only once a year, at Easter, and people do not seem generally to have exceeded this requirement. Bossy argues that the ritual of an annual Easter communion, which in theory at least brought together the whole community, was nevertheless a "more plausible embodiment of the unity of Christians than the more frequent and more devout communions of the Counter-Reformation."[20] Bossy has a point here, for during the Counter-Reformation communion did become a very personal act, closely related to individual contrition and penance. One might argue, however, that for the French Catholic laity, the large, fine loaves of holy bread shared out each week among the congregation were a more accessible symbol of community than the thin, dry, and rarely partaken communion wafer.

This is not to disparage the role of the Eucharist in sixteenth-century French Catholicism. Eucharistic devotion, which should not be equated simply with the taking of Holy Communion, had become increasingly important in Catholic worship during the later middle ages.[21] It was cultivated through special masses, through the propagation of eucharistic miracles, through processions in which the conse-crated host was publicly displayed, and through confraternities specially devoted to the Blessed Sacrament. For both the clergy and the laity, Christ's corporeal presence in the Eucharist was an important article of faith. Whether or not they ever thought about the meaning of the words, many people probably knew the vernacular prayer for the elevation of the host, in which the equations of godhead, host, and flesh are spelled out: "Je te salue, vray Seigneur du monde, parolle du Pere, hostie sacrée, vraye vive chair, dieté entiere, vray homme."[22] Moreover, the language of the time, in which the consecrated host was frequently referred to as

"God's body," either in Latin or in the vernacular, suggests that this notion was broadly shared, even if its theological subtleties escaped common understanding.

Paris had two important cults devoted to miracles of the Eucharist. The first, said to have begun in 1274 but in all probability a somewhat later phenomenon, honored a host believed to have miraculously escaped theft by flying into the air, thereby betraying the thief and leading to his capture, after which the host had calmly descended into the hands of the curé of Saint-Gervais. The miracle was commemorated by a stained-glass window and celebrated with a weekly mass of the Blessed Sacrament and an annual procession at the church of Saint-Gervais.[23] The second cult, dating from 1290, was devoted to a host believed miraculously to have bled when pierced by a Jew in an act of ritual desecration. Preserved at Saint-Jean-en-Grève, the host was encased in a golden sun studded with pearls and other precious stones and set into a vermeil reliquary. The story of the "sacred host and the Jew" was told in paintings, tapestries, and statuary, and a mystery play was written about it in the fifteenth century. Although there is no evidence that the play was performed in Paris in the sixteenth century, two published editions of it appeared, and it is known to have been performed in Metz and Laval, so it was certainly not forgotten. In 1535 the miracle was one of the themes for the moralizing paintings that decorated the pont Notre-Dame on the occasion of a city-wide procession against heresy, and throughout the sixteenth century it was memorialized in a high mass celebrated each Thursday at Saint-Jean-en-Grève.[24] The knife with which the host had been pierced was also an object of devotion. It belonged to the monastery church of the Billettes, which was founded on the supposed site of the Jew's house in commemoration of the miracle, and was one of the sacred objects carried by the Billettes in religious processions. According to Calvin, "the poor crazy Parisians had an even greater reverence for the knife than for the host itself."[25]

The feast of Corpus Christi (*Fête-Dieu*) appears in Parisian breviaries as early as 1318.[26] Corpus Christi observances, which included special masses and sermons as well as elaborate processions in which the consecrated host was paraded in jeweled monstrances through tapestry-hung city streets, reinforced the doctrine of the real presence. Additional emphasis was given to this doctrine in 1553, when Henri II ordered that the processions, high masses, sermons, and other solemnities that marked Corpus Christi henceforth be repeated a week later.[27] Paris was too large for Corpus Christi to be celebrated with a single procession, as it was in many smaller towns. We cannot therefore simply borrow Mervyn James's deft analysis of Corpus Christi celebrations in English towns and extend it to the French capital. Social hierarchies were marked out in the ritual order of Parisian processions, but we cannot, following James, claim to see there "the entire structure of precedence and authority" in the city made "visually present." In broader terms, however, we can see that the underlying themes of "social wholeness and social differentiation," the reconciliation of the parts with the whole, that James identified in the English ceremonies apply also to the Parisian case.[28] I will return to the form and ritual of Parisian Corpus Christi processions later in this chapter. For the time being, what is important is simply to keep in mind the underlying symbolism of the real presence, "divided but whole, eaten but never consumed."[29]

The corporate symbolism of the Eucharist made eucharistic devotion appropriate for confraternal as well as communal forms of worship. There were confraternities devoted to the Blessed Sacrament in a number of Parisian churches. According to Jacques du Breul, the confraternity at Saint-Barthélemy, begun in 1518 but only officially founded in 1542, was the first such organization in Paris based on statutes observed in Rome, but after 1546, when Paul III gave all members of this confraternity a one-hundred-days' indulgence if they would take part in Corpus Christi processions, every church in Paris sought to have a similarly privileged association.[30] Members of these confraternities also sponsored special masses. At Saint-Germain-l'Auxerrois, for example, the confraternity sponsored a weekly mass of the Blessed Sacrament at the church's high altar. The *confrères* provided their own silver monstrance to hold the consecrated host and paid stipends to a total of fifteen persons, including six choir boys, to take part in the mass.[31]

Associations of the Blessed Sacrament were not, of course, the only confraternities in which corporate symbolism might be found. Indeed, the whole popularity of confraternal associations in the later middle ages derived from the notion that salvation was at least in part a collective enterprise. Their members participated through their prayers and services in the salvation of their fellows, as well as in the saving of their own souls. In this sense, too, they were "one bread, and one body."

Because there are so few records from which to reconstruct the membership of Parisian confraternities, it is not possible to say with any precision just what social groups took part in confraternal activities and whether membership was rising or falling in the mid-sixteenth century.[32] Du Breul's *Théâtre des antiquitez* gives a distinct impression, however, that confraternal organizations retained an important place in the devotional life of the capital.

The most prestigious of Parisian confraternities was the Grande Confrairie Notre-Dame, founded in the little church of Sainte-Marie-Madeleine on the Ile de la Cité in 1168. Membership in the confraternity was limited to fifty clerics, fifty bourgeois, and fifty bourgeoises. The latter were usually named from among the wives of the bourgeois members. Many of the most powerful and prominent men in the city belonged to the Grande Confrairie Notre-Dame in the sixteenth century. Each layman was paired with a cleric for special prayers and works of piety. When a member fell seriously ill, the others were to gather at his or her bedside for a special vigil of prayer. If the member died, they were to take part in special services and to offer prayers for the deceased member's soul every day for a week. The confraternal banquet, held every other year, was noted for its "monastic sobriety and modesty."[33]

Mutual prayer and pious works were supposed to be the principles upon which all confraternities were founded. Not all confraternities, however, shared the Grande Confrairie's reputation for "monastic sobriety and modesty." The annual banquet sponsored by the confraternity of the Pilgrims of Saint-Jacques had declined by the later sixteenth century from a simple repast consisting of a little beef with rice and cheese to a sumptuous meal where the wine flowed "without measure," lascivious conversation abounded, and "old pilgrims" were reported dancing lewdly in the street. Reprimanded by Parlement in 1584, the Pilgrims of Saint-Jacques were ordered to return to the frugal "philosophers' banquet" deemed appropriate for a confraternal gathering.[34]

Artisanal and professional confraternities, on the other hand, were denied the right to have any banquets at all. Abolished by order of François I in 1539 because of the fear that they were serving as a basis of labor agitation, these associations gradually reestablished themselves after 1541, when the merchant drapers received permission to resume religious services at their chapel in the church of the Innocents. Despite the prohibition against banquets and other assemblies for secular purposes, artisanal confraternities appear to have continued to play an important role as religious and charitable associations.[35] The confraternity dedicated to Saint Anne, the jeweler's organization, still chose a "Prince of the May" and presented gifts at the high altar of Notre-Dame at midnight on 1 May. In addition, members of this confraternity retained the exclusive privilege of carrying the reliquary casket of Saint Marcel in public processions.[36] As much merchants as craftsmen, the jewelers were an elite corporation, but other artisanal groups had similar privileges. The leather curriers (*corroyeurs*), for instance, had the exclusive right to carry the reliquary of Saint Merry in that parish's processions.[37] The surgeons, on the other hand, made a distinctive charitable contribution by tending the sick free of charge on the first Monday of each month outside of the church of Saint-Côme-Saint-Damien, where their confraternity was housed.[38]

Some confraternities offered holy bread in their religious services. Here, as in the parish services, the corporate and communal symbolism is self-evident. The use of holy bread in confraternal ceremonies was not, however, unanimously approved by parish priests. In a little tract published in 1578, René Benoist, curé of Saint-Eustache, criticized the distribution of holy bread by confraternities on the ground that it might confuse the common people, who, mistaking this bread for the bread of Holy Communion, would think they had fulfilled their Easter duty and cease attending parish services.[39] The same criticism that the holy bread might be mistaken for the Eucharist could have been leveled at the parish custom, but apparently it was not. The reason is that behind the criticism of the confraternities was a drive to strengthen the parish as the focus of religious devotion. The distribution of the holy bread after parish mass was a welcome custom because it encouraged parochial unity; it was unwelcome in confraternal practice because it was feared that confraternal worship might distract people from parochial worship, thereby removing them from the supervision of their pastor and confessor.

The emphasis on parochial duties, usually considered a hallmark of the Counter-Reformation church, was underscored by Pierre Dyvolé in a sermon preached in 1558. Stressing the need to attend mass in one's own parish at least once a week, Dyvolé insisted that "since ancient times, the church has excommunicated those who let three Sundays pass without attending parochial mass, unless they have a valid reason."[40] We should not however take the campaign to get people to focus their devotional life on the parish, instead of attending only confraternal masses or chasing around Paris to hear the most recently fashionable preachers (as one curé chided his flock), as a sign that parish ties were weak.[41] On the contrary, there is evidence that parochial life in Paris was intense, particularly among social elites, who had more stable patterns of residence and consequently tended to become more closely associated with a single parish than did the popular classes. Pierre Chaunu's students, studying testamentary patterns in sixteenth-century Paris, found that more than three-quarters of the people who asked to be buried in a church named a parish church as their preferred place of burial (69 percent in the parish where they currently resided; 7 percent in a parish where they had previously resided and where other family members were buried). Only 24 percent chose to be buried in one of Paris's many convent churches. These were nearly always nobles, but even burial in a parish church was a privilege of the elite—of those who had served their churches as vestrymen, contributed funds for their building and upkeep, and founded masses for their own souls and those of family members.[42]

The structures of parish life encouraged participation by well-to-do parishioners. It was standard practice for the parishioners to meet at least once a year to review the vestry books and choose new lay wardens or vestrymen (*marguilliers*), but in some parishes there were more frequent meetings of select groups of parishioners as well. The "*notables paroissiens*" of Saint-Etienne-du-Mont, for example, met after mass on the last Sunday of each month to discuss the affairs of the parish.[43] The vestry book of Saint-Merry does not indicate that meetings were held on a regular basis, but it does show that such important business as the commissioning of a pulpit or rood screen was always discussed at relatively large group meetings and not merely decided by the vestrymen. Until an office was completed for the vestrymen of Saint-Merry in 1563, these meetings were held in the home of one of the notable parishioners.[44]

Evidence of the ties that humbler people had with their parishes is harder to come by, but an examination of wills suggests that these ties were often strong. After Saint Michael the Archangel and Saints Peter and Paul, parish patrons were the saints most commonly invoked in Parisian testaments in the clause in which the testator confided his or her soul after death to God and other members of the heavenly host.[45] Moreover, testators very often requested commemorative masses at their parish churches, even if they also requested services at convent churches, and they frequently made charitable donations to their parish priest, the vestry, and parish confraternities. To cite just one example, Marie de Fourmancourt, the widow of a secondhand dealer, not only ordered three complete services, each consisting of thirteen low masses, to be said in her parish church of Saint-André-des-Arts following her death, but she also ordered a low mass said every week for a year and specifically named the priest who was to celebrate it. The same priest was made an executor of her testament. In addition, she left twenty sous to the confraternity of the Blessed Sacrament in her parish, in order that she might be included in confraternal prayers.[46]

The emphasis on parochial worship, intended to keep individuals under the eye of their pastor and confessor, can be placed in the larger context of a campaign for greater public order and a more austere morality that was being waged in tandem by Catholic clergy and royal magistrates in the middle and later decades of the sixteenth century. The laws forbidding artisanal confraternities from holding banquets and other assembles were part of the same campaign. So was a parlementary order issued in 1551 intended to regulate behavior at parish dances and festivals.

Citing past incidents of violence, abduction, and unseemly behavior, the court commanded that people attending such festivities conduct themselves modestly and forbade them to bear arms or to wear masks or disguises.[47] It would be a mistake, however, to see the campaign for order and "decency" as having been aimed primarily at the common folk.[48] It was aimed at least as much at social elites. The legislation cited above, for example, was directed primarily against young nobles and their lackeys, who were notorious for invading public festivities masked and bearing swords, in search of a little fun.[49] Sumptuary laws and pamphlet literature were also directed against the sartorial excesses, lascivious behavior, and apparent lack of religious devotion of some of the elites.

In sermons preached in the late 1560s and early 1570s, Simon Vigor complained bitterly about the failure of "*les grands*" to attend mass on a regular basis and affirmed that true Christianity had always resided in the simple populace, which had always understood the Lord's teachings better than the great.[50] René Benoist, in a treatise published in 1564, criticized the indifference of nobles and magistrates, who should, on the contrary, "be the first to honor and serve God, who exalted them and raised them above other people." Benoist also directed some sharp words at the "dames et demoyselles" who came to mass in the company of their young admirers, their hearts burning with the "fires of Cupid" rather than being filled with the love of God.[51] He further criticized "*les grands*" for refusing to take part in processions, which they preferred to watch from the comfort of rented windows along the processional route, or, if they did take part, for doing so without true devotion.[52] He had the same objection to the behavior of his fellow clergymen during processions. He accused them of idly watching passers-by instead of chanting or praying with proper reverence. Earlier sermons and treatises are less explicit in their social criticism, although Francois Le Picart and Pierre Dyvolé both devoted passages of their sermons to the discussion of proper clerical morality.[53] Nevertheless, there is little reason to believe that Le Picart, dean of Saint-Germain-l'Auxerrois, was addressing himself primarily to the populace when he warned that Paris threatened to become another Sodom and Gomorrah and preached continence and a retreat from the sins of the flesh.[54]

The theme of Sodom and Gomorrah in Le Picart's sermon is a reminder of the importance of collective behavior to sixteenth-century Catholics. Just as one might benefit from the prayers of others, so might one be threatened by their sins, which could bring down the wrath of God upon an entire people. This theme assumes increasing importance with the development of the religious conflicts, but it is already evident at mid-century. Only united in one Christian community could Parisians hope to find favor in the eyes of God. This idea is clearly expressed in a sermon preached by Claude Despence at Saint-Séverin in 1557. Citing Psalm 89 Despence spoke first of the joy and benediction that occur when the people are one in their praise of God. What jubilation when all of a parish, all of a diocese, is without division and heresy!

> If then we raise our hands and heart to our Lord, . . . if we raise our understanding
> with good works, Jesus Christ will make the Earth shake so hard that the walls of

Hell and heresy will fall in and the devils be vanquished. The evil spirit of all the world and all trouble will cease; all wars will end. . . . [55]

We cannot understand the French Catholic reaction to religious schism unless we can comprehend that, for the sixteenth-century Parisian, religious unity—personally felt and publicly displayed—was not just an ideal, but a vital condition for individual and collective salvation. Society was perceived as an organic whole, "one bread, and one body."

The City, the Saints, and the Blessed Sacrament

"It is not enough to believe to be saved," wrote René Benoist in the 1560s, "one must also make profession of one's beliefs." Taking part in a religious procession was, in Benoist's terms, a public profession of faith, a way of marking out a distinctive community of Christian believers. It was a way of imitating Christ, who carried his cross publicly through the streets of Jerusalem.[56] Many Parisian processions were not, however, purely religious occasions celebrating the holy days of the Christian calendar. Rather, they were ordered by the king or the city to pray for the success of the king's armies, implore an end to heavy rains, or otherwise solicit divine intervention in secular affairs. These processions reflect a merging of wordly and religious aims and demonstrate well the way in which Catholic beliefs, monarchical politics, and civic identity were mutually reinforcing elements of Parisian culture. On one level at least, the processions were elaborate programs for self-representation by which the cultural elites, both clerical and lay, represented themselves and their ideologies to the common people who gathered to watch.

Our sources seldom reveal popular reaction to the processions, though we occasionally hear that the people were moved to "humility and devotion" or even to "fervent tears"—testimony, however imprecise, to the emotional impact generated by the visceral experience of being part of a crowd swept up in a common mood and purpose.[57] For the most part, we have to rely on our imaginations to visualize the impression the great processions must have made on spectators and participants. We can see from city registers that some of these processions were tremendously long—it takes five columns of print just to list the corporate participants and the major relics carried in one procession in 1535, and the list does not even enumerate individual parishes or their relics—but we can only imagine the awesome impact of a seemingly endless parade of jeweled reliquaries, gold crosses, and polychromed saints carried through the streets by barefooted monks, liveried artisans, somber church wardens, and scarlet-robed princes of the church.[58] We have to imagine the intensity of the sound generated in narrow streets by the constant tolling of church bells, the chanting of hymns and anthems, and the steady roll of drums and pipes that announced the passage of the king and to visualize the spectators, crowding every window of the houses on the processional route and jamming every intersection and square, so that all of the city's archers and a supplemental guard as well had to be called out to help keep order.[59]

With some help from imagination, the complex etiquette of urban religious processions can offer important insights into the relationship between the sacred and the secular in the value systems of sixteenth-century Parisians. We shall look first at the ordinary processions that took place regularly within individual parishes and then more closely examine three particular forms of ritual activity: processions to implore the intercession of Saint Geneviève, the patron saint of Paris; processions to appeal for divine aid or to give thanks for victories in war; and processions of the Blessed Sacrament for the purpose of combatting heresy. I will argue that these three types of processions, distinct in origin and ceremony, came together in 1568, at the outset of the third religious war, in a deliberate attempt to mask the waning authority of a weak, young king by evoking metaphorically the symbolic values of everlasting kingship under the auspices of divine sanction and in the name of religious truth.

Let us begin with a broad picture of the city's processional tradition. Each parish church had its own processional calendar, marking out the days of its patron saints as well as the common holy days of the Christian year. In the parish of Saint-Jacques-de-la-Boucherie, for example, there were eight occasions annually on which the curé and his attendants were required to make a solemn progress through the streets of the parish, in addition to five holy days on which the procession merely circled the exterior of the church. These processions marked the feast days of the church's patrons, Saint Jacques le Majeur and Saint Jacques le Mineur (Saint James the Great and Saint James the Less), as well as such holy days as Ash Wednesday, Palm Sunday, and Ascension Thursday. Each of these processions had its assigned relics and ornaments, and each took a somewhat different path through streets hung with tapestries for the occasion. For all of them, church bells tolled from the moment the procession left the church porch until it returned. In the course of the year, virtually every street in the parish was marked out. The Corpus Christi procession circumscribed the entire parish, which straddled the Seine and included part of the Ile de la Cité as well as a good portion of the old mercantile heart of the city. Three dozen garlands of red roses were ordered each year to deck the cross, monstrance, and heads of the clerics and laymen who participated in the Corpus Christi procession.[60] The neighboring parish of Saint-Merry apparently celebrated Corpus Christi with an even larger procession, for it required nine dozen garlands and eight large bouquets annually.[61]

In addition to processions in each parish, Corpus Christi was celebrated with processions from the parish churches to Notre-Dame. When the king was in Paris, Corpus Christi celebrations were even more elaborate than usual. In 1567, for instance, Charles IX and his court joined the procession from Saint-Germain-l'Auxerrois, the royal parish, to the cathedral. Four princes of the blood carried the canopy that covered the monstrance bearing the consecrated host. The king and his mother walked immediately behind, in the position of honor always occupied by the participants with the highest rank.[62]

Processions from one church or monastery to another had both ecclesiastical and spiritual purposes. Some were forms of homage and reminders of the lines of authority that bound one ecclesiastical institution to another. The six parishes that were dependencies of Saint-Martin-des-Champs, for example, were obliged on each

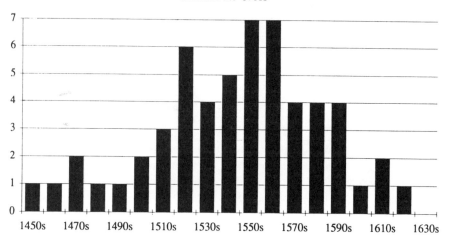

Figure 2–1. Graph showing the number of processions of the relics of Saint Geneviève held during each decade between 1450 and 1640. (Derived from the list of processions in Pinet, *Le culte de Sainte Geneviève*, pp. 75ff.)

of the three Rogation Days that preceded Ascension to go in solemn procession to that priory, from there to accompany the monks of Saint-Martin to the churches where they traditionally sang mass on these days.[63] The same reason, but also a desire to express gratitude, explains the annual procession that the priests and parishioners of Saint-Nicolas-des-Champs made to the priory of Saint-Martin-des-Champs on the feast day of Saint Cecilia. They went to express their thanks for the relics of Saint Cecilia, which had been given them by the monks of Saint-Martin, but, as their parish was a dependency of the priory, their visit was also a gesture of obeisance.[64] Other processions were marks of respect between independent clerical agencies or of homage to their respective patron saints. When the Faculty of Theology and the monks of Saint-Germain-des-Prés at last settled years of disputes over the pré aux Clercs in 1554, the reconciliation was solemnized by a procession from the university to Saint-Germain.[65]

In times of crisis, the regular processional calendar was augmented by additional processions to convent churches or other places with holy meaning. When natural disaster threatened—whether from drought, flooding, plague, or other causes—the first and primary appeal was always to Saint Geneviève, the "ancient guardian of Paris."[66] The cult of Saint Geneviève appears to have reached its peak in the sixteenth century, when forty-six processions of the saint's relics were held (as compared with five in the fourteenth century, eleven in the fifteenth, seven in the seventeenth, and two in the eighteenth century).[67] Indeed, as Figure 2–1 illustrates, it reached its peak in the 1550s and 1560s, precisely at the moment the religious conflicts moved into crisis.

An elaborate etiquette governed the ceremonies by which the saint's relics, preserved in a thirteenth-century vermeil casket, were taken down from their normal resting place in the abbey dedicated to her and paraded through the streets of the city. Whenever possible, there were processions in each of the city's parishes the week before the general procession, and the monks of Sainte-Geneviève always prepared for the event by three days of fasting and prayer vigils that ended with Holy Communion.[68] The ceremony itself took place in several stages. The city officers gathered around seven in the morning at the city hall and, accompanied by anywhere from several dozen to several hundred bourgeois notables, went in procession to the cathedral, where they joined with other processions coming from parish and convent churches. The relics of Saint Marcel, another patron of the city, were then brought out from Notre-Dame and the entire group proceeded up the rue Saint-Jacques to Sainte-Geneviève. According to tradition, Saint Geneviève could not come out unless Saint Marcel came to fetch her.[69] Meanwhile, the members of the sovereign court were making their own procession from the Palais de Justice to Sainte-Geneviève. From the abbey, the combined parades returned through the rue Saint-Jacques to Notre-Dame, where the ceremony culminated in a high mass.

The order of the procession followed a long-established pattern. The mendicant orders, with their banners and relics, led, followed by delegations representing the parish churches. After them came the clergy attached to Notre-Dame, sharing the roadway with the monks of Sainte-Geneviève, which served to demonstrate the equal standing of the two ecclesiastical institutions. The bishop of Paris and the abbot of Sainte-Geneviève likewise walked side by side directly after the reliquary caskets of their respective saints, with the lieutenant civil and other officers of the Châtelet walking on the wings to serve as honor guard for the precious relics. Privileged to carry their patron's relics in the procession, the members of the confraternity of Saint Geneviève, like the monks of the abbey, had prepared for the procession with prayer and Holy Communion. Garlanded with flowers, they walked barefoot and were robed only in simple white tunics. The abbot and his monks were similarly garbed. By contrast, the bishop of Paris normally wore his most splendid pontifical attire. Monarchical authority was represented by the officers of Parlement, who followed after the bishop and the abbot in their finest scarlet robes and shared the pavement with the officers of the Hôtel de Ville, outfitted in their best livery of red and tan.[70]

Although Protestants mocked Parisian Catholics for believing that Saint Geneviève could make it rain or, if it rained too much, make it stop raining, the saint's intercessory powers were highly regarded in the city.[71] Indeed, if we choose to believe diarists and city registers, Geneviève's record in the 1550s and 1560s was a good one. A procession held in 1551 because of too much rain was followed by "fine weather that lasted a full six weeks."[72] In 1555, the weather cleared up on the very day of the procession and two weeks passed without rain.[73] In 1560, Saint Geneviève seems not to have answered the city's prayers. Two processions were held, on the 16 June and again two weeks later, but heavy rains continued throughout the month of July.[74] This did not destroy confidence in the saint, however, and the procession held in 1564 was followed by fine weather.[75] Accounts of a procession held in 1566 do not mention a change in weather, but they do record that a star appeared in the sky during the procession and shone there for about a quarter of an hour. This was taken as a good omen.[76] Finally, in 1567, when Paris was suffering from the more unusual problem of a hot, dry summer, the skies opened during the procession and poured down the sorely needed rains.[77]

The faith Parisians showed in Saint Geneviève is of course rooted in the Catholic tradition of the veneration of saints. In Catholic teaching, such ritual objects as relics are intended to increase devotion by encouraging people to direct their prayers to the saint whose relics were being displayed, thereby securing the saint's intercession in obtaining more easily from God the things for which the individuals prayed. It is clear that city officers understood the role of Saint Geneviève in this way. City records explicitly refer to her as the city's "advocate" and express the hope that the devotion demonstrated in processions of her relics will move her to plead with God on the city's behalf.[78] It is more difficult to determine whether the common people understood this too, or whether, attributing to the saint's relics the sort of "magic" powers the Protestants decried as Catholic "superstition," they regarded them as potent objects in and of themselves.

We must wonder what went through the minds of the people who threw themselves forward to try to touch the casket of Saint Geneviève as it passed. Did they commonly understand that they were to address their prayers to the saints themselves and not to their image or relics? The fact that René Benoist devoted several pages of the little catechism he published in 1569 to explaining how to pray to the saints suggests that there may have been some confusion on this point.[79] On the other hand, he may have been responding to the Protestant critique more than to a perceived problem among his parishioners. Gentian Hervet, in a little treatise published in 1561, scoffed at the notion that anyone could be so simple-minded as to confuse the saints' images with that which they represented. Denouncing as absurd the Protestant accusation that the Catholics worshiped idols, Hervet asserted that "there is no little ninny [*si petite femmelette*] who does not know well that images are only made for the remembrance of saints, who are not themselves adored as gods, the more reason that their images are not either."[80] There is little cause, then, to think that Catholic theologians would have condemned as excessive or superstitious the devotion that sixteenth-century Parisians showed the saints. Parisian Catholics saw the saints as protectors and patrons, but this did not prevent them from recognizing Jesus Christ as their principal source of help and hope or from addressing him or God the Father directly in their prayers.[81]

Processions of the relics of Saint Geneviève were colorful rituals, rich with symbolism. They were, as Benoist would have it, public professions of faith, and the beauty of the pagentry must indeed have stimulated a rich chorus of prayer. Even passive viewers would have found it hard to resist being drawn in by the subliminal appeal to unity and commitment. Protectress of the community, Saint Geneviève seems to have had a particularly close association with communal and collective forms of piety. The confraternity privileged to carry her relics in civic processions was dominated by bourgeois notables, but the parish confraternities that adopted her as their patron seem to have been nonrestrictive beneficent organizations open to men and women irrespective of social status.[82] The confraternity of Saints Christopher and Geneviève in the parish of Saint-Sulpice, for example, was open to anyone who cared to join and is said to have constituted a sort of "mutual aid society" whose members promised to assist one another in times of sickness.[83] On the other hand, Saint Geneviève does not seem to have inspired a great deal of individual or personal devotion. She does not figure in Pierre Chaunu's list of saints commonly invoked in testaments, nor is there a rich repertory of prayers addressed to her suffrage. Indeed, even books of hours published in Paris for local usage only rarely include prayers to Saint Geneviève.[84] In similar fashion, Saint Denis, the patron saint of the monarchy, was normally invoked in connection with monarchical affairs and not personal ones.

Traditionally, before the king of France went off to war, he went to the abbey of Saint-Denis north of the city to participate in an elaborate procession in which the relics of that saint and his companion martyrs were taken down from their resting place in the abbey church, paraded around the cloister, and returned to the church to be placed before the high altar. Except on occasions when the north of France was threatened with invasion, in which case the relics were taken into Paris for safekeeping, they remained on display at the altar of Saint-Denis until the war was over and the king came back to the abbey church for a service of thanksgiving. It is characteristic of these processions that the king took part in them wearing his royal robes, while his principal attendants carried the regalia. The king's sword was carried unsheathed, traditionally by the constable, followed by the scepter, the hand of justice (*main de justice*), and the coronation crown. In this way, not just the person of the king but the symbols of monarchical authority were represented.

City registers specify that the purpose of these processions was "to make devout prayers to God to give victory to the king against his enemies" or to "give thanks to God, distributor of victories, and to blessed martyrs Saint Denis and his companions, intercessors for [the king]."[85] These were rituals of homage and honor, then, and occasions of prayers for intercession. They had a clearly political purpose in that they placed the king and his cause under divine protection and, by giving thanks for royal victories, identified monarchical triumphs with the divine will. And yet—unlike the other processions that I have described—they were not public occasions. They took place entirely within the confines of the abbey of Saint-Denis, and the principal participants were members of the clergy and courtiers. Only the officers of the sovereign courts and the Bureau de la ville, including a group of bourgeois notables, represented the other estates of the kingdom.[86] The participation of Parisian representatives was nevertheless important, because it strengthened their ties to the royal enterprise, associating them with the king's cause in his wars (and probably also helping to ensure their willingness to provide funds for his campaigns). More public ceremonies to pray for divine assistance when the king went to war or to give thanks for victories and the cessation of hostilities were held in the city of Paris. Victories in war, for example, were celebrated with a *Te Deum* at Notre-Dame and proclamations of peace with a general procession between the Sainte-Chapelle and Notre-Dame. There were also more secular festivities, such as bonfires on the place de Grève and in each quartier.[87]

The procession held on 9 July 1559 to appeal for the life of Henri II, wounded while jousting ten days earlier, typifies the ceremonial response in the capital to political crisis.[88] Sometimes Saint Geneviève was invoked, as she was in 1544, when the danger of invasion by the imperial armies was so great that the carts of fleeing Parisians jammed the procession's path up the rue Saint-Jacques.[89] More typically, political crisis was met with a procession that circled the Ile de la Cité, progressing from the Sainte-Chapelle to Notre-Dame and back, the same processional route that was used to mark royal triumphs and proclamations of peace.

Housed in the old royal palace, for several centuries already the Palais de Justice, the Sainte-Chapelle was quite naturally associated with monarchical authority. A processional route that circled the Ile de la Cité, the ancient heart of the city, to link the Sainte-Chapelle with the cathedral of Notre-Dame was weighty with a symbolism that was simultaneously monarchical and Catholic, yet tinged as well with the local patriotism that was in no small part the product of these identities.

The order for these processions was similar to that employed in the processions of the relics of Saint Geneviève; that is to say, the mendicant orders led, followed by delegations representing the city's parishes, and the clergy from Notre-Dame and the Sainte-Chapelle walking side by side. The relics from these churches came next, followed by the bishop of Paris and any other high-ranking churchmen or nobles who happened to take part. The officers of Parlement, on the right, sharing the roadway with the officers of the Bureau de la ville, on the left, brought up the rear. Different relics and ornaments were carried in different processions. During the reign of François I, the most commonly carried relic was a piece of the True Cross.[90] The processions became more elaborate during the reign of Henri II. When the king was injured in 1559, the caskets of Saint Geneviève and Saint Marcel were brought out and carried in the procession, as, significantly, were the reliquary heads of two kings of France, Saint Louis and Charlemagne.[91]

The weakening of the monarchy with the religious wars made the need for the symbolic display of authority still greater. In 1568, when Charles IX, having just recovered from a serious illness, prepared to go to war against the Huguenots, all the emblems of royalty were paraded. In addition to the relics already mentioned, the casket of Saint Denis, brought into the city in September 1567 because of the danger from the Huguenot armies, was carried in the procession. The place of honor was assigned to the consecrated host, carried by the cardinal of Lorraine, escorted by the cardinals of Guise and Bourbon, under a canopy supported by the four Montmorency brothers. Immediately after came princes of the blood bearing the hand of justice, the scepter, and the royal crown. The regalia was followed by the king himself, on horseback because he was still too weak to walk.[92]

Although there is no evidence, one might suspect that the hand of Catherine de Medici, with her strong love of ceremony and keen instinct for symbolic values, lay behind the ceremonial innovations this procession displays. The appeal to symbolic majesty would appear to have been a deliberate attempt to mask the waning authority of the Valois kings. It would appear, moreover, that the procession achieved its desired effect of transcending the reality of a weak, young king by evoking metaphorically the symbolic values of unchanging, everlasting kingship. To borrow from Ernst Kantorowicz's classic analysis of *The King's Two Bodies*, the procession of 1568 succeeded in substituting the image of the "body politic" for the "body natural" of the king.[93] The evidence for the success of this substitution is indirect but suggestive.

François Grin, a canon of Saint-Victor, recorded in his journal account of the procession of 1568 that one of the sacred objects that was carried there was the "holy ampoule of Rheims."[94] This seems to be a mistake, for no other sources mention the holy ampoule containing the sacred oil used for the consecration of

French kings. The error is nonetheless significant. Grin's mention of the ampoule of Rheims shows how closely the ritual objects carried in this procession were identified with monarchical authority. Said to have been carried down from heaven on the wings of a dove for the baptism of Clovis, the first Christian king of the Franks, the holy ampoule of Rheims was a key legitimizing element in the French kings' claim to rule by divine right. As Ralph Giesey has explained, the king's consecration with this oil reenacted a double myth, "the myth of the providential sanction of Frankish kingship" and, by extension, "the myth of the chosen people."[95] The holy ampoule was thus an exceedingly powerful symbol, conveying at one and the same time the king's right to rule, the special favor God showed the French people, and their mission to preserve his holy religion. Grin seems personally to have witnessed—probably even to have taken part in—the 1568 procession. The fact that he believed afterwards that the holy ampoule had been paraded there strongly suggests that the cumulative effect of the symbolic objects displayed in the procession was to evoke the sense of divine right, special favor, and sacred mission associated with the anointing of French kings. It suggests that the procession succeeded in conjuring the images and stimulating the passions necessary to strengthen a worried and divided people about to engage, for the third time in six years, in a bloody civil war.

How was this illusion accomplished? There were two key innovations in the procession of 1568. Borrowed from other forms of religious procession, they were juxtaposed in such a way as to give a new significance to each. The first was the carrying of the regalia—the hand of justice, the scepter, and the crown—which had never before been done in a religious procession outside of the confines of the abbey of Saint-Denis. The second was the display of the Eucharist, which had never been done in a procession whose primary purpose was to pray for the king's health and his fortunes in war. Of these two innovations, the latter is perhaps the more significant. The Blessed Sacrament had come to assume an important emblematic role in the struggle against heresy, and it was almost inevitable that this powerful symbol of Catholic unity should eventually be appropriated to the royal cause in the civil wars. Let us look back briefly to see how the display of the Eucharist became identified with the struggle against heresy in Paris.

The first procession against heresy in the capital occurred in 1528 to expiate a sacrilege committed against a statue of the Virgin affixed to a wall in the rue aux Juifs. Although François I took part personally in the procession, it was neither elaborate nor ritually complex. After mass at the neighboring church of Sainte-Catherine, the processional party, bearing lighted candles, proceeded to the site of the sacrilege, where the king placed a new, silver-plated statue of the Virgin Mary in the empty niche.[96] Popular reaction to the event was naive. Placed in the church of Saint-Gervais, where it was known as "Notre-Dame-de-Souffrance" or "Notre-Dame-de-Bonne-Délivrance," the desecrated Virgin attracted the prayers of pregnant women.[97] The broken statue was believed to have acquired miraculous powers as a result of its persecution, and it was rumored that a woman praying before it felt the baby that was dead in her womb quicken and come back to life. As symbols of unjust persecution, both this statue and the one that replaced it—which was also subsequently desecrated and replaced—had emblematic value in the struggle against heresy. The symbol of the desecrated Virgin was soon overshadowed, however, by the symbol of the consecrated host.

In January 1535, a much more elaborate procession took place against the heretics, who were accused of having "blasphemed God of the Blessed Sacrament of the altar" by the posting of placards against the mass. Ordered by the king as a measure to combat Protestant proselytizing, this seems to have been the first procession outside of Corpus Christi in which the Blessed Sacrament was carried. It was, in fact, the most elaborate religious procession the city had seen to date. In addition to the usual preparations of cleaning the streets and hanging tapestries in front of the houses where the procession was to pass, the king ordered that each of the householders along the route stand outside his house bearing a lighted torch while the procession passed. The pont Notre-Dame, which the procession was to cross, was canopied with green garlands and decorated with narrative paintings depicting religious themes. Significantly, one of these paintings illustrated the story of the miraculous bleeding host of Saint-Jean-en-Grève. The use of the consecrated host as a symbol of Catholic triumph over the evil designs of nonbelievers was thus clearly set out in the programmatic design of the procession.[98]

The procession was orchestrated, moreover, with the Eucharist as its central metaphor and eucharistic devotion its primary gesture. The list of relics carried in the procession is enormously long and includes the Crown of Thorns, the tip of the lance that pierced Christ's side, a drop of Christ's blood, a piece of his robe, and a drop of milk from the Virgin Mary, as well as the more commonly displayed pieces of the True Cross. In addition, the reliquary caskets of Saint Magloire, Saint Martin, Saint Eloi, and Saint Germain were brought out to join the more frequently paraded reliquaries of the city's patrons, Saints Marcel and Geneviève. Pride of place, however, went to the Eucharist, which was carried by the bishop of Paris under a canopy borne by four princes of the blood and immediately followed by the king. Walking alone, bare-headed and carrying a burning torch, François I forsook the appurtenances of royal majesty—the symbols of office and covering canopy to which he had a right—to present himself as a solitary and humble Christian. This deliberate self-effacement emphasized that it was the Blessed Sacrament that was the focal point of the procession.

During the procession, moreover, there were four stations or resting places, at each of which the bishop of Paris put down the monstrance bearing the Eucharist, while the king stepped forward and, after handing his torch to the cardinal of Lorraine, joined his hands and bowed in prayer. The king's display of piety impressed his people tremendously. The city recorder was convinced that "no Jew or infidel seeing the example of the Prince, and after him of his people, could fail to be converted to the [Catholic] faith."[99]

The processional route itself placed special emphasis on the Sacrament of the altar. The general procession originated at Saint-Germain-l'Auxerrois, which, as the royal parish, was given the honor of providing the host that was used in the procession to Notre-Dame. This meant that all the participants had first to make individual processions to bring their precious relics to Saint-Germain-l'Auxerrois, where they merged into a single procession with the monstrance containing the

Eucharist as its climactic center. Even the reliquary of Saint Germain, which, the city recorder noted, had never before left the precincts of Saint-Germain-des-Prés, and the caskets of Saints Marcel and Geneviève, which traditionally moved only between Notre-Dame and the Left Bank abbey of Sainte-Geneviève, were brought over for the occasion. This was done in homage to the Blessed Sacrament, for the etiquette that governed the movements of the saints' relics was every bit as rich in gestures of deference as the etiquette of the king's court.[100] The honor paid the consecrated host can be explained as a result of this hierarchical thinking. As the body of Christ, the Eucharist necessarily took precedence over the saints. More particularly, as the body of the glorified Christ, the Eucharist also took precedence over relics associated with the body of the human Christ, such as the vial enclosing a drop of his blood. The etiquette for the procession thus affirmed and underscored the doctrine of the real presence.

The public part of the procession ended with high mass at Notre-Dame, but many in the watching crowds stayed on to witness the execution by burning of six convicted heretics at two sites near the processional path. In the meantime, the officers of Parlement, the Châtelet, the Hôtel de Ville, and the university dined at the bishop's palace with the king, who took the occasion to remind them of their responsibility to help protect the faith. The king made his position clear when he said that he wanted the heretical errors banished from his kingdom, ''in such manner that if one of the arms of my body was infected with this corruption, I would cut it off, and if my children were tainted with it, I would myself offer them in sacrifice.''[101] In this way, the king put into words the purging of the social body that the day's events had dramatized.

When Henri II became king, one of the first things he did after his formal entry into his capital in 1549 was to order a procession against heresy. The procession of 1535, for which he had helped carry the canopy over the eucharistic host, was clearly the model for the procession of 1549. Since the royal family was staying at the hôtel des Tournelles, the neighboring church of Saint-Paul was used as the starting place for the procession. The list of precious relics seems somewhat shorter than for the 1535 procession, but it contains many of the same items, including the Crown of Thorns, pieces of the True Cross, and the reliquary caskets of Saints Marcel and Geneviève. As in the earlier procession, the Blessed Sacrament was the focal point of the ritual parade. The king and queen, candles in hand, followed behind. Later that same day, after high mass at Notre-Dame and a round of speeches, convicted heretics were burned at three locations in the city. The king himself attended the executions in the rue Saint-Antoine and admonished the prisoners to recant.[102]

During the next ten years, the king was largely preoccupied with his wars against the Hapsburgs, and there were no general processions against heresy of the scale and splendor of the processions of 1535 and 1549. There was one procession against heresy in 1551 in which the relics of Saint Geneviève were carried to the Sainte-Chapelle and then accompanied by the Blessed Sacrament to Notre-Dame. The king took part personally in this ceremony, but it did not match the processions of 1535 or 1549 for drama or display.[103] Instead, what became more important at this time were processions to expiate sacrileges in Parisian churches and churchyards. At least four such processions took place in the early 1550s. Three resulted from attacks on statues of the Virgin Mary and followed the pattern of the expiatory procession of 1528. The fourth, which occurred in 1553, was to expiate a sacrilege committed against a consecrated host in the church of Saint-Honoré.[104] The pattern established at this time continued into the religious wars, when sacrileges against the host became a characteristic form of religious violence and expiatory processions an obligatory response.[105] Indeed, one of the opening gestures in the first religious war was an elaborate procession of the Blessed Sacrament to reconsecrate the church of Saint-Médard, desecrated in religious riots six months earlier.[106]

Religious processions thus served a didactic function, reinforcing the lessons of the Mass about the meaning and importance of the Eucharist. The image of François I or Henri II devoutly following the consecrated host must inevitably have remained in the minds of people who witnessed these events, particularly those who later in the same day had watched the execution of convicted heretics. But at the same time that they educated, the processions inflamed. They ritually enacted a vision in which civic, monarchical, and Catholic symbols merged; the body social, the body politic, and the body of Christ were so closely intertwined as to be inseparable. As events were later to prove, it was easier for most Parisians to break the link to the monarchy than to the image of a unified church. If the king had two bodies, Christ had but one. The mortal, "natural body" of the king could be cast out, while the enduring principle of kingship, the "body politic," was retained. The body of Christ—the unity of Christian believers—allowed for no such separation.

3

The Intensification of
Religious Hatreds, 1557–1562

Only by describing the chain of events that led to the murderous paroxysm that convulsed Paris in August 1572 can we begin to grasp the depth of religious hatreds and their potential for violence. Accordingly, the next four chapters will adopt a narrative mode of presentation. They will retain an analytical subtext where incidents of popular violence are concerned, for our story can only progress if we ask not just *what* happened but *why* these events occurred. Certain analytical questions will, however, be postponed until later chapters so as not to impede the narrative flow. We shall return later to the problem of the Parisian Calvinists. Who adopted the new faith and why? How did they react to the terror of persecution? We shall also return to take a closer look at the Catholic clergy, the magistrates, and the militia—groups that in one way or another bore responsibility for keeping peace in the city. How did they respond to the escalating violence, and on whom did they place the blame? Did they seek to quench popular passions or to inflame them all the more? Finally, we will ask about the consequences these events had for the individuals engulfed by them, for the city, and for the state. How did the religious conflicts affect people as citizens and as subjects? How, in the end, did they affect the larger course of French history? Before we can ask these questions we need a clearer picture of the sequence of events through which the religious hatreds deepened and their potential for violence intensified.

To begin at the beginning we would have to go back beyond the first influx of Lutheran ideas and their condemnation by the Sorbonne in 1521. But our purpose here is not to give a history of Protestantism in France to 1572. Rather, we shall take up the story only after the underground current of French Protestantism became sufficiently permeated with Calvinist teachings to lead to the formation of clandestine daughter churches modeled after Calvin's own church in Geneva. This occurred in Paris in 1555, when a Reformed church was officially founded. Still shrouded in secrecy, the new church became increasingly bold in its proselytism. As the clandestine gatherings became larger, the level of public opposition increased. The first large-scale riots against the new religion took place in 1557. We shall begin our narrative there.

The Breakdown of Order, 1557–1560

On the night of 4 September 1557, three or four hundred men and women gathered in secret in a house in the rue Saint-Jacques for Bible reading, worship, and the celebration of the Lord's Supper according to the rites of the Church of Geneva. Although they came quietly and in small groups, their arrival was observed by some student priests, residents of the collège du Plessis across the street. When the meeting ended, the worshipers found a crowd gathered outside the door that used threats and stones to drive back those trying to leave. For many in attendance, however, fear of the police, who had been summoned, was greater than fear of the people. Protected by the swords of the noblemen among them, some of the worshipers broke through the crowd and made their escape, although the clamor was attracting an ever larger and more vehement audience. When the authorities arrived, they arrested the individuals that remained in the house. About one hundred and thirty persons, many of them women, had not dared to attempt flight. In the end, however, even those that stayed behind had to face the crowds. Charged with holding an illicit meeting, they were bound together and led off to the Châtelet through a hail of insults, as the people in the streets tore at their clothes, tugged at their hair, and smeared dirt in their faces.[1]

This was not the first time that Catholic Parisians had demonstrated their hatred for the followers of the new religion, but it does mark a new dimension to that hatred. In the past, the Catholic fervor of the Parisian populace had been shown by the enthusiasm with which they turned out to watch the execution of condemned heretics or their participation in processions to expiate sacrileges, but acts of violence against persons suspected of the new faith had been few in number and small in scale.[2] After the affair of the rue Saint-Jacques, such acts multiplied. The increase is not fortuitous; it follows a path clearly marked out by broader political developments. This chapter will trace the complex interrelations between popular violence and monarchical politics in the period between the riot in the rue Saint-Jacques and the beginning of the first religious war in 1562. Succeeding chapters will follow these developments through Saint Bartholomew's Day.

The emotional climate for the affair of the rue Saint-Jacques was engendered by the disastrous defeat of the French forces under Constable Montmorency outside Saint-Quentin on 10 August 1557 and the subsequent taking of that town by the Spanish on 27 August. With the king and the greatest part of the French army still in Italy and less than one hundred miles of open plain lying between the Spanish troops and Paris, the fall of Saint-Quentin awakened a chilling fear that the Hapsburgs might put an end to their long wars with France by taking the French capital.[3] City officials reacted to the threat by reinforcing local defenses, setting watch for spies, and calling up the militia, which was still organized on the basis of trades. The review of city troops, however, did little to ease the fear. When the militia was assembled, it was found that there were not enough arms to go around: companies had to lend one another their pikes in order to complete the parade of colors.[4] With a show of more spirit than force, the hastily assembled troops held a general parade on the fairgrounds outside the porte Saint-Denis on 5 September, the day after the affair of the rue Saint-Jacques.[5] Under the circumstances, it is not surprising that the military threat and the activities of the Calvinists became somehow entwined in the popular imagination. Among the slanders hurled at the worshipers of the rue Saint-Jacques was the accusation that they were responsible for France's defeat.[6]

After the affair of the rue Saint-Jacques, the Protestants met for a time only in small groups and with a great concern for secrecy. In February 1558, the minister Macard wrote to Calvin that he had to preach five times a day because his flock was so scattered. In early March, Macard was able to report that people were showing a bit more courage, but his next letter is again pessimistic, explaining on behalf of his followers that "while they greatly feared the voracious *commissaires*, who were everywhere pursuing their prey, they had an even greater fear of the populace, whose rage was excited by the sermons of the priests." In spite of their fears, Macard and his fellow Calvinists continued to visit the prisoners of the rue Saint-Jacques in jail and to encouraged them to remain firm in their faith. Many of the prisoners had already submitted to the pressures of their judges and families and had secured their release by recanting. By February, only about twenty-five of the original one hundred and thirty remained in jail, and many of these later weakened under the king's threat to cut out their tongues and burn them alive.[7]

Despite these trials, the Calvinist movement had by May gathered the strength for more public displays of faith. On five successive evenings, Calvinists assembled to sing psalms on the pré aux Clercs, outside the porte Saint-Germain. Some important nobles, including the king of Navarre, were reputed to be among the singers, and large crowds—part admiring, part scornful—turned out to watch. Exaggerated reports of the size and character of these gatherings excited the wrath of Henri II, who had been told that more than eight hundred "Lutherans" (as all Protestants were still commonly called) had assembled in arms on the pré aux Clercs and that they threatened an uprising. The continued war with Spain made the suspicion of sedition particularly irritating to the king and dangerous to the Calvinists. They had been willing to court martyrdom in the affair of the rue Saint-Jacques, but they recognized that it would do their cause no good to appear guilty of subversive enterprises against the state. They consequently complied with Henri's order to cease the gatherings on the pré aux Clercs.[8]

The king's anger did not, however, abate. He ordered stiffer measures taken against the Protestants, and he redoubled his efforts to extricate himself from the foreign war that was distracting him from the religious troubles at home.[9] The Calvinists returned to secret services in secluded places outside the city or, in small groups, in private houses. On at least one occasion, in September 1558, they narrowly escaped a repetition of the affair of the rue Saint-Jacques. The city guard discovered their meeting place near the city wall, but before the guard could make its move, a frightened Calvinist fired his pistol (an accident, claimed Macard in his report to Calvin, adding that fortunately no one was hurt). The shot scared away the converging crowd, and the Calvinists were able to make their escape through a convenient hole in the city wall.[10]

The Treaty of Cateau-Cambrésis, signed on 3 April 1559, finally put an end to the Hapsburg-Valois wars and allowed Henri II to return his attention to the financial and religious crises that troubled his kingdom. The religious problems were taken up at a special session, or *mercuriale*, of the Parlement of Paris, some of whose members were accused of dealing too leniently with the heretics. On 10 June, Henri attended in person to hear why Parlement had failed to register his most recent law against the "Lutherans." By the end of the session, five magistrates had been arrested for their religious opinions. Among them was the counselor Anne Du Bourg, who had spoken at length against the royal policy of persecution and, in the process, so outraged the king that Henri swore he would see Du Bourg burn.[11]

Du Bourg was burned, but Henri was not there to see him. The king died exactly a month after the famous session of 10 June in an accident that was of immeasurable importance for French history. Taking part in a tournament joust during the festivities for the marriage of his daughter Elisabeth to Philip II, Henri was pierced in the eye by his opponent's splintered lance and died as a result of the infection. The accident deprived France of a mature, adult king and opened the way for the rampant factionalism that was to lead within three years to civil war.

One of the most immediate results of Henri's death was an increase in the policy of religious persecution, as the cardinal of Lorraine and his brother, the duc de Guise, came to power through the influence their niece, Mary Stuart, had over her young husband, King François II. The Guises had long argued that sterner measures were needed to put an end to the Protestant heresy. Their new power at court can be seen in an increase in the number of arrests and executions for heresy during the eighteen-month reign of François II (1559–1560) and in the series of harsh new laws that were passed during this period. Even before Henri's death, however, there was an increase in the number of arrests for heresy. Many of these arrests apparently resulted from denunciations made by a couple of apprentices who had quarreled with their Calvinist masters. As early as October 1558, Macard had been warned that defectors had turned over a list of names to the magistrates and that these names were now in the hands of the cardinal of Lorraine, who intended to use it to put an end to the new sect. It was hoped that the first arrests would lead to a chain of denunciations that would spread through the whole underground community.[12]

Parlementary records show how the magistrates hoped to enlarge the network of suspects. They interrogated arrested persons intently, demanding that they name others they had seen at secret services. They also sometimes sentenced condemned heretics to be "put to the question," as the form of torture most commonly used at this time was called, in order to extract further information. Thus, for example, on 18 August 1559, the court sentenced Marguerite Le Riche, the wife of a bookseller in the university quarter, to be put to the "*question extraordinaire*" to make her disclose the names of her "accomplices" in heretical practices. They also wanted her to identify the house in the faubourg Saint-Victor where she had attended Easter services. The judges gave orders for Le Riche's execution at the same time that they ordered her torture, but they forbade the attending officers to tell her this, believing that she would give a fuller confession if she thought it would save her from the stake.[13]

Large and tumultuous crowds turned out for the execution of prisoners like Le Riche. To punish blasphemy—and to prevent condemned heretics from using their last moments to preach to the assembled masses—the judges sometimes ordered the prisoners' tongues cut out before they were tied to the stake.[14] Most, like

Marguerite Le Riche, were merely gagged to enforce their silence. In fact, the judges often moderated the cruel punishment of burning at the stake, the form of execution traditionally ordered for the crime of heresy, by having the prisoner strangled before he or she felt the flames, but in some cases this act of clemency was ordered only if the prisoner showed signs of repentance.[15]

The crowds could be moved by the steadfastness of the religious prisoners, but that did not stop them from being hostile in the extreme. On at least one occasion, residents of the place Maubert, one of the most common sites for executions, themselves gathered the wood and laid the fire for the heretic's burning.[16] And on more than one occasion, the crowd became so unruly that it threatened to take the prisoner out of the hands of the executioners and attend to the burning itself.[17] As the religious conflicts progressed, there were enough incidents of unruly mobs tearing down the bodies of executed heretics in order to mutilate them, drag them through the streets, or subject them to other atrocities that laws had to be passed forbidding such behavior.[18] Even in this early stage of the conflicts, however, a participatory element in the street theater of public executions is obvious.

The new laws that were passed against religious dissidence in the fall of 1559 also encouraged the people to participate in the repression of heresy. In addition to extending the punishments for this crime to include the death sentence for attendance at illicit assemblies and the razing of houses where such assemblies took place, the laws encouraged people to keep watch on their neighbors. Individuals who knew where the assemblies were held and failed to tell the authorities were threatened with death, while informers were promised immunity from prosecution and a share in the properties confiscated from convicted heretics. Landlords were made responsible for inquiring into the religious practices of their tenants, and the *commissaires* and *quarteniers* were ordered to go into the houses of their districts to gather information on the religious practices of their inhabitants and to be certain that they attended mass each Sunday.[19]

The Protestant publicist Régnier de La Planche also describes certain popular practices that were not prescribed by the authorities but were nonetheless used to identify dissenters. Local youths set up images of the Virgin Mary on city street corners and accosted passers-by when they failed to genuflect. They took up collections for the lighting of candles or the saying of masses before saints' images and intimidated anyone who hesitated to contribute. And they turned on accused "Lutherans" with a kind of vigilante spirit that very easily got out of hand.[20]

In March 1559, for example, a riot broke out in the cemetery of the Innocents when a group of people emerging from a sermon in the church overheard one man call another a "Lutheran." Immediately, people threw themselves on the accused man, who had no chance to defend himself and backed into the church for sanctuary. His assailants pursued him there. Two passers-by who tried to intervene were themselves assaulted, and one died as a consequence of his attempted good deed.[21] A similar incident took place in the church of Saint-Eustache when a crowd turned upon a schoolboy whom an old lady accused of being a "Lutheran" and mocking the services, and in December 1559, several supposed "Lutherans" were killed in a riot at Saint-Médard. According to Jean de La Fosse, the curé of Saint-Barthélemy, the "Lutherans" had tried to attack the church. Several persons with previous records for religious dissidence were arrested in the aftermath of the affair, but the records do not allow us to know with any certainty just what occurred.[22]

Whatever the true story behind the Saint-Médard incident, the accusation that "Lutherans" had attacked the church is important here, for it allows us to see the incident from the viewpoint of sixteenth-century Catholics. We must remember that the "Lutheran heresy" was not for sixteenth-century Parisians a mere failure of religious orthodoxy; it was a threat to the social order and a danger to the entire community. The Protestants were believed to be not only religious deviants, but also immoral and seditious.[23]

The belief that the Protestants were debauched is clearly evident in the memoirs of the priest of Provins, Claude Haton, who dwells at length on the sexual activities thought to take place at Calvinist assemblies, in particular the "*charité fraternelle et voluptueuse*" said to be enjoyed after the candles were extinguished. Haton asserts that such activities took place at the assembly in the rue Saint-Jacques. The authorities arrived before the "*charité fraternelle*" was completed, he says, and the ungallant "brothers" left their poor "sisters" in danger. "*Mesdames de la Charité*" were quite embarrassed, leers Haton, to be caught in such circumstances; so were the authorities when they learned the identities of the highborn ladies they had captured. Haton wrongly adds that the ladies were allowed to leave and only men were taken prisoner. He also errs in saying that most were punished lightly and that the harshest penalty was the galleys, since we know that at least nine persons—including one woman of noble birth—were executed as a consequence of the affair of the rue Saint-Jacques. The errors, however, are of a piece with the salacious tone with which Haton recounts these events and with his conclusion that it was "carnal pleasure" that was the real motive for the gathering.[24]

Haton was by no means alone in attributing immoral behavior to the Protestants, and it was not just in the gutters that such rumors were spread. In 1560, Antoine de Mouchy, a respected theologian, rector of the University of Paris, and an official "inquisitor for the faith," published a pamphlet with the very serious title of *Response à quelque apologie que les heretiques ces jours passés ont mis en avant* in which he made accusations very similar to those put forth by Haton.[25] But it was not just debauchery that the Protestants were believed to practice. They were also accused of plotting against the crown. Haton avers that "all the heretics and Lutherans in the kingdom" were involved in a plot to kill the king because they believed him to be a tyrant and a persecutor of true Christians, and he blames them for an attempt that was made on Henri II's life in 1558 as he left mass at the Sainte-Chapelle.[26] Jean de la Vacquerie, in his *Catholique remonstrance* of 1560, accuses the Protestants of conspiring to burn Paris as part of their revolt against the crown. Similar accusations can be found in other works of Catholic propaganda.[27]

Catholic polemicists helped spread the stories of the Protestants' sinful and seditious behavior, but there is little evidence that the stories originated with them. In most cases it appears that the polemicists were circulating—perhaps elaborating upon, and certainly lending credence to—rumors already current in the city. Though we cannot trace such rumors as the ritual promiscuity of the Calvinists to any specific origin, we can comprehend how traditional beliefs that linked sexual misbehavior to heresy could combine with the observed practice of clandestine, nocturnal meetings to lead to whispered gossip and salacious tales about the nature of these gatherings.[28] The vague notions thus formed had a way of appearing to be confirmed by subsequent events. The rumors of Calvinist debauchery, for example, received apparent confirmation in 1559, when the two apprentices whose denunciations started the chain of Protestant arrests rounded out their confessions with a detailed description of orgiastic behavior at an Easter service in a house in the place Maubert. According to La Planche, the apprentices even named specific individuals they had recognized as taking part in these events; one claimed himself to have coupled "two or three times" with a beautiful young daughter of the lawyer who owned the house.[29] We have only polemical accounts of these events, so it is impossible to know under what circumstances these "confessions" were obtained. It is clear, however, that the stories spread quickly, both at court and in the city, for the precise reason that they served to justify the harsh repression of the new faith.

The rumor that the Protestants plotted to burn down the city of Paris appears to have gained currency in late 1559, as the trial of the Protestant parlementaire Anne Du Bourg reached its climax.[30] On the evening of 12 December, President Minard, one of the magistrates most outspoken in his attacks on Du Bourg, was shot and killed as he returned home from the Palais de Justice. Minard's death had immediate repercussions in the city. The word went around that ten men had taken part in the attack, and the authorities made haste to investigate the conspiracy. They ordered the city gates closed while they conducted a house-to-house search for the culprits. The investigations led to the arrest of a Scot named Robert Stuard, who was not only charged with Minard's death but also with plotting to release Du Bourg from prison and conspiring to set fire to the city. Nothing came of these accusations. Stuard admitted nothing, even under torture. Du Bourg denied all knowledge of the plot, and so did the other suspects that were rounded up for interrogation. The agitation of the authorities, however, was quickly transmitted to the people—they heard the rumors, saw the closed gates, were party to the searches. They also witnessed the special precautions taken for Du Bourg's execution on 23 December. Ironically, the added guards that had been posted to prevent Du Bourg's rescue were called upon instead to protect him from the violence of the Catholic crowds.[31]

In March 1560, news that Protestant conspirators had plotted to seize the king at Amboise sent a new wave of fear over the capital. Once again emergency measures were taken: Gates were closed, guards were reinforced, and house-to-house searches were instituted. Strangers who could not provide a good reason for their presence in the city were ordered to leave within twenty-four hours. Constable Montmorency and his son, the maréchal, governor of Paris and the Ile-de-France, came to Paris personally to supervise security measures and ensure that the city remained calm. The lieutenant civil confiscated a few weapons as a result of the searches, but the authorities found no real cause for alarm. The emergency measures themselves, however, increased the level of suspicion and increased tensions in the city.[32]

One manifestation of these tensions is evident in a request addressed to Parlement in July 1560 by the residents of the faubourgs Saint-Jacques and Notre-Dame-des-Champs. Complaining of "vagabonds," arms-bearing strangers, and illicit assem-

blies, the residents of the faubourgs asked Parlement for permission to arm themselves so that they might apprehend these dangerous strangers and bring them to
justice.[33] Permission was granted, but it was evident to at least some persons in
positions of authority that arming the Parisian citizenry was a dangerous way to
try to keep order. In August, the king responded to continued unrest in the capital
by advising Parlement not to close the city gates or reinforce the city guard unless
it was absolutely necessary.[34] We can see here the beginning of a long series of
vacillations, hesitations, and internal conflicts, as different authorities sought the
best means to ensure both order and tranquility in the volatile capital.

Another manifestation of the continuing tensions is evident in the riot that broke
out during the execution in July 1560 of Martin Lhomme, a printer convicted of
publishing seditious pamphlets. Lhomme had been arrested in June, when authorities
investigating another case discovered under his bed a pamphlet entitled *Le Tigre*
directed against the cardinal of Lorraine. A large crowd turned out to see Lhomme
hanged and the condemned booklets burned on the place Maubert. As the crowd
grew more and more unruly, an unknown man was heard to make some remarks
that inadvertently turned the crowd's wrath from Martin Lhomme to himself. Some
nearby priests, overhearing his words, called him a "Huguenard" (the word Huguenot had just come into use); the crowd assaulted him, and the authorities imprisoned him. Four days later, the stranger, whose name was Robert Delors, was
pronounced guilty of blaspheming against God and "the Glorious Virgin Mary"
and provoking public scandal and sedition. He was executed that same day on the
place Maubert, on the very spot where Martin Lhomme had been hanged.[35]

According to La Planche, the stranger had not even known the reason for
Lhomme's execution, and his only motive in intervening had been humanitarian.
"What's this, my friends?" La Planche reports him saying. "Isn't it enough that
he die? Let the executioner do his job. Do you want to torment him even more
than the sentence calls for?" There is of course no way to prove the accuracy of
these words, nor of the opinions La Planche attributes to Delors's judge, a man
named Lyon, whom he says was overheard telling his friends that he had executed
Delors in hopes of pacifying the cardinal of Lorraine, who was angry that the author
of *Le Tigre* had not yet been found.[36] La Planche had good sources in the Parlement;
he is accurate in such details as the name of Delors's judge. We must remember,
however, that he was also a Protestant polemicist, and his remarks about the cardinal
of Lorraine inevitably reflect the Protestants' growing hatred of the Guises, who
were believed to be behind the policy of persecution.

The Failure of Moderation

The role of the Guises and their policy of religious persecution in provoking the
emergence of the Huguenots as a political and military faction is by now a familiar
episode in the history of the French Reformation. What is essential to my story
here is the emergence of a moderate party and a consequent change in religious
politics.

Even during the reign of François II, Catherine de Medici had encouraged the development of a moderate faction at court in order to dilute the power of the Guises. When she became regent upon the death of François II in December 1560, she continued to support the policies of the moderates. This, she believed, was the best way to maintain peace in the troubled kingdom and so to preserve the crown for her young son Charles IX.[37] Among the policies Catherine supported was an easing of the persecution of Protestants. This change in religious policy was to have important consequences in the city of Paris.

One of the early successes of the moderates had been in forcing a call for the Estates General. By the time the Estates met in December 1560, the unexpected death of François II had considerably strengthened the moderates' position. The opening address of Chancellor Michel de L'Hôpital, himself a leading moderate, expresses well the compromise this middle party hoped to achieve. Without approving of the new religion—indeed, without even believing that two religions could in the long run coexist peacefully in one kingdom—L'Hôpital chided the Catholics for the violence of their intolerance and the Protestants for the impatience of their reforming zeal. He urged that Protestants and Catholics alike look to a church council for the resolution of their differences; in the meantime, both groups should cultivate restraint.[38] Careful to explain that provisional toleration of religious differences was not intended to encourage sedition, L'Hôpital threatened grave reprisals against those who disturbed the tranquility of their cities on the pretext of religion. At the time, however, the warning against disturbing the peace seemed a less important message than the relaxation of measures against the followers of the new faith.

Although still forbidden to hold public assemblies, the Calvinists profited from the less repressive atmosphere to meet more often and more openly. According to La Fosse, they even held Easter services in the great hall of the Palais de Justice.[39] The Catholic populace reacted to this provocation by increasing their harassment of Protestants, and by the end of April 1561 several violent incidents had put a serious strain on the policy of moderation. On 14 April, there were clashes between Catholic crowds and Protestant worshipers near the church of Saint-Eustache and outside the city walls at Popincourt, a favorite place for Calvinist preaching.

These incidents, one of which resulted in fourteen arrests, convinced Parlement to ask the king for greater power to deal with the unrest that appeared to be "growing from day to day." The king replied to Parlement's request on 19 April with a very temperate edict, which forbade his subjects to injure or provoke anyone on account of their religion. The edict went on to threaten severe punishment for seditious conduct, but its principal intent was to promote calm by ordering toleration of what took place in private and forbidding public disturbances.[40] By the time the edict reached Paris, however, there had already been further violence.

On 24 April, a crowd had gathered on the pré aux Clercs to attack a house where Calvinist assemblies were known to be held. The principal tenant, the seigneur de Longjumeau, complained to Parlement, which responded with an order outlawing acts of violence motivated by religious sentiments. The same act forbade the carrying of weapons on the pré aux Clercs and the holding of illicit assemblies. Proclaimed in Paris on 26 April, the order was ineffectual. The very next day a more violent riot broke out around Longjumeau's house, and he and his friends (three hundred of them, according to the Catholic Brulart) proved ready to meet force with force. By the end of the fray, several persons lay dead. Catholic memorialists reported that the attacking "commune" suffered fatalities, Longjumeau told Parlement that he lost one man, and parlementary records offer evidence that at least one innocent bystander—a neighborhood woman who had been standing in her own doorway with a child in her arms—was killed by a stray bullet.[41]

In order to put a stop to the violence, Parlement ordered special security measures taken. The order of 26 April was renewed, and Longjumeau was commanded to leave town. The crown, notified of the affair, sent the king of Navarre to Paris to oversee peacekeeping measures and to conduct an inquiry. One of Navarre's first gestures was to call together all the parish priests, along with other representatives of the Catholic clergy, in order to warn them against stirring up the people with their sermons. In general, however, it was Parlement that set the ground rules for the restoration of order. The orders of 26 and 28 April, which threatened to treat persons found in illicit assemblies as rebels guilty of *lèse majesté*, became the basis for a renewed persecution of religious dissidents.[42]

By mid-May, the Venetian Ambassador, Suriano, was able to report that "in consequence of . . . the severe measures taken against the rioters, who had caused the disturbances in the city, the fear of mischief was greatly diminishing." Suriano found the Catholics heartened by the recent turn of events and the Protestants seriously alarmed. Prominent Calvinists went into hiding or left the city, while a number of moderate sympathizers found it prudent to make a public display of religious orthodoxy. Suriano gave the people of Paris a great deal of credit for the altered religious climate. In his opinion, "the change which had taken place in the religious question had been greatly promoted by various representations made both in Paris and at Court. For the population of this City, which was very numerous, was entirely Catholic, and opposed to all change." Suriano also credited the magistrates of Parlement and the doctors of the Sorbonne with bringing Navarre around to their way of viewing the dangers of heresy.[43]

The officers of the Hôtel de Ville likewise favored a tightening of the laws against heresy. Meeting on 2 May to discuss the recent unrest, the city officers passed an ordinance restating previous laws against illicit assemblies and illegal weapons and ordering that there was to be no preaching of the new doctrines, "but that the word of God was to be preached in the churches and parishes of the city by learned men, trained in theology." Violators of this ordinance would be charged with *lèse majesté*, and they might be proceeded against summarily and without due process of the law.[44]

The laws passed by the city officers reflected public opinion, which was strongly opposed to the royal policy of moderation. The royal edict of 19 April, which provided that no one was to be disturbed on account of his religion, was commonly taken to mean that "the fullest liberty was given to everyone to profess the religion he chose," and Parisians were outraged by the king's apparent willingness to tolerate heresy.[45] Parlement drew the same meaning from the edict, which seemed by its very refusal to countenance persecution "to approve religious diversity." On 11 May, the officers of Parlement sent the king a stern remonstrance, reminding him that religious schism had never before been tolerated in the French kingdom and arguing that the best way to put a stop to the sedition was to "cut the root, which is religious division." Parlement urged the king to announce that he intended to live and die in the faith in which he and his predecessors had been baptized, and he intended his subjects to do the same. In this way, with God's grace, the kingdom would know peace. Objecting to the clauses in the edict that forbade people to gather outside houses where illicit assemblies were taking place, Parlement shifted the blame to those within and called for an end to illicit preaching and the enforcement of old laws forbidding such assemblies.[46]

The edict that the parlementaires wanted the king to issue against Protestant assemblies was not forthcoming until July. In the intervening two months, the king and his counselors hesitated, weighing the arguments of the Calvinists, who were pressing for further signs of toleration (in June they asked to be allowed to build churches), against those of the militant Catholics, who wished the religious repression heightened.[47] During this period, Paris remained tense, but precautionary measures instituted by the authorities prevented serious disorders. On 3 June, the lieutenant criminel relayed to Parlement the chancellor's warning that children, who were mimicking their elders and playing at religious processions, should be forbidden to continue the practice of parading crosses through the streets because of the danger of provoking riots.[48] Special security measures were also taken for the Corpus Christi processions, which occurred at about the same time, because it was feared that the Protestants would attempt some sort of sacrilege against the consecrated host. As it happened, it was the Catholics who disturbed the peace. A crowd attacked the house of an artisan who was believed to be a follower of the new religion because he had not hung out the customary tapestry for the procession.[49] Another display of Catholic militancy occured when the Protestants' request to build churches was made known in the city. According to Suriano, the bishop of Paris attempted to counter the Protestants' boast of having great numbers of followers by asking everyone in the city to make a public profession of faith, but so many thousands had turned out to register as Catholics and to offer "their property and their lives in support of the Roman Catholic faith" that the proceedings had to be stopped "in order to prevent any open dissensions in the city."[50]

The king's edict, which was registered in Parlement on 31 July, failed to put an end to the tensions. Too severe to please the Protestants, it was too liberal for the militant Catholics. The edict expressly forbade assemblies, whether public or private, where there was preaching of the new doctrines or where the sacraments were administered in any manner except the traditional forms, but it also reiterated prohibitions against provoking or injuring anyone on account of their religion. This irritated the Catholics, as did a clause that cautioned Catholic preachers not to promote unrest by their sermons and one that forbade "enrollments, signatures" and other actions tending toward factionalism and conspiracy—a clear rejection of the kind of Catholic oath the bishop of Paris had recently urged. Moreover, because the edict was described as provisional, until a church council could settle the religious conflicts, the Catholics believed that the Protestants would ignore it and "not only would not renounce their opinions but would persist in them the more, in the hope that within a short time this decision would be reversed."[51]

There was some justice to the Catholics' fear. The edict did not put a stop to

Calvinist preaching. By autumn the Protestants were meeting more boldly than ever before. Etienne Pasquier, a moderate Catholic, reported that eight or nine thousand people attended Calvinist services outside the porte Saint-Antoine in October and that, on All Saints' Eve, a high noble family openly held services in their Paris town house.[52] The Protestants had been encouraged by the relatively open mind that the queen mother had shown them. Catherine had called for a meeting between Catholic and Protestant theologians in the faint hope that by sitting down together they might still find a way to reconcile religious differences. To no one's great surprise, the attempt at compromise failed. The Colloquy of Poissy, which began in September, was dismissed in mid-October after six weeks of increasingly futile discussions. The Protestants, meanwhile, had seized upon the invitation to Poissy to step up their proselytizing in nearby Paris. Even after the failure of the colloquy, they retained a measure of the queen's good will, and they traded upon her sympathies to expand their evangelical efforts. When Catholics protested against the increasingly public Calvinist preaching, the Protestants replied that Catherine had given them permission to assemble, as long as groups that met within the city contained no more than twenty-five people and those that met outside the walls behaved with decorum. The queen had even ordered officers of the watch (*guet*) to stand guard around the Protestant assemblies to ensure that no unrest occurred.[53]

The Huguenot military leader and tactician François de La Noue offers an interesting assessment of this period of popular evangelizing, which he attributes to the deliberate decision on the part of Condé and other Huguenot leaders to try to enlarge their base in what was, along with the court, one of the two "great lights" of France. Although at the time it had seemed that the tactic was producing "an abundance of fruits"—La Noue reports that some assemblies attracted audiences of thirty thousand—in retrospect it was clear that the effort had come too late. Comparing the sudden popularity of Protestant preaching to a grass fire that flames brightly but quickly burns out, La Noue concluded that most of those attending the Parisian assemblies had been drawn by a love of novelty and not a sincere desire for reform. Their interest quickly faded, and they returned to their old ways and beliefs. In La Noue's opinion, the period of open and aggressive preaching produced few long-term converts; at the same time, it fed the hatred felt by the Huguenots' enemies.[54]

Indeed, the boldness with which the Calvinists met and the protection they seemed to enjoy infuriated Parisian Catholics. In spite of royal letters forbidding name calling, rock throwing, and other forms of aggression, violence was common.[55] On 12 October, angry Catholics closed the city gates against the large number of people that had gone out to hear Calvinist preachers in the northeastern suburbs. Several persons were grievously injured as the Calvinists attempted to fight their way back into the city.[56] A week later, the king sent orders that the Parisians were to turn in their arms at the Hôtel de Ville. Here was another blow to the Catholic population: Calvinist noblemen were seen attending the assemblies of the new religion in arms; their services were guarded by officers of the watch; and yet the people of Paris, who prided themselves on their political and religious loyalties, were to be denied the right of self-defense.[57]

For they did believe that the issue was self-defense. Brulart, describing the

Calvinist ministers as themselves bearing arms, wrote that the followers of the new faith "held most of the city in subjection," and Suriano reported rumors that the Calvinists planned to seize the abbey of Saint-Germain or at least the Carthusian house in the faubourg Saint-Jacques. According to Suriano, the Catholics had placed armed men in these and other city churches because they feared some sort of action on the part of the Huguenots. The king's orders to disarm were a response to these activities and an attempt to ward off the conflict that threatened.[58]

Catholic preachers, who had been urging their listeners to take up arms to defend their churches from the heretics, turned their venom against the crown as well. A Carmelite preaching at Saint-Benoît was reported to have compared the situation in the kingdom to that of two children who, playing with an apple, are about to let it be snatched by a third. Another cleric, in a public debate at the Sorbonne, defended the proposition that it was in the power of the pope to excommunicate a king and free his people from their obligation of loyalty if he was found to favor heretics. Ordered to look into these and other incidents, Parlement by the end of November was investigating reports of seditious preaching in the parishes of Saint-Benoît, Saint-Séverin, Saint-Germain-l'Auxerrois, Saint-Eustache, Saint-Merry, and Saint-Jacques-de-la-Boucherie—some of the most important parishes in the city—and at the Sorbonne itself.[59]

In December, the crackdown on inflammatory preaching nearly led to riots. A friar of the Minim order, Jean de Hans, was accused of fomenting sedition in the Advent sermons he preached in the parish church of Saint-Barthélemy. During the night of 9 December, de Hans was summarily arrested and dragged off to the court at Saint-Germain. The city of Paris howled with anger. The Hôtel de Ville dispatched a troop of notable merchants to plead with the king for the return of "their" friar, while Parlement ordered the city guard and the Châtelet officers to calm the excited crowds and to tell them that the cleric was taken on the explicit orders of the king. Meanwhile, the king dispatched troops to prevent a full-scale riot in the city. He also freed de Hans, who was escorted triumphantly back to the city by the delegation of merchants. The following day, the parishioners of Saint-Barthélemy organized a procession to thank God for this sign of his favor.[60]

Two weeks later, the fragile order that prevailed in the city was shattered by the violent clash between the Huguenots worshiping in the faubourg Saint-Marcel at a house known as the Patriarche and the Catholics of the neighboring church of Saint-Médard. It is hard to know just who touched off the melee. The best reconstruction of the event seems to be that the Protestants, whose services had been interrupted by the tolling bells of Saint-Médard, sent over some envoys to ask that the bells be silenced. The Catholics did not immediately agree and an argument ensued. Meanwhile, more men came over from the Patriarche to find out what was happening. The parishioners of Saint-Médard thought they were being attacked, and a battle broke out that resulted in serious injuries—even deaths, the Catholics claimed—and in acts of sacrilege and pillage. Heads were knocked off the statues of saints, crosses were broken, and chalices stolen or defiled.[61]

I shall not attempt here to reconcile the contradictions between Protestant and Catholic accounts of the event. What is important is that the Catholics of Saint-Médard sincerely believed they had been attacked. Just as their preachers had been warning them, the Huguenots had broken into their church and defiled the things they held sacred.

Not surprisingly, in the aftermath of the event, other parishes in the city demanded arms to protect themselves from such "surprises."[62] Furthermore, the Catholics believed that the special guards that had been raised at public expense to help keep peace in the city had joined in the battle on the Huguenot side, and they were scandalized to learn that no Huguenots had been arrested for their part in the affair but that more than thirty Catholics—including six priests—had been taken as prisoners to jails of the Châtelet. The prisoners were released two days later, and a full and impartial investigation was ordered by Parlement. Nonetheless, in the popular mind, the incident was a blatant piece of Huguenot brutality and a proof of their growing power. Brulart wrote that there were "three or four thousand" armed men milling about in the streets near the church of Saint-Médard, "holding in subjection" the local residents, and a Catholic tract published in 1562 describes the Huguenots as parading through the streets in battle order, crying, "The Gospel, the Gospel; where are the idolatrous papists?"[63]

The Saint-Médard affair was still on everyone's mind when, on 17 January 1562, a new edict of toleration was announced. The edict allowed the practice of the new religion under certain constraints and as a temporary measure, until a church council could resolve the religious differences.[64] Although the edict still forbade Protestants to assemble inside city walls, it was unacceptable to Parisian Catholics. The city council, the clergy, and the doctors of the Sorbonne all protested to the king, as did a special delegation of Parisian merchants, acting on their own initiative.[65] Parlement also remonstrated with the king and only registered the edict after having twice received royal orders (*lettres de jussion*) to this effect.[66] Parlement was subjected to other pressures as well as to the king's displeasure. On 4 March, about four hundred armed men had gathered in the courtyard of the Palais to protest the delay in the edict's registration. Brulart and other memorialists cite this attempt at intimidation as an important factor in Parlement's eventual decision to register the offensive edict.[67]

On 16 March, the entry of the duc de Guise, fresh from his violent confrontation with the Protestants gathered for worship at Vassy, provided the occasion for a vivid display of the political and religious sentiments of the people of Paris. A military hero as well as a staunch Catholic, Guise was welcomed as the man who would put an end to the Huguenots' insolence. His entry was well staged. He deliberately chose to enter through the porte Saint-Denis, traditionally used for royal entries, in order to give an impression of power and authority. And, indeed, he was greeted royally. He was met by an impressive entourage of nobles, city officers, and bourgeois. The crowds that lined the streets to view his entry shouted their joy—and their hatred of the Huguenots.[68]

In the weeks that followed, tensions in Paris reached new highs. A bloody riot took place on 20 March, when a Catholic crowd attempted to disinter a corpse that had been buried according to Reformed rites in the Cemetery of the Innocents.[69] The situation was aggravated by the fact that, at the moment that Guise arrived, the Protestant leader Condé was in Paris to seek redress for Vassy, where twenty-three Protestants had been killed and more than a hundred injured. Condé's followers, as well as those of Guise, had flocked to the city.[70] Parisian Protestants were convinced that the Catholic leaders planned the same fate for them as for the worshipers at Vassy. Their reaction to the massacre was thus not limited to registering formal protests at court; they began to take up arms in the defense of their faith.[71]

Easter week, which began on 22 March with the traditional Palm Sunday processions, provided numerous occasions for clashes between the rival factions. Pasquier described the processions as a scene of "chaos and confusion" in which "pistol shots and cannons served as carillons." Pierre de Paschal similarly observed that "one heard so often the retort of firearms that it seemed that Paris was a frontier town."[72]

The confrontation that everyone expected was prevented by the city's new governor, the cardinal of Bourbon, who persuaded both Condé and Guise to leave Paris.[73] Condé left on the twenty-third, retiring to one of his properties. Guise left on the following day. He went with his allies of the Catholic Triumvirate, Constable Anne de Montmorency and the Maréchal de Saint-André, to Fontainebleau, where he took the king under his protection—or, as Condé saw it, into captivity.[74] In the opinion of most historians, these were the events that made war inevitable. They were also the events that set the terms for the confrontation. As Pasquier pointed out, Condé placed himself at a grave disadvantage when he abandoned not only the king but also the capital to his enemies.[75]

Pasquier had in mind the long-term consequences of this event, which placed the Huguenots in the position of rebels against the crown, but it was equally true in the short term that this action cleared the way for bloody reprisals against the Huguenots still in Paris. On 4 April, Constable Montmorency came back to Paris from the court and, accompanied by his soldiers, proceeded to destroy the two principal sites of Reformed preaching in the Paris suburbs. To the great delight of the Parisian populace, he made a bonfire of the pulpit and benches found in the house known as Jerusalem in the faubourg Saint-Jacques. Then he did the same at the house in the northeastern suburbs known as Popincourt. The next day, which was a Sunday, a great crowd gathered at Popincourt to complete the destruction. They tore the house to pieces and brought the rubble into the center of the city, to the place de Grève, where, to jubilant cries that "God has not forgotten the people of Paris," they set fire to it.[76]

On 6 April, the king was brought back into the city. Within a week, he had issued a special declaration exempting Paris and its suburbs from the January edict and forbidding any exercise of the new religion in this area.[77] This special exception, which was repeated in every edict of toleration or pacification down to the Edict of Nantes, was prompted by the protests of the city's civil and religious authorities. More important, it was forced upon the king by the unruliness of the Parisian populace. A sign of the failure of the politics of moderation, it represents a clear victory for the Parisians in their struggle against the new religion.

4

War and Peace, 1562–1567

The history of Paris during the first religious war is a study in the psychology of fear. The physical destruction that resulted from the war was, in both the long and the short run, less damaging than the psychological effects of the war. The actual fighting only briefly touched the Paris area. For three weeks in late November and early December 1562, Condé's army threatened the capital; but for more than six months prior to this time, the city lived in a state of anticipatory dread, and for more than six months after the army's departure, the city was convulsed by spasms of retributory violence. The return to order was, moreover, handicapped by a new danger, for even while the first religious war was being fought, Paris was entering into a subsistence crisis more serious than any that had been experienced for over a century. The tensions built up during the war were consequently never entirely dissipated, and the entire period from 1562 to 1567 must be seen as a period of crisis.

Fear and Anticipation

Throughout the spring of 1562, the king insisted on his desire for his people to live together in peace. Repeated efforts were made to negotiate a settlement with the Huguenots, who had seized Orleans during the first week in April. The people of Paris were not content, however, to wait upon the success or failure of these negotiations. They talked of nothing but war, and they insisted that preparations be made for the defense of the capital, which they considered a prime target for Condé's armies. The Parisians had already taken up arms during Easter week, but now they insisted on forming a new militia and systematizing internal security.[1]

By the beginning of May, there was a heady combination of fear and anticipation in the city. The Huguenots had taken Tours, Blois, Rouen, and other major cities, and the Parisians were certain that Condé would attempt to seize the capital too. When Catherine decided on 13 May to take the young king back out of the city, no one slept at night for fear of being surprised by the enemy. On 16 May, a noisy quarrel between a couple of boatmen at four in the morning put the city into a panic. People grabbed up their arms, dragged heavy chains across the streets, and prepared to fight, just as if the Huguenot army were at the city gates.[2]

On 26 May, on the ground that the king was leaving to fight the rebels and the city would consequently be vulnerable to Huguenot plots, all Protestants were ordered to leave Paris within forty-eight hours.[3] Many had already chosen to leave, but others had remained in order to protect their property or because they had no place to go. The captains of the city's newly formed militia were charged with identifying the individuals in their quartiers who were "notorious" for their religious beliefs. Inhabitants of each quartier met in special assemblies to denounce suspicious persons. These individuals were ordered to sign a formal confession of faith or to leave the city immediately.[4]

The cardinal of Lorraine contributed to the swell of emotion by choosing personally to preach the Corpus Christi sermons at Notre-Dame and Saint-Germain-l'Auxerrois. According to Pasquier, the cardinal alternated days for Corpus Christi week, which began on 28 May, with Jean de Hans, the Minim whose Advent sermons had nearly provoked riots six months earlier. For his first sermon at Saint-Germain, Lorraine took as his subject the real presence in the Eucharist, an appropriate theme for the holiday and one guaranteed to stimulate partisan feelings. Pasquier recorded that the enormous crowds that turned out to hear the cardinal went away tremendously impressed by his message that "it was better to die, and to give the last drop of blood, than to permit . . . another religion to be established in France." In Pasquier's opinion, the cardinal's sermons "greatly excited the people to arms."[5]

Religious processions and other forms of "street theater," such as the burning of books in the place Maubert, further excited popular emotions. The participation of the city's new troops, along with companies of old soldiers from the Hapsburg wars, gave a decidedly military air to Corpus Christi processions. In the rue Saint-Denis, a spectator was attacked and killed when he was heard to disparage the procession as idolatry.[6] On 14 June, a solemn procession of the Blessed Sacrament was held to reconsecrate the church of Saint-Médard, defiled by the Huguenots in December's riots. In order to prevent a possible attack on the Eucharist, an armed man was stationed outside each house on the processional route from the abbey of Sainte-Geneviève to Saint-Médard. Again the captains of the city's new forces participated as a body, and, so that there was no mistaking the symbolic association between the procession and the campaign against heresy, a sermon was preached on the site of the Patriarche, where the Protestants had formerly held their services.[7] The following Wednesday, all the city's churches held individual processions against heresy, and on Sunday there was a citywide procession of the relics of Saint Geneviève to pray for victory against the heretics.[8]

Word of Huguenot victories elsewhere in France reinforced the passions stirred by the symbolic display of Catholic militance, and in the weeks that followed all semblance of order broke down. A carelessly worded ordinance issued by Parlement on 30 June contributed to the growing lawlessness by seeming to authorize popular violence against the Huguenots. The ordinance was issued in response to Huguenot pillaging of Catholic churches and houses in the nearby town of Meaux. Anyone who took part in this action was declared by the king's lieutenant and Parlement to be guilty of *lèse majesté* and rebellion and was as a consequence subject to death. Citing edicts issued by François I, the court ordered that anyone caught sacking churches or houses might be "torn to pieces" by the people without fear of legal reprisals.[9] Many people took this declaration as permission to launch a free-for-all attack on anyone suspected of the new religion. Reputed Huguenots were struck down in the streets. Sometimes mock trials were held, as the attackers grilled their prisoners on their religious beliefs and killed them on the spot when they were not satisfied with the answers. Officials who tried to intervene were themselves in danger, and attempts to legislate an end to the killings met with violent protests. As one memorialist described it, "The people wanted nothing less than permission to kill and exterminate the Huguenots without any form of trial; but the consequence was too dangerous." He implies that permission might have been given, had the city not been already dangerously close to anarchy.[10]

Behind this violence was fear. The Parisians feared that a Huguenot seizure of nearby Meaux would mean "the establishment of a new Geneva ten leagues from the kingdom's capital."[11] They feared for their food supply, much of which was imported from the rich agricultural area east of the capital. It would be so easy to cut off the river that was the city's lifeline. They also feared more directly for their lives. By early fall, rumors were circulating that the Huguenots intended to take Paris by surprise and slit the throats of the city's residents.[12] The first president of Parlement, who reported these fears in a special session on 10 September, had his own particular dread. He feared what would happen within Paris if the Huguenots succeeded even temporarily in cutting off the food supply of the capital. The Parisians were already in despair, he said, because of their fear of a surprise attack, and "a people in despair is not easy to pacify." There was a grave danger that, if the people had to go hungry for even three days, they might act "like mad men or crazy people" and attack their magistrates and fellow citizens.[13] Where Parisian authorities were concerned, the problem of dealing with the Huguenots could never be separated from the problem of public order.

Security measures taken in the fall of 1562 reflect this dual concern. On 16 September, orders were given for any Parisians who had grain or wine stored on their country estates to bring these supplies into the city. This was followed by other measures intended to ease the fear of food shortages. At the same time, all persons suspected of being followers of the new religion were ordered to leave Paris, even if they had made an official profession of faith to a Catholic official. This measure, which was intended to ease both the fear of a Huguenot "surprise" and the danger of Catholic unrest, was followed up by a number of ordinances ordering the search and seizure of suspects and weapons.[14] Because the task of policing the city for suspects was too large (and potentially too dangerous) for the commissaires of the Châtelet, the captains of the dizaines, the principal officers of the special militia that had been formed in the spring, were ordered to make at least weekly searches of the houses of their districts. They were to arrest any unknown persons without legitimate business in Paris and anyone whose name was on the lists of suspected Protestants. They were also to seize any horses or arms belonging to these persons and to turn them in to the Hôtel de Ville. The commissaires were to assist in these searches, and a weekly report was to be made to the Bureau de la ville.[15]

As a result of these orders, there was a tremendous increase in the number of persons arrested for reasons having to do with religion.[16] By the end of October, prison conditions were deplorable. In the Conciergerie, religious prisoners were indiscriminately thrown into the dungeons, where there was no possibility of communicating with those who might secure their release.[17] In the Petit Châtelet, the jailers could not afford to feed the large number of persons who were being detained, and by the end of November prisoners were reported to be starving to death.[18] Many of those arrested claimed that they were not Huguenots but rather were good Catholics and had not been ordered to leave the city. Such individuals had to bear the burden of proof and to demonstrate their innocence by securing the testimony of twelve or fifteen of their nearest neighbors.[19] Parish priests were also called upon to testify in favor of accused parishioners. The priests contributed to the round-up of suspects as well, however, by making denunciations a part of the ritual of confession. They told their parishioners that they must "ease their consciences" by confessing the names of any persons they had seen attending Protestant services, and at least some priests insisted that the verbal confession be followed up by a written denunciation.[20]

Many abuses occurred. Jealousy, revenge, or other base motives could easily provoke a false arrest. The more aggressive captains sometimes continued to harass residents of their districts even after they had been ordered to leave them alone. Sometimes they simply allowed their victims to languish in jail without filing formal charges against them.[21] The behavior of the captains will be discussed in more detail in a later chapter. What is important here is to understand how the attempts to police the city in fact contributed to the climate of unrest by adding to the sense of omnipresent danger. If there was somewhat less overt violence in fall than there had been in spring and early summer, it was only because the driving out of all known Protestants had left fewer suspects to attack. Violent incidents were nevertheless still common, and on a number of occasions the captains had to arrest men or women in order to save them from the fury of the crowds.[22]

The Enemy at the City Gates

In early November, with the loss of Rouen added to an already weakened position in the Loire valley, Condé decided to gamble on an assault on the capital. Reinforced by the German mercenaries that d'Andelot had raised, Condé's army took Etampes, just thirty miles to the south of Paris, on 13 November and proceeded to march on to Corbeil. Strongly defended because of its key position on the river Seine, Corbeil resisted the Huguenots' attack and slowed them in their progress toward the capital.[23] While Condé's army wreaked havoc on the towns and villages to the south, the Parisians were able to overcome their panic and strengthen the city's defenses. Most important, the delay gave Guise and the Constable Montmorency time to arrive, which gave an immediate boost to the Parisians' courage.[24]

The new Venetian ambassador, Barbaro, is scornful in his depiction of the initial attempts of municipal officers to prepare the city's defenses. Emphasizing their fear, he comments on the futility of their plans and the ineffectiveness of their actions. The Parisians proposed drastic measures: they would raze the suburbs to leave a clear field for the fighting, they would reinforce the city's fortifications, and they would assemble large numbers of troops. In fact, however, "they had done nothing but march all day round the walls with troops and engineers, professing their intention of doing great things if they were allowed time."[25] Meanwhile, residents of the southern suburbs were pouring into Paris, increasing the confusion.[26] The influx of refugees combined with the loss in Etampes of an important grain depot and the pillaging of the fields south of the capital to bring about a sharp rise in food prices, and this too added to the sense of alarm.

Somehow, a semblance of order was maintained. The militia began regular exercises, the night watch was reinforced, and conscripts were assembled to dig trenches and place artillery in preparation for the expected battle.[27] In the end, however, no battle took place. Although Barbaro reported on 22 November that "it appeared impossible that some disturbance should not take place in the city, both on account of the vicinity of the enemy, and of the stoppage of supplies," the queen had taken steps toward negotiations, and while the possibility of negotiation lasted only a few skirmishes disturbed the tense wait.[28]

On 6 December the Parisians had the thrill of being asked to send out part of their militia to assist Guise in keeping watch over the faubourg Saint-Jacques, because expected reinforcements to the king's armies had not yet arrived. The account of this event in the city registers is naively boastful, relating how the city's captains and their troops were "so well equipped that they excited the admiration of the Swiss and other soldiers in the king's pay." The Parisians liked to think that the practice rounds Guise had them fire terrified the enemy, but Pierre Paschal is perhaps more accurate in noting that these shots rather signified to Condé's men that the attempt to negotiate a peace had failed.[29]

When Spanish and Gascon troops arrived the next day to reinforce the king's defenses, Condé withdrew and marched his troops off to the west, where the king's army met them on 19 December for the ultimately decisive battle of Dreux. On 20 December, word reached Paris that Condé had defeated the king's army, the constable had been killed, and Guise and Saint-André had taken flight. This false news created a flurry of panic, before the truth of royal victory reached Paris the next morning, and the fear turned to joy.[30]

Catherine's response to the defeat of Condé at Dreux was to seek once more to negotiate an end to the war. The Parisians, on the other hand, however happy to have the immediate threat dispelled, were not ready to approve a negotiated peace if it meant allowing the practice of two religions in the kingdom. On 5 January 1563, in response to a letter from the queen which mentioned her desire for peace, the Bureau de la ville wrote to "supplicate her in all humility" to use the victory of Dreux as a lesson to the rebels that there could be but one religion in the kingdom. The city fathers warned that as long as the new religion was tolerated in any part of the king's lands, its adherents would have reason to meet together, to gather strength, and ultimately to fight again.[31] This letter was a clear warning that the experience of war had not persuaded the Parisians of the need for compromise or moderation.

In the eyes of some observers at least, the obstinacy of the Parisians was a major obstacle to peace. On 17 January, the English ambassador wrote Queen Elizabeth that three things prevented an agreement from being reached. The first was the Huguenots' fear of entrapment; the second was the ambition of the Guises, which fed upon the troubles; and "the third is the Parisians, who say they will not change their religion, or receive the Huguenots amongst them, whom they have expelled."[32] The Parisians demonstrated their opposition to any solution except the decisive defeat of the Huguenots by their refusal to publish an edict issued after the victory of Dreux that promised amnesty to any Protestants returning to the Catholic faith and by their continued—even intensified—persecution of religious suspects.[33]

Afraid that the Huguenots might try to slip back into the city, Parisian authorities renewed orders for regular searches and tightened up the guard of the city gates. No one was allowed to enter without a passport. The volume of arrests for January and February 1563 testifies to the diligence with which these orders were carried out.[34] Suspicion was everywhere—one man claimed to have been seized while attending mass at Notre-Dame—and, indeed, even the most ostentatious observance of Catholic ceremonies no longer sufficed as a demonstration of religious orthodoxy.[35] Court records show the difficulty that suspects had in clearing their names; even a person presumably cleared of suspicion by the presentation of the required testimony from neighbors and priests was normally subjected to weekly searches and denied the right to possess arms or to serve in the local militia, for which he was required instead to provide a substitute.[36]

However rigorous the official justice, it was less terrifying than the "justice" meted out by the crowds. The new English ambassador, Sir Thomas Smith, who was not yet inured to the ways of the Parisian populace, wrote with some alarm that "they in Paris every day murder one or another for Huguenots. It is enough if a boy, when he sees a man in the street, but cries '*Voyla ung Huguenot*,' and straight the idle vagabonds, and such as cry things to sell, and crocheters, set upon him with stones; and then come out the handicraftsmen and idle apprentices with swords, and thrust him through with a thousand wounds."[37] The job of the authorities was complicated by the danger these crowds presented. If the city's guardsmen sometimes had to make arrests to save innocent people from the wrath of the crowds, on other occasions they found their suspects snatched from them and subjected to various indignities by the people on the streets.

The explosion of gunpowder stored in the Arsenal on the night of 28 January created grave problems for Parisian authorities. The powder exploded with a force that toppled chimneys and broke windows in nearby houses, and a raging fire ensued. As a crowd gathered to watch, word spread that the Huguenots were responsible for the deed. By the time the maréchal de Montmorency, the prévôt des marchands, and other authorities arrived, the people were attacking anyone who might have been involved. At least one man was killed. Although the authorities quickly realized the fire was accidental, serious disturbances continued for more than a week. The city's official account admits to three more deaths in the days that followed the fire.[38] The English ambassador put the total higher, but as a newcomer, a stranger, and a man who was himself threatened by the crowds, Smith may not be entirely accurate here. He may also be stretching things—though not by very much—when he says that neither Montmorency nor the prévôt des marchands and échevins "dared do anything against the people, but let them do what they would.''[39] In fact, the city officers and other authorities did take limited defensive action; they convinced the crowds to release several persons, and they placed guards in threatened houses. Somewhat belatedly, on 3 February, Parlement ordered an end to all violence and took steps to increase the *corps de garde*.[40] Still, one can understand why Catherine de Medici felt it necessary on 7 February to express her extreme displeasure at the state of affairs in the capital and why on 8 February she advised the maréchal de Montmorency to station more troops in the city.[41] The local officers were obviously either unwilling or unable to take the steps needed to control the populace.

The role of the municipal officials in maintaining order in Paris will be taken up in detail in a later chapter. In the meantime, however, it is necessary to make a few comments on the predicament the city magistrates faced. Although some of the city officials had relatives who were Protestants or were even themselves drawn to the new faith, the great majority shared the religious sentiments of the Parisian populace: they were fervant Catholics who opposed the practice of two religions in the kingdom. At the same time, the city magistrates knew they had not only a responsibility for maintaining order but also a personal interest in doing so. They could not allow the populace too much license without endangering the hierarchical system on which their own privileged positions rested. Although they might condone a certain amount of popular unrest as a means of signaling to the king the city's firm opposition to a policy of compromise with the Huguenots, they could not afford to allow this unrest to escalate uncontrollably. It should also be remembered that most of the city officials were simultaneously members of the royal bureaucracy. Having benefited professionally from the king's favor, they did not want to lose this precious advantage by too rashly opposing the royal will. Torn by conflicting pressures, the city officials attempted to negotiate a difficult path between the dictates of personal conscience, the demands of royal policy, and the realities of urban discontent.

This complex interplay of competing forces is evident in the city's response to the news in late February that the duc de Guise had been felled by an assassin's bullet. City officials hastened to send a reassuring reply to Catherine's letter of 25 February enjoining them to keep a firm hand so that the death of the Catholic hero did not spark riots, but there was an immense amount of anger in the city. This anger was directed against the crown as well as against the Huguenots, and it was felt by the bourgeoisie as well as the populace. Catherine predictably had seized upon the occasion of Guise's death to step up negotiations for peace, and the word was out in Paris that the articles being discussed were ''very harmful to the Roman Catholic Church.''[42] The outpouring of grief at Guise's death—a display that astonished even the usually unflappable Venetian ambassador—was occasioned by the fear of a dishonorable peace as well as by a sincere regret for a fallen hero.[43] As Sir Thomas Smith wrote of ''the great lamentation'' in Paris, ''they now say themselves that they are utterly undone; and as their greatest champion is overthrown, the Huguenots will have all.''[44]

Whatever precautions the city may have taken in response to Guise's death, they were insufficient. A new round of popular violence broke out. In one incident, a crowd seized a recently arrested woman from the militia captain who was con-

Figure 4–1. The execution of Jean Poltrot de Meré, drawn and quartered on the place de Grève on 18 March 1563. (Phot. Bibl. nat. Paris.)

ducting her to the Conciergerie. Killing her, the people stripped her naked and, crying out that she was a Huguenot, dragged her through the streets from the porte Saint-Denis to the Halles.[45] I have found no evidence to support Smith's assertion in his dispatch of 8 March that "the populace, who now bear rule [in Paris], broke open the prisons and killed all therein," but the special security precautions that had to be taken—including the daily stationing of six armed men in every dizaine "to prevent scandalous attacks or murders"—testify to the seriousness of the unrest.[46]

On 18 March, the people were given the opportunity for a vicarious release of their anger. Guise's assassin, Jean Poltrot de Meré, was publicly executed on the place de Grève in an elaborate spectacle of retributory justice. An enormous crowd gathered before the Hôtel de Ville to watch Poltrot's painful death. First mutilated by red-hot pincers, the assassin was harnessed to four horses to be drawn and quartered. After his death and dismemberment, his head was placed on a lance before the Hôtel de Ville, his severed limbs were posted outside the four principal gates of the city, and his trunk was reduced to ashes in a fire on the place de Grève.[47] The ritual reduction of his corpse served at one and the same time to signal a triumph over the enemy, a warning against future betrayal, and a purging of the social body threatened by his crimes.

On the day following Poltrot's execution, the Parisians turned out for a very different sort of ceremony. With the permission of the queen mother, the city sponsored an elaborate funeral procession for the slain duc de Guise. The procession stands out from other princely funerals of the era because of the massive participation of the Parisian bourgeoisie and because of the air of defiant militancy that the bourgeoisie imparted to it. After the twenty-two town criers, who led the cortege with their ringing bells, came a great number of merchants and bourgeois bearing flaming torches. Four hundred bourgeois citizens joined the city officers following the prévôt des marchands and échevins, while thousands of others took part in their capacity of militiamen. Although there were sizable groups of clerics and nobles in the procession, the tone was set by the carefully orchestrated parading of the city militia. Rank after rank of captains and their lieutenants alternated with blocs of bourgeois harquebusiers and pikemen, helmeted and in chain mail, their weapons reversed.[48] Jean de La Fosse thought there must have been ten to twelve thousand armed men on parade.[49] Like the violence of the populace in the wake of Guise's death, this display of bourgeois might was a political gesture, a deliberate statement that the city looked upon the duke as its fallen leader and continued to support the policies for which he had stood.

The Parisians' opposition to a compromise peace was, however, to come to naught. At the very moment that Guise's coffin was being paraded through the streets of Paris, the final touches were being put on an edict of pacification. Negotiated by Condé and Constable Montmorency, the edict signed at Amboise on 19 March 1563 gave the Calvinists freedom of conscience and certain limited rights of worship. For the most part, the right to hold Protestant services applied only to noble households, but the Calvinists were also allowed to hold religious services in one city in each *bailliage* and in those towns that they had controlled just prior to the peace. They were not permitted to build temples, and they could not hold services anywhere in Paris or the surrounding *vicomté* and *prévôté*, although residents of the city were to be allowed to return unmolested to their homes.[50]

Two princes of the blood, the cardinal de Bourbon and the duc de Montpensier, were dispatched to Paris to oversee the registration and publication of the edict, for its violent rejection was very much feared. In a special session on 27 March, the officers of Parlement agreed to register the edict but still hesitated to publish it.[51] Public reaction when the edict finally was published on 30 March shows that these apprehensions were justified. Turning upon the town criers, whose job it was to announce the peace, the people pelted them with mud and put them in fear for their lives.[52]

Retributory Violence

The violence continued throughout the spring and the first half of summer. The coincidence of the peace with the Easter season, always a time when religious feeling ran high, did not help matters. Nor did the attempt of Parisian Protestants to return to their homes in the city, as the edict promised they might. On 7 April the prévôt des marchands reprimanded the militia captains for their failure to keep order—for the murders and other atrocities that were being committed daily. On Easter Sunday, 11 April, the city received even stronger reprimands from the queen mother and from the king himself. Referring in particular to the murder of two prisoners who were snatched from the hands of their guards, the king ordered the city to put a stop to the violence and to observe the edict of pacification.[53] The city officials responded to the king's reprimand by putting the blame for the prisoners' murder on the guards who had escorted them to jail. The guards had, the city admitted, publicly declared their prisoners to be Huguenots who had borne arms against the king. This explanation, which amounts to a confession of the inability of city officials to control the angry populace, was apparently considered sufficient. The city made no effort to track down the individuals who had instigated the seizure of the prisoners, although it is worth noting that greater precautions were ordered in later transfers of prisoners.[54]

At the same time, the officials of the Bureau de la ville refused even to attempt to enforce the provisions of the Edict of Amboise that promised those of the new religion that they might return to their homes and work. The city followed instead the lead of Parlement, which had warned the Calvinists not to try to return to Paris until after Easter, after the foreign troops had left the country and things had calmed down a bit.[55] The attitude of the parlementaires is further revealed by the order given on 7 April for the jailer of the Conciergerie to make a list of all of the religious prisoners who were unwilling to submit to the traditional Easter obligations of confession, absolution, and communion. A secret clause specified that those prisoners who refused this proof of Catholic practice were to be thrown in the dungeons, while those who submitted were to be allowed the freedom of the Conciergerie's open courtyard.[56] The official reason given for this order was to avoid "scandal and inconvenience," which suggests a fear of popular unrest and a realization that the yard of the Conciergerie was not very secure. This reasoning is justifiable. The order nonetheless reveals the limits of Parlement's willingness to support the liberty of conscience promised in the edict of toleration.

The summer of 1563 was a difficult one. The Corpus Christi celebrations were marred by outbursts of violence, and the attempts of Protestants to return to their homes continued to provoke vengeful acts. Moreover, the officials of the Hôtel de Ville engaged in a prolonged controversy with the militia, which refused to lay down its arms in spite of the king's repeated orders. Gradually, however, the capital returned to a state of relative calm.

Economic Tensions

During the next few years, economic issues competed in importance with political ones. Political and religious tensions did not fade away completely, and, indeed, by 1566 they were again on the rise. Even in the comparatively peaceful year of 1564, religious tensions are evident in the struggle of returning Huguenots to reclaim properties and positions taken from them during their absence.[57] They are also evident in occasional incidents of violence, such as that which occurred in April 1564, when the maréchal de Montmorency's men intervened to prevent an angry crowd from disinterring a Huguenot corpse buried at night, in accordance with a royal edict of December 1563, in the Cemetery of the Innocents.[58] The level of violence, however, was considerably lower. Catholic Parisians disliked the maréchal de Montmorency, whom they accused of being overly sympathetic to the Huguenots, but by and large they respected his authority.[59] As the king's lieutenant for Paris, the maréchal took a particularly active role in maintaining order in the city during the tour of the provinces that took Charles IX and his mother away from the vicinity of the capital for more than two years (March 1564–May 1566). Historians make much of the skirmish that took place between the maréchal's men and the retinue of the cardinal of Lorraine on 8 January 1565, and this incident is indeed significant as evidence of the reawakening of the quarrels between the houses of Montmorency and Guise. It is worth noting, however, that this conflict, which was occasioned by the cardinal's defiance of a royal ban on entering Paris in arms, did not involve the Parisian populace in any important way. Some bourgeois partisans of the Guises joined the cardinal's escort before it reached the city, but they do not appear to have been involved in the subsequent scuffle, and, by all accounts, the common people were unmoved by the quarrel.[60] There was considerable agitation in the city two weeks later, when Admiral Coligny entered the city at the invitation of the maréchal, who had requested his assistance in maintaining order. A rumor even circulated that the admiral's men intended to pillage the capital.[61] And yet the city remained calm. Opinion was expressed in the form of posters and pamphlets rather than in public disturbances and riot.

Parisian Protestants took advantage of this period of relative calm quietly to rebuild their force in the city. The illicit renewal of the Reformed Church of Paris, and the role this church played in the recrudescence of religious tensions that touched off the second war, will be discussed in the next chapter. For the time being, it is more important to establish that, from the perspective of most contemporary observers, the crucial issues in the period between 1563 and 1567 were not religious but economic ones. Already during the first religious war, Paris was entering into a serious subsistence crisis. The summer of 1562 was so cold and wet that the crops rotted in the fields. The plague raged in Paris for more than a year and, in the estimate of Claude Haton, who saw these natural disaster as signs of God's wrath, caused more than 25,000 deaths.[62]

During the first war, then, Parisan authorities had to cope not only with the religious conflicts but with the additional problems of scarcity and contagion. Grain prices, already unusually high at the start of the war because of previous bad harvests, reached the unprecedented level of 9 *livres tournois* per *setier* (approximately 156 liters), more than double the average prewar price, by December 1562.[63] To the bad weather and plague, which kept some of the grain from ever reaching the markets, we must add pillaging by troops quartered in the grain belt around Paris.[64]

Prices eased in the aftermath of the war, and it appeared that they were returning to normal. In 1564, however, a new sequence of natural disaster began. A part of the crop was destroyed by rain before it could be brought in from the fields. Then came a winter so cold that the wine froze in the cellars and peasants were found dead in their fields. François Grin calls this the "year of three winters." The rivers, which were such solid ice in December that a man could walk across them, flowed furiously when they finally thawed.[65] The Seine overflowed its banks, and it was a long time before the river was safely navigable and provisions could be brought into the city.[66] Meanwhile, it was apparent from the unusually cold spring that the 1565 harvest would be poor. By June, the king had issued orders to prohibit the export of grain, and by late August, when the price of wheat reached 11 livres per setier, the city was actively engaged in attempts to import supplies from places as distant as Sweden and Danzig.[67]

The subsistence crisis brought the fear of sedition to the city. Municipal records candidly reveal that the city fathers wanted to supply grain to the needy because they feared that the needy would otherwise try to help themselves to the supplies they believed were stored in the houses of the rich. The city officials were worried that the poor, not finding any grain, would "use violence on the properties and persons of the weak, which would be a beginning of riot and sedition that could only be appeased by arms."[68] Attempts to bring in supplies from a distance were frustrated, however, by the extent of the area affected by the scarcity and by the difficulties of transport. An early freeze in the north meant that the promised grain from Danzig could not delivered before spring. In the meantime, the city tried to cope with a great influx of paupers. Rules for the policing of the poor were tightened, and a tax was levied on the bourgeoisie to pay for alms.[69]

Grain prices remained high, averaging 9 or 10 livres per setier, through the next spring. The promise of a good crop in 1566 caused tensions to ease a bit, but prices had not yet begun to fall noticeably when torrential rains once again wiped out the crop. In July 1566, the price of wheat topped 21 livres per setier—more than five times the average price for any period prior to 1561.[70] The danger of grain riots appeared acute. Carts were burned on their way to market, and, in order to protect the bakers, who were inevitably blamed for the high price of bread, the city had to station armed guards in the markets of the popular quarters of the city. Desperate measures were taken: convents, barns, and private homes were searched for hidden stores, and officials were sent out to commandeer grain from the countryside in order to provision the capital.[71] By August, sufficient grain had been procured to cause prices to begin to drop, but the crisis was not really over. Prices remained at a level that was roughly double that of the prewar average.[72]

The significance of this crisis is twofold. In the first place, it is important to recognize that this period between the wars was one of merely relative calm and stability. In fact, it was a very troubled period in which all the socio-economic tensions already present in the city were aggravated. Second, the crisis fueled popular hatreds as the second religious war broke out in autumn of 1567.

5

The Renewal of War and the
Failure of Peace, 1567–1572

Between the renewal of religious war in October 1567 and the brutal massacre of 24 August 1572, France went through two more cycles of war and peace. The unity of this period and its coherence as a part of the story of Saint Bartholomew's Day lie not, however, in the oscillation between war and peace but rather in the gradual emergence during this period of many of the distinctive elements—the symbols, victims, and agents—that were to characterize the massacre itself. The white arm bands and paper crosses worn by those who took part in the bloodshed of Saint Bartholomew's Day first appear in the tumultuous unrest that marked the start of the second war in 1567. The outrages to which Coligny's corpse was subjected in 1572 mimic the mutilation of a straw effigy of the admiral exposed in Paris in 1569. Not just Coligny but lesser figures begin to find their way onto the scene. Some of the Huguenots who lost their lives on Saint Bartholomew's Day make earlier appearances as victims of harassment or assault; some of the men accused of being killers in 1572 appear as militia officers patrolling the streets during the second and third wars. This background has been neglected in previous accounts of Saint Bartholomew's Day, yet it provides the crucial context for understanding how the massacres took place. Let us begin with the buildup of religious hatreds that preceded the second religious war.

The Second and Third Religious Wars

The compromise peace signed at Amboise in March 1563 brought an end to overt warfare but did not resolve the religious quarrels. The intense hostility with which the Parisian populace initially greeted the Peace of Amboise gradually faded; people laid down their arms and permitted Huguenots to return to the capital, and yet the city remained alive with suspicion. Despite the hostile atmosphere, Catholics and Protestants alike managed to resume a semblance of ordinary life. The Protestants, insisting on the promised right to live untroubled in their own houses with freedom of conscience, returned to their homes and jobs. When necessary, they applied to the courts and required the magistrates to secure the return of confiscated properties or to oust the Catholic incumbents who had taken advantage of their absence to acquire their leases or assume their official functions.[1]

The Huguenots insisted on scrupulous observance of the edict of pacification, however, only when it was to their own advantage. The Reformed Church of Paris, dissolved in March 1563 in compliance with a clause in the Treaty of Amboise forbidding any exercise of the Reformed religion in the city, prévôté, or vicomté of Paris, was clandestinely revived just six months later. One of the Parisian ministers, Antoine de la Roche de Chandieu, though himself too well recognized to return to the capital, recorded in his journal on 16 September that "the Church of Paris is reconstituted, and its organization reestablished insofar as the current circumstances permit."[2] At first meeting only in small groups and in great secrecy, the Huguenots became bolder in time. They even held an illegal national synod in the capital in December 1565.[3]

Members of the Reformed community in Paris revived their church in violation of the law because they felt that they were being quietly strangled by the edict of pacification. They were angry with Condé for having agreed to peace on terms that favored the Huguenot nobility at the expense of the Huguenot city dwellers. They thought that he had been shortsighted and that, by agreeing that the Protestants should have only one church in each administrative district, or bailliage, and none at all in the capital, he had not only permitted a large proportion of the faithful to be deprived of the exercise of their religion but also sacrificed the evangelical potential of the church. Denied opportunity for future growth, the Reformed church would be condemned to a slow, painful death. To avoid this fate, it was necessary to carry on the church's evangelical mission even where this was forbidden by law. It was necessary to retain some kind of base among the citizenry from which pressure for change might later be applied.[4]

Moreover, despite continued protestations that the king had no intention of renouncing the edict of pacification, it soon became evident that Catherine de Medici wanted the Peace of Amboise to be interpreted in as restrictive a sense as possible where Huguenot rights were concerned. In June 1563, Reformed preaching was banned from royal palaces and the court.[5] In December, a detailed "interpretive" edict placed a number of new restrictions on the Protestants' rights to worship. Most important for Parisians was a clause that forbade residents of the capital to go out to nearby bailliages to attend services established there.[6] Catherine also tried to ensure that the site chosen for the one authorized place of preaching in each bailliage was in a small and obscure location, well removed from any population centers. She ordered the maréchal de Montmorency to transfer the place of preaching that had been established in the bailliage of Senlis from Pontoise to some "small city" in that district.[7] Nemours and Melun were also deemed unsuitable sites for reasons that seem directly related to the importance of these towns, and Fontaine-bleau, where the duchess of Ferrara had purchased a house with the specific intention of having it used for preaching, was outlawed as being too near the court.[8] In this way, Catherine effectively removed Reformed preaching from a number of the larger towns in the region of the capital. In doing so, she aggravated Protestant fears that she intended to deny them a popular base.

The ministers and elders of the Reformed Church of Paris responded to this threat largely by working underground. New ministers whose faces were not familiar to Parisian Catholics worked clandestinely within the city. Better-known ministers were sent to secret locations outside of the capital, where people could go to hear sermons and receive the sacraments in comparative safety, even though it was illegal to do so. The Parisian ministers lived in constant fear of "traitors and spies."[9] Even at the presumably safe distance of Geneva, Theodore Beza burned most of the letters that reached him from French reformers—an inestimable loss for historians, and a mark of the risks Beza believed his French colleagues ran.[10] Parisian Protestants had two reasons to fear betrayal. The first was the danger to personal safety, the risk of provoking the Parisian populace to renewed incidents of assault and pillage. The second and still more worrisome danger was the risk of upsetting the ever-precarious peace and provoking a new civil war on terms and timing unfavorable to the Protestant cause.

And yet, from time to time, whatever the peril, the Parisian church had to assert its existence. It had to proclaim that it had not been crushed, although it remained, in Chandieu's words, "afflicted and beneath the relics of the cross," struggling to support a burden that other Reformed churches had been allowed to set down.[11] One such self-assertion occurred in May 1565 when Condé's chaplain held public services in the prince's house in Paris.[12] A second occurred eighteen months later, when one of the chaplains to the queen of Navarre again defied the edicts by preaching publicly to a large audience in Paris. By this time, religious tensions were clearly mounting, partly as a reaction to the wave of iconoclasm that had swept over the neighboring Low Countries in the summer of 1566, and partly due to more local events.

Parisian Catholics were angered by evidence that the city's Protestants were continuing to practice their faith, even if it was outside the city walls. On two occasions in September 1566 Catholic crowds greeted Huguenots returning from services outside the city with catcalls, stones, and swords.[13] When the queen of Navarre's chaplain preached publicly within the walls just two months later, a storm of bitter protest broke loose. Placards were posted around the city urging the people to violence. "Cut them down, . . . burn them, . . . kill them without a qualm," exhorted one such placard:

> Hang and strangle them,
> So that death can strap them in,
> And dissolve them into the earth,
> Because they haven't wanted to live
> According to the church of Saint Peter.[14]

Indeed, it is hard to know whether the curé of Saint-Paul, Simon Vigor, was delivering a threat or a warning when he "said to the king in the name of the chief of the city of Paris, that if the Huguenots were suffered to preach in the city against the edicts, they would take them and burn them all."[15] Whatever the intention of Vigor's message, the Catholic outcry prompted new measures against the Protestant community and stimulated an effort to root out the ministers known to be living secretly in Paris. Marin Delamare, one of the pastors of the underground church, wrote to Beza in January 1567 that Vigor had done all he could to "inflame" the king against them, but he and his brethern had not ceased their work. Delamare hoped "the smoke would clear," but he predicted that, unless God showed great mercy, a new period of troubles would soon be at hand.[16]

Delamare's fears were well founded. It was disingenuous, however, to blame the Catholics alone for the threat to peace. Whatever justification the Huguenots might have had for their actions, they were straining the patience of the Catholic population. In late March, Catherine de Medici instructed the maréchal de Montmorency to impress upon Parisian Protestants that they must in the future "conduct themselves more modestly," because there was great trouble to be feared if they continued to violate the edict of pacification."[17] The warning had little effect. The more the Protestants feared the loss of their already limited rights, the more determined they were to carry on their clandestine activities. In April, Chandieu, who had remained in Lyons because it was thought too dangerous for him in Paris, set out for the capital with the intention of resuming his ministry there.[18] By June, Charles IX was receiving frequent complaints about secret assemblies, preaching, baptisms, marriages, and the collection of funds on the part of Parisian Protestants. Letters patent issued 1 June repeated the king's express prohibitions against any exercise whatsoever of the Reformed religion in the city and suburbs of Paris and threatened severe penalties for violation of these laws.[19]

More worrisome to the Protestants than the king's threats, however, were signs that French Catholics were taking up arms. Religious violence was becoming increasingly common. Corpus Christi was once again disrupted by riots, and the king deemed it necessary to have armed men ready to assist the officials charged with keeping order in the capital.[20] To this end, in mid-July, Charles IX invited the prévôt des marchands and échevins to appoint one hundred men from each quartier to a new peacekeeping force. Heads of household wherever possible, they were to be supplied with all sorts of weapons except firearms and to serve under the command of bourgeois notables, or "*centeniers*," chosen by the king from a list of nominees supplied by the city officials.[21] Although the new troops might in theory have been called upon to repress Catholic as well as Protestant-inspired acts of violence, they were clearly seen as an anti-Protestant force, and their presence was worrisome to the Huguenots.[22] Moreover, the king had seized upon the excuse offered by the passage of the duke of Alva's troops along France's eastern border to raise new companies of French and Swiss guards. The Protestants, knowing full well that Alva's army was intended to quell the religious unrest in the Netherlands, did not trust the king's explanation that he feared to be surprised by the old Spanish enemy. They suspected that the six thousand Swiss troops whose arrival the king was awaiting were to be directed instead against themselves. Indeed, they feared that the kings of France and Spain might ally in a joint campaign against the Calvinist dissidents that troubled both of their realms.[23] By mid-September, amid persistent rumors that the king was about to revoke the edict of pacification, Parisian Protestants began to sell their belongings and leave town.[24]

As it happened, it was the Protestants who broke the peace. Convinced that the Catholics were just waiting for an opportune moment to launch an attack against them, they determined to seize the initiative. Their plan was to intervene militarily to prevent the arrival of the king's new Swiss troops, to separate the king from his arch-Catholic advisers (in particular the cardinal of Lorraine), and to convince him to reconsider Protestant grievances.[25] To accomplish these ends, Huguenot forces gathered in arms in the vicinity of Meaux, near where the court was staying at Monceaux. As with the attempt to seize François II at Amboise, however, word of the conspiracy leaked out. The royal party retired in haste to the safety of Catholic Paris. The plot was aborted and with it any chance for an amicable entente between the Huguenot leaders and the king, who, with some reason, interpreted the failed coup as an attempt against the crown and angrily rejected the Huguenots' protestations of loyalty. The argument that the Protestants were trying to save the king from his evil advisers was no more convincing than it had been in 1560, and Charles IX was not quick to forgive the Huguenots for forcing him to run for cover in his capital. Attempts were made to negotiate a settlement that would avoid a return to arms, but neither party was in the mood for compromise. The Protestants, having lost a desperate gamble through their failure to seize the king, were forced to carry through with the war they had thereby provoked. In the words of the Huguenot captain François de La Noue, they decided to save themselves "with their arms instead of their feet."[26]

Taking a lesson from the first civil war, when they had learned that it was easier to seize a city than to hold it, the Huguenots resolved this time to take few cities, but important ones.[27] And so they determined to capture Paris. While continuing to discuss the terms under which they would lay down their arms, they took several towns in the Paris basin and prepared to invest the capital. On the night of 1 October, they burned a dozen or more windmills outside the porte Saint-Denis. The flames of the burning mills could be seen from across the city, and the Parisians, thinking they had been attacked, rushed to take up their weapons, which had been returned to them two days earlier.[28] Convinced after the abortive "surprise of Meaux" that the Huguenots, "insatiable for royal and human blood," were capable of any treachery, Parisian Catholics readily believed stories that the Protestants had accomplices within the walls prepared to set fire to their own houses in order to see the city burn.[29] When a rumor went around that fagots and powder had been found concealed in several locations, the newly armed Catholics began to break down the doors of Protestant houses in search of the presumed conspirators.[30] Most Protestants had already left the city; those who had stayed behind and were discovered suffered arrest, assault, or even death.[31] Fear coupled with anger to produce a night of frenzied violence during which Parisian Catholics defended their city by striking out blindly at the enemy they believed was concealed within it.

The best insight we have into the Catholic view of these events comes from an anonymous observer who told of receiving orders to keep a good watch through the night—to have arms at the ready, buckets of water near the door, and a lantern shining until daylight,

> to fight with one hand and defend yourself with the other. It was permitted in these circumstances, following the counsel of Christ, to sell one's tunic and purchase a sword. That night they found in the street the skin of a man who had been flayed, which terrified pious souls. If someone said a word in favor of the authors of the rebellion, it was permitted to kill him, which was the fate of many.[32]

In many respects this night and the days that followed constituted a rehearsal for the massacre that was to occur five years later. Unless we believe in omens, we can consider the discovery of the flayed skin—the symbol of Saint Bartholomew, who was martyred by being skinned alive—as an ironic, if gruesome, coincidence. One of the key symbols associated with Saint Bartholomew's Day did, however, appear at this time. According to Etienne Pasquier, anyone who did not put the sign of a white cross on his hat was in danger of being killed.[33] Five years later, white crosses marked the Catholic crowds on Saint Bartholomew's Day. More crucially, we can see the appearance already in 1567 of a state of mind characteristic of those who took part in the massacres. Our anonymous observer's words testify not only to an unquestioning belief in the rumors of impending treachery but also to a conviction that the retributory violence had been officially sanctioned. By his account, "it was permitted" to kill not only rebels but anyone who "said a word in favor of [them]." Elsewhere in his description of events, he tells of a royal edict ordering all Catholic men and women to display the sign of the cross prominently on their persons, "otherwise they would be put to death on the spot."[34] We have already had Pasquier's testimony that people found it prudent to don white crosses or other visible signs of Catholic affiliation, but there is no evidence of a royal edict to this effect. Indeed, it is extremely unlikely that such an edict was issued. Why, then, did people like our anonymous informant believe that it had? The answer lies in the psychology of fear, a subject to which we shall inevitably return.

Despite Catholic apprehensions, the Protestants did not try to enter Paris. The firearms, rocks, and chains the Parisians had prepared for their defense were not needed. A new worry, however, arose. The Huguenots had cut off the entrances to the city and were prepared to starve it into submission. Paris had not yet recovered from the interwar scarcity, and this new threat to the grain supply drove its Catholic citizens into a frenzy.[35] Their anger increased through the month of October, as the futile negotiations dragged on and the shortage of foodstuffs became acute. Much of the anger was directed against the maréchal de Montmorency and his father, the constable, who had charge of the defense of the capital. Parisian Catholics even accused the Montmorencys of treason when Charenton, a point through which much of the city's grain supply necessarily flowed, fell into Huguenot hands. Rumors linked the maréchal to the treacherous capitulation of Charenton's garrison.[36] According to Jacques-Auguste de Thou, if the king had not been in Paris, there would have been an uprising.[37]

The threat of popular violence eventually pushed the constable to take the offensive. His troops made several sorties, which allowed Paris to be provisioned, although, again according to de Thou, "the people did not on that account cease to murmur."[38] On 10 November, Montmorency finally led his army out to battle. The aged constable received mortal wounds that day on the plain of Saint-Denis, but the battle itself was not decisive. The Huguenots were forced to give up their plan of starving the Parisians into submission, but they were by no means defeated. They moved their armies off to the east to await the German princes who had promised to come to their aid. Meanwhile, negotiations began again for a settlement and end to war.[39]

If Catherine was willing to talk of peace, the Parisians were not. Public opinion in the city was strongly opposed to a negotiated settlement.[40] The English ambassador wrote in December that the Parisian magistrates had offered the queen mother great sums of money if she would continue the war. In January he wrote that she had to keep the continuing negotiations secret for fear of offending the Parisian bourgeoisie, which had already contributed six hundred thousand francs to the war effort.[41] The Parisians wanted to fight on to a clear victory—to eliminate the Huguenots from the kingdom once and for all. An anonymous pamphlet published in February 1568 summed up the popular view that it was morally and tactically wrong to make any attempt to treat with the "seditious rebels," who aimed at nothing less than the "entire subversion and ruin of the state." The same pamphleteer made use of a familiar metaphor when he wrote that "rebellion is the true cancer of a state, which cannot be cured or removed by gentle means" but rather must be "cut back and uprooted" by means of "the sword." A negotiated peace could only result in the king being despised and threatened; it would leave him in perennial danger from new seditious enterprises.[42]

Despite Parisian opposition, peace was made in March 1568. The Huguenots' position was sufficiently strong for the peace to be concluded on terms favorable to their party. The Peace of Longjumeau confirmed the conditions set out in the Peace of Amboise four years earlier, without any of the later modifications that had gradually restricted the Protestants' rights to worship. It also promised a complete amnesty for Condé and his followers, and, in order to rid the country as quickly as possible of the German troops who had come to Condé's aid, the king promised to pay their wages.[43]

The Parisian populace bitterly resented the concessions made in the Peace of Longjumeau.[44] An anonymous poem in the form of an echo sums up the popular sentiment in Paris in the spring of 1568: "Pour traicter ceste paix, que gaigne notre Royne?" And the echo: "Hayne."[45] The Parisians' resentment was encouraged by Catholic preachers, who raged against the peace in their Lenten sermons. As recounted by Haton, the sermons predicted dire consequences for the king if he did not cease to support false prophets. Haton insisted that the preachers did not urge the people to rebellion, but they did warn that the Huguenots would destroy France "if they were not exterminated by force of arms."[46]

Whether or not propagandists and preachers can be blamed for encouraging popular violence—a subject that will be taken up in a later chapter—some people did demonstrate their opposition to the Treaty of Longjumeau by sacking Protestant houses and assaulting those Huguenots who dared to return to the city. One of Beza's correspondents informed him that six houses had been pillaged on the very day the peace was announced, and late in April, a month after the treaty was signed, an English agent wrote that there was "the appearance of greater trouble than before."[47] In May two men were killed in a riot in the rue Saint-Antoine.[48] Special troops patrolled the city on holidays, and an armed guard accompanied the Corpus Christi procession, but still the violence continued. On 7 August the English ambassador wrote to the queen that "more have been murdered since the publishing of the peace than were all these last troubles."[49]

The Peace of Longjumeau could not last. Neither side disarmed. The third war, which began in late August 1568, was in effect a continuation of the second.[50]

Although Paris was not a major scene of the fighting in this new war, tensions in the city remained high. In November 1568 city officials were sufficiently frightened that a Huguenot attack might occur that they ordered all the houses outside the northern gates torn down so that the enemy could not find shelter in the shadow of the walls. Emergency measures were put into effect, and regular searches were made for Huguenots and hidden arms.[51] It is clear throughout this period, however, that a Huguenot attack was not the only danger that worried city authorities. All through the second and third wars—as in the interval between—they struggled to prevent mob violence. Ordinances against pillaging and public disturbance were issued over and over again.[52]

Many Parisian Protestants left the city at the outset of the second war and did not return until after the conclusion of the third. Most fled of their own accord when they heard news of the failed attempt to take the king at Meaux; the remainder were ordered to leave on 2 October. Repeated injunctions forbade them to return until after the Peace of Longjumeau.[53] During the third war, Protestant residents who had not been combatants during the previous wars were allowed to remain in the city, but they were subject to severe restrictions and were usually required to post a bond to guarantee good behavior. Men whose living depended on daily labor were permitted to go to work, but they were not allowed out on Sundays or holidays. The other Huguenot residents were forbidden to leave their houses at any time. They had to send servants out to do their regular shopping and errands; in an emergency, they could secure special passes from the officers of their quartier.[54] These measures were intended to prevent violence on the part of the city's Catholics as well as to eliminate danger from the Protestants themselves. Records of Huguenots arrested during the second war indicate that law officers often had to intervene to save the Huguenots from menacing crowds.[55] Similar attacks occurred during the third war. The most dramatic incident of this sort was the assault on Philippe and Richard de Gastines, who were arrested in January 1569 on the charge of celebrating a Protestant Lord's Supper in their house in the rue Saint-Denis.

Haton may have exaggerated when he said that fifty people were killed in the riot that accompanied the arrests, but other sources confirm that the seizure of the Gastines, along with several of their relatives and neighbors, took place amid widespread public disturbances.[56] Haton reported that this incident was followed by three more collective attacks on Protestants. "The Huguenots were so hated by the Parisian populace that, if the king and authorities had let them have their way, there would not have been one [Huguenot] in the whole city who was not attacked."[57] Jacques-Auguste de Thou added that crowds of people followed after the magistrates of Parlement, heckling and harassing them, while this case was being judged. In his opinion, the crowds so pressured the justices that they eventually pronounced a death sentence against the Gastines and their neighbor Nicolas Croquet for a crime that would ordinarily have warranted banishment or a mere fine.[58]

On 1 July 1569, in accordance with a sentence rendered by Parlement the previous day, Philippe and Richard de Gastines and Nicolas Croquet were hanged on the place de Grève for taking part in illicit assemblies and the rite of the Lord's Supper.[59] Their properties were confiscated, as was common with executed criminals, but, in an exceptional measure of reprisal, the house of Philippe de Gastines (in which the assemblies were said to have taken place) was torn down. On its site was erected a monument in the form of a massive stone pyramid topped by a cross. This monument was to become an important symbol of the religious hatreds of the Parisian populace.

The people were given another symbol in the summer of 1569 when Admiral Coligny, the leader of the Huguenot party after the death of Condé in the battle of Jarnac (March 1569), was hanged in effigy in the place de Grève. In a move that was at least partly motivated by the desire to confiscate his properties to the profit of a penurious crown, Parlement convicted Coligny of *lèse-majesté* and sentenced him to be dragged on a wooden frame through the streets of Paris to the place de Grève, there to be hanged and strangled. Since Coligny was out of reach of Parisian justice at the time the sentence was pronounced, it was carried out on a straw dummy dressed in his colors and painted to resemble him.[60] Haton recounted that the effigy and Coligny's coat of arms hung in the place de Grève until after the conclusion of peace. He saw them there on several occasions. When rain ruined the dummy's face, it was replaced with a painting of Coligny that hung from the gallows on a chain and told passers-by of his crimes. What remained of the effigy was taken to the gallows of Montfaucon where it joined the decaying corpses of executed criminals.[61]

This symbolic execution became reality on Saint Bartholomew's Day, when the real corpse of Coligny, the first victim of the massacre, was dragged through the streets, mutilated, and eventually hung by its feet (the head having been cut off) at Montfaucon. Haton added that the youths responsible for these acts conducted a mock trial of the admiral, "just as if they had been judges," and sentenced him to the punishment pronounced by the court three years earlier.[62]

The Failed Peace of Saint-Germain

Even more than the effigy of Coligny, the cross that marked the destruction of Philippe de Gastines's house became a symbol of Parisian resistance to any form of toleration or peaceful coexistence with the Huguenot enemy. The Peace of Saint-Germain, which ended the third religious war in August 1570 was, like the earlier peace treaties of Amboise and Longjumeau, bitterly opposed by the city's populace. Once again, Parisians protested orders to disarm and to allow Protestants to return to their homes.[63] One of the clauses of the edict of pacification specified that all monuments to the persecution of Huguenots were to be demolished and the properties on which the monuments stood returned to their owners.[64] The people of Paris, however, refused to allow the cross of Gastines to be torn down.

City officials, fearing sedition, ignored the king's orders to remove the cross through the fall of 1571.[65] By early December the king's anger was great enough to force the officials to act. In a compromise move intended to appease the populace and yet obey the king, city magistrates made plans to transfer the cross-topped pyramid to the Cemetery of the Innocents. They tried to justify the move by explaining that the cross was being moved from profane to sacred ground, but Catholic preachers interpreted the action rather as an attempt to obliterate the memory of Christ's passion, and in their sermons the preachers condemned the removal of the monument.[66]

Because of the high level of tension, preparations for moving the cross had to be made under armed guard. Even so, when the workers retired at night, youths came in and destroyed their labor. On 8 December, twenty-five or thirty men were stationed in the cemetery to protect the foundations that had been dug for the pyramid. Attacked by a crowd that broke down the cemetery's locked gates, they fled under a hail of stones.[67] That night the city called on all of its forces to maintain order and prevent sedition. The prévôt des marchands commanded householders to take up arms and station themselves in their doorways, where they were to await further orders. He told heads of household to keep watch on their children and servants and instructed heads of colleges to keep their students inside. He sent the city's professional guards to strategic stations, and ordered special reinforcements for the quartier Saint-Denis adjacent to the cemetery. Finally, Catholic priests were told to admonish their parishioners and warn them against sedition.[68]

The precautions proved insufficient. Sunday afternoon, a crowd gathered again around the Cemetery of the Innocents, where it once again stoned the guards and forced them to flee. Another crowd beseiged the house of the quartenier for the rue Saint-Denis. Refusing to obey the orders to stay quietly in their homes, the people wanted to string up the chains traditionally provided for the city's defense. That same afternoon, the mistress of the Golden Hammer on the pont Notre-Dame, suspected of having lobbied for the removal of the cross of Gastines, came to the Hôtel de Ville to complain that a great number of people were throwing rocks at her house and trying to break into it.[69] The city sent troops, who dispersed the crowds and made several arrests, but the assistance they provided was of short duration. Members of the crowd freed the prisoners as they were being taken to jail and then chased after the lieutenant responsible for their arrest, stoning him until he reached the shelter of his own home. They later returned to pillage the Golden Hammer and the houses of several other known Huguenots.[70]

Additional security measures went into effect Sunday night, and through continued vigilance on the part of city officials, Paris remained calm for the rest of the week. The following Sunday, people were again ordered to stay in their houses, while the heads of household kept watch. The king, meanwhile, became more and more angry as city officials, aware that they had only a tenuous grasp on public order, continued to postpone moving the cross. When the king threatened to send troops to see that his will was enforced, city magistrates finally decided that the transfer could be postponed no longer.[71] Late on the night of 19 December, the cross was moved. Those responsible for the transfer, thinking that all was quiet, retired without leaving a guard, but by six the next morning, the crowds had gathered again. Only quick action by the prévôt des marchands prevented the people from seizing weapons stored in the Hôtel de Ville. The crowds went on to attack the Golden Hammer again and to sack a neighboring house, the Pearl, which was also occupied by Protestant tenants. At one point they appeared to be heading for the Palais de Justice, whose gates were pulled shut in a panic, but this proved to be a false alarm. They did, however, set fire to belongings that had been emptied from the Golden Hammer and the Pearl. They also burned a house in the rue Saint-Denis owned by the heirs of the Gastines. Fifteen men worked from nine in the morning until eleven at night to put out this fire and to ensure that it did not spead to neighboring houses.[72]

According to Jacques Faye, the house was burned not only because it belonged to the Gastines family but also because the ironsmith who lived there had lent some tools to those responsible for moving the cross. Faye also remarked that the crowds burned the belongings from the Golden Hammer to show that they pillaged not to enrich themselves but to "punish the lady of the house." The crowd believed that she had gone to Coligny and convinced him to pressure the king into tearing down the cross.[73] Other sources confirm the rioters' intention to punish the relatives of the Gastines because they were believed responsible, along with Coligny, for the decision to move the cross.[74]

The same specificity of targets appears in the Saint Bartholomew's Day massacre. The inhabitants of the Golden Hammer were among the first victims of the crowd's violence on 24 August, as were the inhabitants of the Pearl and other houses attacked in the riot of the cross of Gastines.[75] Indeed, a great many of the victims of Saint Bartholomew's Day can be identified as participants in earlier quarrels or conflicts. We find the wife of Richard de Gastines on the lists of the murdered, along with an innkeeper accused of harboring fugitive Protestants, a quartenier removed from office for his religious beliefs, and a clockmaker who successfully appealed the sentence of beating and banishment handed down by the prévôt de Paris in 1569.[76] The common people who were victims of the massacres may seem anonymous from a distance of four hundred years, but they were not anonymous to their murderers. They were neighbors and acquaintances. Their houses were known by the signs of their absence during the troubles or by the regular visits of Châtelet officers. Paris's Protestants were a marked people, a familiar enemy.

The inability of the civil magistrates to maintain order in times of crisis and the provocative sermons of Catholic preachers, themes that occur repeatedly in the cross of Gastines riots, will be subjected to closer scrutiny in later chapters. For the time being, let us simply follow the thread of events down to Saint Bartholomew's Day, for the anger generated by the cross of Gastines affair did not dissipate after the December riots but persisted well into the new year. Although the city repaired the damage that had been done to the Golden Hammer and the Pearl, passers-by continued to deface the houses with mud and filth. On 7 February 1572, the prévôt des marchands ordered the inhabitants of the pont Notre-Dame to keep a watch out and intervene when necessary to prevent such acts of vandalism.[77] On 16 February, Charles IX asked Parlement for copies of the proceedings and judgments rendered by that court and the Châtelet against persons arrested in the riots. With some reason, the king suspected that the courts had been lax in prosecuting those responsible for the affair. He had since the beginning of the riots been pressing for prompt and exemplary justice, and with little result. One man, a poor cobbler named Paul Rousselet, had been arrested and condemned to death for participating in the first riot. The notes from Rousselet's final interrogation in Parlement indicate, however, that he was only a minor participant. Rousselet admitted to having thrown one or two stones but denied any further part in the events of 9 December. His judges asked questions designed to place him at the scene of the incident and to elicit the names of people who might have incited him to throw stones, but the judges obviously knew Rousselet was not a ringleader. His condemnation by the lieutenant civil, which was brought up to Parlement on 20 December, was intended as a warning to the people and a demonstration of diligence to placate the king.[78]

Even so, the judges feared to execute Rousselet while feelings were running so high. The case was postponed until after the holidays.[79] In the meantime, several other people were arrested for possessing goods taken from pillaged houses. The evidence suggests that their roles were even more marginal than Rousselet's. The goods were of little value—in one case amounting only to a pot of butter—and the judges were acutely aware that they had no way to disprove the claims made by the accused that they had found the stolen items in the street or taken them from fleeing pillagers but had not themselves entered the violated houses or participated in their sack. Nevertheless, in early January, after new letters from the king urging prompt justice, Parlement upheld the sentence condemning Rousselet to be hanged on the place de Grève and sentenced three men accused of possessing stolen goods to watch Rousselet's execution and then to be publicly whipped and banished from the city.[80]

The judges of Parlement seem to have been troubled by these sentences and well aware that people who bore more serious responsibility for the riots had escaped punishment. They reprimanded the lieutenants civil and criminel for having arrested only "*belistres*" (idlers or ne'er-do-wells) and accused them of lack of diligence for their failure to apprehend the people who had actually invaded the Huguenot houses and set fire to their belongings. For his part, the lieutenant criminel insisted that he and the other officers of the Châtelet had done everything possible to find the authors of the riots but to no avail. He believed that "there were no authors, but rather that the people, seeing the cross torn down, were roused."

Contemporary accounts agree on this point. Guillaume Aubert, a lawyer in Parlement, explicitly denied that there was "any plot or conspiracy" and characterized the events as "a sudden tumult raised by the people, irritated to see that the cross had been removed against their wishes." According to Aubert, "people of the better sort and good Catholics were thoroughly annoyed by the tumult."[81] Jacques Faye likewise dismissed the participants in the riots as rabble and warned his correspondent in a letter describing these events not to exaggerate their importance.[82] The official report that Parlement sent to the king on 22 December also emphasized that only members of the lower classes had been seen to participate in the riots. No heads of household or "*gens de qualité*" had taken part, wrote the parlementaires, but only poor people, "laborers, women, and children who had no arms but stones and sticks."[83] Bernard Fortia, one of the parlementaires commissioned to report on the riots, was still more explicit on this point. Fortia noted that the people gathered around the fire on the pont Notre-Dame "had neither leggings nor shoes," though it was December, and that "the poor laborers [*gagnedeniers*] are the cause of all of the trouble."[84]

The king, moreover, seems to have accepted these conclusions. Although he sent word to the city after the first riots that he knew perfectly well that "the little people [*les petitz et menuz du peuple*] do not put their hand to something like this unless they are pushed and supported in it by the big [*des gros*]," he later described the participants in the riots as "just some knaves, like picklocks and other idlers," for whom the excitement over the moving of the cross was "a pretext to pillage and plunder."[85]

The general consensus that the riots had no real leadership or organization is important, for some historians have suggested that the cross of Gastines affair was not a spontaneous uprising but rather was provoked by enemies of the religious peace such as the Spanish ambassador or agents of the Guises.[86] There may be a small kernel of truth to this suggestion, at least where the Spanish ambassador, Don Francès de Alava, was concerned. Charles IX did complain to the French ambassador in Madrid that Alava, whose recall he had requested some months earlier, was using the issue of the cross to stir up trouble in Paris.[87] There are also rumors of a build up of Guise forces in Paris in the fall of 1571, and it is thus possible that Guise partisans helped stir the populace to oppose the transfer of the cross.[88] We should not, however, exaggerate the part that these provocateurs—if such they were—might have played in the cross of Gastines affair. At most, the Spanish ambassador and Guise agents took advantage of already present, long-festering hatreds and encouraged their expression. They pointed to a symbol—the cross of Gastines—and made it a focus and a rallying point for otherwise diffuse discontents. The significance of these events does not lie in secret plots and covert maneuvers but rather in the very facility with which the Parisian populace, given a target and a symbol, could be stirred to violence. It is the volatility of Paris, not the agility of secret agents, that is demonstrated here.

Building Anger against the Crown

The lesson of Parisian volatility seems to have been lost on the king. The angry letters that Charles wrote from the comfortable distance of the Loire valley, letters in which he insisted on the immediate restoration of order and the summary punishment of the authors of the sedition, show how little he could empathize with his magistrates' fear of reigniting still-smouldering passions by public executions and other displays of royal authority. They show how poorly Charles comprehended the intensity of anti-Huguenot feelings in his capital; how little he understood that these feelings were gradually being turned against his family and himself.

The removal of the cross of Gastines was not the only grievance Parisians had against the king during the two years between the Peace of Saint-Germain and Saint Bartholomew's Day. First and foremost, they were angered by the fiscal burdens the king's seemingly futile wars had made necessary.[89] The economic disruption caused by the wars combined with continued bad harvests and high prices to create serious economic hardships. Moreover, as had happened in 1568, as soon as the Peace of Saint-Germain was signed, the king had turned to his capital for the money urgently needed to pay off the foreign mercenaries who had come to the aid of the Huguenot armies.[90] The people of Paris did not have the money the king demanded and resented the very purpose of the imposition. They also resented the frivolous display in which the Valois court, despite its penury, continued to indulge. Contemporary accounts show their growing tendency to be critical, even cynical, in their references to the king and court. For example, when the royal family moved into the newly rebuilt Louvre, as yet incomplete in March 1571, Jean de La Fosse noted in his journal that Charles IX's predecessors had never enjoyed such luxury in their buildings, "even though the kingdom was never in such poverty as that caused by the civil wars."[91]

Through the fall of 1571, city officers struggled to ward off the king's demands for the sums still due on the tax assessment imposed in the aftermath of the Peace of Saint-Germain. Initially set at six hundred thousand livres, the tax had been cut in half after repeated remonstrances on the part of the city, but it remained very difficult to collect. Finally, in January 1572, the king forgave the last one hundred thousand livres of the assessment on the condition that the city pay immediately the other fifty thousand livres that was due. In order to scrape together that final amount, the city in March threatened to seize the properties of delinquent taxpayers and even to quarter troops on those that owed substantial sums. And yet, by May, the king was pressuring the city for a new assessment of two hundred thousand livres.[92]

At the same time, the king was resorting to other expedients to raise the money needed to cover his debts. These fiscal devices too left their mark on the city. François I had begun the practice of using the Paris Hôtel de Ville as an agency through which to issue annuities backed by the income due the royal domain from various taxes and fees. This practice proved a convenient way for the crown to raise ready cash, even though it meant mortgaging future income, and it was continued and expanded by François's successors. Initially, at least, there were plenty of potential buyers. *Rentes sur l'Hôtel de Ville* became a popular form of investment for the bourgeoisie and royal magistrates. During the reign of Charles IX, however, particularly during the second and third religious wars, the rentes were issued in amounts that far exceeded public demand. On more than one occasion, the city had to coerce wealthy citizens to purchase annuities they did not want. As a consequence of the mounting level of indebtedness and the unsound policies that went along with it, public confidence in the rentes evaporated. By 1571, the king had to turn to private financiers, or *partisans*, for the funds he needed. These partisans advanced the required cash and in return received title to rentes, which they then disposed of as they wished, collecting the interest until purchasers were found.[93] This allowed the king to keep on borrowing, while ever more distant and tenuous sources of income were assigned as the funds from which the rentes were to be paid. The Hôtel de Ville, which had loaned its name and its fiscal credibility to these operations, was left with the problem of collecting the funds with which the interest was to be paid. Royal officers and bourgeois citizens, who by this time frequently had a third or more of their wealth invested in rentes sur l'Hôtel de Ville, were justifiably worried that the whole system would collapse. They suspected that the partisans—who were by and large the same Italian financiers known to have made inordinate profits as tax farmers and moneylenders—would continue to prosper because they were too wealthy and powerful for the king to risk offending, whereas their own investments would be lost.

In addition, some people nourished grudges because of direct financial losses suffered as a consequence of the Peace of Saint-Germain. Prominent among this group were the Catholics who had purchased offices confiscated from Huguenots in 1568. These offices were returned to their previous owners by the terms of the peace. The empty state of the treasury meant, however, that little or no compensation was paid to the Catholics summarily deprived of their recently acquired positions. The move was thus an affront to both pocketbook and pride.[94] Individuals who had paid high premiums to acquire the leases to houses whose Protestant tenants had fled the city at the start of the second war were similarly affected by the order to return these properties to their previous tenants after the Peace of Saint-Germain. In principle, the Catholic tenants received partial compensation for their displacement in the form of a tax levied on the returning Huguenots for reentry into their leases, but even if this money actually reached the displaced Catholics—and it is not at all clear that it did—it only partially moderated their sense of grievance. Nor did the city's offer to give them them preference when new leases became available serve to ease the sense of resentment against a peace treaty deemed to favor the rebels at the expense of the king's loyal subjects.[95]

Economic grievances thus merged with anger over religious issues to alienate the Parisians from their rulers. As yet, the king received little direct criticism for the policies that people opposed. The queen mother shouldered most of the blame. Charles IX, twenty years old at the time of the Peace of Saint-Germain, was excused on the grounds of his youth and on the assumption that his mother continued to dominate affairs of state. In March 1570, for example, Parlement conducted an investigation into rumors of seditious preaching in the parish church of Saint-Nicolas-des-Champs. A Franciscan was said to have preached that "the kingdom had fallen to the distaff" (that is so say, fallen into the hands of a woman), and that "the distaff should be burned." The same friar was accused of criticizing the new bishop of Paris, Pierre de Gondi, for having entered his office "not through the door but through the window,"[96] an allusion to the favoritism enjoyed by Gondi and his siblings, the children of an Italian banker whose wife was a close confidante of Catherine de Medici.[97]

The anti-Italian feeling manifest by educated people in sarcastic comments and witty aphorisms was translated at popular levels into a virulent xenophobia. Already in 1569 the Venetian ambassador reported that, because of the hated tax programs, Italians were so detested in Paris that they could not go out in the streets in safety.[98] In the spring of 1572, the xenophobia became hysterical. There was a rash of attacks on Italians, who were accused of the ritual murder of little children. On 20 June, officers of the city guard rescued one Italian from an angry crowd. Three others were found to have been seriously injured. There was no foundation for the accusations of ritual murder. The corpse of one young boy was found, which excited the crowd greatly, but the child proved to have died of a long illness. His corpse had been left at the edge of the cemetery by his father, who was too poor to bury him.[99]

Anger against the Valois monarchy lay very close to the surface in the anti-Italian riots. Vile rumors circulated that the purpose of the ritual murders was to secure blood with which to cure the duc d'Anjou of some secret illness. Some people said it was the queen herself that needed the innocents' blood.[100] There may also have been an element of scapegoating here, with the Italians feeling the lash of hatreds that, because of orders for the strict enforcement of the edict of pacification, could not be vented on the Huguenots.[101] Coligny had returned to court in September 1571. He had been given a generous pension and readmitted to the king's council. This angered the Catholic populace, which continued to view Coligny as a perfidious rebel, and they quickly came to believe that he exercised an undue and pernicious influence on the young king.[102] N. M. Sutherland has argued that this view of Coligny is mistaken; the king resisted much of Coligny's counsel and temporized on issues of supreme importance to him. Moreover, the admiral spent only five weeks at court between his return in September 1571 and August 1572, so he could hardly have had the influence often imputed to him.[103] People did not see it this way, however. They noted that the Guises ostentatiously left court at the same time that Coligny returned, they noted the king's new insistence on the strict enforcement of the Peace of Saint-Germain, and they drew their own conclusions.[104] The riots of the cross of Gastines must be seen in this context as well. It was Coligny who insisted that the cross must be removed, and the riots were an expression of opposition to his presumed influence with the king. The news that Charles IX planned to marry his sister to the Huguenot prince of Navarre furthered the suspicion that the Huguenots were in power at court, as did rumors of a possible French invasion of the Netherlands or even a war against Spain.

When a Huguenot army under Louis of Nassau invaded Hainaut and seized Valenciennes and Mons in May 1572 in support of the Netherlandish rebels, these rumors appeared to be confirmed. Jean de La Fosse recorded in his journal that Charles IX was said to be secretly assisting the invasion and had been promised the county of Flanders when the Protestant victory was assured.[105] There is diplomatic evidence that Charles may indeed have consented to such a pact and only disavowed the project when its failure appeared certain, so the rumors were well founded. The opportunity to take advantage of the momentary weakness of the old Hapsburg enemy, whose subjects were in rebellion, as well as the notion of uniting his own divided people in a new foreign war, seems to have appealed to the young king.[106] The Catholic population of Paris could not, however, share this enthusiasm. War in the Netherlands could only aggravate the continuing economic distress. Moreover, the old Hapsburg-Valois rivalries had little resonance among the common people, who were shocked at the notion of allying with heretics to fight another Catholic king.[107]

As the marriage between Marguerite de Valois and Henri de Navarre passed from rumored possibility to accomplished fact, tensions grew. Here was a new theme for the Catholic preachers, who told their listeners that God would surely be avenged for the impiety of this perverse union.[108] One source tells of a woman, described as a nun or lay sister, who went around Paris shortly before the wedding saying that she had been sent by God to tell the Parisians that their city would be destroyed if they did not kill all the Huguenots.[109] These ravings only added to the anxiety the Parisians felt at seeing a large number of Huguenots gathered in and around the capital for the wedding and their anger at reports that religious services were being held in Huguenot circles.[110]

Tensions rose to a fever pitch on August 22 when Coligny was wounded by shots fired from the window of a house near his lodgings in the rue de Béthisy. City officers feared a riot and took steps to diffuse the tension. Merchants who had closed their shops because they feared disturbances were ordered to reopen them; people who had taken up arms were ordered to put them down. Bourgeois guardsmen were stationed at the gates of the city, but they were given no arms and told only to keep watch over anyone who entered. Only the professional officers of the city's guard were allowed to take up their weapons, and they were cautioned to cause as little stir as possible when they assembled.[111] The precautions were futile. By 23 August, the rumor that the Protestants demanded revenge for the attack on Coligny was making the rounds of the city. Once again anger was coupled with fear.

This was the situation in Paris on Saint Bartholomew's Eve. The next events are obscure. The accounts we have of them are partisan, contradictory, and frustratingly incomplete. As Henri Dubief has pointed out, "all the history of Saint Bartholomew's Day rests on suspect sources."[112] I shall try despite these handicaps to reconstruct a logical sequence of events, but many things will never be known for certain. One thing should, however, be clear from the foregoing account: the immense danger that popular passions, building for so long, could be ignited by the slightest spark.

6

The Massacre in Paris

This chapter will recount the version of events leading up to Saint Bartholomew's Day that seems to me most plausible. Like most historians, I find the abortive attempt on Coligny's life on 22 August the key point from which to begin this narration. The admiral had remained in Paris after the wedding of Henri de Navarre and Marguerite de Valois only in order to present to the king some petitions concerning violations of the Peace of Saint-Germain. He was shot as he returned from a meeting with Charles IX in the Louvre. A chance move—variously reported as bending to adjust a shoe, stopping to open a letter, or turning to spit in the street—saved Coligny's life. Wounded in one arm and the opposite hand, he was brought to the safety of his lodgings by the Huguenot nobles who accompanied him, while his would-be assassin, usually identified as Charles de Louviers, Sieur de Maurevert, fled through the rear entrance of the house in which he had lain in wait. Historians, following contemporary accounts, have most often accused Catherine de Medici of hiring Maurevert and initiating this attempt on Coligny's life. Sometimes the duc d'Anjou and the Guises are made to share this responsibility with Catherine, but she is the one most often named.[1] Intensely jealous of the influence the admiral had acquired with the king, Catherine is said to have plotted Coligny's death in order to prevent him from leading France into a war with Spain.[2] This view has been disputed by N. M. Sutherland, who has argued, in my opinion convincingly, that such a move would have been inconsistent with Catherine's larger political aims. Catherine had spent more than ten years trying to preserve peace and authority for her sons by balancing Catholic and Protestant power in the kingdom, and there is little reason to believe that she would suddenly have abandoned these consistently held policies and ordered the death of the Protestant leader, a move which could be predicted to lead to a renewal of the civil wars and a return to power of Catholic extremists. Moreover, the theory of her insane jealousy appears groundless when one considers that Coligny was rarely at court between September 1571 and August 1572 and thus could hardly have had the king under his sway.[3]

If not Catherine, then who? No certain answer can be given to this question. At the time these events took place, no one really knew who was responsible for them. Ambassadorial accounts, journal entries, and, later, memoirs were tissues of conjecture, heavily colored by their authors' preconceptions and prejudices. It can be argued, however, that the most likely candidates are one or more members of the Guise family, who still blamed Coligny for the death in 1563 of François, duc

Figure 6–1. The massacre of Saint Bartholomew's Day. This engraving simultaneously shows the assassination attempt on Admiral Coligny on August 22, his killing on August 24, and the massacre that followed. Center left: Coligny, on horseback, is shot as he reads a letter. Upper right: he is attacked in his bed, thrown from the window, and dragged off through the street below. (Phot. Bibl. nat. Paris.)

de Guise, or possibly the duke of Alva, who wanted to prevent Coligny from leading his forces into the Netherlands.[4] It is also conceivable that the assassin, Maurevert, acted on his own initiative. Maurevert is believed to have killed Coligny's trusted lieutenant, the seigneur de Mouy, in 1569, in an abortive attempt on the admiral's life, and he may have decided to strike again at the admiral before the latter could exact revenge for the murder of Mouy.[5] In the end, the identity of the person or persons responsible for the initial attempt on Coligny's life is less important than the fact that this attempt was in all probability the result of a personal hatred or vendetta and not a part of a larger plan to eliminate the Huguenot leaders. Here again, Sutherland's argument is convincing. The strike against Coligny makes no sense as the first step in a larger assassination plot, since it could be guaranteed to put the Huguenots on the alert at the very moment when an unsuspecting torpor would best have served the assassins' ends.[6]

Indeed, the attempt on Coligny's life was a key event precisely because of the violent reaction it provoked among his followers, still gathered in Paris for the royal wedding. Had the shots actually killed the admiral, it is probable that the Huguenot nobility would immediately have left Paris and prepared for a new civil war. But Coligny did not die, and he refused to take the advice of those who urged him to leave the city before his assassins returned to finish their task. He placed his trust in the king's protection and his promise to find and promptly punish the authors of the crime. This meant that Coligny's followers also remained in Paris, where they fed off of one another's anger, becoming more and more outspoken in their threats of vengeance. It meant that the city was in an uproar, as the Huguenot threats were rumored about and magnified, fueling the anger of the Catholic populace. And it meant that the Huguenot leadership, collected in the Catholic capital, presented a convenient target for a "preemptive strike" intended to eliminate the retribution they threatened.

Targets and Motives

It is in this light, as a preemptive strike, that the massacre must be viewed. According to Gaspard de Saulx de Tavannes, the king and his council, meeting in the Louvre on 23 August, concluded that civil war was inevitable and that "it was better to win a battle in Paris, where all the leaders were, than to risk it in the field and fall into a dangerous and uncertain war."[7] Whatever questions one might have about the veracity of Tavannes's memoirs, which were in fact written by his son, there is a ring of truth to the sentiment expressed here. We must take seriously Catholic fears that the Protestants intended to begin a new war by an uprising in the city of Paris and a coup against the royal family. It was to receive instructions concerning a Huguenot plot that the prévôt des marchands, Jean Le Charron, was ordered to the Louvre late on the night of 23 August.[8] The same excuse was given in the king's first attempts to explain the massacres to Protestant princes. Charles IX claimed to have received word on 23 August that Huguenot troops stationed outside of the city were marching on the capital and that the Protestants intended that very night to seize the royal family in the Louvre and eliminate the Catholic leadership.[9]

This explanation was immediately dismissed by the Protestants as a culpable fabrication—an attempt to foist off onto the Huguenots the blame for their own ruin—and historians have generally viewed the suggestion that the Huguenots would attempt a coup against the king on the hostile territory of his fiercely Catholic capital as too farfetched to warrant serious consideration.[10] We should not, however, dismiss the fear of a Huguenot coup so lightly. There may in fact be an important element of truth to this claim—not that the Protestants really intended to seize the king, but that Charles sincerely believed rumors to this effect.

There is evidence that stories of Huguenot reprisals did begin to circulate soon after the attack on Coligny. Jean de La Fosse recounts that on 23 August the word spread that the Huguenots intended to cut the king's throat, kill his brothers, and pillage the city of Paris.[11] Haton reports similar rumors.[12] One could discount this evidence as being tainted by hindsight—we have no proof that La Fosse kept his journal on a day-to-day basis, and Haton's memoirs were definitely composed at a later date. Besides, both men were ardent Catholics inclined to believe the worst of the Huguenots. Still, given the highly charged emotional climate that followed the attempt on Coligny's life, it would be surprising if such rumors were *not* being spread through the city and the court.

Furthermore, it is entirely plausible that the king, already intimidated by Coligny's demands for justice and by the haughty demeanor of the angry nobles who attended him, should have found the rumors credible. Charles could not help but remember the Huguenots' earlier attempt to capture him at Monceaux or their attempt to seize his brother, François II, at Amboise, and he might easily have been convinced that they would try this tactic once again. As we shall see, the orders the king gave the prévôt des marchands on the night of 23 August would seem to confirm this fear of an impending Huguenot coup. But even if this was not the case—if Charles did not have reason to fear an immediate Protestant attack—he did have reason to fear a new civil war, and the temptation to ward off this danger or at least to tilt the odds in favor of the crown by destroying the Huguenot leadership, might well have proved irresistible. The plan of action that led to the massacre may have been made under the impulse of panic, in vital terror of an impending Huguenot attack, or it may have resulted from a more calculated desire to destroy the Huguenots' force by annihilating their leadership. Either way, it was the result of a sudden, impulsive decision and not a carefully nurtured plot.[13] Either way, the plan was laid without thinking through the potential consequences.

From this standpoint, it does not really matter who it was that convinced Charles to order the Huguenot leaders killed. The queen mother, Anjou, the comte de Retz, and the duc de Guise have been variously accused; the truth will never be known. Everyone who was party to these events had reason later to lie, to present his or her own role in the best possible light, and there is no independent, impartial evidence. Once again, assigning responsibility for the decision is less important than analyzing its consequences. Sometime in the afternoon or evening of 23 August it was agreed that the Huguenot leaders must die.

Once this decision was made, hasty plans had to be made for its execution. It is well established, both by accounts of the plans and by the evidence of later events, that the primary responsibility for the assassination of the Huguenot leaders was given to the king's Swiss and French guards and to those of the duc d'Anjou under the command of the ducs de Guise and d'Aumale and other Catholic leaders.[14] The roles of the Paris city officers and the militia have proved more difficult to delineate. We know that Charles IX summoned the prévôt des marchands, Jean Le Charron, to the Louvre late on the night of 23 August and informed him, in the presence of the queen mother, Anjou, and "other princes and nobles," that the Huguenots were planning a coup against the king, the state, and the city of Paris. Charles related certain threats that had been addressed to him that very day by Huguenot leaders and gave Le Charron orders for the security of the royal family and "the peace, repose and tranquility of the city and his subjects."[15] More specifically, Charles ordered Le Charron to seize the keys to all of the gates of the city and carefully to lock them so that no one could enter or leave, to draw all the boats on the Seine over to the Right Bank, where they were to be chained so that no one could use them, and to distribute weapons to the militia officers and all citizens capable of bearing arms. He was to have these men ready at the militia's usual gathering points, where they would receive additional orders in case of necessity. Furthermore, he and the échevins were to call up the city artillery and have it ready on the place de Grève and inside city hall, in order to defend the building or to be used elsewhere as the need might arise.

The final paragraph of the city's account of this midnight meeting in the Louvre indicates that the king gave Le Charron several other instructions, both for him personally and for the échevins and other city officers—an ambiguous statement that some historians have taken to be a tactful (or squeamish) way of saying that orders to participate in the massacre were also conveyed. The main argument in favor of this interpretation is that the scale of the massacre was too great for it to have been simply the product of a popular uprising. Historians also cite Jacques-Auguste de Thou and other sixteenth-century informants who claimed that such orders were given. The scale of the massacre does not in itself constitute a proof of official origins, however, and we have no more reason to trust sources like de Thou on this particular aspect of the secret meetings held in the Louvre than on other details they presume to give about what occurred in these meetings, which they did not attend and only heard about secondhand.[16]

If we look at the logic of the situation, rather than relying on accounts we know to be untrustworthy, we will, I think, find it hard to accept allegations that the city officials and militia took part in the massacre as a direct result of royal orders. It is certainly possible that Charles told Le Charron in confidence about the attack that was planned against the Huguenot leaders, but I think it unlikely that he invited the city's participation.[17] If the attack was aimed only at the Huguenot leaders, the kings' troops and those of his brother provided adequate manpower for the job, and there was more to lose than to gain by calling the poorly trained and undisciplined city militia to share in the slaughter. Rather, both the initial orders and the commands subsequently issued from the Hôtel de Ville seem to confirm that the city forces were called out as a precautionary measure, in case something went wrong in the attack against the Huguenot leaders and back-up force was needed. The placement of the city's artillery in front of the Hôtel de Ville makes sense only in this context. The artillery was brought forth when an uprising or popular sedition was feared; it was brought out, for example, for the cross of Gastines riots.[18] But what use was heavy artillery in a plan to murder the Huguenots in their beds?

According to city registers, Le Charron met with the échevins, the city councilors and quarteniers, and other city officials on his return to the Hôtel de Ville. Together, they endeavored "as best they could" to carry out the king's commands, while reporting back regularly on their progress. The necessary written orders to summon the captains of the archers, crossbowmen, and harquebusiers, as well as orders summoning the bourgeoisie to arms, did not go out until "the next day," that is to say, Sunday, 24 August, "very early in the morning."[19] It would be useful to know the time more precisely, but, in any event, if we consider the logistics of the situation, it is highly improbable that the city's guardsmen could have assembled in the large, crowded, and unlit city in time to take part as a concerted force in the massacre. All accounts of the massacre place Coligny's murder some time before dawn—usually about four in the morning—which can hardly have given the captains time to summon their forces, distribute weapons, and issue orders, much less to have their orders carried out.[20] Some of the more extremist militia captains and guardsmen did take part in the general massacre that ensued, but there is no evidence that this was pursuant to orders from either the king or the prévôt des marchands.[21] Quite the contrary, at eleven on Sunday morning, the prévôt des marchands was remonstrating with the king, informing him that members of the royal household and soldiers of the king's guard, as well as all sorts of other people who had mixed themselves among them, were pillaging and sacking houses and killing people in the streets.[22] Why would the city's highest officer have made such a complaint if the killing was officially sanctioned? Rather, it seems that events were not proceeding according to plan, that the killing was both unexpected and unsettling to the city's highest officials. Sunday afternoon, in response to the king's command to put a stop to the "pillaging, sacking of houses, and murders," the prévôt des marchands issued orders to all citizens who had taken up arms to lay them down again and to return quietly home and stay there.[23] There is no denying that these orders were ineffectual. It took nearly a week of repeated commands, regular patrols by city officials, and sentinels posted outside Protestant houses to regain some semblance of peace in the city.

I will argue in a later chapter that there was a radical faction within the miltia that had become increasingly uncontrollable as the religious wars progressed and that, on Saint Bartholomew's Day, as on other occasions, these men contributed more to the explosion of violence than to the maintenance of civil order in the capital. On the whole, however, I believe that the officials of the Hôtel de Ville and the guardsmen under their command tried to behave responsibly and that they were simply overwhelmed by the popular fury. The massacre of Saint Bartholomew's Day was an unplanned—though not unforseeable—explosion of hatred and fear touched off by the events surrounding the attempt to kill Coligny. In the end, the best explanation for these events is the simplest one.

The Swiss guard, breaking down the door to the house where Coligny was lodged, must have made enough noise to cause a stir in the already watchful neighborhood. Indeed, the account believed to come from one of the captains of the Swiss guard relates that the house was well defended by the troops put there earlier to ensure Coligny's safety and that there was considerable fighting before the attackers could gain entry.[24] Many sources also say that when Coligny was killed the tocsin was rung at Saint-Germain-l'Auxerrois as a sign for the general massacre to begin. Whether or not this is true—and there is some ambiguity about just where the tocsin was rung and when—the noises from the attack on Coligny's lodgings would have sufficed to rouse the neighborhood.[25] Given the earlier rumors, Catholics would naturally have associated the noises with the anticipated Huguenot attack. The many Protestant noblemen lodged in nearby streets would have taken the same noises for an attack on the admiral and very likely tried to come to his defense. Terror and confusion would have brought the quartier Saint-Germain-l'Auxerrois to the combustion point and spread from there to the city at large.

If we look at these events in context, we can see the contagious quality of fear. At the same time that Guise and the Swiss guard were preparing to kill Coligny, the city was attempting to muster its defenses against a feared Huguenot attack. The night was not as dark and still as usual. People were knocking on doors to summon their neighbors to arms, they were bringing out weapons, perhaps stretching chains across the streets, though there is no good evidence that preparations advanced this far. We must remember what had occurred five years earlier, when the Huguenots lit up the sky with burning windmills. The magnitude of violence was less on the earlier occasion, but the pattern of popular reaction was much the same. On that occasion too, the Parisians had turned on their Protestant neighbors, imagining them to be the accomplices of illusory troops that were massing outside of the walls.

Why did the events of 1567 end with just a few deaths and those of 1572 with several thousand? Two answers are necessary here. The first is well established; the second more problematical but, in my opinion, key. In the first place, the intervening years had done much to exacerbate and little to resolve the hatreds already felt in 1567. The situation was inherently more explosive. Second, I would postulate that in 1572 there was an added spark. A few reckless words served to ignite the conflagration.

The words were spoken by the duc de Guise upon leaving Coligny's lodgings. Encouraging his troops to carry on with their task, Guise reminded them that they killed by the king's command. The five words, "it is the king's command," overhead by others in the confused excitement of the darkened street, spread like wildfire. Taken to mean that the king had commanded the death of all of the Huguenots, these words transformed private passions into public duty. They authorized actions that many people might otherwise have held in check and allowed them to view themselves as soldiers and citizens fighting to protect their city and king, and not as murderers and rabble, wantonly sacking and killing. I believe that such authorization—or the conviction that it had been given—was psychologically necessary before the massacre could take place, that people had been primed by polemical sermons and writings to believe that the king could and should order the annihilation of heretics, and that many sincerely believed that he had given precisely this order.[26]

It is not necessary to accept exaggerated stories of the duc de Guise racing through the city shouting, "kill them, kill them all; for it is the king's command," to believe that the last five words, or words like them, probably were spoken. Goulart's relation of the massacre, although distorted by a hatred of Guise, probably comes close to the truth where he places in the duke's mouth the following speech: "Courage, soldiers; we have begun well; let us go on to others, for the king commands it."[27] Goulart adds that Guise repeated in a loud voice, "the king commands it; it is the king's will; it is his express commandment." This may be true, but such repetition was not necessary. Five small words were enough. Throughout the city were men who were willing to believe—happy to believe—that the time had come to wipe out past humiliations, to restore France to divine favor by purging her of the heretics who had infected her for so long.

The Popular Fury

From the quartier of Saint-Germain-l'Auxerrois and the Louvre, where archers of the king's guard dispatched the Huguenot nobles attendant upon Henri de Navarre and the prince of Condé, the massacre spread south and east in the city. Activated by the wild rumor that the king had ordered all the Huguenots killed, militiamen and civilians joined in an orgy of murder and looting that lasted for nearly a week. It is difficult to establish a chronology for the violence, which spread rapidly in the early hours of Sunday morning and continued through much of the day but appears to have diminished somewhat by late afternoon, perhaps as a consequence of the orders issued by both the city and the king for everyone to lay down weapons and return to their homes.[28] Monday morning, however, the killing took up again, as roving groups of armed men sought out Huguenots hidden by friends or relatives, attacked prisoners being escorted to the Conciergerie, and sacked the houses of those missing or dead.

The first non-noble victims appear to have been wealthy Huguenot merchants like Mathurin Lussault, the queen mother's jeweler, whose house adjoined the cloister of Saint-Germain-l'Auxerrois, and Phillippe Le Doux, who lived on the rue de la Vieille-Monnaie, near Saint-Jacques de la Boucherie. Nicolas Le Mercier and his family on the pont Notre-Dame also appear to have been among the massacre's early victims. Having already been objects of the popular fury in the riot of the cross of Gastines, they were obvious targets for murder on Saint Bartholomew's Day.

According to Goulart, Mathurin Lussault, hearing his doorbell ring in the night, went to open the door and was immediately pierced through by a sword. Lussault's son, coming downstairs when he heard the noise, was also struck by a sword but managed to escape into the street. He died when the neighbor with whom he sought shelter refused to open the door and left him standing defenseless before his assailants. Lussault's wife Françoise Baillet died a slower and more painful death. On hearing of the fate of her husband and son, she first climbed to the attic and tried to jump to safety in the courtyard next door, but fell clumsily and broke both legs. Moreover, the open window betrayed her flight, and her pursuers so threatened the neighbor who had hidden her in his cellar that he disclosed her hiding place. "Then they took her and dragged her by the hair a long way through the streets, and spying the gold bracelets on her arms, without having the patience to unfasten them, cut off her wrists." Pierced through by a metal rod intended for roasting meats, she was dragged through the streets for several hours before her body was dumped in the river. "The two hands remained in the street for several days," Goulart tells us, "and were gnawed upon by dogs."[29]

There is, of course, no way to verify the accuracy of the events narrated here. We can, however, confirm from Lussault's inventory prepared after his death that he and his wife "were killed on [August] 24 with those of the so-called Reformed religion and the greater part of their properties pillaged by the populace." Ironically, the inventory was compiled at the orders of the queen mother's chancellor, Martin de Beaune. Some items of silverware and jewelry belonging to Catherine de Medici and her daughter Marguerite had been confided to Lussault for repairs and were believed to have been taken in the sack of his house.[30]

Pillage was also a motive in the deaths of Phillippe Le Doux and his wife. Goulart describes how Le Doux was killed in his bed. His wife, who was so close to delivery of the couple's twenty-first child that the midwife was already present, was killed despite her pleas to allow the child to be born before she died. Attempting to escape her assailants, she climbed to the attic, where she was caught, stabbed in the abdomen with a dagger, and thrown into the street below. The half-born infant, its head poking out of its mother's mutilated body, was left to die in the gutter.[31]

Once again, we cannot confirm the gruesome details of the murders, but we do have an unpublished source not only confirming that Le Doux and his wife died during the first night of the massacre but also giving important insights into the popular killings. The book of *sentences*, or judgments, of the prévôt des marchands contains a partial transcript from a lawsuit involving properties allegedly taken from Le Doux's house.[32] Although fragmentary, the transcript shows that the *sergent de bande* of Le Doux's dixaine, Pierre Coullon, along with several accomplices, was suspected of having stolen several thousand écus from trunks in the house. The stories told by the witnesses, who were all neighbors and for the most part members of the dixaine's bourgeois guard, suggest that instead of installing men in the house to prevent looting, as the city had ordered, Coullon and his friends had ransacked the house in search of the four thousand écus rumored to be hidden there. Several witnesses describe being chased out of the house by Coullon and his accomplices and only half-glimpsing broken trunks and belongings scattered about, but one, Guillaume de La Faye, describes Coullon searching through a wardrobe, his hands deep in the pockets of clothing found there, and saying, "Look, look and see if you will find something."

We may suspect that Coullon's pillaging was motivated by personal revenge or professional jealousy, for he and Philippe Le Doux were neighbors and practitioners of a common trade. Both men were *passementiers*, dealers in the gold braid and embroidered trims that decorated the fashionable clothing of the era, but Le Doux was much more successful financially than Coullon. The tax levied on Le Doux in 1571 was 120 livres, a sum paid only by the mercantile elite and prosperous magistates. By contrast, Coullon, whose name is fourth above Le Doux's on the tax list for the rue de la Vieille-Monnaie, was taxed at one hundred sous, a mere five livres. Coullon's principal accomplices, Thierry de Saint-Laurent and Jean Poignant, likewise residents of the rue de la Vieille-Monnaie, were taxed at six and ten livres respectively.[33]

On the other hand, it also appears from La Faye's testimony that the four thousand écus that Coullon was suspected of taking belonged not to Le Doux but to a Huguenot gentleman who was staying in the house. Another witness identified this gentleman as "a man named La Roche who claimed to belong to the King of Navarre," and recounted how La Roche had promised before dying that he would "make rich" whomever would save his life. Was it perhaps on account of this gentleman, then, and not Le Doux himself, that a guard was set outside the house in the early hours of the morning of 24 August? The sources are not clear on this. Several witnesses testified that they had been summoned to guard Le Doux's house, but they do not tell us why. Once again it is La Faye whose testimony is the most precise.

He said that he was called upon about two in the morning by Thierry de Saint-Laurent and Pierre Coullon to guard the house of Philippe Le Doux so that no one might leave and that, when the tocsin sounded, they were to be killed ["'que l'on les tuast''], which was done, and the aforesaid Le Doux and his wife and others were killed by the populace ["par la commune''] and, this done, Coullon com manded everyone to leave the house and [said] that it was necessary to draw up an inventory on behalf of the poor children [of the deceased] and that it was necessary to call their uncle, who lived in the rue Aubry le Boucher, and in fact they all did leave except for seven or eight who remained in the house with the aforesaid Pierre Coullon.[34]

If it answers some questions, La Faye's testimony raises others. Is he evasive about the murders ("que l'on les tuast'') and determined to blame them on the populace so as to avoid admitting his own role in the affair? None of the other witnesses mention that an order was given to kill the residents of the house; nor do they mention the sounding of the tocsin. Is La Faye simply more forthcoming than they, or did he receive different orders? Or did he perhaps just imagine afterwards that the order to kill was given? Unfortunately, we will never know. Nor will we know, if indeed La Faye was given this order, whether Coullon invented it or whether he received it from his superiors and, if so, how far up the chain of command it began.

One final comment should be made about this testimony. One of the witnesses in this case refers to bottles of wine being brought out of Le Doux's house for those standing guard outside. It is a small point but a potentially significant one: many of those who took part in the events of Saint Bartholomew's Day were doubtless fortified by drink. This does not excuse but may help explain such barbaric acts as cutting off a woman's wrists to remove her gold bracelets. Descriptions of such cruelties abound in narratives of the massacre. Protestant accounts in particular stressed the abusive treatment of women and children. As in the accounts cited above, the deaths of Huguenot women are commonly described in more detail than those of the men, especially if the women were young and beautiful, or pregnant.[35] The children are described witnessing their parents' death, as in the account of the two little sons of Richard de Gastines, who cried "until the blood came out of their noses and mouths'' as they watched their mother's murder on the pont aux Meuniers, or the account of the youngest daughter of Nicolas Le Mercier and his wife, who was dipped "stark naked in the blood of her massacred mother and father, with horrible threats that, if ever she became a Huguenot, the same would happen to her.''[36]

The propaganda motives of the Protestants who published these accounts are clear. They wanted to dehumanize their enemies—to show how brutally they vi-olated all human and sacred laws, how like animals they were in their blood lust. And yet we cannot dismiss the horrible tales of painful death as being merely Protestant propaganda. Many of the stories, if they cannot be confirmed from independent sources, nevertheless retain a ring of truth and are validated by their resemblance to earlier incidents in the religious wars (and to the inhuman tortures that continue to be a feature of aggravated religious and ethnic conflicts). We know that women were dragged through the streets by their hair and that bodies were pitched into the Seine during earlier incidents of popular violence; there is every reason to believe that such things—and worse—occurred during the immensely more disordered events of Saint Bartholomew's Day.

I would agree with Janine Garrisson-Estèbe that there was a ritual aspect to these killings but even more with Natalie Davis that the "rites of violence" enacted here did not spring up from the collective unconscious, where they had been buried since the dawn of time, but rather "were drawn from a store of punitive or purificatory traditions current in sixteenth-century France."[37] If we can see the acting out of a sacerdotal role in the "baptism" of Nicolas Le Mercier's daughter in the blood of her parents, we can see the acting out of magisterial roles in a number of stories of Huguenot deaths. When residents of the Latin Quarter burned a poor bookbinder in a bonfire of his books before dragging him "half dead" to the river, they were mimicking the execution by burning that was the traditional punishment for heresy.[38] When youths from the crowd mutilated Coligny's dead body—cutting off his head, his hands, and his genitals—and then dragged it through the streets, set fire to it, and dumped it in the river, they were acting out a confused ritual of humiliation, as well as parodying the forms of royal justice. According to Claude Haton, the youths conducted Coligny's trial as they dragged him along, "just as if they were judges and officers of the court," and they repeated their sentence against him at all the major intersections of the city before burning him as a Huguenot and heretic. When they got tired of these activities, they tossed the corpse in the river, but then, deciding that it was not worthy of being food for the fish, they hauled it out again. Eventually the royal hangman, acting on the orders of Parlement, which had confirmed the sentence pronounced against the admiral in 1569, dragged what was left of the body out to the gallows of Montfaucon, "to be meat and carrion for maggots and crows."[39]

The violence of Saint Bartholomew's Day was didactic and coercive as well as vindictive. There are numerous accounts of Parisian Catholics attempting to force their Huguenot captives to recite Catholic prayers or go to mass. Goulart tells how Antoine Merlanchon's murderers exhorted him to "invoke the Virgin Mary and the saints and to renounce his religion" before they dealt their final blows and how a neighboring tradesman offered protection to Mathurin Lussault's sixteen-year-old servant if she would promise to go to mass, only to turn her over to Lussault's killers when she refused.[40] The old woman who hid the minister Pierre Merlin's five-year-old son took pleasure in teaching him to say the Hail Mary and to kiss saints' images, though she also practiced a more conventional form of blackmail in refusing to return the lad to his mother until she had received five hundred écus for her services.[41]

There is other evidence of extortion. In addition to the unverifiable incidents recounted in the *Histoire des martyrs*, there is a good case recorded in the unpublished proceedings of the Bureau de la ville. Less than a month after Saint Bartholomew's Day, André Pynet, an innkeeper on the rue des Prouvelles, described for the prévôt des marchands how the governor of pages in the duc d'Anjou's stables and another gentleman in Anjou's service had seized Jean Lat, a Huguenot guest at his inn, "the day that looting and pillage were permitted in Paris against those of the new opinion." They would have killed him, "as was permitted," had Lat not promised them a ransom of one thousand écus. Unfortunately, city officials were more interested in collecting the substantial sums of money owed by Lat, a tax farmer, than they were in his personal fate. The records do not tell whether the ransom was paid and the bargain kept.[42]

The picture that emerges from these stories of murder, pillage, and extortion is black indeed, but we must not imagine that Paris was completely devoid of Catholic citizens willing to shelter their Huguenot neighbors out of pure compassion or goodness of heart. Charlotte d'Arbaleste was protected by a succession of Catholic kinsmen and acquaintances in a harrowing but eventually successful attempt to escape from Paris.[43] The man she was later to marry, Philippe de Mornay, was sheltered first by his host at the Golden Compass in the rue Saint-Jacques, where he had taken rooms for the royal marriage, and then by his family's solicitor, who lived off the rue Saint-Martin. Mornay left the Golden Compass on the morning of Monday, 25 August, when his host, a man named Poret, "a Roman Catholic but a man of conscience," warned him that "he could not save him but rather would be ruined himself, which he would not have lamented if he could have guaranteed [Mornay's safety]."[44] Murderers were already at work next door in the house of the bookseller Oudin Petit when Mornay slipped out of the Golden Compass and crossed the city to the solicitor's house. The solicitor, whose name was Girard, withstood several visits from local militia officers who came to ask about any strangers he might be harboring, but it was obvious to Mornay, who had been joined by several of his serving men, that everyone was endangered by his presence, so he left early the next morning, accompanied by one of Girard's clerks, who had volunteered to help him get out of the city and claimed acquaintance with some of the guards at the porte Saint-Martin. As it happened, the young clerk was nearly the cause of Mornay's arrest, for he had left Girard's house so abruptly that he was still wearing his slippers, which awakened suspicions among the guards posted at the city gates. We cannot doubt, however, that his intentions were good and his motives generous.[45]

Renée Burlamaqui tells another story of disinterested assistance in relating how her nursemaid's husband, Jean Madame, attempting to escape the house where he was cornered by fleeing over adjacent roofs, at last climbed into a strange house, where he encountered a serving maid who gave him something to eat and hid him until morning, when she ushered him out into the street after first affixing to his hat a white paper cross so that he would be taken for a Catholic.[46] Burlamaqui herself and her two young siblings received aid from several Catholic Parisians, most notably the duc de Guise, who housed them, along with other fugitive Huguenots, for a week in his Paris townhouse. Burlamaqui's parents meanwhile found refuge with the duc de Bouillon, who had saved his own life by agreeing to go to mass and tried—without insisting—to convince those he sheltered to do the same. When the parents learned that Guise planned to have the three children rebaptized in the Catholic church, they hastily reclaimed their young.[47]

The composite picture that emerges from such accounts of protection and escape suggests that a minority—probably a relatively small minority—of Parisian citizens actively participated in the massacre. Roaming the city in small, fierce bands, they assaulted suspected Protestants in the streets, searched them out in their homes, and demanded entry to houses where they might be hiding, while the largely passive majority remained behind closed doors, afraid either to participate in or to protest against the activities of their peers. This does not mean that the mass of bystanders were innocent of complicity in the crimes; many approved of the killing without taking part in it, and, if some showed the courage to hide fugitive Huguenots, very few were willing to continue extending this protection when it involved any personal risk. I will return in Chapter 10 to the problem of the split between active participants and those who disliked but feared to oppose the massacre. For the time being, two points need to be made. First, it can be seen that the atmosphere in the city at the time of Saint Bartholomew's Day was such that even those who detested the massacre feared to oppose it. Second, the fact that the duc de Guise, the notorious leader of the attack on Coligny, opened his house to fugitive Huguenots is yet another piece of evidence that the massacre was never intended to encompass the mass of Parisian Protestants but rather was aimed at a selective few—the military leadership—and then got out of hand.

At the same time, the violence that broke out on Saint Bartholomew's Day was more than the continuation on a larger scale of the violence already evident in the religious conflicts. The radicalization of Catholic and Huguenot polemics during the first decade of the religious wars effected both quantitative and qualitative changes in the willingness of people to act upon their murderous impulses. Popular poetry and placards urged Catholic Parisians to envision violent solutions to the religious quarrels: "cut them down, . . . burn them, . . . kill them without a qualm."[48] The unimaginable was first put into words and then acted out.[49] Moreover, as Chapter 9 will show, Catholic preachers in Paris, rather than using their moral authority to quell the tensions caused by religious differences, actually encouraged recourse to violence by describing the extermination of heresy as a necessary purging of the social body. They helped created an atmosphere of apocalyptic fervor that allowed normal social restraints to be breached.

Joachim Opser de Wyl, a Swiss student studying with the Jesuits at the collège de Clermont, reflects popular attitudes toward the massacre when he says in a letter, written on 26 August, that "everyone agrees in praising the prudence and magnanimity of the king, who, after by his kindness and indulgence having so to speak fattened up the heretics like cattle, suddenly had their throats cut by his soldiers."[50] Although at one point Opser referred to the events as a "horrible tragedy," his whole tone was one of exaltation.[51] He interpreted the sudden blossoming of a hawthorn tree, long-dormant in the Cemetery of the Innocents, as a visible sign of divine approval, a sign that the true religion was to be reestablished throughout the kingdom.

Other pious Catholics shared Opser's delight in the "miracle of the hawthorn tree." They gathered to stare at the unexpected sight, to pray, and to touch the tree with their rosary beads or other sacred objects. They brought their sick to view the hawthorn and so be healed. And, like Opser, they interpreted the miracle as a sign that God approved "the Catholic sedition and the death of his great enemy the admiral."[52] Some chroniclers also attached a special meaning to the crosses that everyone affixed to their hats as a sign of Catholic allegiance. By God's grace, they said, where one cross has been torn down, many thousand have now sprung up.[53] What better reminder of how closely the events of Saint Bartholomew's Day were connected to other events in the recent past?

7

The Underground Church

About six o'clock on the morning of Sunday, 24 August 1572, Pierre de La Place, a president of the Cour des aides and a known member of the Reformed Church of Paris, received his first warning about the massacre that was taking place in the city. His initial impulse was to flee, but, finding that none of his Catholic neighbors would take him in, he came back to his house and returned to his usual Sunday routine. Gathering together the members of his family and those servants who had not already run away, he first led them in prayer and then read a chapter from the book of Job. He followed the Bible reading with Calvin's sermon on the same passage from Job and then gave his own little exhortation on the "justice and mercy of God." Concluding with another prayer, he prepared himself and his family "to endure all sorts of torments, even death, rather than to do anything contrary to the honor of God."

The next day President de La Place was ordered to appear before the king, who, he was told, wished to speak to him about the affairs of "those of the Religion." Replying that he would be happy before "departing from this world" to have the opportunity to account for his actions to His Majesty, but that it appeared impossible for him to come to the Louvre on account of the massacre, La Place refused to submit to the command until troops were supplied to protect him from the mobs in the streets. A guard was supplied, and he agreed to go. Before leaving his house, La Place took a moment to reprove the lack of faith shown by his eldest son, who had affixed the white cross of the Catholics to his hat, and to counsel his wife to keep the honor and fear of God ever in her mind. Then, calmly and in good spirits, he walked out into the street. Almost immediately, La Place was set upon by a group of men who had lain in wait for him. They struck without regard for the ten or twelve archers who were supposed to serve as his guard and, in the words of the martyrologist, killed him "like a poor lamb."

The story of President de La Place's martyrdom, first recounted by Simon Goulart in his *Mémoires de l'estat de Charles neufiesme* in 1578 but subsequently incorporated into Jean Crespin's often republished *Histoire des martyrs*, has become a part of the Huguenot legend, an inspirational story of faith in the midst of persecution and a model of Calvinist piety.[1] The contemporary reader, however, is likely to find the story vaguely disturbing. The qualities of faith that steeled a man for martyrdom are not qualities we readily understand, and we find it hard to empathize with La Place's quiet submission to an unjust fate. We are reluctant to accept this exemplary figure as fully representative of Parisian Protestantism, and yet we find it difficult to penetrate the aura of legend that surrounds the history of the Reformed church in Paris. The victims of Saint Bartholomew's Day have been mythologized into exemplars for later generations of French Protestants; the refugees, apostates, and other survivors have largely been forgotten.

Moreover, the conditions of secrecy under which Parisian Protestants were forced to live have meant that they left few records from which to reconstruct the essential elements of their daily life and faith. They left no registers of consistory proceedings, no lists of baptisms or marriages, no sermons by local pastors. Hated by the Catholic populace and forbidden to practice their religion, Parisian Protestants withdrew into the privacy of a clandestine community that left as few traces as possible of its existence. We have seen the Catholics parade their faith in elaborate processions through the city; it is harder to catch a glimpse of Protestants filing silently out of the town gates to hear a sermon, slipping into a nearby house under cover of darkness to gather in prayer, or purchasing forbidden books from merchants who shared their faith. Only in rare moments of defiance or during that brief period when Catherine de Medici's experiment with toleration had not yet culminated in civil war did their psalms echo in city streets or ring out in the fields beyond the walls. We have to struggle to hear their voices or follow their path, and yet we can, if we are willing to use indirect sorts of evidence as well as direct testimony, recover more of their hidden experience than we might think.

It is the purpose of this chapter and the next to replace the pious legends of the *Histoire des martyrs* with a more realistic picture of the underground community that struggled for existence during the first decade of the religious wars, to ask who was drawn to Calvinist ideas in this fiercely Catholic city, and why. What sort of community took shape under the cloak of secrecy imposed by the laws that forbade the Reformed church to exist? What bonds held it together, and how was it nurtured and maintained despite its clandestine situation? How in the end did it respond to the accumulated pressures of persecution?

The Appeal of the New Religion

Because there are no surviving records of Protestant church membership in Paris, it is impossible to gauge accurately the size or to reconstruct the social composition of the church in the period prior to Saint Bartholomew's Day. We can, however, use the lists of persons booked into the prison of the Conciergerie on charges of "heresy" or "the new opinion" to get a rough approximation of the sort of individuals that were attracted to the Protestant faith during the first decade of the religious wars. There are problems with using this data. Some persons were doubtless falsely accused or erroneously booked on charges of heresy, but we have no means of identifying these people or eliminating them from our tally. Moreover, we must recognize that the Protestant population was not stable but shifted with the severity of the persecutions. We will never be able to identify the Protestants who fled the city at the first sign of trouble, nor those who remained quietly in their houses. Despite these problems, the arrest records are a valuable source

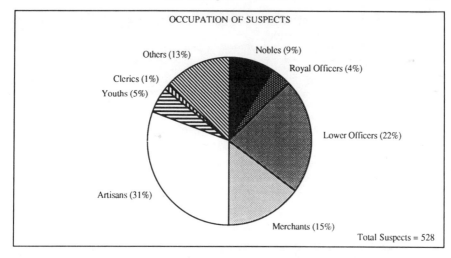

OCCUPATION OF SUSPECTS

Others (13%)

Nobles (9%)

Royal Officers (4%)

Clerics (1%)

Youths (5%)

Lower Officers (22%)

Artisans (31%)

Merchants (15%)

Total Suspects = 528

Figure 7–1. Professed occupation of 528 suspects held in the Conciergerie on the charge of heresy between 1564 and 1572. (Based on arrests recorded in APP, A[b] 1–4.)

of information on religious dissidents and merit closer study. The data they provide compare favorably with the data that emerge from studies of the Protestant communities in other French cities, and the identification of many of the suspects as members of the Protestant community can be corroborated by the qualitatively richer evidence contained in the dossiers of Paris's two known Protestant notaries.

Figures 7–1 to 7–5 summarize the results of my evaluation of the religious suspects listed in the arrest records (*écrous*) of the Conciergerie for the period between 1564, when the first records are preserved, and 1572.[2] Figure 7–1 shows the social or occupational distribution of the 528 religious suspects for whom these qualities were listed in the arrest records. (For the fifty-six female suspects, the status or occupation is that of the husband or father.) Nine percent of the suspects were noblemen or women identifying themselves at least as "écuyers" or "damoiselles." This high proportion reflects both the large number of nobles drawn to Paris by the court and the very high level of animosity directed against nobles because of their visibility in the Protestant faction. These nobles, I would add, were not necessarily members of the Paris church; half of the people in this group did not give a Parisian residence (whereas three out of four of the suspects taken as a whole resided in the capital).

Four percent of the detainees were royal officers of a level of distinction at least equal to that of the king's lieutenant in a bailliage. A far greater proportion—22 percent—held lesser offices as lawyers or *greffiers* in the sovereign courts or were members of liberal professions, such as doctors, teachers, or solicitors. Persons who identified themselves as merchants and "bourgeois" made up 15 percent of the detainees, while master and journeymen artisans, at 31 percent, made up the largest single group. There were a few students (3 percent) and a few clerics (1 percent). The categories grouped as "Others" are a mixed lot: 7 percent were domestic servants, 3 percent were soldiers, and 3 percent were unskilled day laborers or claimed to have no occupation.

The association between Protestantism and some level of education or skill, already perceptible in these bare statistics, becomes even clearer when we look more closely at the artisans who were arrested for religious reasons. If we follow the classification suggested by Natalie Davis, only nine of 172 arrested artisans (5 percent) were members of the elite trades identified as having *very high* rates of literacy (apothecaries, surgeons, and printers), but 42 percent were members of trades associated with *high* rates of literacy (painters, musicians, taverners, metal and goldworkers). Thirty-four percent belonged to trades with *average*, or middling, literacy rates (furriers, leather workers, or members of the textile and clothing trades); and only 19 percent belonged to the construction, provisioning, and transport trades associated with relatively *low* levels of literacy, even though these categories made up a very large part of the artisanal population of the city.[3]

On the whole, the Conciergerie records suggest that the Protestant faith attracted the same sorts of individuals in Paris as it attracted in other French cities. If we make allowances for the different occupational structures of different cities and the biases and uncertainties of the sources, the results shown in Figure 7–1 resemble the profiles of the Protestant communities described by Natalie Davis for Lyons, Philip Benedict for Rouen, and Joan Davies for Toulouse.[4] In all these cities, the "new religion" drew its adherents from a broad social spectrum in which only the lowest strata—unskilled workers, day laborers, and the very poor—were conspicuously underrepresented. It appealed to well-educated, high-status artisans like printers, jewelers, and locksmiths, more than to less-educated, lower-status groups like masons, bakers, or boatmen.

It is difficult to generalize about the appeal of Protestantism at higher social levels, but it does seem that, in Paris as in other cities, the new religion had a relatively strong attraction for members of the liberal professions—especially doctors and lawyers—and low or middle-level officials, while the higher magistrates, perhaps because they had so much of a stake in the status quo, were less likely to depart from the traditional faith (or maybe they were just quicker to return to it when the going got rough). Similarly, we find proportionately more religious suspects among the middling merchants—the shopkeepers of the Palais de Justice or the pont Notre-Dame—than among the mercantile elite. With a few prominent exceptions, the merchants whose names appear on city registers as bourgeois notables, civic officers, and judges in the consular court are not to be found on the lists of religious suspects.

The écrous reveal two other things about the individuals arrested on suspicion of heresy. First, if we look at the place of origin of the 473 individuals for whom this data is available (Figure 7–2), we find that 33 percent were born in Paris, 16 percent were native to other parts of the Ile-de-France, 15 percent were from neighboring areas in Normandy, the North, and Champagne, 18 percent were from Maine and the Loire valley, while only 16 percent came from more distant regions of France, and 3 percent were foreigners. Although one's initial impression here may be that the proportion of native Parisians is very low, these figures are not at all abnormal for an early modern city where in-migration was a common phenom-

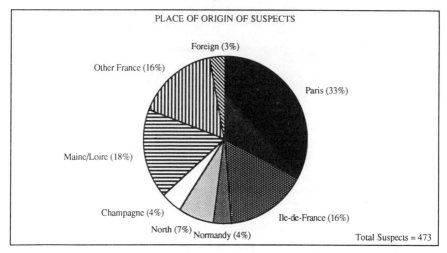

PLACE OF ORIGIN OF SUSPECTS

Foreign (3%)

Other France (16%)

Paris (33%)

Maine/Loire (18%)

Champagne (4%)

North (7%)

Normandy (4%)

Ile-de-France (16%)

Total Suspects = 473

Figure 7–2. Place of origin of 473 suspects held in the Conciergerie on the charge of heresy between 1564 and 1572. (Based on arrests recorded in APP, A^b 1–4.)

enon.[5] Moreover, one would expect that the traditional fear of strangers, much accentuated by the emotional climate of the religious wars, would result in a high percentage of outsiders among the religious suspects. The proportion of nonnatives among the suspects and their distribution—their tendency to come from regions north of the Loire—is nevertheless reminiscent of long-term migration patterns. The one unusual thing here might be the relatively high proportion of migrants from the Maine and the Loire regions, which can be attributed to the successes of the Protestant armies in these areas during the first part of the religious wars and a consequent suspicion of anyone who might have come from Orleans, Blois, Tours, or other cities that had fallen to the Huguenots.

The second point concerns the residential patterns of the religious suspects within Paris. Although one in four of the 399 suspects who gave an identifiable place of residence in Paris claimed to live in either the Left Bank quartier of Saint-Séverin or the adjoining faubourg Saint-Germain (which thereby earned the nickname of "Little Geneva"), it is clear from the information in Figures 7–3 to 7–5 that Parisian Protestants did not all cluster into this one neighborhood.[6] There was also a high concentration of religious suspects (that is, a high proportion of suspects by comparison with the total population) in the Right Bank quartier of Sainte-Avoye, and there were significant concentrations in the region of the university (Sainte-Geneviève), on the Ile de la Cité (Notre-Dame), and in the area north and west of the Louvre (Saint-Honoré).

More research needs to be done on these favored quartiers and on the clusters of Protestants within them. It would be interesting to establish whether Protestants tended to move to these quartiers becaused they seemed safer or appeared to offer more opportunities for fellowship with their coreligionists or whether, by contrast, persons already living in these quartiers were drawn into the new religion by the evangelizing of their neighbors and friends. In the meantime, we should rather take

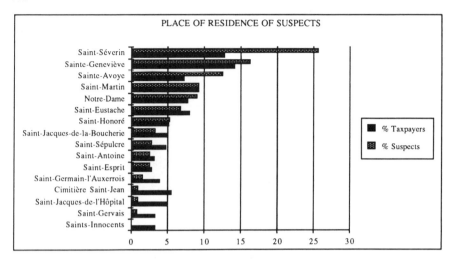

Figure 7–3. Percentage of religious suspects who resided in each quartier (shaded bar) and percentage of taxpayers listed on the 1571 tax rolls who lived in each quartier (black bar). (Based on arrests recorded in APP, A^b 1–4.)

note of the broad distribution of accused Protestants through the city. These figures show that Parisian Protestants (or at least those accused of Protestantism) were not, except in their religious choice, a group apart. They did not stand out from the city's residents as a whole in either their geographical origins or their choice of residential locations. Equally important, they were, like other urban groups of French Protestants that have been analyzed, concentrated in the skilled crafts and educated professions.

Merely determining who the Protestants were, where they came from, and where they lived in Paris cannot bring the community to life for us. Religious choice, and the willingness to sacrifice oneself for this choice, was a matter of profound faith and not just occupation or domicile. And yet the question of why people converted to Protestantism has proved difficult for the historian to answer. It is easier to show that Protestantism exerted its greatest appeal among certain social groups than to explain just what it was in the Protestant message that appealed to these people. For Parisian Protestants in particular, there is little direct evidence about the reasons for conversion. The rare accounts we have of conversions tend to place more emphasis on the conviction of truth that the convert experienced than on the specific aspects of the Protestant message from which this conviction derived. Despite the scanty nature of the evidence, several generalizations can be made. In the first place, it is clear that the conversion of French Protestants involved both the rejection of Catholic religious practices as corrupt and somehow fraudulent or ineffective and the affirmation and explicit acceptance of Protestant teachings.

French Protestants were vociferous in rejecting Catholic practices as "superstition" and "idolatry," and they made this as clear in their actions—in their avoidance of Catholic ceremonies, their refusal to hang out tapestries for Corpus Christi processions, their quiet nighttime burials—as in their words. They were

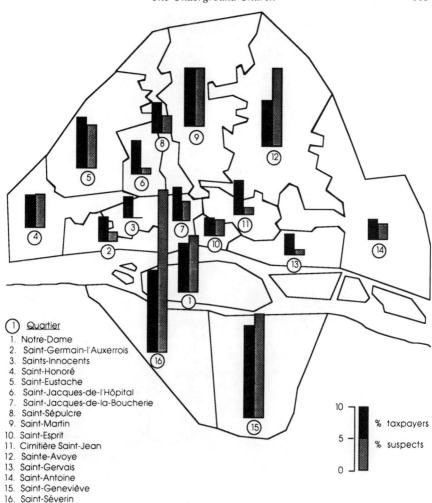

1. Notre-Dame
2. Saint-Germain-l'Auxerrois
3. Saints-Innocents
4. Saint-Honoré
5. Saint-Eustache
6. Saint-Jacques-de-l'Hôpital
7. Saint-Jacques-de-la-Boucherie
8. Saint-Sépulcre
9. Saint-Martin
10. Saint-Esprit
11. Cirnitière Saint-Jean
12. Sainte-Avoye
13. Saint-Gervais
14. Saint-Antoine
15. Saint-Geneviève
16. Saint-Séverin

PLACE OF RESIDENCE OF SUSPECTS

Figure 7–4. Percentage of religious suspects who resided in each quartier (shaded bar) and percentage of taxpayers listed on the 1571 tax rolls who lived in each quartier (black bar). (Based on arrests recorded in APP, Aᵇ 1–4.)

more reserved about expressing the deeply held tenets of their faith, but we can find in the wills of Parisian Protestants ample evidence that the doctrine of justification by faith was at the heart of their belief. The ritual invocation by which Christian believers, before ordering the disposal of their mortal remains and property, confided their souls to God was developed in Protestant wills into an eloquent expression of trust in God's promised gift of eternal life and belief that this gift was acquired uniquely through the death and passion of Jesus Christ and not through any personal merit or effort. Protestant testators eliminated the references Catholics

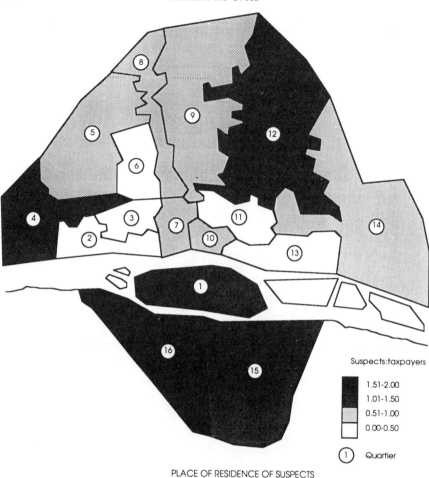

Suspects:taxpayers

■ 1.51–2.00

▦ 1.01–1.50

▨ 0.51–1.00

□ 0.00–0.50

① Quartier

PLACE OF RESIDENCE OF SUSPECTS

Figure 7–5. The relationship between religious suspects and taxpayers computed as a ratio, with the darkest-colored quartiers having the highest density of religious suspects in relation to the taxpaying population at large. (Based on arrests recorded in APP, A[b] 1–4.)

traditionally made to the intercession of the Virgin Mary and the saints and expressed their desire for their sins to be forgiven in the direct context of the ''merit'' acquired by the death of Christ.[7] Some testators even explicitly asked that God ''not enter into accounts with this poor and miserable sinner but accept the death and passion of his son, our savior Jesus Christ, as the sole and unique satisfaction for [the testator's] faults and sins.''[8] Over time, these invocations became somewhat conventionalized, as Catholic invocations had tended to become; and yet there is enough variation among them to show that they were sincere expressions of belief and not simply formulas imposed by the notaries.

The same belief in justification by faith alone is expressed in a letter a Protestant convert sent to her Catholic niece to explain her conversion. ''I now cast aside my merits and good intentions,'' she wrote, ''and cling solely to the promises that God made in his son Jesus Christ.'' The anonymous letter writer, who appears to have been a gentlewoman, also justifies her conversion in terms of the failure of the Catholic clergy to teach her fundamental Christian doctrine: "Won't you have pity on me who, at the age of forty-nine, didn't even know the Creed that Jesus Christ gave his Apostles to teach us the articles of our faith?'' She adds that "when I was on the other side, I adored what I didn't know; now I adore what I know,'' and expresses the wish that she could see her niece and share with her what she has learned from hearing and reading scripture. "Although I have retained only a little, I hope you will agree that it is more than when I heard only Latin, of which I understood nothing.''[9] For this woman at least, the rituals of unreformed Catholicism had failed to provide spiritual satisfaction.

A conviction that the Catholic church was failing in its spiritual mission did not in itself, however, suffice to bring about a conversion to the new faith; nor did a simple acquaintance with the new ideas. A "conversion experience,'' which new converts would have described as an awakening of their minds to the gift of God's grace, was also necessary, and many years could separate the initial acquaintance with Reformed ideas from the conviction of their truth and determination to act that were necessary to complete the experience of conversion. This is perhaps best illustrated by the story recounted by Charlotte d'Arbaleste of the conversion of her father, Guy d'Arbaleste, a president of the Paris Chambre des comptes. Arbaleste had become acquainted with Protestant ideas in his youth, having during a study trip to Germany heard Protestant sermons and even a disputation in which Luther personally took part. In his daughter's words, "he had thus learnt something of the abuses in the Roman Church, but he had never been instructed in the true religion.''[10] His conversion occurred when, at the start of the first religious war, he found himself falsely accused of Protestantism. "Finding himself persecuted for a religion which he had never professed, [he] recognized the goodness of God which thus manifested itself, and took steps to receive instruction.'' After being tutored in the faith by ministers of the Reformed church, "he made public profession of the true religion, and God gave him grace to remain steadfast in it to the last breath of his life.''[11]

It is significant that Arbaleste experienced his conversion under the pressures of persecution, which he interpreted as a sign of the "goodness of God''; it is significant also that the living out of his faith is included as an integral part of the conversion story. The need to live out one's faith—to make gradual progress toward sanctification through personal effort and active commitment—is an important part of Calvin's teaching, and the close association we have seen in Arbaleste's story between the change of heart that marked the initial decision to follow the Reformed faith and the lifelong process of sanctification that ensued is also evident in other narratives of Calvinist conversions. It is perhaps best expressed in the autobiographical memoirs of Pompée Diodati.

Diodati was Italian by birth, and he may at first seem an inappropriate example to use to illustrate the characteristics of Parisian Protestantism. We have already seen, however, that Parisian Protestants were not a group apart, either within their own city or by comparison with Protestants in other French towns, and it thus seems reasonable to use examples of conversions illustrative of French Protestantism even if they are not specifically Parisian cases. But can we use an Italian example? We can, I think, in this case. Diodati's childhood experience in Lucca as the son of a mother who concealed her evangelical faith because of the hostile atmosphere of her intensely Catholic town was not unlike the experience of Parisians raised under similar circumstances. More important, Diodati's conversion occurred in France, in Lyons, where he happened to travel on business just at the moment that the Huguenots seized control of the government and publicly established the Reformed faith. He was converted by the preaching of French ministers, and he stayed in Lyons for six months to deepen his knowledge of the new religion. He moved to Paris, where he had relatives in the Italian merchant colony, in 1566. Although a foreigner, he became part of the Reformed community there. He soon moved his family out to nearby Luzarches to escape the hostile atmosphere of the city, but he remained in close contact with the Paris church and attended its services whenever he could. The second and third religious wars turned Diodati and his family into refugees, as they did the other Protestants of Paris, but he returned each time to Luzarches and, whenever possible, to the services and fellowship of the Paris church, until Saint Bartholomew's Day, when he took the road of exile a final time. He ended, as many Parisian Protestants did, in Geneva. By experience, then, if not by birth, Pompée Diodati fits well into the community I am seeking to describe.[12]

Diodati recounts in his memoirs how his mother had instructed him in the "true religion" from an early age. He knew and approved its teachings but lacked the necessary zeal to abandon his native land, where he enjoyed considerable personal and political standing, until, at the age of twenty, "the providence of God" brought him to Lyons, in order to bestow upon him "a rich treasure, which I was not expecting."[13] He began at last to appreciate

> the great grace that God bestowed upon me in the knowledge that he had given me; such that by assiduously attending sermons, the Lord managed in this way to germinate the seed of his word, which until then had been kept hidden and unfruitful; with the result that from that time forward, I was entirely resolved to shake off the yoke of the Antichrist, and dedicate myself totally to the pure service of God; and since that time, not withstanding various difficulties and the great dangers to which I found myself exposed on this account, I have never committed any action contrary to this holy resolution, for which the sole honor is due to God, recognizing that I am myself entirely incapable of carrying out the least of the resolutions or actions that God has formed in me.[14]

These words were written many years later, after Diodati had finally brought himself and his family to a safe refuge in Geneva. As such, we can assume that Diodati's choice of words and images reflects his long steeping in Calvin's language and theology. Moreover, the fact that Diodati recorded this experience in a memoir intended for his descendants suggests that he has shaped and tailored his experience as a moral lesson for his heirs. It is not necessary, however, to dismiss Diodati's story on this account. The persecution he suffered—his flights into exile, the repeated pillaging and theft of his property—and the spirit in which he endured these sufferings testify to the sincerity of his conversion, and the version he gives of this change of heart is probably as accurate as memory would allow. The metaphor of the seed emphasizes that the insights gained in Lyons were just the start of a long process of growth. The seed had to be nourished by "assiduous" attendance at sermons, and its development had to be reflected outwardly in the conformity of his life to the "holy resolution" he had taken. At the same time, Diodati is thoroughly Calvinistic not only in giving all of the credit for the initial insight, or knowledge, to the grace of God, but also in emphasizing his total inability to carry out the resolution on his own.

Diodati's initial reluctance to sacrifice opportunities for wealth and status was shared by many French Protestants. Charlotte d'Arbaleste's first husband, Jean de Pas, sieur de Feuquères, fell ill as he agonized over the choice between the profession of a religion he had come to recognize as the "truth" and his career in the service of the French kings: "He felt himself on the road to advancement in the court and on the point of acquiring honours and wealth which he could never hope to possess if he made confession of the truth."[15] He at last made his choice on the basis of study and prayer and because he could not resist the conviction that he had to follow his God and not his king. According to Arbaleste's account, Feuquères made his decision after meditating on the Second Psalm, in which he read that "kings and princes more often than not leagued themselves against God and against Christ his beloved King." "Determined to forget all worldly considerations," he resolved immediately to cease attending Catholic services and to "profess the truth."[16] The rest of his life was devoted to the Huguenot cause, first by participating in the conspiracy of Amboise and then as an officer in the Huguenot armies. For Feuquères, these were not worldly, or political activities, but religious ones.

Nicolas Pithou, a brother of the humanist jurist Pierre Pithou, was also a reluctant convert, a covert believer who nevertheless found it impossible to profess openly his faith until a serious illness brought forcibly home the conviction that the price of this cowardice was eternal damnation. Fearful of losing his property and social standing, Pithou continued to attend mass (or, as he put it, "to kiss the baboon; that is, to do homage to the beast on Sundays"), even though he accepted in his heart "the pure word of God."[17] A lawyer and a notable of Troyes, Pithou confessed that he "feared men more than God" until his illness brought home the lesson of Luke 9:26: "For whosoever shall be ashamed of me and my words, of him shall the Son of man be ashamed, when he shall come in his own glory." Although wracked by fever, he could think of nothing except "the just judgment of God" and the penalty he would suffer for having, as it were, "trampled beneath [his] feet the precious gift he had been given."[18] Pithou finally unburdened his heart to a minister who was brought to his bedside. Immediately he felt as though a heavy weight had been lifted, and he began to pray more ardently to God than ever before, promising that if he lived he would never again participate in the "abominations of the papacy," and that he would move to a place where he could serve God in "all purity and freedom of conscience."[19] He believed, moreover, that this prayer was answered, for straightaway he began to hear, like a voice continually in his ear, the words of the Thirtieth Psalm, in the rhymed French version of Marot's psalter. The words of the psalm ("I cried unto thee, and thou hast healed me") were like an omen, a sign of forgiveness, and, indeed, his fever broke that very day and he began to get better. The following year, Nicolas Pithou, his health fully recovered, moved with his wife to Geneva. He later returned to his native town to serve as its minister.

If men like Diodati, Feuquères, and Pithou were torn between their religious convictions and their prospects for worldly advancement, women were often torn between their religious beliefs and their family responsibilities, especially if they were the first member of their family to convert. To practice their faith might mean defying a Catholic husband; it might mean exposing the entire family to persecution. Did they dare? Had they the right? These were burdensome decisions to make.[20] Indeed, we must recognize that, in places like Paris, where Protestants were isolated and outnumbered by a hostile Catholic majority, there were a great many obstacles to conversion. In areas where there was a territorial Reformation, becoming Protestant, for many people, may have been a way of following the path of least resistance. In Catholic cities like Paris, it was not. It was a conscious and often very difficult choice. Because the new religion was proscribed by law, converts had to be willing to sacrifice opportunities for social and financial advancement, to defy or overcome the opposition of other family members, and to surmount a very natural fear of persecution. Only the unshakable conviction that this was the expression of God's will and the unique path to salvation allowed people to triumph over their doubts and set about the difficult process of making their lives conform to their beliefs.

Two sorts of structures, those of the church and those of the community, assisted Calvinists in the crucial process of sanctification. Let us look at the first of these structures as it existed in Paris in the first decade of the religious wars.

The Underground Church

Founded in 1555, the Reformed Church of Paris was simultaneously a local creation, a part of a national confederation of churches, and a part of an international movement with its roots in Calvinist Geneva. These elements were sometimes in balance and sometimes in tension, but all three contributed to the distinctive shape that Parisian Protestantism was to assume. Though I wish here to emphasize the local aspects of the story—the formation of the Paris congregation and its reaction to persecution and proscription—I cannot remove it from its national and international contexts. The Genevan connection in particular is important, for the Parisians drew from Geneva all their doctrines, most of their institutional structures, and, initially at least, an important part of their personnel. Much of the clandestine literature— the psalters and Bibles and theological treatises—by which Parisian Protestants nourished their faith was smuggled in from Geneva, and many members of the Parisian community had friends and family who had emigrated to Calvin's city on a hill. Indeed, there was a constant, albeit very secret, traffic between the two cities, both because of the needs of the underground church and because of the personal ties that still linked the Genevan refugees to their Parisian families and friends.

Calvin himself is the key to the Genevan connection. Driven into exile in the persecutory backlash stirred up by a sermon preached in 1533 by Nicolas Cop, the rector of the University of Paris and a close personal friend, Calvin could never entirely abandon his native France or his hope of seeing it converted to the true religion. Even as he struggled to establish a godly order among the recalcitrant Genevans, he directed a part of his thoughts and words back to his homeland. He dedicated the first editions of his *Institutes of the Christian Religion*, published in Latin in 1536 and in French translation in 1541, to François I and carried on a voluminous correspondence with reformers, converts, and would-be converts worshiping in secrecy in his beloved land. He welcomed French refugees to Geneva, even though it strained relations with the native-born citizenry, and encouraged the clandestine spread of his writings in France, though this too must have worried his Genevan hosts, ever fearful of provoking the anger of the Catholic giants that surrounded them. Circulated privately from hand to hand and expounded by proselytes returning from study trips or visits to Geneva, Calvin's teachings found a receptive audience in the secret circles of the French reform movement and exercised an important—indeed, a determinant—influence on the institutional structures and doctrines adopted by French Protestants when they were ready to form churches of their own.

In Paris this moment came in 1555, when a handful of converts, after years of clandestine meetings for discussion, psalm singing, and Bible reading, chose one of their members to act as minister and organized a consistory after the Genevan model.[21] Little is known about the first years of the Paris church, except that it grew quickly and additional ministers soon were needed. The initial choice, a young man from Angers by the name of Jean Le Maçon (generally known as La Rivière), was a good one. Converted to Protestantism during visits to Geneva and Lausanne, La Rivière was an active and conscientious pastor to his new congregation. Its needs, however, soon exceeded the capacities of any single individual, particularly given the awkward secrecy in which the fledgling church was forced to operate.[22] In 1556 Calvin, who had been following developments in Paris with interest, was able to send help in the form of an experienced minister named François de Morel, sieur de Collonges. In addition to assisting La Rivière with his pastoral duties, Morel gathered together some of the most promising young converts and began to train them for the ministry. Among this group was Antoine de la Roche-Chandieu, who served as catechist for his fellow students at the informal seminary organized by Morel and within the year was chosen as the second regular pastor of the Paris church.[23] A third regular pastor, Jean de Lestre, was chosen from among the seminarians late in 1557. Geneva also sent more help, but, like Morel, these men—Gaspard Carmel, Nicolas Des Gailars, and Jean Macard, among others—served only temporarily, before moving on to other French churches or back to Geneva, which needed them too.[24]

The ministers sent out from Geneva were part of an active missionary movement that began as soon as Calvin's own position in that city was secure. According to the registers of the Genevan Company of Pastors, eighty-eight men were trained in the ministry and secretly sent to congregations that requested them in France between 1555 and the beginning of the religious wars in 1562, but there were others as well who spent time in Geneva before taking up the ministry in France.[25] French churches sometimes sponsored theology students at the Genevan Academy (founded in 1559) with the understanding that the students, once trained, would return to serve as their pastors. Among the early ministers recruited from the Paris congregation, however, only Gabriel D'Amours seems to have enjoyed a prolonged period of study at the Academy, where he was enrolled from 1559 to 1562.[26] This was due to circumstances and not to indifference or lack of desire. The Paris church was simply too pressed for men to part willingly with anyone who might serve it. Chandieu and de Lestre, trained in Paris by Morel, appear to have made brief stays in Geneva before taking up their pastoral duties, but each was absent from the French capital for only a few months.[27] Even La Rivière, already an experienced minister, nourished a strong desire to imbibe Calvin's teachings at their source, but the request he made early in 1557 for two years' leave to study theology in Geneva, although personally endorsed by Calvin, was apparently denied. La Rivière continued to serve his Paris flock, despite declining health and recurrent bouts of fever. Only in October 1558 was he able to visit Geneva, and he was back in Paris within the year.[28]

The flow of men between Geneva and France tightened the links already forged between the Genevan and French reforms. In 1557 Calvin wrote a confession of faith that was sent to Henri II on behalf of the French churches, and in 1559 Genevan ministers took an active role in the national synod that gave the French Reformed churches a more complete confession of faith and a common ecclesiastical code, or "discipline." The French churches continued to ask the advice of the Genevan Company of Pastors on questions of church governance, and they repeatedly solicited their help in articulating and defending doctrinal positions.[29] Even more than Calvin, Theodore Beza became the spokesman for French Protestants. He headed the delegation of Calvinist ministers to the Colloquy of Poissy in 1561 and defended the French churches in numerous treatises and tracts. Consulted on political as well as religious matters, he was the acknowledged if unofficial leader of the French Reformed churches for nearly half a century.

The Genevan Company of Pastors was ambivalent about its role with regard to France. In principle, the pastors believed that all churches should be on an equal footing, and they did not wish to make Geneva another Rome. Moreover, they recognized the dangers that overt interference in French affairs might pose for the safety of their little state. At the same time, they were possessed by a missionary spirit, convinced of the truth of their own doctrine, and unwilling to countenance any deviation from that truth. As such, they found themselves inescapably drawn into both the internal debates and the external conflicts of the French Reformed churches.[30]

Calvin's reaction to the knowledge that representatives of the French Reformed churches intended to gather in Paris in May 1559 for a national meeting in order to draw up a common confession of faith and an ecclesiastical discipline reveals this ambivalence well. Calvin learned that the French churches had called a national synod only a very short time before the meeting was to begin, and he was annoyed that they had not first sought his counsel. He quickly dispatched Nicolas Des Gallars to represent the Genevan Company but lacked even the time to send written instructions with Des Gallars. He also thought that, given the unsettled political conditions in France, the plan of publishing the discipline was a rash and inopportune one.[31] The meeting proceeded as planned, however, and, despite Calvin's fears, the documents drawn up there were thoroughly consistent with his teachings. As it happened, the discipline was not presented to Henri II because of his unexpected death only a month after the synod ended. It was, however, presented to François II in June 1560, in an attempt to demonstrate to the young king that, contrary to rumors provoked by the Conspiracy of Amboise, the Protestants were true and loyal subjects.[32]

The Confession of Faith of 1559 and the discipline, begun in that year but elaborated and extended until it reached its definitive form in 1571, were—and remain—fundamental statements of French Reformed ecclesiology. As such, they can serve to illuminate the theological premises on which French Protestants built their church and the institutional structures they elaborated on this base. The confession of faith defines the true church as ''an assembly of believers who agree among themselves to follow God's word, and the pure religion which dependeth on it, and who profit by it during their whole life, increasing and confirming themselves in the fear of God.''[33] These words are taken directly from the epistolatory confession that Calvin sent to Henri II in 1557 and reflect both the Calvinist understanding of the church as a holy community—a gathering of the faithful—and Calvin's characteristic emphasis on leading a godly life.[34] Reliance on God's grace, implicit here but explicit in the next lines of the article, is coupled with the need to strive daily to mold one's outer life to reflect the truth within.

The authors of the 1559 confession conceded (as Calvin did not in his 1557 missive to the king) that ''among the faithful there be some hypocrites, or despisers of God, or ill-livers.'' Their wickedness could not, however, ''blot out the name of the church.''[35] This was a response to the charge inevitably leveled against any church that claimed to gather God's elect. How presumptuous to claim to know whom God has chosen to save, and how embarrassing when one of the saints publicly lapsed into sin. The only defense was to posit a duality in which the worldly church—the visible congregation—was distinct from the true church—the invisible assembly of the elect. The question of how to recognize that one was among the elect was later to become a troublesome issue for Calvinists. The authors of the confession, however, were more worried about the immense pools of sinfulness outside their church than the pockets of sinners within. The confession of faith explicitly condemned ''assemblies in the papacy'' because ''the pure word of God is banished out of them'' and denounced Catholic sacraments as ''corrupted, counterfeited, falsified, or utterly abolished.''[36] No timid subterfuges were allowed. Attending Catholic services cut one off from the body of Christ. So did contenting oneself with private devotions. The confession affirmed the need for all Christians to ''submit themselves unto the common instruction, and to the yoke of Jesus Christ [wherever] he shall have established the true discipline, although the edicts of earthly magistrates be contrary thereunto.''[37] This refusal to tolerate the timid, who, although recognizing the true religion, were not ready to declare openly for it has its root in the same central tenet from which the vital force of Calvin's activism springs: it is not enough to know the truth; one must act upon it.

To act upon the truth, to accept the ''yoke of Christ,'' meant to submit to being instructed by its pastors, watched over by its elders, and censured by its consistory. Discipline was necessary to protect against the corruptions and vanities of worldly life, among which Calvinists included dancing, card-playing, and other common pastimes. Turning away from such worldly pleasures was a part of the necessary progress toward sanctification. But discipline was also necessary to protect against backsliding and erroneous doctrine. Lapses in doctrine were judged especially harshly because they threatened the unity of God's church. "Heretics, despisers of God, rebels against the consistory" and "traitors to the church" were not to be handled with the same quiet discretion as other sinners but rather were publicly to be charged, so that the congregation might withdraw from their fellowship and avoid contaminating itself with their false opinions. Moreover, they were not just to be denied communion as punishment for their sins but rather to be excommunicated entirely and banished from the church.

Because of the great pressures under which members of the French Reformed churches were forced to live, some compassion was shown toward backsliders who, having abjured their faith under the stress of persecution, recognized their error and sought readmission. An example was made of them, however, and they were required to express publicly their repentance before being taken back into the church.[38] Timid converts who, although admitted to membership in the church, refused to take the sacraments were to be judged according the consistory's best insight into their motives. If they were deemed to be exceedingly scrupulous or as yet uncertain in their beliefs, they were to be given some time to grow in their faith. On the other hand, if they were judged to be abstaining from the sacraments "through fear of being obliged to renounce all idolatry," they were, after first being admonished, to be expelled and cut off from the church.[39]

If there was thus some small concession to the difficulty of the times, it should nevertheless be clear that the ministers and elders responsible for the French Reformed discipline were as insistent as Calvin upon the need for total commitment on the part of church members. Their theological principles did not allow for anything less than total dedication, and, what is more, they knew their church could not survive if its members were too faint-hearted to brave the dangers of persecution. They were willing to practice their religion in secret, even to have members take an oath not to reveal the names of their fellows, but they were not willing to allow their members to go through the motions of Catholic practice, even when such subterfuges might guarantee their safety.[40] Calvin directed some of his angriest words against "Nicodemites" who believed that they could worship the true faith in private while continuing outwardly to attend Catholic services, and Parisian Protestants shared this conviction.[41] This is shown repeatedly in Protestant accounts of Saint Bartholomew's Day, in which the narrators take pride in recounting how they stubbornly refused to attend Catholic mass even though it seemed at the time the only way to save their lives.[42] Pompée Diodati refused even the more innocent subterfuge of donning a white cross so as to be taken for a Catholic; Pierre de La Place castigated his son for succumbing to this same act of concealment.[43] The son of the minister Pierre Merlin was reproached by his parents for years for having allowed the old woman with whom he had been placed in hiding to teach him to recite the Hail Mary and to "kiss idols," even though he was only six years old at the time.[44]

The institutional structures of the French Reformed churches, in which ecclesiastical functions were divided among the four offices of pastors, teachers, elders, and deacons, were borrowed from the Genevan model (itself based on Bucer's church in Strasbourg). The larger framework for a national church could not, of course, be directly fashioned on the model of the Genevan city-republic, but the French churches did find in the organizational structures of the Genevan church the hierarchical principles on which to base their own presbyterian organization. The churches were grouped into colloquies and provinces, which were to meet regularly to discuss matters of common interest. At the top of the hierarchical structure stood the national synod which, meeting once a year, had final jurisdiction over all ecclesiastical matters. Individual churches were prohibited from taking any action "in which the interest or damage of other churches shall be comprised, without the advice and consent of the provincial synod, if it may possibly be convened." Even in an emergency, each church was expected to communicate as soon as possible with its neighbors.[45]

A common front was very necessary to the French Reformed churches. The synodical structure was aimed at achieving both the appearance and the reality of this common front, as was the requirement for close cooperation among churches. Thus, for example, after the massacre of Vassy, the Parisian church not only sent a delegation to the king to protest Guise's brutal action, but also one of its ministers wrote to the neighboring churches to ask them to send delegations to court as well and, in turn, to pass on this urgent message to their own nearest neighbors. As La Rivière wrote to the church of Angers, "we would like all the churches, or at least a great number of them, to come make the same clamor at court, so as to show the bond that is among us and how many people are affected by such an inhuman act."[46] At the same time, La Rivière warned the other churches that further attacks were likely. Those responsible for Vassy were determined to effect a massacre of the Paris assembly if they could catch them off guard. The Reformed churches should both look to their own safety and prepare to come to the aid of the first assailed.[47]

Because of the need for secrecy forced on the Paris church by popular hatreds and official persecution, little is known about the day-to-day administration of church affairs during the first decade of the religious wars. During the first war, most of the ministers, as well as a great many Protestant laymen, took refuge in Protestant-held Orleans. It was there that the Paris consistory met on 26 March 1563 formally to disband the church in accordance with the provisions of the Edict of Amboise— provisions that Chandieu and the other ministers had vigorously but unsuccessfully opposed. At the time of their disbanding, the members of the consistory prayed that God might grant them grace soon to reestablish their church, and indeed within six months—almost as soon as it was safe for Protestant Parisians to return to their homes—the church was reestablished, though it was not yet possible for the ministers to return. The Protestants met, as they had during the worst periods of persecution before the war, in small groups and with great secrecy. Sometime later,

new ministers, who would not be recognized by Parisian Catholics, were slipped
into the city.[48] Even so, they rarely dared to hold formal services or to administer
the sacraments. For these purposes, meeting places were established in secret locations in the neighboring countryside.

A royal edict published in December 1563 made it illegal for Parisian Protestants
to leave the city for the purpose of attending religious services, but this did not put
a stop to the clandestine assemblies.[49] We can catch occasional glimpses in judicial
records of Parisian Protestants making their way to Montévrain, near Lagny in Brie,
about thirty kilometers from the capital, to be married, have their children baptized,
or participate in the Lord's Supper.[50] The names of Brie-Comte-Robert, Loisy-en-
Brie, and "La Forest" also occur in various records. (The latter may refer to Paris
itself, or it may be a code name for another outlying location.[51]) Parisian Protestants
also sometimes had recourse to the chaplains assigned to the households of important
nobles. Some of these chaplains were forced to travel widely in the course of their
duties, but others seem to have been relatively fixed in their placement and thus
accessible to Parisian Protestants. The chaplain of the marquise de Rothelin at
Blandy, near Melun, for example, was instrumental in the conversion of Guy
d'Arbaleste.[52]

We can glean from Beza's correspondance that Jean de L'Espine was the principal minister assigned to Montévrain; there may have been others working out of
that church as well, especially after the third war, when the duchess of Ferrara,
with whom de L'Espine had taken refuge in Montargis, seemed determined to keep
him at her side.[53] We can also find the names of a number of other ministers attached
to the Parisian church during the first decade of the wars in Beza's letters, synodal
records, and other documents: Guillaume Houbracque had a clandestine church
somewhere in the environs of Paris; Hugues Sureau Du Rosier was somewhere near
Melun at the time of Saint Bartholomew's Day. Roland Capito (usually known as
de la Cousture), Théophile de Banos, François de Cherpont, Pierre Garnier, Marin
Delamare, Gabriel D'Amours, Antoine de la Faye, and Pierre Merlin de l'Espérandière were also attached to the Paris church for all or part of this period, but it
is impossible to determine just how long or where each man served. The rapid
turnover was due both to the activity of the Paris church and to the dangerous
conditions in which it operated. A minister who was too widely recognized—as
Chandieu and La Rivière had become—had to be sent away.[54]

Despite repressive laws and popular hostility, the situation was not unremittingly
grim. There appears to have been a period of relative respite in 1565 and 1566.
The prefatory epistle to Jean de L'Espine's *Traitté consolatoire*, published in Lyons
in 1565, refers to the peace that the church at that moment enjoyed. Merlin was
able to write Chandieu in April 1566 that things were going "rather better than
worse," and Delamare informed Beza in September of that year that church affairs
were in "good peace," though they desperately needed more ministers (itself a
sign of growth and prosperity).[55]

Even in this time of relative peace, however, the members of the Reformed
church were forced to pay for their lack of religious conformity. Writing in February
1566 to his brother Philippe, then in Toulouse, Jean Canaye recounted the material
problems the family had suffered for its faith. Their silverware had been confiscated,

their creditors refused payment; even the city refused to pay the interest due on the rentes they held on the Hôtel de Ville. "We can only wait in patience," he concluded stoically, "until the hand of God provides the issue that it pleases him to give us from so many miseries and calamities."[56]

The peaceful interlude, moreover, was of short duration. By the end of 1566, popular hatreds had once again flared and legal repression increased. A concerted search for Protestant ministers was begun, largely because one of Jeanne d'Albret's chaplains had had the temerity to preach a public sermon at Christmastide, but also because of a spate of complaints from Parisian Catholics, who claimed that the ministers were commonly seen in the capital and that they were boldly plotting mischief against the king. Simon Vigor, the curé of Saint-Eustache, spread the word that Sureau Du Rosier, arrested in Paris in June 1566 but subsequently released for lack of evidence, had written a book justifying the assassination of the king.[57] Vigor also claimed that fifty or sixty ministers and "a great many unknown people" had met in Paris in August on the pretext of a synod in order to plot a coup against the king.[58] Such accusations forced the Reformed church still further underground.

Like the pastoral functions of the church, its consistory was revived in the autumn of 1563, but little information has survived about the organizational and disciplinary matters taken up at its meetings.[59] Beza's correspondence with ministers in Chalons, Troyes, and Orleans during the period between the first and second religious wars shows an active concern for reinforcing church order through the disciplining of members guilty of adultery, fornication, and other sins of the flesh, but the only disciplinary issue mentioned in connection with the Paris church relates to ecclesiastical principles rather than to personal conduct.[60] The issue involved was a long dispute over a proposal that the French churches adopt a more congregational form of ecclesiastical governance. The principal figure in the dispute was a man named Jean Morély, a native Parisian who had lived for some years in Geneva when he first made his proposal in 1562. Morély's ideas were vigorously opposed by the Genevan pastors, who claimed that the changes he proposed would destroy all church discipline, and the book in which he initially propagated his ideas was condemned by the French national synod that met at Orleans in 1562. Morély had some sympathizers in France, however, and so the controversy continued. Excommunicated by the Genevan consistory, he returned to France and affiliated himself with the Paris church, which showed itself reluctant to take the disciplinary measures against him that the Genevan ministers deemed necessary. Indeed, Morély's initiative seems to have divided the Paris consistory, which held out against pressure from Geneva to deny him communion and to censure his supporters.[61] The Morély affair was still being debated at the national synod of Nîmes in 1572, and the internal dissension it caused seemed at times even to endanger the French church.[62] The eventual victory of the anti-Morély, pro-Geneva faction in the dispute says something about the locus of power in the French church and its commitment to Genevan ways, but unfortunately it offers fewer insights than one might like into the processes of decision making within the Paris consistory. It is nevertheless significant that, through all of the terrible trials posed by the church's illegal situation in the years after 1563, the Paris church was not merely struggling to survive but was engaged in a heated debate over the forms of ecclesiastical governance.

A final aspect of Reformed church operations during the first decade of the religious wars about which we can glean some small bits of information concerns its poor-relief system. We know that the church had some sort of system for poor relief already in 1558 and that in December 1561 a plan for a formal *Bureau des pauvres* was elaborated and eight bourgeois churchmen were appointed as overseers. Twelve deacons, six from Left Bank and six from Right Bank quartiers, were charged with collecting alms after each religious service. The eight bourgeois overseers (elected for two-year terms), along with four members of the consistory (chosen anew each month), were charged with drawing up lists of impoverished church members, investigating their needs, and distributing funds. As a safeguard against corruption—a consequence, no doubt, of the discovery in 1558 that one of the deacons was embezzling monies intended for the poor—one of the bourgeois overseers was to hold the common funds, another to keep the books, and a third to inspect them each week. As a additional precaution, the deacons were expected to visit on a weekly basis all of the church members receiving aid, so as to certify both their need and their receipt of alms.[63] Testamentary bequests to the Bureau des pauvres in 1564 and 1565 indicate that the organization survived the crisis of the first religious war, though there is no way to judge how effective its operation was or how many poor people it served.[64] From our perspective, however, the significance of the Bureau des pauvres, like the significance of the Morély affair, lies less in its impact or effectiveness than in the demonstration that, despite persecution and the tumult of the wars, the members of the Reformed Church of Paris still actively sought to create and maintain the institutions they deemed necessary to living out their faith.

Although we can admire the tenacity of the Protestants who struggled to maintain the institutions they believed necessary to their faith, we cannot help but recognize that the conditions of proscription and secrecy severely weakened these institutions. People could not attend religious services regularly, and every time they did attend services they took a great risk. Three people went to their deaths in 1569 for the private celebration of a Protestant Lord's Supper in a house in the rue Saint-Denis, and Montévrain, which seems to have been the most important of the clandestine meeting places outside of Paris, was a full thirty kilometers away.[65] Although the structures of the Reformed Church survived the first religious war, its members were often thrown back on their own resources.

Under these circumstances, the private reading of scripture and familial forms of worship assumed a special importance. The image with which this chapter began of Pierre de La Place calmly leading his household in worship on the morning of Saint Bartholomew's Day may be idealized, but there is truth to the image as well. Calvinists encouraged familial worship because they attached a great importance to the process of learning and growing in the faith. Under ordinary circumstances, however, such services would never have been held on Sunday mornings, when the family was supposed to have gathered in church. The services that President de La Place conducted were a substitute for and not a supplement to the regular gathering of the Reformed Church of Paris. We must look beyond the institutions of the church if we are to have a full picture of the sources from which Parisian Protestants nourished their faith.

8

The Shadow of God's Wings

The underground community that grew up around the Reformed church was one of the most important resources its members possessed in their struggle to maintain their faith. Though scattered across the city, Parisian Protestants were linked by a web of horizontal and vertical ties that joined them in fellowship and mutual assistance. They were united by personal ties of marriage and friendship and by a variety of legal, commercial, and financial services. Protestant booksellers risked their lives to smuggle in the Bibles, psalters, and religious literature by which their coreligionists nourished their faith; Protestant notaries candidly recorded the effects of the religious divisions on their lives. Indeed, the best evidence we have of the ties that united this clandestine community comes from the surviving records of the two avowedly Protestant notaries who operated in Paris during the first decade of the religious wars. Accordingly, the first part of this chapter will be devoted largely to the analysis of these records.

The Bonds of Community

Eustache Goguier and Antoine Leal both began their notarial practices in the 1550s. Interrupted by exile during each of the religious wars, their practices continued until shortly before Saint Bartholomew's Day.[1] I have not been able to determine at what point Goguier and Leal turned Protestant. Both men appear to have had some Protestants among their clients by about 1559, but the real transition in the nature of their clienteles appears to have taken place as a result of the first religious war. After returning to Paris in 1563, they practiced almost exclusively among their coreligionists. More records have survived for Leal (twelve volumes of minutes for the period 1560 to 1572) than for Goguier (five volumes for the same period), but they are best analyzed together because the clienteles they represent are overlapping and complementary. Leal, who lived on the rue Saint-Germain-l'Auxerrois, drew many of his clients from the localized and relatively dense Protestant community of his own neighborhood. Goguier, who lived further east on the Right Bank, on the rue Saint-Avoye, drew from a broad geographical and social spectrum and seems to have counted more of the Protestant nobles among his clients. Together the records of Leal and Goguier give us a picture of the Protestant community in

Paris during the period prior to Saint Bartholomew's Day that, although still incomplete, is nevertheless richly instructive.[2]

The contracts registered by Goguier and Leal amply document the many ties
of kinship that linked members of the Protestant community. It seems logical that
from the start Protestant ideas in France traveled the paths of kin and friendship,
as new converts confided in and shared their faith with those who were closest to
them, but it is hard to prove this. It is easier to demonstrate that, once a clandestine
community of Protestant believers started to take shape, the members of this community began to reinforce their ties through the bonds of matrimony. We can trace
in the marriage contracts recorded by Goguier and Leal a dense network of family
relationships. Not only the principal parties but also a very large share of the
witnesses to the marriage contracts they recorded between 1563 and 1571 can be
identified as members of the Protestant community. In other contracts we can see
members of these same families assisting one another with loans, engaging in
business agreements, or taking in one another's children as servants and apprentices.

The ties of kinship within this community can best be illustrated by a few
examples of cases in which the Protestant sympathies of parties listed in a marriage
contract can be confirmed by such evidence as arrest records or mention in Protestant
martyrologies. Let us take as our first example the marriage contract of 24 October
1571 by which Geneviève de Montault, the widow of a haberdasher in the Palais
de Justice, promised her daughter Jeanne de Louvain to Guillaume Le Tellier, a
merchant draper.[3] Of the seven witnesses to the contract, six can confidently be
identified as members of the Protestant community. Thibault Cressé, a jeweler who
signed the contract as a friend of Le Tellier, was arrested on charges of heresy and
carrying weapons during the first religious war and released only after the Peace
of Amboise. Cressé also had his house pillaged during the riots of the cross of
Gastines and again on Saint Bartholomew's Day, but he somehow survived the
massacre.[4] Olivier de Montault, a merchant haberdasher and Jeanne de Louvain's
maternal uncle, was arrested on charges of heresy in January 1569 and subsequently
released with instructions to obey the king's edicts.[5] He is listed in the *Histoire
des martyrs* among the victims of Saint Bartholomew's Day, as was the clockmaker
Jean Greban, another witness to the Louvain–Le Tellier contract. Greban was
arrested on religious charges at least twice in 1569.[6] He was the father of Alphons
Greban, who also witnessed the contract and was Jeanne de Louvain's brother-in-
law by virtue of his marriage in January 1571 to her sister Marie. The last identifiable
witness is Valentin Morin, another haberdasher in the Palais de Justice and the
father-in-law of Geneviève de Montault's son, Nicolas de Louvain. Morin escaped
the massacre of Saint Bartholomew's Day and registered as a resident of Geneva
on 1 January 1573.[7] It may, in fact, be due to information that he brought with
him, or that later reached him, that the fate of many of his friends and relatives
was recorded in the *Histoire des martyrs*. Figure 8–1 illustrates these and other
Protestant connections of the Montault–Louvain family.

A second example takes as its documentary source the marriage contract of 10
October 1564 between Claude Le Mercier and Agnès de Gastines. All ten of the
participants in and witnesses to this marriage can be identified as members of the
Reformed church community. Claude was the son of Nicolas Le Mercier and Claude

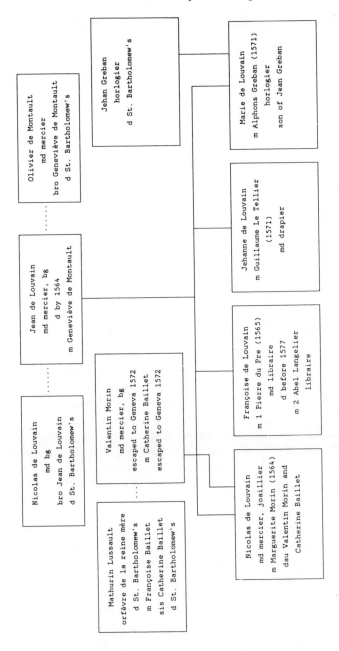

Figure 8–1. Family tree showing the alliances of the children of Jean de Louvain and Geneviève de Montault. Key to abbreviations: bg, bourgeois; bro, brother; d, died; dau, daughter; m, married; md, marchand; sis, sister.

Lenfant, whose house on the pont Notre-Dame, the Golden Hammer, was repeatedly sacked in the riots of the cross of Gastines. Agnès's father, Jean de Gastines, was dead and she was living with her uncle Philippe de Gastines at the time of her marriage. Philippe was a principal in the contract and promised Agnès certain testamentary bequests and payment for her services as a wedding portion. His son Richard and brother François served as witnesses. All three were convicted in 1569 of holding illicit services in Philippe's house in the rue Saint-Denis. Philippe and Richard, it will be remembered, were executed for their participation in these services. François, who recanted and returned to the Catholic Church, was only banished.[8] The third witness on Agnès's behalf was Rodolphe Delor, Philippe de Gastines's son-in-law and a doctor affiliated with the University of Paris. Delor's religious convictions cost him his position with the Faculty of Medicine in 1562, though he was allowed to resume his office after the war was over. He died before Saint Bartholomew's Day, but his widow, Catherine de Gastines, and his daughter Marguerite, both avowed Protestants, were arrested in the course of these events and forced to abjure their faith.[9] In addition to his parents, the parties appearing on behalf of Claude Le Mercier in his marriage contract included his uncle, named Claude Lenfant like his mother, and Jean Carré, a *marchand pourpointier*. A haberdasher in the Palais de Justice, Lenfant was arrested on charges of heresy in May 1569 and only released seven months later.[10] Carré is not mentioned in the arrest records, but he does appear as a kinsman and witness at two other Protestant weddings and he apprenticed his son to a known member of the Reformed community, so he too can confidently be presumed to have been a part of this group.[11]

The ties of family between the Le Merciers and the Gastines were further reinforced when a daughter of Nicolas Le Mercier and Claude Lenfant married Philippe de Gastines's younger son Jacques. Arrested at the same time as his father and brother Richard, Jacques de Gastines was given a life term in the galleys for his part in the religious services in the rue Saint-Denis.[12] He would have been released from this sentence as a consequence of the edict of Saint-Germain. In February 1571, Jacques de Gastines and his wife Marie Le Mercier entered into a business partnership with Marie's parents and moved in with them at the Golden Hammer. These family connections explain why Claude Lenfant campaigned so actively for the removal of the cross of Gastines and the return of properties confiscated from the Gastines family to their rightful heirs. They also explain why the Golden Hammer was attacked and pillaged in the riots over the removal of the cross, and why it was attacked again on Saint Bartholomew's Day, when all of the inhabitants except one young daughter of the Le Merciers were killed.[13] The Le Mercier's son Claude, who was not living at the Golden Hammer in 1572 but rather in the rue Saint-Denis, also survived the massacre. Recanting his faith, Claude Le Mercier swore his loyalty to the Catholic church.[14] Figure 8–2 illustrates the network of Protestant affiliation that had the Gastines and Le Merciers at its core.

Besides being linked by marriage and friendship, Parisian Protestants were bound up in a close web of mutual service. One key aspect of this service was the sale of clandestine books. The booksellers had a dangerous job but an important one, made even more necessary by the inability of Parisian Protestants to satisfy

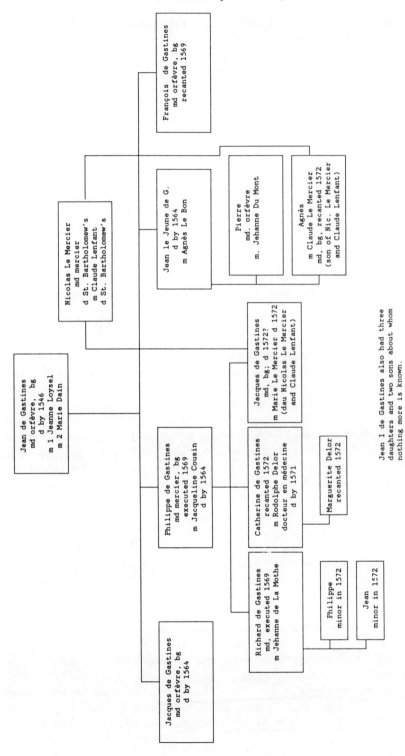

Figure 8–2. Family tree showing the connections between the families of Philippe de Gastines and Nicolas Le Mercier. (For key to abbreviations, see Figure 8–1.)

their hunger for spiritual growth through regular attendance at sermons and public services. An important trade in Protestant literature—in French-language Bibles, psalters, commentaries, and, to a lesser degree, works of controversy—was carried on through the Protestant underground during the first decade of the religious wars. Two types of men were responsible for this trade. The first were itinerant book peddlers, or *colporteurs*, usually poor men with little local standing, who smuggled in books, arranged for their sale, and then—if they were lucky—disappeared again.[15] The second were established booksellers or printer-booksellers who carried on their clandestine trade under the cover of a legitimate publishing enterprise. It is the second group that interests us here, for, in addition to the service they provided, they had strong personal ties to the broader Protestant community.

Parisian printer-booksellers occasionally published their own illicit works during the 1560s, but for the most part they preferred to import forbidden literature from Geneva, Lyons (during the time it was under Protestant domination), or other Protestant cities. They shipped the books to Paris disguised as other merchandise and hoped they would not be discovered during routine inspections of goods imported into the capital. It was a risky operation but less dangerous than tying up one's presses and one's shop with the printing of books or pamphlets whose discovery could mean instant arrest.[16]

Typical of the established printer-booksellers was Richard Breton, who made his public living by printing instructional and classical works while secretly carrying on a trade in prohibited books. Breton first fell under the suspicion of the Parisian authorities in 1559.[17] In 1562 a quantity of censured books was found in his house and he was ordered arrested, along with his wife and half a dozen presumed associates in the illicit trade. Since Breton had already left town on account of the religious conflicts, proceedings against him continued in abstentia. The confiscated books were publicly burned in front of his house. In fact, the proceedings in Parlement had no permanent legal effect. They were "erased from the record" as a result of the Peace of Amboise. (They are crossed out but still legible in the parlementary registers; doubtless they stayed in people's minds in the same way.[18]) Breton also lost some books to confiscation in 1563 because his landlord, Nicolas Chesneau (an important publisher of Catholic polemics), claimed recompense for two quarters of rent that had gone unpaid because of Breton's absence.[19] Despite his losses, Breton continued in his clandestine trade when he returned to Paris after the first war. The inventory that Eustache Goguier made of Breton's property after his death in 1571 includes more than a thousand volumes of illicit religious writings, from French-language Bibles to the latest installment of Crespin's *Histoire des martyrs*.[20]

Breton also published at least one Protestant book, a 1562 edition of Clément Marot and Theodore Beza's versification of the Psalms. He must have hastily completed the book in the brief period of relative toleration that preceded the first religious war. He was one of nineteen Parisian printers who contracted in February 1562 to publish an edition of the Psalms for which the Lyonnais printer Antoine Vincent, taking advantage of Catherine de Medici's short-lived plan of conciliating the Protestants, had secured a royal privilege late in 1561. By the terms of the contract, the printers were to pay the Bureau des pauvres of the Reformed Church of Paris an 8 percent royalty on all of their sales.[21] The agreement was ill-timed; with the onset of war in March 1562, most of the editions were never produced. Breton's is one of only a handful of known editions of the Marot-Beza psalter published in Paris in 1562.[22]

Though it was largely a dead letter, the contract serves as a good starting point for identifying Parisian printers and booksellers with Protestant sympathies in 1562. We can document earlier connections with Protestantism—or at least with the printing and sale of Protestant literature—for three of the men who signed the contract and later connections for at least another eleven. Nine of the men were ordered arrested on one or more occasions between 1560 and 1570 on charges of producing and selling unauthorized books. One actually was arrested on at least three separate occasions.[23] We can, moreover, document personal connections with the Protestant community for at least eight of these printers.[24] Pierre du Pre, for example, was a part of the underground community of Protestants that had its nucleus in the Palais de Justice. He married a daughter of Geneviève de Montault in 1565, thereby acquiring ties of kinship with Nicolas de Louvain, Valentin Morin, and other Protestant merchants in the Palais (see above, Figure 8–1). In order to contract this marriage, du Pre had to cut himself off from his own Catholic family; his mother refused to consent to the union.[25] Among the witnesses to the marriage contract was the bookseller Felix Guibert, whose name also figures on the list of printers contracting to publish the psalter for Antoine Vincent.

Two of the booksellers who signed the contract are mentioned in Crespin's *Histoire des martyrs*. Charles Perier barely escaped with his life on Saint Bartholomew's Day; Oudin Petit perished in the massacre.[26] The ties of both men to the Protestant community can be documented through the records of Goguier and Leal. Perier, a son-in-law of the humanist printer Chrétien Wechel, married his daughter to the bookseller Guillaume Aubray in 1571 in a contract that uses recognizably Protestant formulas.[27] Oudin Petit's second wife came from a Protestant family, and she herself was Protestant until she recanted after Saint Bartholomew's Day. At least four of the children from Petit's first marriage were also Protestants.[28] His son Jean married into a politically active Huguenot family—his wife's stepfather had his property confiscated in 1569 for having borne arms against the king—and Jean was himself engaged in smuggling Protestant literature into Paris in partnership with Jean Le Preux, another bookseller whose name figures on the list of men engaging to publish the psalter in 1562.[29] Le Preux seems to have occupied himself primarily with the Genevan end of the partnership formed with Jean Petit in 1565. He married the stepdaughter of a Genevan bookseller and made his residence in that city and later in Lausanne.[30] Jean Le Preux's brother François was also engaged in clandestine publishing activities. Arrested with Charles Perier on charges of publishing a scandalous tract in 1565, François Le Preux was sentenced to a public beating and banished from the kingdom, whereupon he too retired to Geneva. He later married a daughter of the Genevan printer Henri Estienne.[31]

It has sometimes been argued that printers and booksellers were guided largely by economics in their choice of what to print and sell and that we cannot make assumptions about the personal beliefs of the men working in the publishing trades by surveying the literature they produced and sold. As a general rule this may be true; we can however confirm that many of if not all the men who sold Protestant books in Paris during the decade prior to Saint Bartholomew's Day shared the religious convictions of their clientele and were not motivated simply by a desire for profit.[32] For men like Richard Breton, Charles Perier, and Jean Petit, engaging in the clandestine sale of Protestant literature was a part of the process of living out their faith.[33]

Even where the Protestants' special needs did not set them apart from the population at large, as their desire to purchase forbidden books obviously did, they seem to have formed close ties. They did business together, borrowed money from one another, stood as guarantors for loans, and otherwise assisted one another in legal and financial dealings. The Protestants were too small a group and too scattered to be economically independent of the larger Catholic population, but they seem to have dealt by preference with one another. Thus, for example, although Mathurin Lussault's principal client as a jeweler was the queen mother, when it came time to have his country home enlarged he chose a mason who was also a coreligionist to do the job.[34] Similarly, we find that Louis Bertrand, the seigneur de Popincourt, dealt with the Protestant merchant Thibault Le Maire when he wished to dispose of a large quantity of family jewels; the printer Charles Perier bought his paper from his coreligionist Guillaume Le Bé; and the artisan gilder Louis Massicault rented his lodgings from the Protestant treasury official Claude Tardif.[35]

In the sixteenth century, loans were sometimes made as simple advances of money secured by properties given over to the safekeeping of a third party but were more often disguised as the sale and repurchase of a rente, or annuity, as a way of getting around usury laws that prohibited the loaning of money at interest.[36] Typical of this sort of transaction is the sale of a rente in the amount of 50 livres by Nicolas Le Mercier and Claude Lenfant to Antoine de La Planche, a chancellory official, in February 1566 and its repurchase just three months later. By this contract, the Le Merciers received 600 livres cash from La Planche at an interest rate of 50 livres (8.33 percent) annually. The fact that they repaid the sum—repurchased the rente— just three months later suggests that the transaction was from the beginning a concealed loan and was never intended as a permanent transfer of property.[37]

The ties formed in this way cut across the social hierarchy. Agreements might be made between equals or between persons of different social standing. Important noblemen employed Protestant merchants to act as their agents in the collection of rents and in other financial affairs.[38] The nobles also borrowed money from the merchants, since, like most of France's rich noblemen, they seem to have been perennially short of cash. Thus we find François de Coligny, sieur d'Andelot, employing the Protestant merchants Jean and Philippe Canaye to collect the 12,000 écus owed him by Pierre Asserat in Toulouse. The fact that on the very next day Andelot signed over to Jean Canaye his rights to these 12,000 écus in exchange for some consideration not named in the text suggests that the Canayes had advanced Andelot a large sum of money, which they expected to recover (with profit) through the collection of his debts in Toulouse.[39]

Besides arrangements that worked to the mutual benefit of both parties, there is evidence that at least some of the richer and more powerful members of the Reformed community gave their partronage and protection to the poorer and weaker among their coreligionists. We find, for example, that the personal secretary and solicitor to the vidame de Chartres represented a poor carpenter's wife in a lawsuit in Parlement. The woman had been unable for four years to regain possession of the house from which she had fled with her husband and stepchildren during the first religious war. She was unable to force the man who had moved into the house either to vacate it or to pay rent. She did not know where her husband was, and, since the Reformed church was weakest at the lower social levels, she probably did not have a large circle of friends to help bolster her courage and assist her in recovering her rights to her home and to a reasonable rental for the period during which she had been driven from it. In any event, the notion of filing suit in Parlement was probably as alien and potentially frightening to her friends as it was to the woman herself. The willingness of the vidame's secretary to provide this service, whether of his own initiative or on his employer's instructions, reveals an important kind of solidarity within the Reformed community—a solidarity without which recruitment at popular levels, already weak, would have been weaker still.[40]

Another way in which wealthy or middle-class Protestants extended patronage to the poorer members of the Reformed community was by taking in their children as servants. There was an element of prudence in this practice, since it was well known that secret meeting places and the names of many members of the underground church had been betrayed to the cardinal of Lorraine in 1559 by two apprentices from Catholic families, but its importance in structuring the Protestant community should not on this account be denied.[41] Thus, for example, Geneviève Chobart, the daughter of a journeyman wool dyer in the faubourg Saint-Marcel, was a servant in the house of Geneviève Le Bossu, the widow of the wealthy merchant dyer François Gobelin. In 1565, Chobart married Richard Le Melais, a paper seller of modest standing but with extensive ties to the Protestant community.[42] Nicole and Marie Le Melais, Richard's sisters, worked in the house of the merchant Thibault Le Maire, a cousin through his wife Anne Estienne, until they were married in 1564 and 1566 respectively.[43] Family ties, such as those that existed between Nicole and Marie Le Melais and their wealthier cousin Thibault Le Maire, were common between Protestant servants and their masters in Paris. So were ties of family between apprentices and their masters. Thibault Le Melais, the younger brother of Richard, Nicole, and Marie, was apprenticed in 1566 to Jean Verdier, a musical instrument maker and the husband of Thibault's oldest sister.[44] Even where there were no family ties, however, Protestant parents quite naturally preferred to place their children in the homes of their coreligionists. To cite just one example, Jacques de Gastines, shortly after agreeing to go into business with his father-in-law, Nicolas Le Mercier, took as his apprentice Pierre Le Clerc, the fourteen-year-old son of Jean Le Clerc, a solicitor in the Châtelet and later a victim of Saint Bartholomew's Day.[45] As a resident of the much-hated Golden Hammer, Pierre Le Clerc probably met the same fate.

The ties that linked the Protestant community—ties of family, friendship, and service—were in many respects similar to the ties on which the larger Catholic community was built. They were distinctive only in those cases in which they were based exclusively on a shared religious sentiment and did not also build on old associations of business, neighborhood, or kinship. They were, however, partic-

Table 8.1. Religious Books in the Inventory after Death of Richard Breton*

	Number	Percent
Psalms	634	58
New Testament with Psalms	101	9
New Testament alone	28	3
Complete Bible	15	1
Calvin's writings	81	7
Writings of other reformers	93	9
Histoire des martyrs	36	3
History and Controversy	40	4
Miscellaneous	59	5
Total	1087	99

*AN, MC, 299 (2 April 1571): *Inventaire après décès* of Richard Breton. The document has been published in Wildenstein, "L'imprimeur-libraire Richard Breton," pp. 364–379. This table is based on works listed in Breton's inventory for which both titles and quantities can be established.

ularly important to the Protestant community because, under the given conditions of illegality and repression, they afforded a means of communication and a vital network of economic and psychological support. This network was shattered by the events of Saint Bartholomew's Day. The Protestants could no longer help one another; in many cases those who survived did so only because they found Catholic friends or kin willing to take them in. The Protestant community dissolved in August 1572 as death, emigration, and recantation took their toll.

Psalms and Salvation

We have already seen how the Reformed faith was acquired through conversion and how it was fortified by the discipline of the church and the common bonds among its members. At the same time, the resilience of the faith—its ability to make bearable the sufferings of persecution—deserves further comment. We need to penetrate more deeply into those tenets of belief that fostered the qualities of endurance under stress and obedience to a higher truth. How can we do this? We do not have any published sermons, such as we will use to examine the message Parisian Catholics were receiving from the pulpit, and the few letters and memoirs that have been preserved give only scattered hints about the essential character of their authors' beliefs. One avenue is to examine the literature that was smuggled in to help meet the spiritual needs of the underground community.

The inventory of books made after the death of Richard Breton in 1571 offers some clues as to where we should look (Table 8–1). One title clearly stands out above the rest, and that is the book of Psalms. Breton had more than a dozen editions of the Psalms to offer his clients. Beginning at 18 deniers (1½ sou), there was a psalter for every budget and taste. There were handsome quartos in which the Psalms were bound together with the New Testament and cheap pocket editions of the Psalms alone; there were illustrated psalters and verse Psalms with prose commentaries. The selection of psalters suggests that the book had a special significance for Parisian Protestants; the relative importance of the stock of psalters in the overall inventory of religious books confirms this suggestion. Editions of the Psalms alone or of the Psalms published together with the New Testament accounted for two-thirds of the religious books in Breton's stock.[46]

Why did this particular book have such an importance for Parisian Protestants? The question can be answered superficially—in terms of the role the Psalms acquired as a mark of solidarity and defiance on the part of French Protestants—but it must also be explained on a deeper level in terms of the Protestants' identification with the psalmist David, his suffering, and his faith.

The adoption of the book by French Protestants dates back to the brief period when Calvin, having alienated the Genevan city government, served as minister to a French congregation in Strasbourg. Calvin admired Clément Marot's versification of the Psalms, and he had some of them set to music for use as hymns in the religious services he planned for his church. When he returned to Geneva, he carried back with him the slender volume published in 1539 for the use of his Strasbourg congregation. Revised and enlarged in subsequent editions, it became a key text of Reformed spirituality and an active agent of Calvinist militance.

Association of the Psalms with Calvinist Geneva inevitably provoked a reaction in Catholic France, but the reaction was a gradual one. People liked Marot's elegant verses, and they seem initially to have paid little heed to the condemnation of his Psalms by the theologians of the Sorbonne in 1543. Indeed, one historian has counted twenty-five Parisian printings of Marot's *Cinquante psaumes* or *Cinquante-deux psaumes* between the years 1545 and 1550 alone.[47] Most of these were signed editions, which indicates that the publishers had little fear of the censors. As the threat posed by the Genevan "heretics" appeared to increase, however, so too did the disapproval that was registered against the Psalms. The publication in 1551 of a new edition of *Octante-trois psaumes*, thirty-four of them by Théodore Beza, contributed to the bad light in which the Psalms were held, and the scandals that erupted later in the 1550s when Protestants began singing psalms in public gatherings made matters worse still. After the violent riots that broke out on the pré aux Clercs in 1558, Henri II forbade the public singing of psalms.

Each prohibition made the Psalms more precious to French Protestants as a symbol and expression of the true religion, and so they continued to sing them not only in their private services but also publicly in moments of defiance or spiritual need. They were used to disrupt Catholic services and to call attention to Protestant gatherings. They were sung by religious prisoners as they were dragged off to their jails in chains and by convicted heretics on their way to execution. They were used as marching songs by Huguenot armies and to rally the courage of civilians in the wars as well.[48] Agrippa d'Aubigné tells how the minister Daniel Toussain, ambushed by Catholic forces as he was leading a group of nearly 500 Protestants out of Montargis in 1569, knelt in the road and called upon his flock to prepare for their "deliverance" by singing with him the Thirty-first Psalm.[49] The Huguenots of Bourges celebrated their seizure of the city in 1562 by singing Psalm 124; the citizens of Sancerre marked an initial victory in the eventually disastrous siege of 1572–1573 by singing Psalm 144.[50]

If the Psalms had this value for French Protestants, it was because they found in them a language to express their anguish and their faith. Calvin made the Psalms his own; his sermons and letters are filled with their language and imagery. He repeatedly used direct quotations or allusions to the Psalms in the letters he sent to the Paris church in the late 1550s to encourage its members to bear up under the strains of persecution. The advice to take shelter "in the shadow of the wings of God" in a letter written to the Paris church in March 1557 paraphrases Psalm 57: "Yea, in the shadow of thy wings will I make my refuge, until these calamities be overpast." Similarly, the assurance that God cherishes the sufferings of the faithful in a letter written in September of that same year is bolstered by a reference to Psalm 56. "If God sometimes allows the blood of his faithful to be spilled," wrote Calvin, "he nevertheless carefully collects their precious tears."[51] For Calvin's readers, these words would call to mind not only the immediate reference in the psalm ("Put thou my tears into thy bottle: are they not in thy book?") but also the following verses, in which David expresses his confidence in divine protection, offers up his trust, and prays for strength to carry on. Through this one reference to the "precious tears" of the faithful, Calvin evokes the entire attitude of trusting acceptance he would have his followers assume. The use of the Psalms both to instruct and to console is also apparent in a letter written in February 1559 and smuggled in to the prisoners being held in Paris jails on account of their beliefs. Recalling the lines from Psalm 119 that "The bands of the wicked have robbed me: but I have not forgotten thy law," Calvin brings to mind the many other verses of this, the longest psalm, that make it a meditation on the path of righteousness and a prayer for strength in persecution but also a celebration of the joy experienced by those who follow in God's law and the promise of life to his faithful.[52]

Calvin's followers also borrowed the language of the Psalms to express their confidence in divine protection, their conviction of being a chosen people, and their sense of sin. Merlin de l'Espérandière, for example, used the same reference to being sheltered "under the wings of God" that Calvin used in 1557 to describe the situation of the Paris church in 1567.[53] Like Calvin, he used it to express his confidence that a higher protection would see the church through the current wave of persecution. In a more personal vein, Antoine du Croy, the prince of Porcien, used the language of the Psalms to express his sense of unworthiness when he referred in the confession of faith that precedes his will to "my sin and my iniquity, which are, as David says, always before me."[54]

French Protestants attached to the Psalms three levels of meaning. They understood them first within the Old Testament context of David's own sufferings and his eventual triumph over his enemies; second, as prophetic of the sufferings and triumph of Christ; and third, as prophetic of the sufferings and triumph of the church. These three levels of meaning may have been traditional in Biblical exegesis, but the Huguenots' appropriation of the third level of meaning to refer to their actual sufferings and anticipated triumph—the sufferings and triumph of the true church—was unusually direct and immediate. The application of the Psalms to the current situation was not just implicit in the Huguenot psalter but was clearly set out in the prefatory "argument" or caption attached to each psalm.[55] For example, the caption for Psalm 31—the psalm chosen as a prayer for deliverance in the threatened exodus from Montargis—refers first to David's anguish as he was hunted by Saul in the wilderness of Maon but then broadens its message by adding that it depicts the "torments of the faithful," their outrage against their enemies, and their assurance in the goodness of God. It is, the caption concludes, "an excellent psalm in cases of great affliction."[56]

To make the application to the current situation still more explicit, some editions of the Huguenot psalter included a list directing the reader to the most appropriate psalm for each occasion or state of mind. Psalms to use as prayers for a church that was afflicted or enfeebled, oppressed by combat, or held captive by its foes were prominent on the list.[57] Some editions also included a prayer after each psalm. The most popular set of prayers was composed by Augustin Marlorat, briefly a minister in Paris but more closely associated with the church of Rouen, in which city he was martyred in 1562. Many of Marlorat's prayers make direct reference to the enemies that were persecuting the faithful, but they always refer at the same time to the covenant that God made with his chosen people and to his promise never to abandon them.[58]

French Protestants identified with the stripling youth, who, armed only with his faith, defeated the giant Goliath; with David the anointed of God, who maintained his innocence and his trust despite the persecutions that Saul, having rebelled against God, inflicted upon him. David was a warrior as well as a prophet and praise-singer, and the martial imagery in the Psalms had a special resonance for the Huguenots. Psalm 144, the psalm sung in celebration of the victory at Sancerre, begins "Blessed be the Lord my strength, which teacheth my hands to war, and my fingers to fight." Calvin used martial imagery frequently in his letters and sermons, but one is always aware in Calvin's writings of the metaphorical sense in which God is likened to a "shield, wall, or rampart" or a Christian is "called to combat" and advised to take up God's promises as "arms."[59] The Huguenots were more direct in paraphrasing the Psalms to invoke the "God of vengeance" or "the great God of battles."[60] They found in the Psalms a rich treasury of song with which to praise God and console themselves, but they also found there a militant faith and a God that sanctioned holy war. Consider Marlorat's prayer for Psalm 144, which begins:

> Lord God of Armies, who knows that our weakness is so great that we cannot stand up to our enemies unless we are sustained by your admirable force, show those who rise up against us that you are our shield and defender.[61]

This psalm was especially recommended for those who were headed into combat.

The Huguenots did show some ambivalence about the question of whether or not it was justified to make war to defend their faith. The prefatory letter to Pierre Viret's *L'interim fait par dialogues*, published in Lyons in 1565, expresses this ambivalence well. Dedicating his book to Gaspard de Coligny, Viret expounds in his prefatory letter on the paradox attributed to both David (Psalm 37:11) and Jesus Christ (Matthew 5:5) that "the meek shall inherit the earth." Why should the meek inherit the earth, asks Viret, rather than the valiant ones who fight back when injured? He then cites the common proverb that he who acts the sheep gets eaten by the wolf and says this sounds like common sense, but then he seems to reverse himself, declaring this same proverb contrary to the word of God, for "we must consider not only the nature of the sheep and the wolves but also that of the shepherd.'' Experience shows, says Viret, that violence may seem for a time to triumph, but this is not in the end the case. Citing once again Psalm 37, Viret exhorts Coligny (and his readers) to wait for God's assistance and not look to themselves for help: ''For the evildoers shall be cut off: but those that wait upon the Lord, they shall inherit the earth.''[62] When we read further, however, it is apparent that Viret is not urging pacificism here so much as underscoring the need to place one's trust in God, for he goes on to cite Jesus's words, ''Think not that I am come to send peace on earth: I came not to send peace, but a sword'' (Matthew 10:34) and to explain that the reason for this apparent contradiction lies in the contrariness of men, who do not accept God's peace but by their perversity reject it and end in war. Those who continue in the service of God cannot escape the hatred of these troublemakers, but we should know that when God asks us to be like lambs, it is not to make us lose courage but rather so that, by fixing our trust on him as our shepherd, we are not frightened by the force and cruelty of our enemies and so prevented from keeping our obligations to him. We are not to hide in our houses ''like turtles,'' waiting for better times, but rather to go out and serve the glory of God. Viret concludes by citing several reassuring passages from the Psalms, including Psalm 33:12: ''Blessed is the nation whose God is the Lord; and the people whom he hath chosen for his inheritance,'' and Psalm 34:7: ''The angel of the Lord encampeth about them that fear him, and delivereth them.'' The final message, then, is martial and not pacific; the meek lambs are yet soldiers of God. They fight under the banner of the shepherd.[63]

More important even than helping to justify war in the name of religion, however, the Psalms helped to teach the Huguenots to view persecution as a trial imposed by God and a special mark of his covenant. In a variety of forms, the message of treatises written by Huguenot pastors during the war years is the message of Psalm 119:79: ''It is good for me that I have been afflicted; that I might learn thy statutes.'' Chandieu, for example, wrote in the preface to his *Histoire des persecutions et martyrs de l'eglise de Paris*, published in Lyons in 1563, that ''the afflictions that God has sent us are so many marks and signs of his good will toward us and his adoption.''[64] De L'Espine, in his *Traitté consolatoire*, published in Lyons in 1565, couched the same belief in New Testament terms. Taking as his epigraph Romans 8:17 (''And if children, then heirs of God, and joint-heirs with Christ, if so be that we suffer with him''), he urged his readers not to flee affliction or to try to escape it. He reminded them rather that ''persecutions are inevitable to all who wish dutifully to follow Jesus Christ; . . . to be disciples and students of Jesus Christ, we must take his cross on our shoulders and follow him.''[65] In order to make those tribulations less difficult to bear, de L'Espine urged his reader to glory in them and to remember that ''our king'' always goes before us into battle. It is an honor to follow closely after him. Moreover,

> If it is an honor to a captain to abandon his life sooner than to violate the faith he
> has pledged his prince, so is it to a Christian man to keep to the very end that
> [faith] that he has sworn to Jesus Christ and to die rather than to commit or to
> suffer anything that impairs it.[66]

Writing not merely in terms of honor and obligation but also of joy, Daniel Toussain took up the same theme but carried it farther. In a meditation on Psalm

124 composed in Orleans during the interval between the first and second wars, he wrote that "affliction, among other uses, brings the faithful man a special zeal to trust uniquely in Him, and so to experience the effects of his divine force." Toussain expressed his certainty that although "the church since its earliest days has suffered greatly, . . . nothing can destroy it," and he went on to address God familiarly, saying:

> Your poor church is in this world like a lamb in the midst of wolves, like a rose among the thorns. But at the same time, oh great God, we are so happy when he who created heaven and earth shows himself to be on our side. And we see that you are with us when miraculously you deliver us, when daily you uphold us.[67]

The joy of feeling God's presence was a powerful emotion with Toussain, and he wrote with great confidence in God's deliverance.

> Oh happy the man who . . . not seeing any help in the world, looks at God and is assured of being seen by him! The mother often looks at her child with pity, because she cannot help him. But your look, Lord, is efficacious for your children: it is medicine for their ills.[68]

It is easy to see the Calvinist God as a terrible God, who not only wreaks vengeance on his enemies but also inflicts suffering on his faithful so as to test their steadfastness. It is important to recognize, however, that, at least for the generation of French Calvinists that form the object of our study, the terrible majesty of God was balanced by his healing love. To obey God's law was not just an obligation, it was, as Psalm 119 repeatedly tells us, a "delight." God is a powerful father, but he is also "clement, mild, and full of grace [*doux, benin & gracieux*]. Do we need to fear his judgment? On the contrary, we hope to judge the world with him."[69] God does not want to condemn us but rather to save us. "Thus, God's promises and threats, however diverse they may be, all lead to the same end, which is to show us the love that God bears us, and the care he has for our salvation."[70] We are not all given the same measure of faith, but in the end this does not matter, for "we are assured of eternal life as long as there is a single spark of faith in our heart."[71] This is not the anxious, introspective religion frequently associated with later generations of Calvinists, preoccupied with seeking out each mark or sign of election; it is rather a confident, outgoing, and even joyous faith—as it had to be both to take root in the initial period of evangelization and to surmount the persecutions the church was forced to endure.

These fundamental characteristics of the faith of French Protestants help explain two otherwise puzzling aspects of the Huguenots' reaction to Saint Bartholomew's Day. On the one hand, it has been asked why the Huguenots seem to have put up so little resistance to their murderers, and on the other, why so many of the recantations in the wake of the massacres were, if not sincere, at least permanent losses for the French Reformed Church. To address the question of resistance first, it is true that, of the Parisian victims, only the prévôt de la maréchaussée Taverny, who defended his beseiged house with gunfire, is known to have fought for his life.[72] In my opinion, the circumstances of the massacre—the fact that the Huguenots were pulled from their beds unawares; that they were taken in their own houses, scattered across the city with no means to group together to defend themselves—

should provide sufficient explanation for any failure to fight back, at least where the early victims are concerned. We might also take into consideration the false promises of those who offered Huguenots safety and then betrayed them. Indeed, there are many circumstantial factors that could have come into play. But the real answer to the question lies in the nature of the Huguenots' faith. The Huguenots' confidence in the promise of salvation, their acceptance of affliction as a special trial imposed by God, their belief that it was necessary to suffer under the cross, all combined to prepare them to fight a holy war. But they also prepared them for martyrdom. The death of Pierre de La Place, described at the opening of Chapter 7, exemplifies the Huguenot ideal.

What, then, of those who recanted? It should, it seems, be obvious that, whatever the essential confidence of converts to the Reformed religion, it was easier to pray for the honor of being allowed to die in holy combat than it was actually to endure the same fate, easier to admire the church's martyrs than to become one. We have seen that at every trial, from the affair of the rue Saint-Jacques to the arrest of the Gastines, some Protestants recanted under the pressures of persecution. We have seen, for example, that François de Gastines renounced his faith rather than follow his brother Philippe and his nephew Richard to the gallows.[73] Many similar examples could be cited. The greatest test, however, was that posed by the events of Saint Bartholomew's Day. It was here that the belief that persecution was God's way of chastising his elect met its greatest challenge. Many of those who survived the massacres survived with their faith intact. Daniel Toussain, for example, was able to write after Saint Bartholomew's Day that even "in the midst of the greatest fires, [God] consoles and upholds his children," and he recalled God's promise to David that "I will visit their transgression with the rod, and their iniquity with stripes. Nevertheless my lovingkindness will I not utterly take from him, nor suffer my faithfulness to fail."[74] Others similarly accepted the massacre as a chastisement imposed by God and a punishment for sin without losing their faith in God's promise to his chosen people.[75] But for many Huguenots, especially but not uniquely in cities like Paris that felt the full fury of the storm, the magnitude of the calamity was too great. They could not believe that God would allow the slaughter of his children.

The minister Hugues Sureau Du Rosier described his own lapse of faith in these terms. Removed from his church at Orleans on account of the Morély affair, he was serving in a church outside of Paris when the massacre occurred. Captured and imprisoned as he tried to flee, he began to think over the heinousness of the events that had just occurred, which he found to be of an entirely different order of magnitude from the persecutions he had known before:

> I had always believed the past calamities to be so many visitations and rods by which God purged his church, and had always judged them to be the clear marks of the children of God. But inasmuch as in that last [visitation] could be seen the entire ruin of the church, without any sign to which one could attach the slightest hope for reestablishment, I began to see it as evidence of the indignation of God, as if he had declared by this means that he detested and condemned the profession and exercise of our religion . . . , as if he wished entirely to ruin this church and favor instead the Roman.[76]

Du Rosier later had occasion bitterly to regret these words, but the damage could not be undone. A source of great strength, the Huguenots' confidence in being the chosen of God was at the same time a vulnerable point which, skillfully exploited, could lead to abjuration. Du Rosier himself contributed to the exploitation of this vulnerability. His apostasy was a disaster for the Huguenots. The Catholics made much of his return to the fold by publishing his *Confession* and using him to help convert others, including the king of Navarre.

In time, however, the two religions went to war in Du Rosier's breast, and it was the Protestant faith that emerged victorious. He apostatized a second time. Learning that his family had safely escaped from France, he seized the first occasion that offered itself to flee to Protestant ground. In 1574, he published another *Confession* in which he attributed his fall to the temptations of the devil and sorely regretted the damage he had done. He blamed himself not only for his own miserable weakness, his "disloyalty and rebellion against God," but also for having led others to abjure their faith and, not least, for having injured those who had yet remained faithful by appearing to condemn the cause for which their friends and relatives had died. "What trouble," he asked, "have I put into the hearts of those who consoled themselves for the deaths of their relatives and friends, rendering thanks to God, who had given them the honor of suffering for his name?"[77]

But those whose faith had survived the cataclysm of the massacre were not to be shaken by Du Rosier's suggestion that their friends and relatives had died in vain. Memorialized in Crespin's *Histoire des martyrs*, the victims of Saint Bartholomew's Day were incorporated into the Huguenot legend as a source of pride and strength. The belief that persecution was a trial imposed by God remained central to the faith of the survivors, a comfort in their suffering and a means of accepting their tragic losses. It was also a tool—mostly unsuccessful it seems—for luring back the sheep that had strayed, a central chord in pamphlets intended to convince the apostates to return to the true faith.[78]

Du Rosier, on the other hand, though he took up again his cross, never truly returned to the fellowship of the French Reformed church. Although his repentance was formally accepted and his apostasy forgiven by the French ministers gathered in exile in Geneva, they required him to wait some time in "probation and repentance" before being fully readmitted to the church. Whether because of his former colleagues' reluctance to accept him or because of his own inability to live with the constant memory that his faith had faltered when he needed it most, Du Rosier never joined the exile community in Geneva or returned to the ministry. He lived out the three years that remained of his life as a printer's corrector in Frankfurt.[79]

As much as Pierre de La Place, Hugues Sureau Du Rosier is a fitting symbol of the destruction of the Protestant community in Paris as a result of Saint Bartholomew's Day. He represents the broken bonds of church and community, as well as the failure of faith that afflicted a portion—we will never know how large—of the Protestant community. The merchant Jean Rouillé, writing to business acquaintances in Albi a month after Saint Bartholomew's Day, advised them that more than five thousand people in Paris had abjured. Jean de L'Espine wrote ten years later that the French churches had lost more than two-thirds of their members in the "horrible and appalling revolt" that occurred after Saint Bartholomew's Day and that few of the apostates had ever returned.[80] There is no way to know how accurate these estimates may be. Nor is there any way to know how many of the abjurations were sincere.

In fear for their lives, people hastened to sign Catholic professions of faith that they had every intention of repenting at leisure. Some of these people quietly slipped out of Paris at a later date and made their way to Protestant cities like Geneva, where, after appropriate signs of repentance, they were readmitted to the Reformed church and to the communion of their coreligionists.[81] Some quietly remained in Paris and kept their true beliefs to themselves, a new generation of Nicodemites and a root from which a revived church was eventually to grow.[82] Others, whatever their initial intention, never returned to the faith. They could not regain that proud confidence, that conviction of being a chosen people, that had helped them to survive the first decade of the wars.

9

The Bellows of Satan

On 16 December 1562, with Paris suffering from the twin scourges of pestilence and war, Jean de Hans, the Minim whose Advent sermons had caused such a stir the previous year, died of the plague. Most chroniclers of the period, caught up in the furious clash of events that was to lead just four days later to the crucial battle of Dreux, pass over de Hans's death in silence, but the journal of Pierre Paschal includes a disturbing note. Popular admiration for de Hans was so great, Paschal informs us, that despite the danger of contagion Parisian women gathered around his corpse to touch it with their handkerchiefs and rosary beads and so to draw some blessing from his saintliness.[1]

Jean de Hans had made his reputation through courageous and eloquent preaching, through his willingness to speak the truth before the king himself. Haton attributes to his sermons an intensity that seemed to issue from a spirit of prophecy or divine revelation. Known to wear a hair shirt under his Minim habit, de Hans also won respect for his asceticism, which was seen as an implicit rebuke to his more self-indulgent fellow churchmen.[2] These qualities brought Parisians flocking to his sermons and allowed this simple friar to share the pulpits of the most prestigious parishes in the capital with learned doctors of the Sorbonne and prelates of the church. In 1562, for example, he alternated with the cardinal of Lorraine in preaching the Corpus Christi sermons at Saint-Germain-l'Auxerrois.[3] De Hans's career as a preacher was cut short by his early death; he was about thirty when he died. None of his sermons have been preserved. We know him only from reports in memoirs and letters. Even these scattered mentions, however, should alert us to a subject that requires further study, and that is the role of the Catholic clergy in the fratricidal conflicts that we call the religious wars.

Both Protestant and Catholic accounts of the wars tell us that the fiery sermons of Catholic preachers in Paris acted as a stimulus to popular violence against the Huguenots and resistance against the crown. We have already seen, for example, that de Hans's arrest in December 1561, although conducted at night so as to avoid popular disturbances, nearly led to riots in the capital and that his return, with escorts provided by both the king and the city, was greeted by large and triumphant crowds.[4] Haton tells us that the day following de Hans's release so many people came to Saint-Barthélemy, where he was charged with preaching the Advent sermons, that they could not squeeze into the church. The people came to hear what de Hans had said to the king, who was believed to be under the sway of advisers entirely too favorable to the Huguenots, but de Hans turned the people's anger away from the young king and assured them in his sermon that his majesty was a pious and faithful Catholic. When he told them that Charles IX had personally commissioned him to continue to speak out against abuses, not sparing anyone, including his own royal person, the crowd broke into cheers of, "Vive le roi!"

But if popular anger was deflected from the crown, it was only focused more intently on the Huguenots, who were feared more with each passing day.[5] Moreover, the arrest of de Hans served to fortify the courage of the Parisian clergy, made timid by the accusations of seditious preaching that had been levied against them all during the fall, and to convince them that the time had come when they must show themselves willing to suffer and even to die in defense of the Catholic faith. And so, during the four days that de Hans was absent, they spoke out more courageously than ever before against "the abuses perpetrated by the king's governors, the princes and the preachers, and against the enterprises of the Huguenots."[6] According once again to Haton, they showed such zeal that they clamored to share the fate of the imprisoned Minim, and "to suffer with him for the honor of God and of the Catholic church, his bride."[7]

Recounted in such familiar sources as Claude Haton's memoirs, Etienne Pasquier's letters, and the journal of Pierre de Paschal, the story of Jean de Hans is well known to historians of the religious wars, as are numerous other accounts of provocative sermons delivered before and during the wars. For the most part, however, historians have been content simply to repeat the accusations of seditious preaching that appear in the narrative sources. They have made surprisingly little attempt to inquire more seriously into the subject of popular preaching during the wars, and those attempts that have been made have focused on the period of the League and not on the opening decades of the conflicts.[8] It is true that the sources for such a study are not plentiful; the sermons of only a handful of the Parisian preachers active during this period were collected and published, and manuscript sermons for this particular time and place have proved virtually nonexistent. Those sermons that have survived can nevertheless offer rich insights into the character of popular Catholicism and will amply reward our closer scrutiny. They can be supplemented by the vernacular treatises that appeared in large numbers around the onset of the wars and served to explain and justify the Catholic position on the major issues under dispute.

The treatises and sermons published by Parisian preachers are similar in their rhetoric and in the ideas that they advance. Neither source can be counted as truly "popular," if popular must refer to a message aimed at or spread among society's lowest, or most illiterate, groups, but it is not really the basest social levels that interest me here. We do not know just what was said by the most ignorant of the preaching friars or parish clergy to their most ignorant of listeners, but in an important sense, this does not matter. The message delivered to a mixed urban audience by the learned and respected clergy whose sermons and treatises have been preserved is quite disturbing enough. Besides, it is easy to explain—and so to dismiss—the religious violence in Paris as the product of the base passions of an inflamed and fanatical mob. It is more difficult, but ultimately more important, to understand how the message that was being delivered from the Catholic pulpit

Horribles cruautez des Huguenots
en France.

Cacher ne peut le mal qu'il porte en la poictrine
Le Tyran Huguenot ; qui d'enuie matine
Se monstrant comme Juyf ennemy du Seigneur,
Le prestre ayant force à celebrer la Messe,
Misteres prophanant , & le batant sans cesse,
L'a mis finallement à la croix du Sauueur.

Figure 9–1. Scene from a 1562 Catholic polemic against the "Horrible Cruelties of the Huguenots in France" showing a priest being forced to profane the mass he is celebrating. In a simultaneous depiction, the same priest is being beaten, and he is being shot at as he hangs from the crucifix over the altar of his church. (Phot. Bibl. nat. Paris.)

could capture the hearts and minds of those who were not—or at least under other circumstances would not have been—a part of the common mob. Our task in this chapter, then, is to present and analyze Catholic preaching in Paris during the period between the affair of the rue Saint-Jacques and Saint Bartholomew's Day. By what means did the preachers appeal to the popular imagination? What arguments did they advance, and why did their rhetoric prove so inflammatory? Chapter 10 will take up the question of who responded to the message and how it influenced the course of events in the city.

The Message from the Pulpit

One of the most striking characteristics of the sermons and treatises that issued from the Parisian clergy in the late 1550s and 1560s is the new emphasis on explaining Catholic ritual and dogma. One cannot accuse the French clergy of having been slow to respond to the challenge of Protestantism. After all, the learned doctors of the Sorbonne condemned Luther's teachings as early as 1521. But the first responses of French churchmen represented an attempt simply to put a halt to the movement through official condemnation and persecution. Only when the growing threat of Calvinism in the 1550s seemed to elude these direct attempts at elimination did the French clergy begin to address a concerted defense of Catholic teaching to a popular audience. Only when the Calvinist critique of the Mass as an inefficacious and even dangerous ceremony seemed to be reaching too many re-

Horribles cruautez des Huguenots
en France.   ꝛc

Ces Tirans infensez n'eſtants iamais contents,
Inuentent tous les iours autres nouueaux tourments,
A leur ardant couroux ne ſuffit nulle paine:
Ilz s'eſgaient à voir ſouffrir cruelle mort
Aux pauures innocents, qu'ilz font mourir à tort,
Monſtrant par tel tourments leur tant mortele haine.

Figure 9–2. Another plate from
the same polemic shows some of
the cruel tortures the Huguenots
were said to inflict on their Catholic enemies. (Phot. Bibl. nat.
Paris.)

ceptive ears did the Catholic clergy rise to meet the challenge of Protestantism by
explicating essential doctrines of the faith and unveiling some of the "sacred mysteries" of the church.[9] Somewhat belatedly, French clergymen began to recognize
that an ignorant laity was a weak support for a threatened church. They began at
last to respond to the anguished confusion of people like the gentlewoman we
encountered in Chapter 7 who wrote that, before her conversion at the age of forty-
nine, she had "adored what [she] didn't know."[10]

Understandably, the doctrines that received the most ample discussion in the
new vernacular expositions of faith were precisely those that were in greatest dispute.
The issue that received the most attention was the doctrine of the real presence in
the Eucharist. Among the sermons that have been preserved from this period are
several collections on the sacrament of the altar, including a set of twelve sermons
delivered by François Le Picart, dean of Saint-Germain-l'Auxerrois and perhaps
the most popular preacher in Paris during the period before the civil wars (he died
in 1556). Didactic and repetitive, full of references both to scripture and to the
church fathers, Le Picart's sermons on the Mass were nonetheless clear and straight-
forward in their explanation of Catholic teachings. He even introduced the term
"transubstantiation" to his listeners, explaining that although the word itself is not
in the Bible, the doctrine to which it refers most certainly is.[11] Moreover, he placed
his explanation of Catholic teachings into the explicit context of Calvinist "errors."
A similar approach was taken by Pierre Dyvolé in a series of ten sermons on the
Eucharist that were delivered in 1558. Beginning with a discussion of the priesthood
and the vestments worn for the Mass, Dyvolé systematically explained the sym-

bolism and meaning attached to every phrase or gesture in the Mass.[12] Simon Vigor, whose sermons will be discussed in greater detail in the next part of this chapter, was equally systematic in the series of sermons on the Mass that he delivered at Notre-Dame. Vigor began by expounding on the need for sacrifice in religion and spent several sermons explaining the Mass as sacrifice before moving on to the Mass as sacrament and the doctrine of the real presence. All the sermons were laced with direct references to Calvin's *Institutes* and attacks on Calvin himself.[13]

At the same time that the French clergy began to make frequent use of the pulpit for instructing their flock in the faith, they began to publish large numbers of vernacular treatises to serve the same purpose. Books bearing titles like *Alphabet ou instruction chrestienne pour les petis enfans, Catechisme ou sommaire de la foy*, or *Manière d'ouir la messe* set out the fundamental articles of Roman Catholic belief for an audience that was obviously assumed to be sorely lacking in knowledge of the religion it professed.[14] Although some of these books, like the early catechisms, merely listed the articles of faith along with offering the kind of descriptions of the sacraments that had been published earlier in certain books of hours or works of spirituality such as *L'ordinaire des chrestiens* (1495), many went much farther in explaining the symbolism of Catholic ritual in terms of its theological foundations. Books on specific sacraments—particularly the sacrament of the Eucharist, but others as well—poured forth, as did treatises on such contested doctrines as purgatory, fasting during Lent, or the veneration of saints.

René Benoist (Regent Doctor in Theology, curé of Saint-Pierre-des-Arcis in 1566 and Saint-Eustache in 1569) was particularly prolific in this regard. Every year he turned out one or more treatises with pompous and didactic titles like the *Claire probation de la necessaire manducation de la substantielle & reale humanité de Jesus Christ, vray Dieu & vray homme, au s. sacrement de l'autel* (1561). Benoist produced treatises defending many aspects of Catholic doctrine and ritual, and he also wrote sweeping attacks on the "blasphemies" of the heretics and their "corruption" of the faith, but his favorite subjects, the ones to which he returned time and again, were the sacrifice of the Mass and the real presence in the Eucharist.[15]

The inevitable consequence of these sermons and treatises, which combined explanation of Catholic beliefs with vivid denunciations of Calvinist "errors," was to fan the flames of the theological disputes that were at the heart of the Reformation quarrel. They brought the symbols of this dispute out of their theological sanctuaries and into the streets. Even if the explanations of Catholic doctrine were only imperfectly understood by the mass of the population, as was undoubtedly the case, doctrinal issues became familiar as objects of contention and so served as rallying points for popular opinion and action. It is not surprising that religious violence was often provoked by Protestant attacks on Catholic symbols—by acts of iconoclasm or by the Calvinists' mocking of the Catholics' "God of Paste"—and it is no coincidence that this violence escalated around the key holy days of the Christian calendar, with Corpus Christi week, dedicated to the doctrine of the real presence, the most inflammable period of all. Moreover, even if people did not entirely grasp the theological issues at stake, the preachers provided other emotionally powerful arguments about the dangers of heresy and interwove them with their doctrinal defenses.

They defended the church first on the grounds of tradition and authority and told their audiences that the only safety lay in following the established church. Surely it was the devil's mischief that caused the "atheist heretics" to dare to challenge fifteen hundred years of church tradition.[16] This argument carried weight in a time when novelty and innovation were generally feared. More important, however, the Catholic preachers built their defense on the powerful idea of the church united in the body of Christ—an idea that we have already seen to have been central to eucharistic devotion. The church was conceived as an organic unity, with each part necessary to the whole. It was likened to a human body with Christ as its head and the Holy Ghost as its soul.[17] Just as the human body is only recognized as healthy when all of its parts or members are in "mutual sympathy," so the church is healthy only when its members are joined by brotherly love. Hatred and division among Christians, the inevitable products of heresy, consequently represent a rupture of the body of Christ, "which should remain whole on the trunk of the cross."[18] By extension of the corporeal metaphor, heresy is a cancer or gangrene that has to be rooted out.[19] Pierre Dyvolé, for example, employed this metaphor in one of his sermons on the Mass, when he likened sin to disease, which had to be cured by the "medicine" of the priests and the sacraments, and explained that, more serious than other sins, heresy was like a cancerous limb that had to be amputated in order for the rest of the body to be saved.[20]

The corporeal metaphor was not a new weapon in the French battle against the Protestant heresy. Indeed, we have already seen it employed by François I in his speech to Parisian magistrates following the procession against heresy in 1535.[21] What was new in the period between 1557 and 1572 is the frequency with which the metaphor occurs; it became one of the commonplaces of religious polemic. Equally important, it became particularly insidious in this period of increasing religious tension because it could be extended to justify annihilation of the Huguenots in the name of the common good.

Describing the Protestants in Biblical terms as "wild boars" loose in God's vineyard, or as "ravishing wolves" about to devour God's flock, the Catholic preachers warned their audiences that their own safety and salvation were in jeopardy if they continued to tolerate the heretics' presence.[22] The spread of heresy is a sign of God's anger and a warning of his impending judgment, for does not the Bible warn us that "iniquity and error will abound" and that this will be one of the signs that the last days are upon us?[23] But even where the language is not overtly apocalyptic, the conviction of God's anger pervades these sermons and treaties. The schism of the church and civil wars were signs of this anger; so were the natural calamities—the visitations of plague, extremes of climate, wretched harvests, and dearth—that Paris suffered in the 1560s.[24] Writing in 1565, René Benoist described the earth as "sick and almost dead"; it was not producing as it usually did, nor were the streams yielding up as much fish. The air had lost its sweetness and the sun its warmth; the trees were bare of fruit. Insects and other foul beasts covered the earth and filled the skies, while "men of all estates seemed to languish rather than to live":

> In short, it seems that, wanting to punish us, the eternal God, who is our only hope, has turned all of his creatures against man, whom they were created rather

to serve. But this is done in full justice, so that man, misunderstanding and irritating the Lord who created him, by his glory shall be punished by the things that were created and ordered for man's service and profit.[25]

Benoist warned his readers to amend their lives and change their hearts. Even more strongly, he warned them to flee the corruptions of the new doctrine and to chase out the "infidels," "atheists," and "libertines" who were destroying the unity of the church.[26]

The little pamphlet Benoist wrote about the cross of Gastines affair at the end of 1571 delivers the same message of repentance in explicitly apocalyptic terms. God is angry with us, insists Benoist. What could be a clearer sign of God's anger and our impending ruin than that he should allow the cross, the special sign and mark of Christ's protection, to be taken from us?[27] Investing the cross of Gastines with the full weight of the redeeming passion symbolized by Christ's death on the cross, Benoist encouraged his audience to imagine that removal of the cross would trigger divine vengeance and damnation. In doing so, he inevitably raised the stakes involved in defending the cross and helped incite his audience to sedition.

At least this was the view of Parlement, which reprimanded the curé of Saint-Eustache for having by his pamphlet stirred up popular emotions.[28] Benoist, of course, denied having any such intention and insisted that his sole purpose was to urge the people to repentance, to turn away the wrath of God by changing people's consciences. And it is true that he explicitly says that Parisians should take up the "arms of tears and prayer," for they will not be delivered from God's wrath by any human means.[29] The pamphlet nonetheless conveys a message that is ambiguous if not downright seditious when Benoist insinuates that the French king and magistrates have failed in their obligation to defend their holy religion, and suggests that, when society's leaders are guilty of such failures, God sometimes uses the common people as the agents of his vengeance. He puts "force in the heart and stones in the hands of the rude and imbecilic people as executors of his just sentence."[30] Were these words intended as prophecy or as provocation?

If Benoist employs ambiguous language in the cross of Gastines pamphlet, it is because he had learned from previous reprimands just how far he dared to go in stirring up popular emotions. He could get away with much more direct incitements to violence when France was at war with the Huguenots—and when his attack on the heretics did not imply a criticism of the crown. In a treatise written in August 1562 and republished at the time of the third religious war, Benoist invokes a series of Old Testament scenes in which God "animated the people to kill the false prophets without sparing a single one, thereby teaching us how grievously and without mercy the obstinate heretics should be punished and exterminated."[31] He cites Moses's instructions to the Levites to buckle on their swords and go from door to door, and "each one of you kill his brother, his friend, and his kin." Benoist does not fail to mention that, when the Levites returned from their bloody mission, Moses gave them a benediction and told them that they had consecrated their hands to God.[32] Dedicating his work to King Charles IX, Benoist also included an implicit warning in the example of King Ahab, who allowed his country to be given over to idolatry until his people rose up to overturn the idols, but the intent of the piece was not to threaten the young king but rather to enlist his aid in the holy war. Benoist concluded with the corporeal metaphor, addressing the king directly and telling him that he need not fear "to remove and destroy the corrupt elements [*humeurs*] in order to cure the body of [his] kingdom." Heresy is a "pernicious and contagious cancer" for which there is no remedy but the knife.[33]

There are other messages in these sermons and treatises. The political implications in particular deserve further discussion. This can be done most effectively by turning to the more detailed examination of one man's work. The individual who immediately suggests himself for this examination is Simon Vigor, the radical curé of Saint-Paul's parish in the Marais. More than 140 of Vigor's Paris sermons have been collected and published, by far the largest body of writing for this period from any of the Parisian clergy.[34] Published under innocuous titles that conceal their political content and their polemical intent, Vigor's sermons are a much neglected source and provide valuable insights into the tenor of popular Catholicism in the Paris of the late 1560s and early 1570s.

A Radical Preacher: Simon Vigor

Simon Vigor was perhaps the most famous preacher in Paris during the 1560s. Besides serving his own parish of Saint-Paul, he was a frequent guest at the pulpit of other Parisian churches and in other cities of northern France. He delivered the sermon for such important civic occasions as the procession of the relics of Saint Geneviève to implore an end to drought in 1567, the solemnities at Notre-Dame for the death of Elisabeth de Valois in 1568, and the celebration in the same cathedral of the victory of Moncontour in 1569.[35] In 1566, along with Claude de Sainctes, he engaged in an important theological dispute against the Protestant ministers Jean de L'Espine and Hugues Sureau Du Rosier.[36] The popular influence of his preaching was such that at least one accused Huguenot sought to refute the charge of heresy by earnestly swearing to the judges of Parlement he had regularly attended Vigor's sermons.[37] Simon Vigor preached to the king and court as well as to the Parisian populace and bourgeoisie; in 1568 he was one of four clerics named as *prédicateur du roi*.[38] He was also chosen to preach the sermon for the mass that climaxed the elaborate procession against heresy held to mark the opening of the third religious war.[39] He left Paris sometime in 1572 to take up a new position as archbishop of Narbonne, where it was hoped that he would instill a new energy in a Catholic church sorely diminished by Huguenot victories. He died in Narbonne in 1575.[40]

Contemporary observers make frequent mention of Vigor's outspoken and provocative sermons. He was a favorite target for Huguenot satirists, though they found little about him that was amusing and, indeed, were profoundly threatened by his ability to stir public sentiment against the new faith.[41] One Parisian minister, in a letter to Theodore Beza written early in 1567, characterized Vigor as "a true bellows of Satan" and blamed the renewal of persecution that the church was then experiencing in the capital on the impact of a sermon Vigor had preached before the king.[42] Catholic writers also attribute to Vigor an influential role in political events, but they indicate further that his relationship with the monarchy was an ambivalent one. The Huguenots were not the only ones who might be threatened by Vigor's oratory.

Claude Haton first calls our attention to Vigor in December 1561, when he claims that the preacher so scandalized the king's governors by his denunciations of their concilicatory policy toward the Huguenots that they called for his arrest and execution.[43] This was not done, reports Haton, because Vigor's friends convinced him to moderate his attack until the governors' anger had passed. Haton adds, however, that Vigor's example strengthened the will of other preachers and encouraged them to speak out forcefully on the same themes. Vigor also provoked the displeasure of the king and his council early in 1568, when he criticized them for seeking a compromise peace to end the second religious war. According to the English envoy, Sir Henry Norris, Vigor dangerously inflamed popular sentiment against Catherine de Medici, and, when reprimanded for his behavior by the cardinal of Bourbon, refused to take back a word of what he had said.[44]

Why did Charles IX name Vigor as *prédicateur du roi* less than four months after the cleric was reprimanded for speaking out against royal policy? I suspect that the king hoped by his patronage to co-opt Vigor and the three other radical preachers named to his service. If this was his intention, he underestimated the wily curé of Saint-Paul, who, while extremely critical of the king's advisers, was careful never to criticize the king himself. Rather, Vigor praised the monarch and built up his role as defender of the faith. One can sometimes detect irony in this praise, as for example in February 1568, when, in the words of Sir Henry Norris, Vigor "fell in commendation of the king's virtue and constancy, who being counselled, served, and guarded by Huguenots, yet continued Catholic."[45] More insidious than Vigor's irony, however, was the double-edged sword that he placed in the hands of the king. If the king did not use this sword against the Huguenots, it might in the end be turned against him. Let us look more closely at the logic of sedition that emerges from Simon Vigor's sermons.

Through all the sermons runs a single argument that irrevocably binds up religious truth with political behavior. The argument rests on the familiar premise that heresy threatens not just individual salvation but the entire social order. God will punish those who deviate from his teachings or allow such deviations to take place, and his punishment will be collective as well as individual. Invoking the evil of the times as a sign of God's punishment for sin, Vigor argued that to be restored to God's grace it was necessary to cast out the putrid infection of heresy. It was the king's responsibility to see that this was done.

Like other preachers at the time, Vigor thus employed the corporeal metaphor to justify the elimination of heresy.[46] Like other preachers at the time, he interpreted France's afflictions as manifestations of God's wrath. Natural disasters that destroyed the crops in the field, the birth of misshapen monsters, and the spread of heresy itself were signs of God's displeasure and warnings to return to true devotion. When a heavy rain began to pour down upon the procession that had been organized to invoke an end to the cruel drought of 1567, Vigor seized upon this phenomenon as evidence that God does indeed answer the prayers of true believers.[47] He also built upon familiar themes when he used the story of Ahab to underscore the king's responsibility for ridding his kingdom of heresy.[48] We have seen how René Benoist used the same story to warn Charles IX against heresy, but in fact the story of Ahab was already used during the lifetime of Henri II to express the need for the king to rid his kingdom of false gods.[49] Vigor further developed the theme in a sermon in which he praised Josiah, Hezekiah, and David as kings who had purged their kingdoms of heretics. This sermon was preached in the presence of Charles IX.[50]

If Simon Vigor's sermons were especially popular, it was not for the originality of the arguments on which they were founded but rather for the eloquence with which they were preached. Vigor's rhetorical technique was simple but effective. Typically, he began his sermons with a specific text, a bit of dogma, or a comment on the life of the saint whose day was being celebrated. He built from this material a broader statement of Catholic belief or morality, which he presented in such a fashion that its truth appeared self-evident. Only then did he insert the ideas of heresy and political mismanagement. Deploring the terrible violation of the selected principle of belief or morality by those devoted to destroying the word of God, he turned his sermon into a polemic against the Huguenots and against those who tolerated their presence in the kingdom.

Thus, for example, during his last Lent in Paris (which was almost certainly 1572), Vigor began his Ash Wednesday sermon by explaining why it was good to fast. Attacking as hypocrites those who only pretended to fast, he went on to expound upon hypocrisy in general. Hypocrites, he explained, hid their evil under the pretense of doing good. He illustrated this principle with a series of examples: hypocrites allowed soldiers to pillage the poor people and claimed they were defending the public good; they made wicked edicts and hid them under pretty titles like "Edict of Pacification"; they created judgeships in order to make money and claimed it was for the administration of justice. The Huguenots were hypocrites for betraying the king at Meaux; their doctrine was hypocritical in its deceitful pretense of truth. In this manner, Vigor moved from fasting to hypocrisy to a kaleidoscopic political attack.[51]

In a similar fashion, Vigor used the invitation to preach a sermon at Notre-Dame in celebration of the victory of Lepanto to comment on events in Paris in the fall of 1571. Explaining how the defeat of the Turks was a victory against the heretics, Vigor went on to express his regret that, because of the troubles at home, France had not taken part in this great Christian victory. The subject of Christian victory led to an explanation of how Christians had always erected monuments to perpetuate the memory of their triumphs, and this in turn led Vigor to deplore the fact that no monuments had been built to commemorate France's recent victories at Dreux, Saint-Denis, and Moncontour. Worse still, in his opinion, was the idea that, now that peace was made, Catholic victories over the heretics should be forgotten. This showed an ingratitude toward God that would surely be avenged.[52]

Vigor's audience did not need to be told that the real subject of his discourse was one particular monument, the cross of Gastines, or that his real object was to encourage resistance to the king's orders that the monument be torn down in compliance with the Peace of Saint-Germain. "They talk of removing the cross," said Vigor, in his first direct reference to the monument, "because it is a mark of ignominy and a memorial of the wars and past troubles."[53] This, in Vigor's opinion, showed the falseness of the Huguenots' religion. Instead of being ashamed of the cross and demanding that it be destroyed, the Huguenots should have honored it as a memorial to the three martyrs whose deaths it commemorated. The Catholics, Vigor inferred, had an even better reason for insisting that the cross be maintained, for to allow it to be uprooted now would cut short the praise of God, diminish his glory, and provoke his wrath.

By the time Vigor delivered this sermon on 4 November 1571, Parisian officials, claiming to fear popular unrest, had already delayed for more than a year the removal of the cross of Gastines ordered by the edict of pacification of August 1570. The king was becoming impatient with the Parisians' resistance, and tensions were beginning to grow. Vigor's sermon, with its prediction that God would punish those who permitted his monuments to be despoiled, encouraged the spirit of defiance that culminated in the riots that broke out in December 1571, after city officials finally gave in to Charles IX's demands and had the cross removed.

The sermon of 4 November was not Vigor's only intervention into the affair of the cross of Gastines. Jean de La Fosse tells us that Vigor's first Advent sermon for 1571 earned him a reprimand from Parlement because he preached that the Parisians' objections to removal of the cross were a sign of their zeal toward God. Denying that he had any intention of moving the people to disobey their king, Vigor nonetheless insisted that he, like the Parisian populace, could not believe that the king himself wanted the monument torn down.[54] Vigor adopted here the traditional ruse of feigning to believe that the king was badly advised or poorly informed by his ministers, so that the monarch's own just nature would not appear to be called into doubt.

In addition to opposing the removal of the cross in his sermons, Vigor was one of three delegates from the Paris chapter who went before first the maréchal de Montmorency, as governor for Paris, and then before the king himself to plead for the cross to be left in place. Charles IX took advantage of the delegation to send a general reprimand to the Parisian clergy, which he characterized as "seditious."[55] Parlement also summoned a group of local preachers to reprove them for having spoken against the king and magistrates when they should instead have been calming the populace.[56] The other clerics defended themselves as Vigor had done, by denying any intent of sedition.[57] It is easy to see, however, that popular reaction to the preaching, which encouraged the Parisians to oppose the removal of the monument, was rather less benign.

Many of Simon Vigor's other sermons reveal the same challenge to authority veiled by a superficial diction of obedience to the king. Vigor spoke out against official policy on several crucial issues related to the wars. He vehemently opposed all attempts at conciliatory policy with regard to the Huguenots. In a sermon preached at Saint-Gervais, he called the most recent edict of pacification an "edict of troubles" and declared it the work of the devil.[58] He warned his listeners to have nothing to do with the heretics who returned to the capital after the peace; they should not mix with the Huguenots socially, even if they were members of the same family—"*fust ce pere ou mere*"—or do any business together. They should not even take their final rest in a common burial ground. In one sermon, moreover, Vigor insisted that landlords who rented houses to the heretics should be excommunicated.[59] Vigor's words directly contradicted the king's orders to allow the Huguenots to return after the peace to their homes and work. They fueled the disorders that plagued the capital in the wake of each war.

In a sermon preached shortly after the Peace of Saint-Germain, Vigor went still further. He warned the Parisians not to allow the Huguenots to return to their city. Insisting that it was impossible for Catholics and Huguenots to live peacefully together, he predicted that the Huguenots, to whose advantage the recent peace had been made, would not in fact rest until they had destroyed the whole kingdom. He identified Paris as both the source of the Huguenot heresy and the true aim of the Huguenots' most malicious designs. Entwining as usual the themes of the sinfulness of contemporary society and the dangers of Huguenot devilry, Vigor called upon the Parisians to "keep a close watch over their city and a close watch over their sins." He warned them not to put down their weapons at the same time that he counseled them to pray.[60] Another sermon, preached about two months after the Peace of Saint-Germain, argues similarly that, if the Huguenots are allowed to return to their homes, "in the end they will kill you, either by poison, or by some other means."[61]

Vigor's conviction that the wars must go on until one side or the other lost irremediably explains the joy with which he greeted the start of the third civil war. In a sermon preached at Notre-Dame following the elaborate procession that consecrated the opening of the third religious war, Vigor celebrated the abolition of the hated edict of pacification, the dismissal of Chancellor Michel de L'Hôpital (whom he identified as the man who "put the knife into the hands of our enemies"), and the revocation of the offices of all Protestant magistrates. He also registered approval for the king's order that any Protestant ministers who did not leave the kingdom within a specified interval might be killed on sight.[62]

Vigor's favorable view of this brutal command derived from his conviction that forcible conversion or extermination were the only real solutions to the problem of heresy. He had not, he explained in a sermon of 1572, always felt this way. Once he had believed it possible to use reason to induce the heretics to return to the true faith, but now he was convinced that such efforts were a waste of time. The king should, he insisted, annul "the damnable edict that allows [the Huguenots] freedom of conscience, and constrain [them] to return to the Catholic church by depriving them of their properties and reinstituting the punishment of execution by burning." This was the only way to keep others from being contaminated by their crime.[63]

Vigor was careful not to tell the Parisian populace to go out themselves and kill the Huguenots ("I am not saying this to sound the tocsin against them, nor to animate you to take up arms").[64] He counseled his listeners instead to pray that God "exterminate" the heretics or punish them "by a bitter death."[65] Accused of being cruel and bloodthirsty, Vigor replied by referring to the New Testament (Galatians 5:12: "I would they were even cut off which trouble you") and the Old (Deuteronomy 13:10: "And thou shalt stone him with stones that he die; because he hath sought to thrust thee away from the Lord thy God"). In Vigor's opinion, any sin that disturbed the public order was punishable by death, and heretics, as the most seditious of all criminals, were the most deserving of death.[66]

It was the link with sedition that made the extermination of heretics the responsibility of the king. The church did not have the temporal power to punish the heretics by death, though it could and should do worse by excommunicating them and turning them over to Satan. It was rather the king, the "minister and executor of God's justice," who had been given the sword to wield against the heretics.[67] The religious wars were consequently not only licit but necessary. In a sermon preached during the third war, Vigor explained that it was a very bad thing for a king to fail in his duty to wage war against the rebels. He argued, moreover, that the king had no right to pardon the heretics, and that if he did so, "it was to be feared that God would take his kingdom from him."[68] Here we feel the second cutting edge of the sword Vigor placed in the hands of the king: If the monarch failed to exterminate the heretics, he was unworthy of his office and deserved to lose his crown. In this way, Vigor sowed seeds of doubt that grew to be harvested during the League.

Vigor may also have nurtured some seeds that grew to a more rapid maturity. During his last Lent in Paris, which all evidence puts at 1572, he preached a sermon in which, citing Saint Augustine, he argued that it was permitted to kill oneself only on the commandment of the king, but that, the moment the king gave this order, it was sinful not to obey it. To illustrate his argument, however, he gave an example of murder, not suicide. He said that "if the king ordered the Admiral [Coligny] killed, it would be wicked not to kill him."[69] With these words, the most popular preacher in Paris legitimized in advance the events of Saint Bartholomew's Day.

A final aspect of Vigor's sermons that deserves to be mentioned is his repeated attack on social elites. Vigor frequently remarked to his listeners that he saw only common people—"*petits*"—in his audience. Only they were faithful in their religious duties, attending mass in their parish churches and taking part in religious processions. It was the people of high social status—"*les grands*"—who had been drawn to heretical doctrines, and "if the simple folk had not maintained their religion better than the great, all of France would have become heretical."[70] In the fall of 1568, Vigor singled out the magistrates of Parlement for the prevalence of heresy among them and named this as one of the greatest causes of France's current misfortunes.[71] He also condemned the nobility for being unwilling to fight against the heretics because they had uncles, nephews, and brothers on the other side. Praising spiritual kinship as the only kind that should be valued, Vigor told those who were reluctant to make war that they "had no religion" and predicted that "one day God will have his vengeance, and will permit this bastard nobility to be overrun by the populace [*commune*]." "I am not telling anyone to do this," he hastened to add, "but that God will permit it." He went on to urge that persons unwilling to fight be deprived of their property to the benefit of those more willing to perform this duty.[72] Stopping short of a direct call to sedition, Vigor nonetheless spoke words that must inevitably have exacerbated social tensions already present in the city and undermined the traditional respect on which the magistracy rested its authority.

Even the Catholic clergy did not escape Vigor's criticism. He attacked nonresident churchmen as "thieves" and bishops who did not preach as "idols," and he criticized the tendency to name rich noblemen to episcopal office instead of choosing bishops for their learning and spiritual qualities and for the good example of their lives.[73] Vigor attributed the spread of heresy to the failures of the Catholic clergy, and he called for real reforms, but his anger was directed against the higher clergy in particular. The Catholic bishops had failed to tend the vine, he said, in an allusion to Psalm 80, and the "wild beasts of Geneva" had entered the vineyard.[74] In another sermon, Vigor explicitly blamed the bishops for all the ills from which France was suffering: "For if they had opposed the heresies, and had said to the king, 'No, we would sooner have our heads cut off than permit [heretical] preaching in our bishoprics,' we would not have a single heretic."[75]

It may seem ironic that the day before he delivered this scathing criticism of the French bishops, Vigor had publicly proclaimed the superiority of religious over temporal authority and defended the right of these same bishops to scrutinize the edicts of the king, but there is no necessary contradiction here.[76] Vigor subscribed fully to the Catholic belief that the human failings of the individual holding church office do not invalidate the sacred character of the office itself. The personal weakness of the French bishops did not alter the fact that the special character of the priesthood gave them the right and responsibility to reprove sin wherever they found it—including the edicts of the king. Indeed, Vigor claimed this right not just for bishops but for the entire priesthood, and it was on this basis that he defended his own audacious statements on political affairs. Refusing to submit to an order of the king's council that forbade preaching on "matters of state," Vigor addressed the king and his council over the heads of his assembled parishioners to announce firmly that "because it is our function to reprove sin, we must speak on matters of state when you offend in them. And if you make evil laws, we will cry out against them."[77]

The French civil wars were wars of deeds, not wars of words. And yet it required words to mobilize the masses to those crucial interventions that on more than one occasion altered the larger course of events. These events stand out in clearer relief if we understand that Parisians were receiving from their parish pulpits the message of Simon Vigor and his brethren. They were being taught not only to hate passionately the heretics that disturbed the peace of the kingdom, but also to question the social hierarchy, the magistracy, and even the monarchy that allowed heresy to persist. Radical preachers like Simon Vigor placed their duty to God's truth above their duty of obedience to the king. Their defiant spirit as well as their words urged their listeners to action. The preachers insisted that they made no call to sedition, but there can be little doubt that this was in fact the message their faithful audience received.

10

The War in the Streets

"One king, one law, one faith." Engraved over the entrance to the Hôtel de Ville, this motto proclaimed the traditional values of the Parisian bourgeoisie. The same triad—one is tempted to say trinity—appears in a royal device that depicts Justicia and Pietas as the twin pillars of monarchy. Particularly favored by Charles IX, this emblem was chosen by city officers to serve as the decorative theme for the visit the king made to the Hôtel de Ville upon the publication of the Peace of Saint-Germain in August 1570. Standing on either side of the main entrance to the city hall, Piety and Justice were personified as beautiful women bearing palm branches and trampling the weapons of war beneath their feet. The iconographic meaning of the decorations was intended to please the king but it profoundly irritated the Parisian people, who wanted to see the sword raised high in the hand of Justice and not trampled under her feet.[1]

The people would have been happier with the iconographic program that Etienne Jodelle adopted when he used the same emblem of Piety and Justice as the basis for a series of sculptures and inscriptions intended to decorate the pyramid of the cross of Gastines. His designs called for placing the twin figures at alternate corners of the pyramid's base, with Piety raising a torch to the cross that topped the monument and Justice raising a sword.[2] This project was never realized because of the order to remove the pyramid, but the contrast between Jodelle's depiction of Justice and that offered by the city's officers symbolizes well the growing distance between Catholic extremists, for whom heresy was the primary danger, and Catholic moderates, for whom the threat of heresy had gradually come to take second place to the threat of anarchy. As the extremists became more firmly convinced that only forced conversion or extermination of the heretics would restore the unity necessary to society, the moderates gradually emerged as champions of public order as the first priority. Remembering that in many minds both tendencies still fought for domination, we can nevertheless identify behind this divergence of opinion two different images of the Christian commonwealth, one founded on religious solidarity, the other rooted in respect for the law.

The story of this widening division is the subject of this chapter, which traces the growth of a rebellious and radical faction within the Paris militia during the first decade of the religious wars and the alienation of this faction from the magistracy—a term I use to encompass the higher officers of the Parlement, the Châtelet, and the Hôtel de Ville—responsible for the maintenance of order in the capital. I will focus on the period that begins with the outbreak of war in the spring of 1562. It is important to remember, however, that many people's opinions about how best to deal with the problem of heresy were only too firmly set by the time that the first armies took to the field. This is shown, for example, by the widespread opposition to the edict of January 1562, which granted limited toleration to followers of the new religion. If we compare the formal protests that were made to the edict of January, we find that some were more strongly worded than others— the manifesto of the Parisian merchants, who threatened to pack up and leave the kingdom rather than to allow the worship of the new religion in their city, is decidedly more emphatic than the remonstrances of Parlement—and we might even at this early stage in the conflicts claim to distinguish between moderate and radical Catholic opinion.[3] Such a distinction would, however, be premature. If there were already in 1562 certain shades of difference in the force with which Parisian Catholics opposed the new religion, it was the experience of civil war that effected the true polarization of opinion and divided Catholics into moderates and radicals. Let us turn, then, to that wartime experience.

The Civic Guard and Catholic Militance

I begin by noting with Denis Richet that from its very origin the function of the Paris militia was ambiguous. Created during the tumultuous weeks that followed the massacre of Vassy, the civic guard was intended, in Richet's words, "both to seek out and arrest suspected heretics and to maintain order against the savage violence of the Catholics."[4] This ambiguity reflects a disparity between the way the militia saw itself and the function that the authorizing magistrates intended for it.

The initiative for the creation of the militia came from some of the more radical citizens of Paris and not from the city's officers. Reacting to the highly charged atmosphere that followed the Huguenots' seizure of Orleans during the first week of April 1562, a group of Parisian merchants and bourgeois had presented the king a petition for the election of captains to oversee the defense of the town. Convinced that Paris was a prime target for Condé's armies and that he already had agents within the walls, they asked as well for permission to undertake a house-to-house search for armed strangers and illicit arms brought in by the Huguenots, "who wanted nothing more than to pillage such a city."[5] The king's council, approving the petitions on 2 May, sent them on to the prévôt des marchands and échevins, who accepted them only after chiding the citizens for taking their requests to the king instead of the municipality. At the same time, the prévôt des marchands and échevins attempted to ensure their own authority over the new captains by explicitly stating this principle of obedience. Search procedures were confided to the quarteniers, who were to be assisted by four "cautious and peaceable" bourgeois.[6] Parlement, which because of its administrative responsibilities in the capital had also to pass on the measures, echoed the caution of the prévôt des marchands and appealed to the need to preserve royal authority and public tranquility.[7] From the outset, then, it appears that the idea of hunting down religious suspects was foremost in the minds of the men who demanded the creation of the civic guard, while the need to preserve order already figured prominently in the thoughts of the city's magistrates.

It was only in July that the militia was officially ordered to assume responsibility for repressing Catholic as well as Protestant violence. The command was given in the context of the continuing deterioration of public order. Tensions had not diminished but rather had grown with the election of captains and the arming of the citizens. The first military parades of the newly formed civic guard coincided with the religious festivities of the Corpus Christi season, when enthusiastic crowds listened to the cardinal of Lorraine preach that it was better to die than to allow another religion to be established in the kingdom. During the month that followed, Catholic Parisians further inflamed their religious hatreds by attending public rebaptisms at Saint-Germain-l'Auxerrois, book burnings in the university quarter, and an elaborate procession for the reconsecration of the church of Saint-Médard.[8]

Meanwhile, the captains began to take practical steps to rid the city of internal enemies. On 27 May, they were ordered to draw up lists of suspected Huguenots. All who refused to sign a profession of Catholic faith were ordered to leave the city.[9] The Huguenot departures did not, however, bring peace, and by early July violent incidents and rioting became so common that special orders had to be given for the repression of sedition. On 4 July, Parlement ordered the militia officers to assist the lieutenants of the Châtelet in putting a stop to the popular violence. On 22 July, the king's lieutenant for Paris directed the militia to establish a daily guard of twelve men in each quartier to ensure that orders forbidding violence against suspected Huguenots were strictly obeyed.[10]

The militia was not, however, an unqualified success as a peacekeeping force. Numerous examples can be cited to show that at least some members of the civic guard were more diligent about hunting heretics than they were about repressing Catholic disorder. The captains of one quartier were reprimanded for failing to rescue two men thrown in the river by an angry crowd.[11] The captain of the faubourg Saint-Denis was accused of deliberately turning a woman prisoner over to a mob, which killed her and dragged her naked corpse through the streets of the city. The woman's husband claimed the captain had permitted the mob this act of vengeance because he (the husband) had refused to pay the bribe the captain demanded.[12]

Surviving evidence does not allow us to judge the truth of this accusation. Although it is almost certain that some captains did profit from their positions through extortion and even theft, the deliberate flaunting of authority would seem to have been a more fundamental characteristic of their behavior than the desire for financial gain. Entrusted with the lists of religious suspects for their dizaines, the captains enjoyed tremendous power. They had the right to go into the houses of their neighbors to search for strangers, weapons, and contraband; they had the power to give—or to withhold—the vital certificate of good behavior that allowed people to move freely about the city; and, of course, they had the authority to arrest and incarcerate religious suspects.[13]

Judicial records suggest that these powers were not infrequently abused. Thrown unceremoniously into the damp cells of the Conciergerie, some prisoners were held for months without communication with family or friends and without formal charges being filed against them.[14] In some cases the captains never were able to produce charges, as happened to Nicolas Richier, who was held for more than two months before the arresting officer acknowledged that he had no evidence against him.[15] Released suspects often had difficulty securing the return of confiscated properties, and Parlement had to issue many orders forbidding the harassment of former prisoners.[16]

Judicial records provide several additional insights into the character of the militia. Most important, they disclose that a small minority of the militia officers were responsible for a very large share of the arrests. During the second and third wars, for which we have more extensive records than for the first, it appears that a few militia officers roamed the city in search of suspects on an almost daily basis, while others took their occasional turn in the rotation of the nightwatch or the guarding of city gates but seldom or never were actually responsible for arrests. Together, just four men accounted for over 40 percent of the 572 persons booked into the Conciergerie for religious crimes between October 1567 and October 1572. Ensign Thomas Croizier alone took part in more than one hundred arrests, and Captain Nicolas Pezou more than eighty—this at a time when there were approximately a hundred and thirty captains and a like number of ensigns.[17]

Moreover, the same names always seem to turn up in connection with the most politically charged arrests. Croizier, for example was responsible for the arrest of Nicolas Croquet and Philippe and Richard de Gastines.[18] Pezou could take credit for Jean de Bordes, receveur général de Limoges, arrested in the courtyard of the Palais de Justice on the charge of "communicating false memoirs in favor of the rebels."[19] He was also in on the arrest of Simon Le Comte, an agent of the Canaye family suspected of channeling funds to the prince of Condé.[20]

The most active members of the militia were seldom notables prominent in the affairs of the city and the state.[21] During each of the wars, the Bureau de la ville received complaints that the "principaulx bourgeois" were refusing to take their turns at the watch, and on at least one occasion the officers of the king were especially singled out for the bad example they set by their dereliction of duty. In July 1563, Captain Grandrue, himself a maître des comptes, reported that the inhabitants of his dizaine refused to continue serving guard duty until the "principal officers of the king and bourgeois" were ordered to take their turn.[22] The officers of the Bureau de la ville and Parlement concurred with these complaints and issued repeated orders for bourgeois citizens to serve personally their appointed watches. The magistrates were not motivated in this by a sense of fair play; they believed that a strong bourgeois presence within the militia would hold in check the turbulence of the artisans who made up the bulk of the city's forces. They counted on the social elite to prevent the disorders that repeatedly occurred among the guardsmen.

The reluctance of the "bonne bourgeoisie" to take a regular part in the activities of the city guard left the militia in the hands of its more radical members and increased the tendency to place Catholic militance before public order. Already in the fall of 1562 the militant core of the civic guard had so identified itself with the Catholic cause that a group of militia captains was willing to challenge the religious orthodoxy of the highest magistrates of the sovereign courts. Insisting that parlementaires were known to have attended clandestine services, the captains demanded that these men be deprived of their offices and forced to leave the city. The people were scandalized, they asserted, that so many "rebels" had still not been brought to justice.[23]

For the militants, participation in the militia was a religious and not just a civic duty. Marching out to the gates, standing watch on the walls, or hunting out suspected Huguenots, they believed themselves to be engaged in a holy war, and they carefully cultivated the auxiliary demonstrations of faith that would make evident their role as soldiers of Christ. They held religious services in the chapel belonging to the city harquebusiers and participated as a group in Corpus Christi processions and in such special processions as the one held for the reconsecration of Saint-Médard in June 1562 or the one held a month later to expiate a sacrilege committed against a statue of the Virgin at the porte Saint-Honoré.[24] The captains even organized their own processions to Sainte-Geneviève in October 1562 and to Notre-Dame in December of the same year.[25] It is striking, moreover, that Thomas Croizier was invited to join the prestigious confraternity of the bearers of the relics of Saint Geneviève in 1568. Nicolas Pezou joined the same select group in 1570.[26] It appears that they were being rewarded for their Catholic militance. It is unfortunate that we do not have better sources for the study of Parisian confraternities during this period, for more information about these organizations might provide important keys to the character of the radicals' faith, the local bases of their power, and the mechanisms through which this power was exercised. As it stands, we can at most postulate that something in the civic and communal character of their religious practices or in the social ties these practices created set them apart from the city's elites, who, as we know, were accused by Simon Vigor and other radical preachers of a certain lack of fervor in their devotions. We are on surer ground, however, if we leave these speculations aside and return to the political and military behavior of the militia's radicals.

Their incipient conflict with the higher authorities of the city and state began to emerge more clearly in the period that follows the peace made at Amboise in March 1563. As has already been seen, the Peace of Amboise was highly unpopular among Parisians, who demonstrated their opposition in repeated acts of violence. Still needed as a peacekeeping force, the militia was not ordered to disband until late August, by which time it had proved itself more of a hindrance than a help in the pacification effort. During this interval, several events placed an increasing strain on relations between the magistrates and the militia. First, the Corpus Christi processions were marred by two murders. One, the killing of an unknown Huguenot, was little remarked, the other, the murder of a gentleman in the suite of Condé, had important repercussions.

This gentleman, whose name was Couppé, was reportedly set upon by four or five hundred armed Parisians as he accompanied the coach of the princesse de Condé out to Vincennes. The following day, the prévôt des marchands was commanded by the king to bring in the men responsible for Couppé's murder, and that very afternoon two of the city's militia captains, Garnier and Tancré, were arrested and charged.[27] On hearing of the arrests, the other militia captains rushed to the Hôtel de Ville. They warned the prévôt des marchands that the people threatened to riot if Tancré and Garnier were not freed. Aware, no doubt, that he was risking the king's displeasure, the prévôt des marchands succumbed to the pressure and ordered the prisoners freed. At the same time, he resolved to go out personally through the dizaines to inform the city guard of the measures deemed necessary to keep the peace. These measures amounted to a nearly total curfew.[28]

The demand to release Tancré and Garnier may be considered the first act in a power struggle that pitted the radicals in the militia against both the king and the Bureau de la ville in the summer and fall of 1563. A second act occurred in late June, when a crowd tore down the body of an executed criminal—a Huguenot condemned for theft, not religion—and, beating it with sticks, dragged it to the Seine. The prévôt des marchands and échevins, who happened to be meeting in a room overlooking the place de Grève, where the action took place, rushed out to intervene. Forcing the people to yield up the mutilated corpse, they arrested two men and four youths and dispersed the crowd.[29] Two days later, the men were summarily judged and sentenced to be hanged. On their way to be executed, however, the men were freed by a mob, which stoned the guards and loosened the prisoners' bonds. In reaction, the city ordered an inquest and fined the militiamen and guards whose negligence was deemed responsible for the incident.[30]

These events left a bitter residue of mutual distrust between the city's highest officers and the more radical members of the citizenry. On 2 July, the city authorized the creation of a special guard to accompany the prévôt de marchands and échevins on their rounds of the city.[31] The authorization, however, came too late, or else the city officers underestimated the force of popular discontent, for just a week later, on 9 July, two échevins, Henri Ladvocat and Claude Le Prestre, were attacked by an unruly crowd as they went out to inspect the guard at the porte Saint-Antoine. The three men charged with inciting this riot were members of the militia and were on duty at the time of the incident. Witnesses testified that the guardsmen had provoked the riot by telling the people that the échevins had come to save the Huguenots, who should be killed and not saved. Taking up the cry of "kill the Huguenots," the crowd, some of whose members were armed, had turned upon the échevins as if they were themselves members of the hated sect. Eventually the militia officers intervened to help rescue the échevins from the violence their own members had provoked.[32]

The refusal of the militiamen to relax their militant anti-Protestantism in the wake of the Peace of Amboise was, however, the most profound source of the tension between the officers of the Hôtel de Ville and the officers of the civic guard.[33] The conflict over disarmament began with a symbolic issue, when, in mid-July, the king and queen mother ordered that the captains responsible for guarding the city gates should no longer parade out to their guard posts with beating drums and flying standards. The king and his mother hoped to reduce tensions in the capital by eliminating the emotion associated with the daily military parades. A number of the captains, however, chose to defy the king's order, which was conveyed to them by their quarteniers on 19 July.[34] The ensign for Captain Desprez not only flew the company's flag over the porte Saint-Jacques, but he also marched his men back through the heart of the city in a procession led by two bagpipers.[35] Qualifying this act as one of deliberate "derision and mockery," the prévôt des marchands tried to reason with the captains, who came en masse to the Hôtel de

Ville to protest against the order. Suspending one captain, who insisted that his men would not march without drums and standards, the prévôt des marchands threatened to send the king the names of anyone who disobeyed the command, but the threat had little effect.[36]

On 11 August, the king warned that if the Parisians continued to flaunt their drums and flags, he would march upon the city with an army that would force their submission to his will.[37] This threat prompted the city officers to redouble their efforts to enforce the king's orders and to attempt to placate him by ensuring him of their good intentions. Inspections were made, and more captains were called to account for their violation of the royal command. Several of the captains explained their disobedience by casting the blame on their men. The officers were ready to obey the king, they reported, but their troops were not. Captain Hugues Theveneau, sent out by the prévôt des marchands to seize the standard his company persisted in flying, reported back his failure. Captain Jean Salvancy relayed his men's insistence that they would abandon their posts before they would consent to take down their flag.[38] For at least some of the militia officers, the spur to radicalism thus came from their subordinates. The captains had to adopt a militant stance in order to retain their leader's role.

The defiant attitude of the Paris militia helped provoke the orders for complete disarmament that were issued upon the king's declaration of his majority at Rouen on 17 August 1563. Charles IX followed up his initial order to lay down arms with a letter informing Paris's city officers of his intention to dismantle the civic guard entirely and to return full responsibility for the nightwatch to the professional troops of the chevalier du guet, whose forces would be increased at city expense. For good measure, the king threatened once again to bring in an army to see that his will was obeyed.[39] During the next several months, city officers attempted to bargain with the king in order to soften this blow.[40] In large measure, the strategy was effective. Charles promised not to bring in his army; but he also reduced by two-thirds the size of the new professional guard, and he permitted the city to keep its citizens' watch, albeit on a much more limited scale. Imposing even these compromise measures on the rebellious militia did not, however, prove an easy task. The prévôt des marchands had to give repeated orders for the surrender of weapons, which were not finally collected until late October.[41]

Through all these negotiations, the city officers can be seen to have acted in defense of the best interests of their fellow citizens. They were, however, forced by their intermediary position to take a stand more conservative than that held by many local residents. Enforcing unpopular orders such as the prohibition on drums and standards and supervising the collection of weapons, they alienated themselves from the members of the community who believed that only a thorough and active repression of the Huguenots could bring about a true end to the religious conflicts. Slowly but surely, a wedge was being driven between the officers of the Hôtel de Ville and the more radical members of the citizenry, including a large part of the civic guard.

During the second and third wars, the wedge was driven in further. When, shortly before the second war, the swell of unrest made additional security measures necessary, the king ordered the creation of a new force of one hundred bourgeois householders in each quartier of the capital. Charles IX showed his lingering distrust of the militia by declaring that officers who had served in the previous troubles were not eligible to command the new forces. When he discovered that, in spite of his orders, six of the sixteen men first named to head the new guard had been captains in 1562–1563, he demanded that they be removed.[42]

The attempt to ensure that cool heads would prevail among the city's peace-keeping forces was abandoned two months later when war broke out on account of the Huguenots' attempt to seize the king at Meaux. On 29 September 1567, Charles IX reestablished the citizen guard as it had existed during the first war. He did not exclude as captains men who had previously served in this capacity but permitted them to be routinely renamed.[43] The only concerns at this point were to rid the city of internal enemies and to stave off a Huguenot attack; for both of these services, militant leadership was highly desirable.

Orders for the guard of the city were relaxed only in small details after the Peace of Longjumeau in March 1568. As after the Peace of Amboise, the militia retained a role that was, in the eyes of some at least, altogether too active. In August 1568, Parlement had to intervene in a quarrel between the militia captains and the commissaires of the Châtelet over the respective jurisdictions of the two peacekeeping forces. Parlement limited the captains to the correction of "military infractions" encountered in their duties as sentinels and in their authorized rounds of the city. "Ordinary justice" was to remain the responsibility of the commissaires, whom the captains were to assist when such aid was requested. The same order specified that the militia officers were subject to the reproval and correction of the commissaires when they exceded the limits of their charge. The burden of the order was thus to keep the militia in line and to prevent its most aggressive members from usurping too much authority.[44]

The success of this order was limited, and when the third war broke out, the radical element in the militia became still more assertive in its role. The third war differed from the second in two important respects. In the first place, the focus of the fighting was away from Paris. Second, the king allowed Huguenots, who had been ordered out of the capital during the first two wars, to remain during the third, as long as they had not previously fought in the rebel army and on condition that they stayed quietly in their houses. This combination of circumstances proved inflammatory. With the danger of rebel attack less acute, many officers of the bourgeois militia became lax about their duties. The militants became still more dominant, and they refused to leave Parisian Protestants in peace.

In November 1568, armed militia officers were found to be organizing book burnings in the streets of the Latin Quarter without the knowledge or permission of the magistrates.[45] In December, the maréchal de Montmorency called the captains to the Louvre to reprove them in the king's name for their "disorders and unaptness to be ruled." He told them that the king had suggested garrisoning four hundred men on the town in order to help keep order, but he trusted that this would not be necessary. According to the English ambassador, the militia officers did not accept this reprimand in silence. The spokesman for the captains replied with a pointed allusion to the city's emblem, saying that "Paris was like a ship, whereof the master neglecting his charge, it is requisite that the pilots do put hand to the helm."[46] The message was clear: if the king did not provide the leadership the radicals wanted, they would themselves take charge.

In January, the captains convinced Parlement to issue stringent new regulations concerning the lodging of Protestants in Paris and its suburbs.[47] This allowed them to step up the pace of arrests and seems to have had as its particular motive the captains' desire to lay their hands on some wealthy Protestants accused of having loaned money to the prince of Condé. The captains may have been correct in their suspicions, since among those caught up in the sweep were the wealthy merchants Jean and Philippe Canaye, whose financial dealings with François de Coligny, sieur d'Andelot, have already been mentioned in another context.[48] Nevertheless, the "extraordinarily bad behavior" of the militiamen (reported by the English ambassador to have arrested forty of Paris's wealthiest Protestants in a very brief period of time) angered the king, who commanded the first president of Parlement to see to it that they made no further arrests without the consent of higher authorities. The king also forbade the captains to assemble unless they were in the presence of his new governor, the duc d'Alençon. Neither of these orders appears to have been enforced.[49] Through most if not all of the third war, the captains met together at least twice a week at the Hôtel de Ville, and many arrests were made on their collective order, that is to say, as a result of suspicions raised at these meetings.[50] They also held special assemblies in their districts for the denunciation of religious suspects.[51]

The credit the captains enjoyed with the Parisian populace gave them an important leverage with Parlement, and one that they did not hesitate to use. On 25 June 1569, they marched on the Palais de Justice to demand the execution of Nicolas Croquet and Richard and Philippe de Gastines. Members of the accompanying crowd are said to have threatened the life of the parlementaire who received them if "justice" was not done in the case, and in fact, although no direct connection can be shown, Croquet and the Gastines were executed (after six months' imprisonment) within the week.[52] In August, the captains used their collective influence to have reinstated one of their members who had been suspended for his unusual cruelty.[53]

The captains appear to have made no protests when the militia was finally disbanded in February 1571, five months after the Peace of Saint-Germain.[54] It is significant, however, that, when riots began in December 1571 over the order to tear down the cross of Gastines, the city officials refused the request of the inhabitants of the most troubled neighborhood to resurrect the militia and put its captains in charge of the peacekeeping efforts. The prévôt des marchands and échevins told the local residents to have their arms ready but to remain in their homes. At the same time, they called out the city's professional troops and garrisoned them at strategic points in the center of town.[55] When the situation worsened a week later, the orders issued by the city were equivocal. The quarteniers were commanded to assemble the bourgeois notables for the purpose of putting an end to the riots, and at least one order explicitly called for the participation of officers from the now disbanded militia, but these men were not given charge of peacekeeping operations, which remained in the hands of the professional troops.[56] On the other hand, when the prévôt des marchands was called to the Louvre late on the night of 23 August

1572 and informed of a Huguenot plot against the king, he was told immediately to call up the "captains, lieutenants, ensigns and bourgeois of the quartiers" and to hold them ready for the king's command.[57] Faced with a Huguenot threat—real or imagined—the militia sprang to life overnight.

Catholic Militants and the Massacre

We cannot know exactly what role the guardsmen played in the events of Saint Bartholomew's Day. Evidence of the popular fury is even more scarce, ambiguous, and contradictory than evidence for the events of the previous two days. I have explained in Chapter 6 why I think it doubtful that the prévôt des marchands gave the militia orders to take part in the killing. It is easy to imagine that some of the extremists among the guardsmen nevertheless seized upon the occasion to give vent to their long-suppressed hatreds and joined the populace in its orgy of murder and pillage, and this indeed seems to have been the case. When the authorities—the king and the prévôt des marchands—called up the militia, they set loose forces they could not contain. They put arms into the hands of angry men and sent them out into a confused situation, where wild rumors abounded and at least some people did have orders to kill. It should not surprise us that some members of the militia came to believe that they too had received such orders.[58]

Protestant accounts of the massacres often include a blanket condemnation of the militia captains for having, as it were, "rolled up their sleeves and bloodied their knives" to encourage their troops. Specific references to members of the militia do not, however, offer much evidence to support this view. Charlotte d'Arbaleste, for example, relates how she was hidden for two days by the captain of one quartier. She claims that he was a brutal man, who tried to convince her to go to mass, and says that she quaked with fear and anger at the sounds of booty being brought into the house. Nonetheless, the captain sheltered her, a kindness that was offered, she explains, because he had married a servant of her mother's. Without belittling the tie of patronage this family connection may have provided, it is hardly likely that Arbaleste would have dared to entrust her life to a man whom she believed had orders to exterminate all Huguenots on sight.[59]

Indeed, in all the narrative sources I have been able to discover, only four militia officers are explicitly named as killers. One, identified by Crespin as the murderer of Richard de Gastines's widow, is only mentioned once, but the other three are readily identifiable as Catholic extremists.[60] Captain colonel Jean Du Perrier, a lawyer in Parlement, named as a murderer by Aubigné and L'Estoile, is the militia officer who was suspended from his functions in June 1569 on the ground of his unusual cruelty. Pierre de L'Estoile brings Du Perrier to our attention again in 1578, when the king had him imprisoned in the château de Loches on suspicion of conspiracy with the Spanish and the duc de Guise.[61] The other two names are ominously familiar: Captain Nicolas Pezou and Ensign Thomas Croizier, the very men responsible for the most arrests during the second and third religious wars, are named by Goulart, de Thou, and Aubigné as having been among the worst of the killers on Saint Bartholomew's Day.

The sources that name Croizier and Pezou are not entirely independent but rather overlap in their common reliance on narrative accounts of the massacre first published by Goulart. Nevertheless, there are enough differences in the specific accusations leveled against the two men to suggest that each of these authors also had access to additional information. All three name Pezou as the militia captain assigned to escort Pierre de La Place to the king and imply that he was responsible for La Place's death at least to the extent that he failed to provide a safe escort for him. De Thou goes farther and explicitly accuses Pezou of betrayal in yielding up La Place to his killers. Aubigné goes even further and accuses him of having wielded the knife that knocked President de La Place from his mule.[62] Goulart and Aubigné both blame Pezou and Croizier for the deaths of a large number of Huguenots who were led off to prison with the understanding that they were being taken there for their safety, but the *Histoire des martyrs* also specifically names Croizier in the deaths of Mathurin Lussault, jeweler to Catherine de Medici, and Jacques Rouillard, a counselor in Parlement and reportedly not even a Huguenot.[63] Jacques-Auguste de Thou repeats the accusation concerning Rouillard and adds the gruesome note that Croizier cut off the parlementaire's head after leaving him for a long time hanging between hope and fear. De Thou includes a personal note here that sets this episode apart from those derived from Goulart and appears to lend it additional veracity. Calling Croizier (mistranslated as "Crucé" in the French edition of the *Histoire*) a "murderer truly deserving of the scaffold," de Thou recalls how he had often heard the man, "raising his arm with an inhuman vanity," boast that "he had killed more than four hundred men with this arm in the carnage [of Saint Bartholomew's Day]."[64]

Can we believe these accounts? Only on a certain level. Each has elements of fantasy, and we need only to compare the versions of Rouillard's death given by Goulart and de Thou to see how willing each of the authors was to twist events to suit his purposes. Goulart name Jacques-Auguste's father, Christophe de Thou, as the instigator of Rouillard's death. Rouillard, Goulart claims, was a man who loved justice, and he was actively pursuing a case of fraud against a fellow counselor in Parlement who was a close friend of President de Thou's. Jacques-Auguste, a loyal son, does not repeat this accusation but proffers instead that Rouillard was a "troubled and quarrelsome man, and an enemy of the commissaires of Paris."[65]

As biased as these sources are, I believe that they do contain elements of truth where the popular massacres are concerned. We cannot trust them on such key events as the midnight meeting in the Louvre, because, as I have already explained, everyone who witnessed those events had cause to lie. Nor can we trust them on the motives the killers might have had in particular instances, as the example just cited shows. But there was less reason to lie about such details as the name of the militia captain charged with escorting President de La Place to the king, and here the narrative accounts seem more reliable. If we disregard the blanket condemnation of the militia, then, and look rather for specific incidents in which its officers were involved, we find that we are not dealing with the militia as a whole but rather with its militant and mutinous core.[66] It is more than a coincidence that the militia officers these sources name as having actively shared in the killing are the very same men who were responsible for the greatest cruelties during previous periods of religious war.

It would further appear from a close reading of even Protestant sources that the highest city officials did not take part in the killing but rather struggled against the forces of disorder. Goulart describes how Jean Le Charron, the prévôt des marchands, visited his fellow president in the Cour des aides Pierre de La Place on the morning of Saint Bartholomew's Day not to arrest him but rather to offer help in barricading his house against the popular onslaught. When Le Charron departed, he left four archers in the house. These men spent the rest of the day and the following night fortifying doorways and blocking up windows with stones. The fact that La Place was ultimately killed cannot be blamed on Le Charron. He was not killed in his own house, after all, but only after he left it in response to a summons from the king.[67]

Even the former prévôt des marchands, Claude Marcel, often accused of having been one of the leaders of the popular massacres, does not seem to merit the vile reputation he has acquired.[68] Goulart describes how, meeting Thoré (the third of the four Montmorency brothers) in the street on the morning of 24 August, Marcel warned him to "take shelter immediately if he valued his life; it wasn't a good day for those of his [the Montmorency] house."[69] Ilja Mieck cites this as an example of Marcel's complicity in the massacres, but it seems to me to have been only sensible advice.[70] It was commonly said that only fear of the maréchal de Montmorency, who had left the city two days before the massacres, kept all four brothers from being included on the list of those who were to be murdered.[71] Whether or not this was true, it is indisputable that, until the storm passed, a member of the Montmorency clan was safer behind locked doors than he was on the streets of Paris.

Mieck also cites a case in which the younger Charles Perier, along with his father and brother, was arrested and brought to Marcel, who, instead of saving them, ordered them taken to prison. Mieck's source here is the *Histoire des martyrs*, which does indeed blame Marcel for Charles Perier's death (the father and brother somehow escaped) and says that the order to take them to the Conciergerie was "a password for throwing them in the river."[72] This last interpolation, however, should not be taken for established fact. It may be true that some prisoners ended in the river instead of jail, but there is no reason to assume that this was what Marcel intended by his order. Many Huguenots were brought to the Conciergerie in the days following the massacre on the assumption that they would be safer there than in their homes. They were forced to recant as the price of their freedom, but they did eventually leave the prison alive.[73] Marcel's order should be taken at face value and not as evidence of complicity in murder. We might also note in Marcel's favor that Jacques-Auguste de Thou recounts one incident in which he did intervene to save a life, that of a daughter of Magdaleine Briçonnet.[74]

In truth, there are some strange inconsistencies in de Thou's account of the events of Saint Bartholomew's Day. Although he follows Goulart closely for most of his description of the midnight meeting attended by Le Charron and Marcel in the Louvre, he places in Marcel's mouth a speech that Goulart attributes to Le Charron, a speech in which the militia captains are apprised of the king's desire for the massacre of the Huguenots and are given their orders for the night. But then, having given Marcel this central role, de Thou says that Marcel was "nonchalant" in executing his own assignment, which was to raise a thousand men to assist Laurens de Maugiron in assassinating the Huguenots quartered outside the walls at Saint-Germain-des-Prés. According to de Thou, Marcel's half-hearted effort explains why Montgomery and other important Huguenot leaders escaped.[75]

If Marcel was a willing participant in—even a leader of—the massacres, why was he so negligent in performing this task? Could it be that Brantôme is right when he says that the city's representatives objected on grounds of conscience to the orders the king gave them during the infamous meeting in the Louvre and that they agreed to cooperate only after having been roundly berated by Tavannes and threatened with hanging?[76] Unfortunately, there is no evidence to confirm this tasty gossip. We must fall back instead on an analysis of de Thou's motives in writing his account of Saint Bartholomew's Day. Here, we might posit the theory that de Thou was trapped into presenting an essentially Protestant version of Saint Bartholomew's Day by his own later position as a Politique rallied to Henri IV. Could de Thou, in a book dedicated to the first Bourbon king, destroy one of the key legends that legitimized the Protestant struggle against the crown—a struggle in which Henri had himself taken part—by revealing that Saint Bartholomew's Day was never intended to exterminate the Huguenots in their entirety, that it was not the pogrom that Protestant propaganda made it out to be? Could he moreover admit to the terrible weakness of constituted authority—the inability to control the urban masses—that had allowed the popular massacre to take place? Better to follow the accepted mythology and affirm the already traditional view that the massacre was the result of a concerted plot on the part of an evil king, his council, and the Catholic leaders of the city of Paris, even if some of the details of the story reveal that this was not entirely the case.[77]

The Lessons of Civil War

In the end, then, de Thou's account, like other narratives of the massacre, is inconclusive and potentially misleading. Instead of trying to piece together a convincing argument about the role of city magistrates from such bits and pieces of dubious evidence, let us return to the larger problem of public order and to the lessons learned from civil war. Having reviewed the respective roles of militiamen and magistrates in the events prior to Saint Bartholomew's Day, we are in a better position to appreciate their reactions to the news of the massacre itself. We can understand, for example, that for many of the militia officers, the wars had offered a new public role and a new status. Marching around the city with flags and drums, manipulating their lists of religious suspects, the militia captains had enjoyed a prestige they had never known before. They not only had had the proud responsibility for keeping the rebels outside the city gates, but they also had felt the satisfaction of sharing in a vital effort to rid their polis of the corruption of heresy and return it to a pristine state. For the magistrates, by contrast, the wars had offered a less positive and more profoundly unsettling experience. They had been constantly reminded of the fragility of civil society and made keenly aware of the narrowing limits of their effective authority. They had seen that the turbulent masses could only too easily escape their attempts at control. The divisions within the militia, its tendency to challenge the constituted authorities, and its unreliability in moments of crisis, had compounded this feeling of insecurity.

Already under strain because of rising prices, difficulties in absorbing a continuing influx of new residents, and an increasingly oligarchical civic authority, the social fabric of Paris was seriously weakened by tensions that divided the Parisian magistrates from the mass of the population during the decade that preceded Saint Bartholomew's Day. Suspicions developed on both sides. On the one hand, the magistates betrayed signs of a class-based fear of an unruly populace. Christophe de Thou betrayed this fear in September 1562, when he warned Parlement that if the Huguenots succeeded in cutting off the capital's food supply, there was a grave danger that the hungry masses would attack their magistrates and fellow citizens.[78] City officials expressed a similar worry during the grain crisis that followed the first religious war.[79] This fear of popular rebellion provoked by economic tensions, a fear common to early modern elites, was seriously aggravated by the political unrest that resulted from the religious crisis.

Parisian magistrates knew that any popular protest—whether it stemmed from the arrest of a favorite preacher, the passing of an unwelcome law, or the removal of a venerated symbol—could quickly turn from its original object to focus instead on the agents responsible for the unpopular act. Witness how quickly the officers of Parlement slammed shut the gates of the Palais de Justice during the riots of the cross of Gastines.[80] Incidents such as the attack on the échevins Claude Le Prestre and Henri Ladvocat taught the magistrates to fear for their personal safety, but most of all they feared that the mask of authority should slip and their true weakness be thereby revealed.

At times this fear resulted in paralysis, a paralysis easily mistaken for deliberate obstructionism, especially when it coincided with the magistrates' known or assumed political stance. Thus, for example, when the officers of Parlement notified the king that they dared not publish the Peace of Amboise, or the prévôt des marchands postponed dissolving the militia after the first religious war, they were accused of willfully defying the crown. The same accusation was made when the lieutenant civil delayed executing the order to move the cross of Gastines or Parlement postponed the public execution of persons arrested in the subsequent riots. And yet, when the full circumstances of each of these incidents are taken into account, it can be seen that the magistrates temporized because they were afraid to take actions whose success they could not guarantee, because any failure would only reveal more clearly the true weakness of civil authority.

With the events of Saint Bartholomew's Day, the full extent of this weakness was nevertheless revealed. If the officers of the Bureau de la ville, the Châtelet, and Parlement failed to regain order in the hours and days that followed the attack on the Protestant leaders, it was not for lack of will but rather for lack of might. With the militia divided and undependable, the magistrates had no force with which to confront the rioting populace. The city's professional troops were too few in number to do more than to accompany the prévôt des marchands and échevins in their ineffective patrols about the city and to try to protect an individual here or to defend a family there, as they did with President de La Place. The orders to lay down weapons and return home repeatedly issued by the prévôt des marchands were unenforced and unenforceable. The frequency with which these orders had to be repeated is itself testimony to the powerlessness of the civil authorities.[81]

I do not say this to excuse the Parisian magistrates from sharing responsibility for the events of August 1572. When the Bureau de la ville gave the order to call out the militia, willingly or not, it became a partner in the crime of Saint Bartholomew's Day. When Parlement accepted without protest the king's claim to have ordered the massacre, the high court magistrates became accomplices as well. Acquiescing to the king's rash move, the Parisian magistrates revealed the fundamental contradiction of their position: a dependence on royal favor that served to color their personal opinions and sometimes also to cloud their professional judgments. But the essential weakness of the magistrates, both civic and parlementary, lay not in their relationship with the king but rather in their relationship with their fellow Parisians, over whom their authority had been seriously weakened by the strains of civil war.[82]

In the minds of the common people, strongly influenced by the preaching and propaganda of militant Catholicism, the magistrates were soft on heresy, perhaps even Protestants themselves. Why else had they ceased to burn the heretics? The limited truth contained in this accusation—there were a few Protestants in the high courts and in the city hall, and a larger number had relatives who belonged to the new faith—obscured the more fundamental reality that the abandonment of the policy of persecution established by Henri II and continued by the Guises during the short reign of François II had made it impossible for Parlement to continue to treat heresy as a capital crime.[83] Even the Edict of Romorantin (May 1560), although intended as a repressive measure, had weakened the ability of Parlement to prosecute religious deviance by separating the religious aspects of heresy from the secular, or political, manifestations of heretical belief. Parlement had retained jurisdiction over the political aspects of heresy—over Protestant preaching and teaching, attendance at illicit assemblies, and possession of forbidden books—but the crime of heresy itself had been returned to the episcopal courts.[84] The edict of July 1561 was another supposedly harsh measure that did little to strengthen Parlement's hand. Although the act forbade Protestant assemblies, it was difficult to enforce this prohibition because the same act forbade inquiry into matters of conscience. Moreover, by applying its prohibitions to the future but not to the past, it forced Parlement to release religious suspects accused of the very acts that it forbade.[85]

The ability of Parlement to prosecute religious dissidence effectively was further compromised by the edict of January 1562 and by the edicts of pacification that concluded each of the first three wars, all of which placed certain limits on Protestant acts of worship but allowed for liberty of conscience. Indeed, parlementary records show only three executions for religious crimes between 1561 and 1569. We have no details on the first of these cases, but the second was for blasphemy and sedition and the third for a sacrilege committed in a Paris church.[86] Heretical belief was in itself no longer a crime, and even as serious a violation of the law as illicit publishing was deemed punishable by beating and banishment and not by execution. The mass of arrests marked "heresy" in the Conciergerie entries for this period involve suspected Protestants arrested during the most critical stages of each of the wars for violations of the laws that restricted their presence or free movement in the capital. Surviving interrogation records for these cases show that the judges questioned the suspects on their actions—what religious assemblies they had attended, where their children had been baptized, and whether or not they had ever partaken of the Protestant rite of the Lord's Supper—and not on their fundamental beliefs. Moreover, in virtually all cases, the suspects were eventually either released without charge or were fined and told to leave the city.[87] Only the strong pressure of public opinion moved the judges to condemn first Lambert Marais, convicted of teaching children Protestant doctrine, and then Nicolas Croquet and the two Gastines in the spring of 1569, and these condemnations remained exceptional.[88]

It was thus a change in royal policy and not a change in parlementary jurisprudence that brought an end to the bonfires of the heretics, but the common people did not appreciate this distinction. Nor did they appreciate the difficulties that were created for the magistrates by the shifts in royal policy—by the reversals that occurred with each new round of war and peace, and by the obligation to enforce the edicts of pacification, however unpopular they might be. The people's view of justice was a simple one. As the radical preachers had repeatedly told them, justice was the sword of secular authority that the French kings had received from God. As agents of the king's justice, the magistrates had the right and obligation to use this sword to restore the religious unity on which the Christian commonwealth must rest.

For the magistrates, on the other hand, the notion of justice was necessarily more complex and incorporated a belief in an orderly state, effectively governed and legitimately ruled. The magistrates shared the conviction that religious unity was a necessary foundation for the state; they had protested the relaxation of persecution in 1561 and pleaded for stronger measures against the Huguenots, and yet, as the wars progressed, many came to believe that religious unity had to be a long-term goal and not an immediate priority if the state was to survive. The zeal manifested in defense of one holy faith came to seem a greater danger than religious division itself, and the fear of heresy receded before the still greater fear of anarchy. At first hesitantly but then more resolutely, the magistrates emerged as defenders of constituted authority. They were willing to enforce the king's edicts even when these edicts violated their Catholic beliefs, because they shared an even stronger belief in a legitimate and orderly state.

In this widening cleavage between divergent images of the Christian commonwealth, one founded on religious solidarity, the other rooted in respect for the law, we can detect the origins of the conflicts that were to dominate in the second half of the civil wars. I would not want to suggest that all magistrates became Catholic moderates and eventually joined forces with the Politique party that emerged from the horrors of Saint Bartholomew's Day. There are too many obvious exceptions to posit such a rule. Nor were all members of the militia religious extremists who ultimately joined the Catholic League. Like the sovereign courts and city government, the militia was divided on the Day of the Barricades (12 May 1588), and it never went over entirely to the radical side. I would, however, argue that the contrasting-outlooks of the Leaguers and their Politique foes took root during the first decade of the civil wars, and that if we would seek to understand this culminating episode in the wars we must look back to these roots and not, as too many historians have done, take up the story only in the 1580s.

The perspective of time can help us to understand some of the social and psychological characteristics of the League much debated in historical literature. Consider, for example, the often remarked prevalence of a middle or "seconde" bourgeoisie in the ranks of the League, while the higher bourgeoisie was more often associated with the Politique party. Was this the product of social conflicts born of frustrated professional ambitions, as Henri Drouot and others after him have suggested?[89] Or was it rather a natural consequence of the fact that many members of the "bourgeoisie seconde" were radicalized by the role they played in the civic guard, while many of the higher bourgeoisie had their religious hatreds tempered by the responsibility for public order they assumed as magistrates? The simpler argument, the one that acknowledges the formative character of the years of religious strife, seems to me the more persuasive one.

Finally, I should add that, if the decade that led up to Saint Bartholomew's Day laid the foundations for political affiliations that were to take shape in the years that followed, the same decade saw the definitive rupture of the civic unities of centuries past. In his study of the "bonnes villes du roi" in the later middle ages, Bernard Chevalier writes that after "the season of Saint Bartholomew's, . . . the gulf remained open between the distant elites [*les 'messieurs'*], suspected of half-heartedness and rejected as secret partisans of a heretic king, and the populace, fanatically attached to all the traditional values."[90] The second level of the bourgeoisie, that which might have served to bridge the gap, "allied with the crowd in these events and seemed to share its tastes, its passions, and its rites of popular culture." In Chevalier's analysis, this alliance was a tactical and contingent one. Nevertheless, for the cities,

> the hour of profound communion was past. Even after the return to calm, . . . nothing was the same as before. The solidarities, the mutual understanding, the confidence with which one group dealt with another, the common vision of the different classes were fractured in the "bonne ville" divided against itself, like a kingdom in peril.[91]

These words describe well the situation in Paris after the events of August 1572.

Conclusion: Paris in the Religious Wars

On 4 September 1572, at the command of Charles IX, a solemn procession of the relics of Saint Geneviève rendered thanks to God for the "defeat of the Huguenots."[1] Jean de La Fosse tells us that the Blessed Sacrament was carried in the procession and that the king took part in it personally, along with his brothers.[2] The procession brought a kind of closure to the events of Saint Bartholomew's Day. Most important, it allowed both king and people to sacralize their actions by placing them under the aegis of divine will. Although he had in his address to Parlement accepted responsibility for the massacre, Charles IX represented himself through this procession as merely the executor of the divine command to rid the kingdom of the pollution of heresy. This at least is how many people, well prepared by the lessons of their radical preachers, interpreted events. As one of many celebratory poems written after Saint Bartholomew's Day expressed it, Charles IX had "accomplished the royal prophecy" in maintaining the "law of the great eternal God." He had been conducted in his actions by the "angel of the great King who directs kings and prolongs their life," and the people gave joyous thanks that "by [the king's] good success the Governor of the heavens has exterminated the cruel admiral."[3]

Yes, the prophecies had been accomplished, and the people—most of them, at least—gave joyous thanks. The violence that they had witnessed, the violence in which they had participated, had come from God and been dedicated back to him; they could look on it not with horror but with pride. One must imagine Thomas Croizier and Nicolas Pezou, the leaders of the militia's radical faction, laying down their bloody weapons to take up the jeweled casket of Saint Geneviève. Like the other members of the confraternity of the bearers of Saint Geneviève, they would have fasted, prayed, and taken communion—which implies confession—before donning white shifts and floral crowns to parade barefoot through the streets. We can only wonder how many in the watching crowd or in the procession itself— among the magistrates, for example—gave a secret shudder of revulsion when they saw brutal killers bearing the relics of the city's patron saint. We might speculate that this revulsion encouraged some Catholics to begin turning away from the collective and communal forms of traditional religious practice to the more interiorized, personal spirituality that was later to emerge with the Counter-Reformation, but such speculation goes beyond the story that I have to tell, for the procession of the relics of Saint Geneviève marks a point of closure for this book as well.

Why end here, when the procession did not in fact mark the end of the violence unleashed on Saint Bartholomew's Day? It trailed on for another month in Paris and, just as an earthquake produces aftershocks, threatened to convulse the capital again at later dates. In mid-November, hasty action had to be taken to ward off a rumored plan to "pillage the best houses in Paris," on the pretext of "finishing off the killing of the Huguenots."[4] Moreover, in spite of the king's direct orders to keep the peace, the wave of murder spread to various provincial cities, where it climaxed at the end of October and produced a total number of victims that may have been three or four times as great as the number killed in the capital.[5] A new civil war began, and in this sense too there was continuity rather than change.

Indeed, traditional history treats Saint Bartholomew's Day as a turning point in the religious conflicts but not as an end in itself. I have chosen to break with this tradition because it seems to me to diminish the significance of the period prior to the massacre to view it as but the first act in a drama that climaxes with the League and eventually resolves itself in the triumph of Henri IV. The earlier period does foreshadow the later one in important ways. As we have seen, the division between Catholic extremists and moderates, or "politiques," has its roots in the first decade of the wars. But this is not the only—or even the principal—lesson of this period, which must be seen as a vitally important episode in the struggle over the Reformation of the Christian faith and not just as an episode in French state-building.

It is equally misleading to view the massacre as an isolated event, one that began with, or shortly before, the shot that was fired at Coligny on 22 August. Only by viewing Saint Bartholomew's Day in the context of the fifteen years of religious conflicts that preceded it, can we appreciate the significance of the massacre not just as a crime on the part of the king—although it was that—but also as a terrible act of faith on the part of an impassioned populace that believed itself to be executing the will of God.[6] Only against this background can we see the gradual build-up of the tensions to which the massacre gave vent—the wearing rhythms of war and uneasy peace, the worrisome undercurrents of famine and plague, the inflamatory sermons that predicted the wrath of a jealous and demanding God. Only against this background can we see the gradual construction of the mental framework that allowed the massacre to take place. We can see it in the Parisians' resistance to every attempt at a truce or a negotiated peace with the Huguenot enemy, in their refusal to allow the Protestants to return to their homes at the end of each war, and in their exaggerated response to such symbolic issues as the order to remove the cross of Gastines. Most of all, we can hear it in the sermons of the popular preachers, who insisted that the task of exterminating heresy was assigned to the king when he was given the sword of secular justice and that the king in turn might call upon his subjects to assist in this task.

At the same time, this perspective allows us to see that not all Parisians were equally receptive to the message of the radical preachers. The popular killings were not the work of the entire Catholic population but rather of an extremist faction that took shape within the militia and gathered adherents among the population at large. Surely some were moved to take part in the killing by the promise of pillage, by the opportunities for private revenge, or by a perverse delight in violence itself—such motives exist in any riot or popular uprising—but these were not the emotions that triggered the massacre, which would not have taken place without the hallucinatory belief that this purge of the heretics was a salutory act commanded by the king and ordained by God.

It may seem strange that I should feel the need so to stress the role of popular religious passions in bringing about and pushing forward the fratricidal wars that divided France against itself in the second half of the sixteenth century. They are, after all, known as the "Wars of Religion." Traditional historical writing has, however, tended to empty these wars of much of their religious content, so that the clash of faiths takes second place to the personal rivalries and political factionalism that divided the noble leaders in the wars. Even in recent histories, the wars tend to be described primarily in terms of the struggle for influence and ultimately control of the crown waged by the noble houses of Montmorency, Bourbon, and Guise.[8] The terms "Catholic" and "Huguenot" are reduced to party names and are used as a kind of shorthand to describe the principal factions. The emphasis in describing each of these parties is on the political strategies through which it operated and not on the religious beliefs that underlay it. The primacy of politics in the wars is also emphasized through a distinction between "political Huguenots" and "religious Huguenots" and through the example made of important nobles who changed camps or showed other signs of acting more out of opportunism than out of true conviction. These distinctions are valid; indeed, they are crucial if we are to understand the meaning of the religious wars in terms of the larger process of French state-building. The complex aims of the noble participants in the wars, the conditions under which they shifted their alliances, their relation to the crown: These are key to understanding the process through which monarchical authority was first dissolved into anarchy and then rebuilt under Henri IV. But, as I have repeatedly said, this is not the only way to view these wars, and the persistent emphasis on long-term political developments has tended to obscure the originality of the religious revolt, its particular character in the period prior to Saint Bartholomew's Day, and even its ultimate effect on the political outcome of the wars.

We are used to viewing the wars of the early modern period as almost uniquely the affair of princes and kings, but the religious wars were different. They had a resonance among the common people that the dynastic wars of the Valois (or the civil wars of the fifteenth century and noble revolts of the seventeenth) did not have. They did not just affect the people in material ways, in terms of higher taxes or devastated fields, but also appeared to threaten the very bases on which civil society was built and the accustomed relationships that linked the individual to the collectivity and to God. As we have seen, the doctrinal differences that separated Catholics and Huguenots in the wars were not perceived by the common people as abstruse scholarly debates but rather as crucial choices between truth and error, between salvation and damnation, between God's favor and his impending wrath. At the popular level, the religious wars represented a crusade against heresy, a crusade that had to be won if civil society was to be preserved and salvation to be assured. The people had a stake in these wars that they did not have in the dynastic squabbles of their kings, and as a consequence, the Wars of Religion had broad repercussions at the popular level.

At the same time, the popular reaction to the wars, experienced at the local level in terms of increased social tensions and new divisions between Catholic extremists and moderates, was reflected back to the level of princes and kings, where it was experienced in very different ways. Catherine de Medici, Charles IX, and the various leaders of the noble factions were not the independent actors they are often made out to be in histories of this period. Rather, they were constrained in their actions by popular pressures—in particular by the pressures exerted by the people of Paris. The fact that the peace treaties that settled each of the wars favored the rights of the Huguenot nobility at the expense of the urban populations is usually blamed on the aristocratic prejudices of the Huguenot leaders. It is nevertheless true that the fierce lobbying of delegations sent from cities like Paris, cities that refused even to consider the prospect of allowing Protestant services within their bounds, made it much harder for Protestant leaders to insist on the right to establish churches in cities outside of their areas of primary strength. As one of the king's most dependable sources of funds when it came to paying the costs of the wars, the city of Paris was in a particularly good position to impress upon the king its determined opposition to any compromise with the Huguenot enemy.

The Parisians intervened in the course of events on numerous occasions. They helped bring on the first religious war by their refusal to accept the toleration edict of January 1562 and by their reaction to the massacre of Vassy a month later. They interfered with the queen mother's attempts to negotiate a truce with the Huguenots at several stages in the war and delayed the peace that eventually was struck. They then helped to undermine the peace by refusing to disarm and by refusing to allow the Huguenots to return to their homes in the capital. They played a comparable role in the second and third wars through their violent reaction to the Huguenots' attempt to seize the king at Monceaux, their objections to any attempts to negotiate peace, their reluctance to lay down their arms, and, once again, their refusal to allow Protestants to return to their homes. More than a year after the peace concluded at Saint-Germain, the cross of Gastines riots demonstrated the persistent refusal of the Parisians to accept the terms of the agreement. Finally, the uncontrolled violence of Saint Bartholomew's Day had a direct impact on the course of subsequent wars. By forcing a hardening of opinion within both the radical Catholic and Protestant camps, at the same time that it precipitated a new current of moderation among those horrified by the barbarity of the slaughter and eager to seek a political solution to the quarrels, the massacre initiated a new stage in the conflicts, one that was not finally resolved until after Henri IV recaptured his rebellious capital in 1594.

"Yes," I can hear my reader say, "but were the people of Paris really the independent actors that you make them out to be? Were they not the puppets of the Guises, the tools of the same noble factions whose independence of action you wish to limit?" There is no doubt that the Guises had clients in Paris. Like other great nobles at the time, they had created a clientele by using their influence to help obtain for their supporters positions in Parlement or other areas of royal service, or by appointing them to positions in their own household.[10] I found surprisingly little evidence, however, of broader patronage extending down to lower social levels or into the parishes. Nor did I find any sign that members of the Guise family were actively furthering the careers of the radical preachers in order to advance the arch-Catholic cause.[11] Quite the contrary, the lines of allegiance appear to have run the opposite direction during this period. That is to say, the Parisians adopted the duc de Guise as their hero and symbol because he was a charismatic figure and because he represented the views they already held. When the duke was assassinated in March 1563, he became still more of a symbol, for his death coincided with the final negotiations for a peace that the Parisians bitterly opposed. The elaborate funeral that the Parisians gave their martyred hero—complete with a procession of the militia, carrying their arms reversed as a symbol of mourning—was a way of protesting the betrayal they saw coming in the Treaty of Amboise, as well as a way of marking the duke's death. As I see it, the people of Paris adopted the Guises, and not the other way around, at least at this early stage of the wars. The Guise family may well have learned to profit from and to manipulate this popularity, but the Parisian populace was nobody's puppet.

Of course the religious wars were *also* very much the affair of great nobles and kings. They would not have taken place had French Protestants not found important protectors within the high nobility and had the Catholic cause not found equally powerful champions within rival noble houses. But it is also true that the great French nobles were accustomed to courtly power games in which the threat and the bluff and ultimately the negotiated compromise were used by all parties to advantage. The factional leaders, especially Condé, tried to continue these practices during the first wars. Given Catherine de Medici's tendency to try to maintain her sons' authority by balancing out the interests of the competing factions, it is very likely that these tactics would have been successful and some compromise for the sharing of power would have been reached had the stakes been merely the traditional ones of political advantage and power. But the religious element in the conflict meant that the stakes had changed. The interests involved were no longer just those of a handful of courtiers and the crown. The spread of the Calvinist Reformation in France and the reactionary rhetoric on the Catholic side had introduced an unpredictable and dangerous element to the nobles' power struggles, for even if the factional leaders remembered the artful rules of negotiation and compromise, the urban populations refused to abide by these rules. Indoctrinated by dogmatic and unforgiving preachers, they saw the religious conflicts in terms of truth and error that admitted no middle position. Most cities were too small to influence the larger course of the wars; they played out before a local audience their bloody dramas of persecution and revenge. Paris, by its size and political importance, was an exception to this rule. Had it not been for the fierce Catholicism of the people of Paris, the Wars of Religion would have taken a very different course. Perhaps they would not have taken place at all.

NOTES

Abbreviations

AEG   Archives d'Etat de Genève

AN   Archives nationales (Paris)

Annales, E.S.C.   *Annales, économies, sociétés, civilisations*

APP   Archives de la Préfecture de police (Paris)

BN   Bibliothèque nationale (Paris)

BHR   *Bibliothèque d'humanisme et renaissance*

BSHParis   *Bulletin de la Société de l'histoire de Paris et de l'Ile-de-France*

BSHPF   *Bulletin de la Société de l'histoire du protestantisme français*

C.O.   *Ioannis Calvini Opera quae supersunt omnia*, ed. G. Baum, E. Cunitz, and E. Reuss, 59 vols. (Brunswick, Germany, 1863–1900)

CSP,F   Great Britain, Public Record Office, *Calendar of State Papers (Foreign Series) of the Reign of Elizabeth*, ed. Joseph Stevenson et al., 28 vols. (London, 1863–1950)

Hist. eccl.   [Theodore Beza], *Histoire ecclésiastique des Eglises réformées au royaume de France*, ed. G. Baum and E. Cunitz, 3 vols. (Nieuwkoop, 1974; reprint of Paris edition, 1883–1889)

MC   Minutier central (Paris)

MSHParis   *Mémoires de la Société de l'histoire de Paris et de l'Ile-de-France*

Reg. BV   François Bonnardot, et al., *Registres des délibérations du Bureau de la ville de Paris*, Histoire générale de Paris, vols. 1–7 (Paris, 1883–1893)

SCC   Simon Vigor, *Sermons catholiques pour tous les jours de caresme & feriés de Pasques, faits en l'eglise S. Estienne du Mont à Paris* (Paris: Gabriel Buon, 1588)

SCP   Simon Vigor, *Sermons catholiques sur les dimanches et festes depuis l'octave de Pasques jusques à l'advent.* 2 vols. (Paris: Nicolas du Fossé, 1597)

SSA   Simon Vigor, *Sermons et predications chrestiennes et catholiques du s. sacrement de l'autel, accommodées pour tous les jours des octaves de la feste Dieu* (Paris: Nicolas Chesneau, 1577)

Introduction

1. Barbara B. Diefendorf, *Paris City Councillors in the Sixteenth Century: The Politics of Patrimony* (Princeton, 1983).

2. Ibid., pp. 73–80.

3. See the related, though by no means identical, accounts published by Simon Goulart in his *Memoires de l'estat de France sous Charles IX* (Middleburg, 1578), reproduced as the ''Relation du massacre de la Saint-Barthélemy'' in the *Archives curieuses de l'histoire de France*, ed. Cimber and Danjou, 1st ser. (Paris, 1835) 7:116; Jacques-Auguste de Thou, *Histoire de Monsieur de Thou des choses arrivées en son temps*, tr. P. Du Ryer (Paris, 1659), 3:658–59; and Théodore-Agrippa d'Aubigné, *L'histoire universelle du sieur d'Aubigné*, 2 vols. in (Maille, 1616–1618), 2:16–17.

4. Antoine-Jean-Victor Le Roux de Lincy, *Recueil de chants historiques français depuis le XIIᵉ jusqu'au XVIIIᵉ siècle*, vol. 2 (Geneva, 1969; reprint of edition of Paris, 1841–1842),

pp. 294–98. Several versions of the original are to be found in BN, Mss. fr. 22560, fols. 179, 181, 186. It should be noted that most of the songs collected here are Protestant satires on contemporary persons and events and that this one should probably be seen as a Protestant attack on the power that Marcel and other rich merchants could exert over the king's purse and not as a Catholic vaunting of military strength. On Marcel's social and political rise, see Diefendorf, *Paris City Councillors*, pp. 95–109.

5. Jacques-Auguste de Thou, *Mémoires depuis 1553 jusqu'en 1601*. Nouvelle collection des mémoires pour servir à l'histoire de France, ed. Michaud and Poujoulat, ser. 1, vol. 11 (Paris, 1838), p. 276.

6. Janine [Garrisson-]Estèbe, *Tocsin pour un massacre: La saison des Saint-Barthélemy* (Paris, 1968), p. 43.

7. Natalie Zemon Davis, "The Rites of Violence: Religious Riot in Sixteenth-Century France," *Past & Present*, no. 59 (1973), reprinted in her *Society and Culture in Early Modern France* (Stanford, 1976), pp. 152–87. Denis Richet, "Aspects socio-culturels des conflits religieux à Paris dans la seconde moitié du XVIe siècle," *Annales, E.S.C.* 32 (1977): 764–89.

8. Philip Benedict, *Rouen during the Wars of Religion* (Cambridge, 1980).

9. Janine Garrisson, *La Saint-Barthélemy* (Brussels, 1987). See also her article, "Le massacre de la Saint-Barthélemy: Qui est responsable?" *L'histoire*, no. 126 (October 1989), pp. 50–55. Jean-Louis Bourgeon, "Les légendes ont la vie dure: A propos de la Saint-Barthélemy et de quelques livres récents," *Revue d'histoire moderne et contemporaine* 34 (1987): 102–16; Bourgeon, "Pour une histoire, enfin, de la Saint-Barthélemy," *Revue historique* 282 (1989): 83–142; and Bourgeon, "Une source sur la Saint-Barthélemy: l'"Histoire de Monsieur de Thou,' relue et décryptée," *BSHPF* 134 (1988): 499–537. Professor Bourgeon also has an article forthcoming, "La fronde parlementaire à la veille de la Saint-Barthélemy," in the *Bibliothèque de l'Ecole des chartes* 148 (1990): 17–89, which I have not had the opportunity to see.

10. Denis Crouzet, *Les guerriers de Dieu: La violence au temps des troubles de religion, vers 1525–vers 1610*, 2 vols. (Paris, 1990). Unfortunately, Crouzet's book appeared after my own manuscript was complete except for this introduction, which (like many introductions) was written last. I am thus unable to profit from some of his very original ideas as much as I might have liked or to make more than a few comparative references or commentaries in my notes. Although I do not in fact see any places where I would have significantly changed my argument if I had read his book earlier, I might have refined it at certain points and certainly could have reinforced it with some of the massive evidence that he cites. I cannot follow Crouzet in all the ramifications of his thesis, in part at least because my own sources tie me to more earthly explanations of certain occurrences, but I admire his book tremendously and applaud the rethinking it forces of a period that has been too long viewed in overly secular terms.

Chapter 1

1. Eustache Knobelsdorf, *Lutetiae descriptio [1543]*, ed. and tr. O. Sauvage (Grenoble, 1978), pp. 65 and 67.

2. Report of Marino Cavalli in Niccolo Tommaseo, *Relations des ambassadeurs vénitiens sur les affaires de France au XVIe s.* (Paris, 1838), 1:261.

3. Thomas Platter, *Description de Paris (1599)*, tr. L. Sieber and M. Weibel (Paris, 1896), p. 8.

4. Reports of Cavalli and Suriano in Tommaseo, *Relations des ambassadeurs vénitiens*, 1:261 and 483.

5. Report of Corero in Tommaseo, *Relations*, 2:113; "Paris en 1596 vu par un Italien (Récit de Fr. Greg. d'Ierni)," *BHSParis* 12 (1885): 169.

6. Jean Jacquart, "Le poids démographique de Paris et de l'Ile-de-France au XVIe siècle," *Annales de démographie historique* (1980): 93–94.

7. Jean-Pierre Babelon, *Nouvelle histoire de Paris: Paris au XVIe siècle* (Paris, 1986), pp. 159–66. Babelon has, in my opinion, overestimated the average number of residents per house and consequently used too large a multiplier in calculating the city's population on the basis of the tax list of 1571. In addition, Babelon assumes that each entry on the tax list denotes a separate house, which is not the case. There are, for example, eighty-eight entries for the sixty-eight houses on the pont Notre-Dame. BN, Mss. fr. 11692, fols. 159v–161r.

8. These estimates follow the curve suggested by Babelon, *Paris au XVIe siècle*, p. 166, but do not reach the same peaks. See also Jacquart, "Le poids démographique de Paris," pp. 90–94.

9. Tommaseo, *Relations des ambassadeurs vénitiens*, p. 263. See also "Paris en 1596," p. 169.

10. "Paris en 1596," p. 169.

11. Ibid., p. 166.

12. Ibid.

13. Babelon, *Paris au XVIe siècle*, p. 219.

14. Ibid., p. 219. On the administration of the Hôtel-Dieu, see *Reg. BV*, 1:108–10.

15. Platter, *Description de Paris*, p. 15. See also Jacques du Breul, *Le théâtre des antiquités de Paris* (Paris, 1612), p. 52.

16. "Paris en 1596," p. 166.

17. Annie Parent, *Les métiers du livre à Paris au XVIe siècle (1535–1560)* (Geneva, 1974), p. 171.

18. Platter, *Description de Paris*, pp. 18–20.

19. Ibid., p. 22.

20. "Paris en 1596," pp. 168–69; Platter, *Description de Paris*, p. 25; and L. A. Van Langeraad and A. Vidier, "Description de Paris par Arnold Van Buchel [1585–1586]," *MSHParis* 26 (1899): 96.

21. Platter, *Description de Paris*, p. 44; Babelon, *Paris au XVIe siècle*, pp. 113–16; David Thomson, *Renaissance Paris: Architecture and Growth, 1475–1600* (Berkeley and Los Angeles, 1984), pp. 73–74.

22. AN, Q^{1*} 1099$^{197B - 204C}$: rent contracts for the pont Notre–Dame.

23. Platter, *Description de Paris*, p. 45.

24. Van Langeraad and Vidier, "Description de Paris," p. 96.

25. Babelon, *Paris au XVIe siècle*, pp. 223–24.

26. Parent, *Les métiers du livre*, p. 171.

27. Van Langeraad and Vidier, "Description de Paris," p. 116.

28. Knobelsdorf, *Lutetiae descriptio*, p. 67; Van Langeraad and Vidier, "Description de Paris," p. 102.

29. Platter, *Description de Paris*, p. 41.

30. Jean Martineau, *Les Halles de Paris des origines à 1789. Evolution matérielle, juridique et économique* (Paris, 1960), pp. 153–63.

31. Platter, *Description de Paris*, p. 38.

32. Du Breul, *Le théâtre des antiquitez*, p. 831.

33. Platter, *Description de Paris*, p. 38.

34. Ibid., p. 40.

35. BN, Mss. fr. 11692. Robert Descimon has recently published a meticulous description of the social geography of Paris, based largely on his study of this manuscript. See "Paris

on the Eve of Saint Bartholomew: Taxation, Privilege, and Social Geography,'' in Philip Benedict, ed., *Urban Society in Ancien Regime France* (London, 1989), pp. 69–104.

36. Platter, *Description de Paris*. For Erasmus's comments on the collège de Montaigu, see his colloquy, "Concerning the Eating of Fishes."

37. Platter, *Description de Paris*, p. 27.

38. Knobelsdorf, *Lutetiae descriptio*, p. 59; cf. François Rabelais, *Gargantua and Pantagruel*, book 1, chapter 23.

39. Parent, *Les métiers du livre*, p. 169.

40. Platter, *Description de Paris*, p. 36; Van Langeraad and Vidier, "Description de Paris,'' p. 110.

41. Van Langeraad and Vidier, "Description de Paris,'' p. 110.

42. "Paris en 1596,'' p. 169; Babelon, *Paris au XVIe siècle*, p. 286.

43. Paris en 1596,'' p. 169; Knobelsdorf, *Lutetiae descriptio*, p. 61; Platter, *Description de Paris*, p. 8.

44. Babelon, *Paris au XVIe siècle*, p. 289, lists the fountains. See also *Reg. BV*, 4:307 (25 June 1554): complaints of Jean Luillier about the noise made by people at the fountain outside his house.

45. Platter, *Description de Paris*, p. 11.

46. Platter, *Description de Paris*, p. 47. Ierni estimated the population of the faubourg Saint-Germain before the last wars at 18,000 ("Paris en 1596,'' p. 167).

47. Babelon, *Paris au XVIe siècle*, pp. 197–98; Emmanuel Le Roy Ladurie and Pierre Couperie, "Les loyers parisiens (1400–1700),'' *Annales, E.S.C.* 25 (1970): 1021; *Reg. BV*, 3:66n: reference to order of September 1544 to tear down houses at Villeneuve, near the porte Saint-Denis, because of advancing imperial armies.

48. Platter, *Description de Paris*, p. 9.

49. Richard Gascon, "L'essor commercial,'' in *Histoire économique et sociale de la France*, ed. Fernand Braudel and Ernest Labrousse, vol. 1: *De 1450 à 1660: L'Etat et la ville* (Paris, 1977), p. 257.

50. Tommaseo, *Relations des ambassadeurs vénitiens*, 1:267.

51. Jean Jacquart, *La crise rurale en Ile-de-France, 1550–1670* (Paris, 1974), p. 117; Yvonne Bézard, *La vie rurale dans le sud de la région parisienne de 1450 à 1560* (Paris, 1929), pp. 75–77.

52. Jacquart, *La crise rurale en Ile-de-France*, p. 117.

53. Gascon, "L'essor commercial,'' in *Histoire économique et sociale*, ed. Braudel and Labrousse, 1:261.

54. Corero in Tommaseo, *Relations des ambassadeurs vénitiens*, 2:141; Jean Meuvret, "Circulation monétaire et utilisation économique de la monnaie dans la France du XVIe et du XVIIe siècle,'' in his *Etudes d'histoire économique: Recueil d'articles* (Paris, 1971), pp. 129–30; and Michel Mollat, *Le commerce maritime normand à la fin du moyen âge. Etude d'histoire économique et sociale* (Paris, 1952), pp. 321–26.

55. Emile Coornaert, *Les Français et le commerce international à Anvers. Fin du XVe, XVIe siècle*, 2 vols. (Paris, 1961), 1:232, 242; and Richard Gascon, *Grand commerce et vie urbaine au XVIe siècle. Lyon et ses marchands (environs de 1520 – environs de 1580)*, 2 vols. (Paris, 1971), 1:69 and 129.

56. Coornaert, *Les Français et le commerce*, 1:242; and Parent, *Les métiers du livre*, pp. 156 and 161. See also Albert Chamberland, "Le commerce d'importation en France au milieu du XVIe siècle d'après un manuscrit de la Bibliothèque nationale,'' *Revue de géographie* 31–33 (1892–1893): 292, for a table of French imports in the mid-sixteenth century.

57. Parent, *Les métiers du livre*, p. 161.

58. Tomasseo, *Relations des ambassadeurs vénitiens*, 1:259.

59. Léon Roulland, "La foire Saint-Germain sous les règnes de Charles IX, de Henri III et de Henri IV," *MSHParis* 3 (1876): 192–96.

60. Robert Descimon, "Structures d'un marché de draperie dans la Languedoc au milieu du XVIᵉ siècle," *Annales, E.S.C.* 30 (1975): 1444. See also Roger Gourmelon, "Etude sur le rayonnement commercial des marchands drapiers parisiens au XVIᵉ siècle," *Bulletin philologique et historique (jusqu'à 1610) du Comité des travaux historiques et scientifiques (1961)* (1963): 264–75.

61. Mollat, *Le commerce maritime normand*, pp. 302 and 327–29; and Gascon, *Grand commerce et vie urbaine*, 1:93–94 and 129.

62. Coornaert, *Les Français et le commerce*, 1:233–35 and 243–44.

63. Gascon, "L'essor commercial," in *Histoire économique et sociale*, ed. Braudel and Labrousse, 1:287; and Coornaert, *Les Français et le commerce*, 1:243.

64. *Reg. BV*, 3:107–8 (23 January 1548).

65. Tommaseo, *Relations des ambassadeurs vénitiens*, 1:263.

66. See, for example, Roland Mousnier, *Les hiérarchies sociales de 1450 à nos jours* (Paris, 1969), or his *Les institutions de France sous la monarchie absolue, 1598–1789*, vol. 1: *Etat et société* (Paris, 1974).

67. Diefendorf, *Paris City Councillors*, pp. 42–52 and 134–51.

68. See, for example, Bernard Chevalier, *Les bonnes villes de France du XIVᵉ au XVIᵉ siècle* (Paris, 1982), pp. 90 and 147.

69. Etienne Martin-Saint-Léon, *Histoire des corporations de métiers depuis leurs origines jusqu'à leur suppression en 1791* (Geneva, 1976; reprint of Paris edition, 1922), p. 290.

70. Ibid. See the lists of membership published by Georges Denière, *La juridiction consulaire de Paris, 1563–1792. Sa création, ses luttes, son administration intérieure, ses usages, et ses moeurs* (Paris, 1872), pp. 87 and 509–10. See also Ronda Larmour, "A Merchant Guild of Sixteenth-Century France: The Grocers of Paris," *Economic History Review* 20 (1967): 472, 472n, and 475–76.

71. Larmour, "A Merchant Guild," p. 471; cf. Coornaert, who does not find the distinction between retail and wholesale merchants useful (*Les Français et le commerce*, 2:32).

72. Parent, *Les métiers du livre*, p. 165.

73. See René de Lespinasse, *Les métiers et corporations de la ville de Paris*, 3 vols. (Paris, 1886–1897), 1:95–96: "Rolles arrêtés au Conseil d'Etat du roy le 5 juilliet 1582," which classifies corporations according to their relative rank. See also Chevalier, *Les bonnes villes*, p. 76.

74. Martin-Saint-Léon, *Histoire des corporations*, pp. 280–84. On fees for mastership in the grocers' corporation, see Larmour, "A Merchant Guild," p. 479.

75. Emile Levasseur, *Histoire des classes ouvrières et de l'industrie en France avant 1789*, 2 vols. (Paris, 1901), 2:118; Emile Coornaert, *Les corporations en France avant 1789* (Paris, 1941), pp. 120–21; and Louis-Marie Michon, "A propos des grèves d'imprimeurs de Paris et de Lyon au XVIᵉ siècle," *Paris et Ile-de-France* 3 (1951): 103–16.

76. Martin-Saint-Léon, *Histoire des corporations*, p. 280.

77. Lespinasse, *Métiers et corporations de Paris*, 1:228 on the *grainiers*, and 3:45–48 on the *liniers-chanviers*, both of which had female wardens; 3:62–71 on the *lingères*, and 296–97 on the *plumassières, chapelières de fleurs*, and *mercières*; passim on women in other corporations.

78. "Paris en 1596," p. 166.

79. AN, H 2065²: miscellaneous city receipts and related documents. See also Alfred Franklin, *Dictionnaire historique des arts, métiers, et professions exercés dans Paris depuis*

le treizième siècle (Paris, 1906), p. 580. More generally on women's work, see Natalie Zemon Davis, "City Women and Religious Change," in her *Society and Culture*, pp. 65–95.

80. See, for example, AN, MC, CXXII, 247 (28 August 1565): apprenticeship of Anthoinette Collart to Gillette Buisson, an embroiderer in gold thread and the wife of a trunk-maker; CXXII 247 (10 March 1566): apprenticeship of Geneviève Blondeau to Magdaleine du Bois, a maker of hoods and headdresses and the wife of a journeyman hosier; CXXII, 1391 (14 March 1561): apprenticeship of Marie du Val to Françoise Prevost, a seamstress and the wife of a dresser of white leather.

81. *Reg. BV*, 5:384 (15 March 1564). See ibid., 385 (16 March 1564), 401 (14 April 1564), and 413 (27 April 1564) for other cases involving "marchandes publiques."

82. See the guild regulations published by Lespinasse, *Métiers et corporations de Paris*. See also *Reg. BV*, 3:194n, 4:9 (30 August 1552), 5:224 (3 July 1563) and 484 (6 January 1565).

83. Beatrice Beech, "Charlotte Guillard: A Sixteenth-Century Business Woman," *Renaissance Quarterly* 26 (1983): 346–47 and 351; see also Michon, "Grèves d'imprimeurs," p. 106, on the number of workers required for each press.

84. Platter, *Description de Paris*, p. 11; *Reg. BV*, 4:132 (18 March 1553) and 285 (22 May 1554), 5:260 (July 1563), 372 (28 February 1564), and 407 (20 April 1564).

85. *Reg. BV*, 4:285n (22 May 1554).

86. Ibid., 2:178 (28 March 1534) and 211–14 (20 January–3 February 1536); 3:26n (23 August 1543) and 45–46 (5 and 16 November 1544); 6:297 (17 March 1571); and Michel Félibien and Guy-Alexis Lobineau, *Histoire de la ville de Paris*, 5 vols. (Paris, 1725), *Preuves*, 2:711–14 (19 November 1544) and 725 (30 June 1545). See also Marcel Fosseyeux, "L'assistance parisienne au milieu du XVIᵉ siècle," *MSHParis* 43 (1916): 83 and 115–19.

87. *Reg. BV*, 3:244–45 (16 April 1551) and 245–46n (18 March 1551).

88. Du Breul, *Le théâtre des antiquitez*, pp. 76–77, gives a good description of the Hôtel-Dieu.

89. Félibien and Lobineau, *Histoire de Paris*, *Preuves*, 2:731 (29 July 1547).

90. Fosseyeux, "L'assistance parisienne," pp. 98–102. On the lepers, see Félibien and Lobineau, *Histoire de Paris*, *Preuves*, 2:816.

91. Jacques Bouillart, *Histoire de l'abbaye royale de Saint Germain des Prez* (Paris, 1724), p. 185. See also Babelon, *Paris au XVIᵉ siècle*, pp. 190–91.

92. *Reg. BV*, 3:252 (13 June 1551), 316 (8–20 July 1552); 4:34–36 (20 October 1552), 193 (4 August 1553), 212 (25 August 1553), 373 (24 July 1555), 438 (July 1556), 464 (January 1557), and 495 (August 1557).

93. Jacquart, *La crise rurale en Ile-de-France*, p. 48.

94. Micheline Baulant, "Prix et salaires à Paris au XVIᵉ siècle. Sources et résultats," *Annales, E.S.C.* 31 (1976): 993.

95. Ibid., p. 992.

96. Diefendorf, *Paris City Councillors*, p. 9.

97. Babelon, *Paris au XVIᵉ siècle*, pp. 263–64 and 271–73; Robert Descimon and Jean Nagle, "Les quartiers de Paris du moyen âge au XVIIIᵉ siècle: évolution d'un espace plurifonctionnel," *Annales, E.S.C.* 34 (1979): 962. See also BN, Mss. fr. 21390, for a list of officers of the Châtelet.

98. Babelon, *Paris au XVIᵉ siècle*, pp. 264–66.

99. Alphonse de Ruble, "François de Montmorency, gouverneur de Paris et de l'Ile-de-France," *MSHParis* 6 (1879): 224; Claude Haton, *Mémoires, contenant le récit des événements accomplis de 1553 à 1582*, ed. Félix Bourquelot, 2 vols. (Paris, 1857), 1:378.

100. See, for example, *Reg. BV*, 3:26n, 245, and 245n, on the reform of the poor relief system.

101. On the early history of the Parisian municipality, see Frédéric Lecaron, "Les origines de la municipalité parisienne," *MSHParis* 7 (1880): 79–174 and 8 (1881): 161–272; and Raymond Cazelles, *Nouvelle histoire de Paris: Paris de la fin du règne de Philippe Auguste à la mort de Charles V, 1223–1380* (Paris, 1972).

102. Diefendorf, *Paris City Councillors*, p. 5; Babelon, *Paris au XVIe siècle*, pp. 119–25; *Reg. BV*, 2:164–165.

103. Diefendorf, *Paris City Councillors*, pp. 19–22.

104. Ibid., p. 19.

105. Descimon and Nagle, "Les quartiers de Paris," p. 962.

106. Descimon and Nagle (ibid., p. 963) would go further: "L'antagonisme entre les privilèges et l'accomplissement des fonctions publiques des quartiers mina de l'intérieur le vieux cadre territorial de la municipalité."

107. *Reg. BV*, 4:494–96, 499 (September 1557): review of troops ordered after the disaster of Saint Quentin.

108. AN, Y 12 (16 July 1566).

109. AN, H 2065^1 and H 2065^2: miscellaneous city receipts and orders, among which are many directed to the captains of the three companies during the years 1568–1572.

110. See, for example, *Reg. BV*, 4:33–35 (October 1552), on the deployment of the guet bourgeois when the emperor's troops in Picardy appeared to threaten Paris.

111. *Reg. BV*, 3:202–7 (13 April 1550) and 207n; 5:9–13 (October to December 1558), 13n (August 1559), 87–88 (1 April 1561), and 88n.

112. Diefendorf, *Paris City Councillors*, pp. 22–29.

113. "Du grand et loyal devoir, fidelité et obeissance des Messieurs de Paris envers le roy et couronne de France," otherwise known as the "Livre des marchands," and generally attributed to Louis Régnier, sieur de La Planche. It is published with his *Histoire de l'estat de France, tant de la république que de la religion sous le règne de François II*, ed. Edouard Mennechet, 2 vols. (Paris, 1836).

114. See Lawrence M. Bryant, *The King and the City in the Parisian Royal Entry Ceremony: Politics, Ritual, and Art in the Renaissance* (Geneva, 1986). See also I. D. McFarlane, *The Entry of Henri II into Paris, 16 June 1549* (Binghamton, NY, 1982) and Victor E. Graham and W. McAllister Johnson, *The Paris Entries of Charles IX and Elisabeth of Austria, 1571* (Toronto, 1974).

115. *Reg. BV*, 3:164–71 (16 June 1549).

116. Ibid., 42 (20 September 1544).

117. Chevalier, *Les bonnes villes*, p. 76.

Chapter 2

1. *Reg. BV*, 5:26–27 (5 April 1559).

2. Ibid., 28 (8 April 1559). On the reliquary of Saint Sebastien, see du Breul, *Le théâtre des antiquitez*, p. 38.

3. *Reg. BV*, 5:33–34 (9 July 1559); 34n (10 July 1559).

4. "Paris en 1596," pp. 167–68. Ierni erred in one detail of the French custom. Not only women but any member of the parish might offer the bread to be blessed. Usually the offering was made by the heads of Parisian households. The tapestries Ierni admired at Saint-Merry were only woven in the 1580s, but the custom of decorating Parisian churches with large tapestries on holy days was a well-established one. On the tapestries at Saint-Merry,

see Amédée Boinet, *Les églises parisiennes*, vol. 1: *Moyen âge et Renaissance* (Paris, 1958), p. 415.

5. [Pierre Dyvolé], *Dix sermons de la saincte messe & ceremonies d'icelle* (Paris: Guillaume de la Noue, 1596), p. 285.

6. Babelon, *Paris au XVIᵉ siècle*, p. 131.

7. On the experience of the Mass for lay folk, see Virginia Reinburg, "Popular Prayers in Late Medieval and Reformation France," unpublished Ph.D. dissertation, Princeton University, 1985, chapter 3.

8. Reinold Theisen, *Mass Liturgy and the Council of Trent* (Collegeville, MN, 1965), p. 17, citing Calvin's "Petit traicté de la Saincte Cene" (1541).

9. Olivier Maillard, *L'histoire de la passion* (Paris: Jean Lambert, 1493), fol. Ciiii [unpaginated].

10. This expectation is expressed in the introduction to *L'ordinaire des chrestiens* (Paris: Antoine Vincent, 1495). The book itself, which explains in some detail the sacraments of baptism and penance but not the Mass, is clearly written for the well-educated lay reader or cleric.

11. Jean-Claude Dhotel, *Les origines du catéchisme moderne d'après les premiers manuels imprimés en France* (Paris, 1967), pp. 36–37; see also Bernard Lord Manning, *The People's Faith in the Time of Wyclif* (The Thirwell Essay, 1917), 2d ed. (Totowa, NJ, 1975), pp. 14–16, on religious practice in late medieval England. For more educated people, Petit composed a very interesting manual entitled *La formation de l'homme et son excellence, et ce qu'il doibt accomplir pour avoir paradis* (Paris: Galliot du Pre, 1536).

12. Dhotel, *Origines du catéchisme moderne*, pp. 29–37.

13. Reinburg, "Popular Prayers," pp. 195–97.

14. Nicolas de Thou, *Manière d'administrer les saincts sacremens de l'eglise, y faire prosne et benedictions, avec instructions convenables pour leur intelligence* (Paris: Jacques Kerver, 1580), fol. 94. See also Christofle Cheffontaines, superior general of the Franciscans, *Traitté de l'exercise de la vraye religion, qu'on doit tenir estant au sacrifice de la divine messe, proposé en un sermon à Paris l'an 1561*, included in René Benoist, *Sermon sur le cantique O Salutaris Hostia, recité en une procession de S. Eustache au couvent des filles religieuses de Saincte Claire, dit l'Ave Maria, à Paris, l'an 1577, apres Pasques* (Paris: Nicolas Chesneau, 1577), p. 45.

15. Reinburg, "Popular Prayers," p. 202. Reinburg emphasizes the role of the kiss of peace, however, where I see the holy bread, for its resemblance to the Eucharist, as the more significant ceremony.

16. [Pierre Floriot], *Traité de la messe de paroisse. Où l'on découvre les grands mysteres cachez sous le voile des ceremonies de la messe publique et solemnelle; & les instructions admirables que Jesus-Christ nous y donne par l'unité de son sacrifice* (Paris, 1679), pp. 322–23.

17. Emond Auger, *La maniere d'ouir la messe avec devotion et fruict spirituel. Ensemble la maniere de bien confesser ses pechez & se disposer à recevoir le corps de nostre Seigneur* (Paris: Nicolas Chesneau, 1571), fol. Di. Floriot, *Traité de la messe*, pp. 329–30. See also *Dictionnaire de théologie catholique*, 11 (1931): 1731–32, s.v. "Pain bénit."

18. *Heures de Nostre Dame à l'usaige de Rome* (Paris: Magdaleine Boursette, [1550]), fol. 165v.

19. John Bossy, "The Mass as a Social Institution, 1200–1700," *Past and Present*, no. 100 (1983): 34.

20. Ibid., p. 53. On the obligations of confession and communion, see René Benoist, *Catechisme ou instruction populaire, contenant les principaux poincts de la religion chrestienne, lesquels tous Chrestiens sont tenus de sçavoir, & suivant l'expresse parole de Dieu*

& *ordonnance de l'eglise catholique, apostolique & romain* (Paris: Guillaume de la Noue, 1569), fol. 8.

21. *Dictionnaire de spiritualité, ascétique et mystique, doctrine et histoire*, vol. 4 (Paris, 1961), s.v. "Eucharistie," especially cols. 1626–27 and 1638. On eucharistic piety in a specifically Parisian setting in the later middle ages, see Jean-Georges Vondrus-Reissner, "Présence réelle et juridiction ecclésiastique dans le diocèse de Paris (fin XVème–1530)," *Histoire, économie et société* 7 (1988): 41–54.

22. *Heures de Nostre Dame* [1550], fol. 147r.

23. Du Breul, *Le théâtre des antiquitez*, pp. 807–8; Boinet, *Eglises parisiennes*, 1:393. Anne Lombard-Jourdain has done an excellent reconstruction of the development of the legend behind this miracle. See her "La naissance d'une légende parisienne: Le miracle du Lendit," *Annales, E.S.C.* 28 (1973): 981–96. The museum collection of the Manufacture des Gobelins in Paris contains a tapestry depicting this miracle; it was woven in the first decade of the sixteenth century for a convent in Angers.

24. *Reg. BV*, 2:196 (21 January 1535); Georges Guiffrey, ed., *Chronique du Roy Françoys Premier* (Paris, 1860), p. 114; du Breul, *Le théâtre des antiquitez*, pp. 812–13; l'Abbé Lebeuf, *Histoire de la ville et de tout le diocèse de Paris*, vol. 6: *Rectifications et additions*, ed. Fernard Bournon (Paris, 1890), pp. 62–67. On works of art portraying the story, see Boinet, *Eglises parisiennes*, 1:337–38 and 341–42; on the mystery play, see Louis Petit de Julleville, *Histoire du théâtre en France: Les mystères*, 2 vols. (Paris, 1901), 2:103–4, 193–94, and 574–76.

25. *Reg. BV*, 2:371 (3 July 1538); Jean Calvin, "Advertissement tres-utile du grand profit qui reviendroit à la chrestienté, s'il se faisoit inventaire de tous les corps saincts & reliques" [usually called the "Petit traité des réliques"] in his *Recueil des opuscules. C'est à dire, petits traictez de M. Jean Calvin* (Geneva: Baptiste Pinereul, 1566), p. 741.

26. *Dictionnaire de spiritualité*, vol. 4, s.v. "Eucharistie," col. 1626.

27. *Reg. BV*, 4:165 (after 6 June 1553).

28. Mervyn James, "Ritual, Drama and Social Body in the Late Medieval English Town," *Past and Present*, no. 98 (1983): 3–29, especially pp. 4–5.

29. John Bossy, *Christianity in the West, 1400–1700* (Oxford and New York, 1985), p. 72.

30. Du Breul, *Le théâtre des antiquitez*, p. 130.

31. AN, L 569 (30 April 1549): agreement between Mc François Le Picart, dean of the church of Saint-Germain-l'Auxerrois, and the "maistres & gouverneurs de la confrérie du Tresprecieulx Sainct Sacrement de l'Autel."

32. In Lyons and Troyes, there does appear to be evidence that confraternity membership was declining in the mid-sixteenth century. See Natalie Zemon Davis, "The Sacred and the Body Social in Sixteenth-Century Lyon," *Past and Present*, no. 90 (1981): 51; and A. N. Galpern, *The Religions of the People in Sixteenth-Century Champagne* (Cambridge, MA, 1976), p. 103.

33. *Le manuel de la grand phrairie des bourgeoys et bourgeoyses de Paris* (Paris, 1534); du Breul, *Le théâtre des antiquitez*, pp. 106–10. The statutes for the "Confrairie des porteurs de la Chasse de Madame Saincte Geneviefve" (1564), by contrast, do not require prayer vigils for dying confrères, but they do require participation in their funeral rites. See BN, Imprimés, 4° Le Senne 14616: Manuscript beginning "En l'honneur de Dieu...," fols. 7–8.

34. Archives de l'Assistance publique, Fonds Saint-Jacques-aux-Pèlerins, liasse 22, pièce 272 (23 July 1584). See also René Benoist, *De l'institution et de l'abus survenu és confrairies populaires avec la reformation nécessaire en icelles* (Paris: Nicolas Chesneau, 1578).

35. Nicolas de La Mare, *Traité de la police*, 2 vols. (Paris, 1705–1710), 1:373–75.

36. Michèle Bimbinet-Privat, "Le commerce de l'orfèvrerie à Paris sous les derniers Valois (1547–1589)," *BSHParis* (1983): 94; Jules-Joseph Guiffrey, "Les Mays de Notre-Dame de Paris, d'après un manuscrit conservé aux Archives nationales," *MSHParis* 13 (1886): 292; du Breul, *Le théâtre des antiquitez*, pp. 26–27.

37. Du Breul, *Le théâtre des antiquitez*, p. 825.

38. Ibid., p. 354; see also Claude-Stephen Le Paulmier, *Ambroise Paré, d'après de nouveaux documents découverts aux Archives nationales et des papiers de famille* (Paris, 1887), p. 30n.

39. Benoist, *De l'institution és confrairies*.

40. Dyvolé, *Dix sermons de la saincte messe*, p. 435.

41. Artus Desiré, *L'origine et source de tous les maux de ce monde par l'incorrection des peres & meres envers leurs enfants, & de l'inobedience d'iceux. Ensemble de la trop grande familiarité & liberté donnée aux servans & servantes, avec un petit discours de la visitation de Dieu envers son peuple chrestien par afflictions de querre, peste & famine* (Paris: Jean Dallier, 1571), fol. 42r.

42. Pierre Chaunu, *La mort à Paris. XVIᵉ, XVIIᵉ et XVIIIᵉ siècles* (Paris, 1978), pp. 324–25.

43. AN, LL 704: "Registre des deliberations des affaires de l'eglise parrochialle Sainct Estienne du Mont" (1560), fol. 3. More generally, see Babelon, *Paris au XVIᵉ siècle*, pp. 383–84.

44. AN, LL 848: "Livre des marguilliers," paroisse Saint-Merry (1528–), fols. 5–9.

45. Chaunu, *La mort à Paris*, pp. 306–7 and 470. My own, less systematic investigation of Catholic testaments in the Minutier central supports the same conclusion.

46. AN, MC, VIII, 95 (28 April 1567).

47. Félibien and Lobineau, *Histoire de Paris, Preuves*, 2:752 (11 July 1551).

48. See, for example, Peter Burke, *Popular Culture in Early Modern Europe* (New York and London, 1978), pp. 207–22, on the "reform of popular culture" said to have characterized the sixteenth and seventeenth centuries.

49. Roulland, "La foire Saint-Germain," pp. 196–97; see also Van Langeraad and Vidier, "Description de Paris," pp. 156 and 171.

50. Simon Vigor, *Sermons et predications chrestiennes et catholiques du s. sacrament de l'autel, accommodées pour tous les jours des octaves de la feste Dieu* [hereafter, *SSA*] (Paris: Nicolas Chesneau, 1577), fol. 62v.

51. René Benoist, *Du sacrifice evangelique, où manifestement est prouvé que la saincte messe est le sacrifice eternelle de la nouvelle loy, que Jesus Christ le premier l'a celebrée & commandé aux ministeres de son eglise* (Paris: Nicolas Chesneau, 1564), fols. 19v–20.

52. René Benoist, *Discours de l'histoire du miracle des Ardents, gueris de Dieu, par les prieres & merites de Saincte Geneviefve à Paris, du temps du regne de Louys le Magnanime, fils de Philippes Roy de France. Avec un petit traicté des processions des chrestiens* (Paris: Thomas Belot, 1568), p. 1.

53. François Le Picart, *Les sermons et instructions chrestiennes pour tous les jours de l'advent jusques à Noel, & tous les dimenches & festes depuis Noel jusques à caresme* (Paris: Nicolas Chesneau, 1566), fol. 11; Dyvolé *Dix sermons de la saincte messe*, pp. 276–77. See also René Benoist, *Brieve response à quelque remonstrance faicte à la roine mere du roy par ceux qui se disent persecutez pour la parolle de Dieu* (Paris: Guillaume Guillard & Amaulry Warencore, 1561), fol. e.

54. Le Picart, *Sermons et instructions chrestiennes*, fol. 77v.

55. BN, Mss. fr. 454, fol. 13r: Sermons preached by Claude Despence at Saint-Séverin in 1557. Seventeenth-century copy.

56. Benoist, *Discours du miracle des Ardents*, pp. 19–20; see also René Benoist, *Traicté des processions des chrestiens, auquel il est discouru pour quoy la croix y est eslevée & portée; premierement pourquoy les chrestiens la porte pour marque & signe* (Paris: Michel de Roigny, 1589), pp. 3–4.

57. François Grin, "Journal de François Grin, religieux de Saint-Victor (1554–1570)," ed. Alphonse de Ruble, *MSHParis* 21 (1894): 22; *Reg. BV*, 2:198 (21 January 1535).

58. *Reg. BV*, 2:197–99 (21 January 1535).

59. On the problems of keeping order, see Théodore Godefroy and Denys Godefroy, *Le cérémonial françoys*, 2 vols. (Paris, 1649), 2:941, 942, 951–52. See also AN, Q^{1*} 1099^{200}, fol. 2r, regarding the rental of city-owned houses on the pont Notre-Dame. A clause in all leases provided that city officials had a right to use the windows of the "première chambre" to view processions that passed on the bridge.

60. AN, LL 788: "Cérémonial de l'église Saint-Jacques-de-la-Boucherie"; parts of this ceremonial have been published by Laurence Fritsch-Pinaud, "La vie paroissiale à Saint-Jacques-de-la-Boucherie au XVe siècle," *Paris et Ile-de-France* 33 (1982): 7–99; see especially pp. 78–81. See also du Breul, *Le théâtre des antiquitez*, p. 863.

61. AN, LL 848, "Livre des marguilliers," fol. 147r.

62. BN, Mss. fr. 4338, fols. 50–51. See also *Reg. BV*, 6:334 (13 June 1571): regulations for the policing of Corpus Christi parades; and James, "Ritual, Drama and Social Body," especially p. 5, on the symbolism of Corpus Christi processions. It should be pointed out, however, that the Corpus Christi procession was not unique in this regard. The same basic rules of precedence held for all Parisian processions. The participants joined in an order that clearly symbolized the social hierarchy and its political head, the king (or, in his absence, the magistracy).

63. Du Breul, *Le théâtre des antiquitez*, p. 865; cf. Fritsch-Pinaud, "La vie paroissiale," p. 87.

64. Du Breul, *Le théâtre des antiquitez*, p. 855.

65. Bouillart, *L'abbaye royale de Saint Germain*, p. 188. By contrast, the clergy attached to Notre-Dame made annual processions to Sainte-Geneviève and Saint-Martin-des-Champs on the feast days of those saints (du Breul, *Le théâtre des antiquitez*, pp. 46–48).

66. The phrase is used by the city recorder. *Reg. BV*, 2:196 (21 January 1535).

67. I have taken my figures from Edouard Pinet, *Le culte de Sainte Geneviève à travers les siècles. La compagnie des porteurs de la chasse de Sainte Geneviève, 1525–1902* (Paris, 1903), pp. 75ff. Pinet's principal source is Ms. 1874 of the Bibliothèque Sainte-Geneviève. Somewhat different figures are given in Chaunu, *La mort à Paris*, p. 215. See also Jacques Dubois and Laure Beaumont-Maillet, *Sainte-Geneviève de Paris: La vie, le culte, l'art* (Paris, 1982), pp. 74–84.

68. It was usually the king, or, in his absence, Parlement that ordered the ceremony to take place. The city had an important role in notifying participants and otherwise helping to organize the event, but the officers of the Bureau de la ville do not seem to have had the authority to initiate the ritual. See *Reg. BV*, 3:252n (10 June 1551): example of a procession ordered by Parlement. Du Breul, *Le théâtre des antiquitez*, pp. 286–90.

69. Dubois and Beaumont-Maillet, *Sainte Geneviève de Paris*, p. 105.

70. This description is based on the entries in the *Reg. BV*, 2:98–99 (10 January 1521); 207–8 (13 January 1535); 281–82 (24 August 1536); and 376 (29 July 1538); 3:252–53 (13 June 1551); 4:37–75 (24 and 25 July 1555) and 438 (July 1556); 5:57–58 (16 June 1560); and 6:185–88 (10 September 1570). On the confraternity of the *porteurs de la chasse de Sainte Geneviève*, see the manuscript copy of the statutes of 1564 in the Le Senne collection on the history of Paris at the Bibliothèque nationale (Imprimés: 4° Le Senne 14616) and the

more synthetic description in Pinet, *Le culte de Sainte Geneviève*. There is also a useful collection of extracts from the records of Parlement concerning the procession in the Bibliothèque Sainte-Geneviève (Ms. 681).

71. For the Protestant view, see Henri Estienne, *Apologie pour Hédodote*, new ed., edited by P. Ristelhuber, 2 vols. (Paris, 1879), 2.310; and Thomas Platter, *Description de Paris*, pp. 24–25.

72. *Reg. BV*, 3:252–53 (13 June 1551).

73. Ibid., 4:375 (25 July 1555).

74. Ibid., 5:57–58, 57n (16 June 1560).

75. Jean de La Fosse, *Journal d'un curé ligueur de Paris sous les trois derniers Valois*, ed. Edouard de Barthélemy (Paris, 1866), p. 68 (23 July 1564).

76. *Reg. BV*, 5:565–66 and 565n (7 July 1566); and Grin, "Journal," pp. 34–35.

77. *Reg. BV*, 5:592 and 592n (22 June 1567).

78. See, for example, *Reg. BV*, 2:207 (13 July 1535).

79. Benoist, *Catechisme ou instruction populaire*, fols. 4v–5r.

80. Gentian Hervet, *Recueil d'aucunes mensonges de Calvin, Melanchthon, Bucere, & autres nouveaux evangelistes de ce temps, par lesquelles seduisans & donnans faulx à entendre aux simples* (Paris: Nicolas Chesneau, 1561), fol. 67r. More generally, fols. 32v–34v and 64r–67r. See also René Benoist, *Traicté catholique des images et du vray usage d'icelles; extraict de la saincte escriture & anciens docteurs de l'eglise* (Paris: Nicolas Chesneau, 1564).

81. See also Chaunu, *La mort à Paris*, p. 311. Based on the evidence of testamentary practice, Chaunu concludes that even in the sixteenth century, Parisian piety was "in spite of everything, very reserved about the intercession of angels and saints" and that the Christocentric teachings of the Counter-Reformation only confirmed a "sobriety" already visible in sixteenth-century religious practices.

82. The confraternity of the porteurs de la chasse de Sainte Geneviève prided itself that its members were from the Six Corps or other important mercantile companies and that many had served in public office as judges in the consular court, members of the Bureau des pauvres, or other civic agencies. See the Le Senne manuscript cited above (BN, 4° Le Senne 14616), p. 22. In the other hand, in his forthcoming thesis for Princeton University, Moshe Sluhousky expects to show that the porteurs were not as important city notables as they claimed to be.

83. Charles Hamel, *Histoire de l'église Saint-Sulpice* (Paris, 1900), p. 10.

84. Chaunu, *La mort à Paris*, p. 470. Prayers addressed to Saint Geneviève are inventoried by Jean Sonet, *Répertoire d'incipit de prières en ancien français* (Geneva, 1956), pp. 118, 400, 403; and Pierre Rézeau, *Répertoire d'incipit des prières françaises à la fin du moyen âge: Addenda et corrigenda aux répertoires de Sonet et Sinclair. Nouveaux incipit* (Geneva, 1986), pp. 243 and 321.

85. *Reg. BV*, 2:321–23 (28 March 1537) and 4:336–38 (royal letter of 7 October 1554).

86. Michel Félibien, *Histoire de l'abbaye royale de Saint Denys en France* (Paris, 1706), pp. 369, 387, 392–93; *Reg. BV*, 2:321–23 (28 March 1537); 4:87–93 (2 January 1553); 317–20 (18–20 July 1554); 336–38 (10 October 1554); 6:289–90 (7 and 8 March 1571). See also Blaise de Montesquiou-Fezensac, *Le trésor de Saint-Denis. Inventaire de 1634* (Paris, 1973), pp. 15–18 and 18n, for occasions on which the relics of Saint Denis were taken into Paris for safekeeping.

87. See, for example, the celebrations ordered for the Peace of Cateau-Cambrésis, *Reg. BV*, 5:26–27 (5 April 1559).

88. Ibid., 5:33–34 (9 July 1559).

89. Ibid., 3:42 (13 September 1544).

90. See, for example, ibid., 2:67 (8 July 1530); or 2:335 (8 October 1537).

91. Ibid., 5:28 (8 April 1559); 5:33–34 (9 July 1559).

92. Ibid., 6:59–60 (28–29 September 1568). See also AN, X^{1a} 1624 (29 September 1568). The procession is also described by Félibien, *L'abbaye-royale de Saint-Denys*, pp. 399–400.

93. Ernst H. Kantorowicz, *The King's Two Bodies: A Study in Medieval Political Theology* (Princeton, 1957).

94. Grin, "Journal," p. 49.

95. Ralph Giesey, "Models of Rulership in French Royal Ceremonial," in *Rites of Power*, ed. Sean Wilentz (Philadelphia, 1985), pp. 41–64, especially p. 43. See also Joseph Strayer, "France: The Holy Land, the Chosen People, and the Most Christian King," in *Action and Conviction in Early Modern Europe: Essays in Memory of E. H. Harbison*, ed. Theodore K. Rabb and Jerrold E. Seigel (Princeton, 1969), pp. 3–16.

96. *Reg. BV*, 2:24–26 (12 June 1528).

97. Fernand Bournon, ed., "Chronique de Pierre Driart, chambrier de Saint-Victor (1522–1535)," *MSHParis* 22 (1895): 133; Boinet, *Eglises parisiennes*, 1:387.

98. *Reg. BV*, 2:195–96 (21 January 1535); more broadly on the procession, 195–99. See also Guiffrey, *Chronique du Roy Françoys Premier*, pp. 113–14; Bournon, "Chronique de Pierre Driart," pp. 175–77; Godefroy and Godefroy, *Le cérémonial françoys*, 2:939–45; Ludovic Lalanne, ed., *Journal d'un bourgeois de Paris sous le règne de François premier (1515–1536)* (Paris, 1854), pp. 442–44. On the sacred host of Saint-Jean-en-Grève, see above, note 24.

99. *Reg. BV*, 2:198.

100. On the etiquette governing the relics of Saint Geneviève, see Dubois and Beaumont-Maillet, *Sainte Geneviève de Paris*, p. 105.

101. The accounts we have of the speech differ somewhat in their exact wording but do not differ significantly in meaning. See Godefroy and Godefroy, *Le cérémonial françoys*, 2:934–35; *Reg. BV*, 2:199; Guiffrey, ed., *Chronique du Roy Françoys Premier*, p. 125.

102. *Reg. BV*, 3:183–85 (4 July 1549); Félibien and Lobineau, *Histoire de Paris, Preuves*, 2:745–46 (4 July 1549). I. D. McFarlane, *The Entry of Henri II into Paris, 16 June 1549* (Binghamton, NY, 1982), pp. 68–69, reproduces the account of Belleforest.

103. Pinet, *Le culte de Sainte Geneviève*, pp. 103–7.

104. Attacks on the Virgin occurred in December 1550 at Notre-Dame; in December 1552 behind the chapel of Saint-Antoine; and in September 1554 in the cemetery of Saint-Nicolas-des-Champs. See Félibien and Lobineau, *Histoire de Paris, Preuves*, 2:748 (10 December 1550), 755 (16 December 1552), and 765–66 (10 September 1554); and *Reg. BV*, 3:233 (14 December 1550) and 4:249 (26 December 1553).

105. See, for example, *Reg. BV*, 5:259 and 259n: procession of 17 July 1563 to Saint-Barthélemy to expiate a profanation of the host; 342: procession of 26 December 1563 to expiate a sacrilege committed in Sainte-Geneviève. The precautions that had to be taken to prevent the spilling of blood during Corpus Christi celebrations also illustrate the emotional tensions associated with eucharistic practices.

106. *Reg. BV*, 5:125–26 (13 and 14 June 1562); see also Grin, "Journal," pp. 22–24.

Chapter 3

1. *Hist. eccl.*, 1:139–56. This is the standard Protestant account, largely derived from Antoine de la Roche Chandieu, *Histoire des persecutions et martyrs de l'eglise de Paris, depuis l'an 1557 jusques au temps du roy Charles neufviesme* (Lyon, 1563) and Jean Crespin, *Histoire des martyrs persecutez et mis à mort pour la verité de l'evangile* (Geneva, 1564).

See also [Pierre de La Place,] *Commentaire de l'estat de la religion & republique soubs les rois Henry & François seconds, & Charles neufieme* (N.p, 1565), fol. 5v. For secondary sources, see Fernand Aubert, "A propos de l'affaire de la rue Saint-Jacques (4–5 septembre 1557) un rapport présenté par l'église de Paris à la délégation helvétique," *BSHPF* 95 (1947): 96–102; Nathanaël Weiss, "L'assemblée de la rue Saint-Jacques, 4–5 septembre 1557," *BSHPF* 65 (1916): 195–235; and Haton, *Mémoires*, 1:47–53.

2. *Journal d'un bourgeois de Paris*, pp. 276–77; Guiffrey, ed., *Chronique du Roy Francoys Premier*, pp. 110–33; Bournon, ed., 'Chronique de Pierre Driart," pp. 79, 113–15, 133, 167, and 172–78; *Hist. eccl.*, 1:35 and 112.

3. *Reg. BV*, 4:493 and 494: reports of the defeat of Saint-Quentin.

4. Ibid., 4:495–98.

5. Ibid., 4:499–500.

6. Etienne Pasquier, *Les oeuvres*, 2 vols. (Amsterdam, 1723), 2:75–76; Aubert, "L'affaire de la rue Saint-Jacques," p. 98; Jean de la Vacquerie, *Catholique remonstrance aux roys et princes chrestiens* (Paris: Nicolas Chesneau, 1560), fol. 27. Grin, "Journal," p. 16, also reports rumors of treason on the part of Coligny, who had been charged with the defense of Saint-Quentin, but it is hard to know what to make of this accusation, since Coligny is generally believed to have converted to Calvinism only during his imprisonment after Saint-Quentin, and he did not actively support the Protestant cause, though some accused him of doing so, for another three years. See Junko Shimizu, *Conflict of Loyalties: Politics and Religion in the Career of Gaspard de Coligny, Admiral of France, 1519–1572* (Geneva, 1970), pp. 25–31.

7. Athanase Coquerel, *Précis de l'histoire de l'Eglise réformée de Paris*, vol. 1: *Première époque* (Paris, 1862), pp. xxv–xxvi (letter of 7 February 1558), xxxvii (letter of 27 March 1558), and lxix (letter of 6 March [1559]).

8. Ibid., pp. xl–xli (letter of 22 May 1558); *Hist. eccl.*, 1:167.

9. On attempts to make peace so as to pursue Protestants: see Coquerel, *Précis*, pp. liv–lv (letter of 26 August 1558), lviii (letter of 24 September 1558), and lxi (letter of 15 October 1558); and Jules Bonnet, "Jean Macard: Un an de ministère à Paris sous Henri II," *BSHPF* 26 (1877): 99. On persecutions resulting from the affair of the pré aux Clercs, see Weiss, "L'assemblée de la rue Saint-Jacques," p. 224, citing AN, X^{2a} 121 (13 August 1558): *amende honorable* of Matthieu Bachellet for "assemblées faictes au pré aux Clercs."

10. Coquerel, *Précis*, pp. xlviii (letter of 11 July 1558) and lvii–lviii (letter of 24 September 1558).

11. On the mercuriale, see Denis-François Sécousse, ed., *Mémoires de Condé, servant d'éclaircissement et de preuves à l'Histoire de M. de Thou*, 6 vols. (London and Paris, 1743–1745), 1:217–304; see also Jules Bonnet, "L'Eglise réformée de Paris sous Henri II. Ministère de François Morel (1558–1559)," *BSHPF* 27 (1878): 443–49. On the belief that the judges were too lenient, see La Vacquerie, *Catholique remonstrance*, fols. 43 and 63–64.

12. On the increase in persecution see La Fosse, *Journal d'un curé ligueur*, pp. 35–39, and Louis Régnier de La Planche, *Histoire de l'estat de France tant de la république que de la religion sous le règne de François II*, edited by J. A. C. Buchon (Paris, 1836), pp. 220–26; 236–37. For some of the edicts and royal letters from this period ordering the repression of heresy, see Robert O. Lindsay and John Neu, *French Political Pamphlets, 1547–1648: A Catalogue of Major Collections in American Libraries* (Madison, 1969), pp. 112–14, especially entries 132, 141, 145, 146, 153, 155, and 156. On the incident regarding the arrested apprentices see also Bonnet, "Ministère de François Morel," p. 45; and Coquerel, *Précis*, p. lxi (letter of 15 October 1558). Jean de la Vacquerie, in his *Catholique remonstrance*, fols. 52v–53r, encouraged the use of denunciations to rid France of its heretics.

13. AN, X^{2a} 125 (19 August 1559). Le Riche had been turned over to the church inquisitors

on 5 May 1559. The bishop's official pronounced on her heresy and returned her to the secular arm for punishment, as was normally done at this time. Alfred Soman has found that the *question préalable* (torture of a condemned person in order to find out the names of his accomplices) was only rarely practiced by the magistrates of the Parlement of Paris. Its use for condemned heretics in 1559 and 1560 is thus another sign of the special rigor of the proceedings against heretics in this period. At the same time, the fact that the Parlement of Paris overturned several sentences by the prévôt of Paris ordering the question préalable for convicted heretics would seem to confirm Soman's point about the reluctance of the high court to order this torture. See Alfred Soman, "La justice criminelle aux XVIe–XVIIe siècles: Le Parlement de Paris et les sièges subalternes," *107e Congrès national des Sociétés savantes, Brest, 1982. Philologie et histoire jusqu'à 1610*, 2 vols. (Paris, 1984), 1:33. Relevant cases include AN, X^{2a} 125 (7 December 1559) and X^{2a} 918 (7 December 1559): case of Jean Geoffroy; and X^{2a} 125 (11 January 1559/1560): case of Jean Le Maistre.

14. Bournon, "Chronique de Pierre Driart," pp. 78 and 113.

15. See, for example, AN, X^{2a} 125 (7 December 1559) and X^{2a} 918 (7 December 1559): case of Jean Geoffroy. On forms of punishment associated with different crimes, see Soman, "Justice criminelle," pp. 29–31. Soman argues convincingly that prisoners sentenced to burning were generally strangled first even if the special clause, or *retentum*, was not added to their sentence.

16. Bonnet, "Ministère de François Morel," p. 436; and Coquerel, p. xlviii (letter of 11 July 1558), which refers to a longer account in a letter (now lost) from Macard to Calvin.

17. La Planche, *Histoire de l'estat de France*, ed. Buchon, pp. 236 and 312–13.

18. AN, X^{2a} 131 (28 June 1563) and X^{2a} 133 (29 February 1564/1565).

19. Sécousse, ed., *Mémoires de Condé*, 1:308–15. It is not clear that informers ever did profit in a significant way from their denunciations. Confiscated properties appear most often to have been ordered sold and the profits used for charitable purposes. See, for example, AN, X^{2a} 125 (7 December 1559): case of Jean Geoffroy; X^{2a} 125 (5 January 1559/1560): case of Pierre Girard; X^{2a} 126 (15 June 1560): request presented by the *procureur général* concerning confiscated properties. See also Bonnet, "Ministère de François Morel," p. 246, citing a letter from Morel.

20. La Planche, *Histoire de l'estat de France*, ed. Buchon, p. 237.

21. *Hist. eccl.*, 1:192–94. The narrative accounts we have of these events may be challenged as partisan, but parlementary records confirm that a riot resulting in serious injuries and at least one death did take place in the church and cemetery of the Innocents on Sunday, 5 March 1559. One year later, two journeymen artisans were sent to the galleys for their part in this incident. A priest was also arrested in the case, but his role is unclear. See AN, X^{2a} 125 (6 April 1559/1560 and 31 May 1560).

22. On the incident at Saint-Eustache, see the *Hist. eccl.*, 1:192–94; on the incident at Saint-Médard, see La Fosse, *Journal d'un curé ligueur*, p. 36. An investigation by the lieutenant criminel into the "assemblies, murders, and violence" that took place at Saint-Médard on the evening of 14 December 1559 resulted in an order to arrest a local *bonnetier* named Nicolas Le Duc, alias "Le Lorrain," and his wife, and two other bonnetiers in the neighborhood. Three of the four suspects had already been arrested four months earlier on charges brought by a local priest, and Le Duc and his wife had previously been convicted of religious offenses, but apparently the charges brought against them for the Saint-Médard affair could not be sustained, for all were released on bail and the affair seems to have been dropped. See AN, X^{2a} 124 (9 August 1559) and 125 (31 December 1559, 30 January, 20 and 22 February, and 6 March 1559/1560).

23. This is clearly expressed in Jean de la Vacquerie's *Catholique remonstrance* and in other polemics that will be discussed in greater detail in Chapter 9.

24. Haton, *Mémoires*, 1:50–53. See also Weiss, "L'assemblée de la rue Saint-Jacques," pp. 215 and 225.

25. G. Wylie Sypher, " 'Faisant ce qu'il leur vient à plaisir': The Image of Protestantism in French Catholic Polemic on the Eve of the Religious Wars," *Sixteenth Century Journal* 11 (1980): 59; more generally on Catholic polemics before the first religious war: pp. 59–84. Also see La Vacquerie, *Catholique remonstrance*, fols 37r–39r; and *Hist. eccl.*, 1:268–71. On de Mouchy's position as inquisitor, see AN, X^{2a} 125 (16 January 1559/1560).

26. Haton, *Mémoires*, 1:86.

27. La Vacquerie, *Catholique remonstrance*, fols. 36r and 37r; see also Sypher, "French Catholic Polemic," pp. 71–73.

28. On the assumed link between heresy and debauchery, see La Vacquerie, *Catholique remonstrance*, fols. 15–16r and 37v–38.

29. La Planche, *Histoire de l'estat de France*, ed. Buchon, pp. 223–24.

30. La Vacquerie, *Catholique remonstrance*, fols. 36r and 37r, refers to two earlier attempts on the part of the Protestants to set fire to the city of Paris, but I have found no evidence that this rumor was widespread before 1559.

31. *Reg. BV*, 5:47 and 47n (23 December 1559); AN, X^{2a} 125 (23 December 1559); La Fosse, *Journal d'un curé ligueur*, p. 35.

32. *Reg. BV*, 5:52–53 and 52–53n (30 March and 6 April 1559/1560); AN, X^{2a} 125 (8 April 1559/1560).

33. AN, X^{2a} 126 (31 July 1560).

34. *Reg. BV*, 5:53n, citing AN, X^{1a} 1595, fol. 166r.

35. The best accounts of these events are by La Fosse, *Journal d'un curé ligueur*, p. 36; and La Planche, *Histoire de l'estat de France*, ed. Buchon, pp. 312–13. The relevant parlementary sources are AN, X^{2a} 126 (28 June and 13 and 18 July 1560). The pamphlet is believed to have been written by François Hotman and has been republished as *"Le Tigre" de 1560. Réproduit pour la première fois en fac-similé*, ed. Charles Read (Geneva, 1970; reprint of Paris edition, 1875).

36. La Planche, *Histoire de l'estat de France*, ed. Buchon, pp. 312–13.

37. Jean-Henri Mariéjol, *La Réforme, la Ligue, l'Edit de Nantes (1559–1598)* (Paris, 1983; originally published in 1904 as vol. 6, pt. 1 of *L'histoire de France des origines à la Révolution*, ed. Ernest Lavisse), p. 46. This is still one of the best narrative accounts of this period, at least as far as the popular violence is concerned.

38. Ibid., pp. 46–48.

39. La Fosse, *Journal d'un curé ligueur*, p. 41; see also Nicolas Brulart, *Journal des choses plus remarquables (1559–1569)*, in *Mémoires de Condé*, ed. Denis-François Sécousse (Paris, 1743), 1:26.

40. AN, X^{1a} 1597 (14 April 1561); Sécousse, ed., *Mémoires de Condé*, 2:332. See also BN, Mss. Dupuy 722, pp. 101–6: Remonstrances of 11 May 1561.

41. AN, X^{1a} 1597 (26 April 1561). Accounts of the events are given by Brulart, *Journal*, p. 26; La Fosse, *Journal d'un curé ligueur*, p. 42; and the British attaché: *CSP,F*, 4:89–90 (letter of 30 April 1561). See also Sécousse, *Memoires de Condé*, 2:341–47. The husband of the woman killed in the riots filed charges against Longjumeau and several other Calvinists he held responsible for her death. See AN, X^{2a} 128 (21 June 1561). More broadly on religious unrest in Paris in the spring of 1561, see Michele Suriano and Marc Antonio Barbaro, *Dispatches* (Publications of the Huguenot Society of London, vol. 6; Lymington, 1891), p. 24 (letter of 2 May 1561).

42. Sécousse, ed., *Mémoires de Condé*, 2:345; *Reg. BV*, 5:90–91 and 90–91n (2 May 1561); *CSP,F*, 4:96 (letter of 4 May 1561).

43. Suriano, *Dispatches*, p. 25 (letters of 14 and 16 May 1561; the latter also signed by Leggi and Cavalli, who were in France on a special mission).

44. *Reg. BV*, 5:91 (5 May 1561).

45. Suriano, *Dispatches*, p. 24 (letter of 2 May 1561).

46. BN, Mss. Dupuy 722, pp. 101–6: Remonstrances of 11 May 1561.

47. Suriano, *Dispatches*, p. 28 (letter of 25 June 1561).

48. Sécousse, ed., *Mémoires de Condé*, 2:369.

49. Suriano, *Dispatches*, pp. 26–27 (letter of 10 June 1561); La Fosse, *Journal d'un curé ligueur*, p. 43.

50. Suriano, *Dispatches*, p. 28 (letter of 25 June 1561).

51. *Edict du roy sur le faict de la religion, publié en la cour de Parlement à Paris le dernier jour de juilliet 1561* (Paris: Jean Dallier, [1561]). Discussed by Suriano, *Dispatches*, pp. 30–33 (letters of 14, 15, and 27 July 1561), and by Pasquier, *Oeuvres*, 2:85–86 (book 4, letter 10).

52. Pasquier, *Oeuvres*, 2:87–88 (book 4, letter 11).

53. Ibid.; Suriano, *Dispatches*, p. 48 (letter of 3 November 1561); BN, Mss. fr., N.a. 8061, fol. 56v. The Protestant view of these events is given in the *Hist. eccl.*, 1:740–41 and 746. More generally, see Mariéjol, *Le Réforme*, pp. 60–64. The best recent account of the Colloquy of Poissy is given by Donald Nugent, *Ecumenism in the Age of the Reformation: The Colloquy of Poissy* (Cambridge, 1974).

54. François de La Noue, *Discours politiques et militaires du Seigneur de la Noue, nouvellement recueillis et mis en lumiere* (Geneva: François Forest, 1587), pp. 549–53.

55. Brulart, *Journal*, pp. 57–59, citing letters of the king dated 16 September 1561. For an example of this popular violence, see AN, X^{2a} 128 (25 October 1561): case of Jean Bonnallet, accused of taking part in a "tumulte" at Saint-Martin-des-Champs on 19 October 1561.

56. La Fosse, *Journal d'un curé ligueur*, p. 44, relates that there were a number of Huguenots killed, but the *Hist. eccl.*, 1:741, claims only injuries, including one *mercier* who was "gravely injured, left for dead, and thrown in a gutter outside the porte de Montmartre."

57. *Reg. BV*, 5:103–4 and 103–4n, citing edict of 21 October 1561; Suriano, *Dispatches*, p. 48 (letter of 3 November 1561); Haton, *Mémoires*, 1:178–79.

58. Brulart, *Journal*, p. 67; Suriano, *Dispatches*, p. 46 (letter of 16 October 1561).

59. For Catholic pleas to take up arms to defend the churches, see Pasquier, *Oeuvres*, 2:90 (book 4, letter 12). On the incidents of seditious preaching at Saint-Benoît, the Sorbonne, and other Paris churches, see BN, Mss. fr., N.a. 8061, fols. 15v–16r, 25–26, 35, 39, 43v–44r, and 55v. See also Sécousse, ed., *Mémoires de Condé*, 2:285–86, citing letters of 2 April 1560/1561 to investigate reports of seditious preaching by a preacher named Fournier in the parishes of Saint-Séverin and Saint-Germain, and 2:532, citing the royal order of 29 November 1561 ordering an investigation into the report of seditious preaching at Saint-Benoît. Catherine de Medici, *Lettres*, ed. Hector de la Ferriere and Baguenault de Puchesse (Paris, 1880), 1:182, also refers to suspicions directed against Fournier in April 1561.

60. AN, X^{1a} 1599 (10 and 12 December 1561); *Reg. BV*, 5:109 (13 December 1561) and 109n; Haton, *Mémoires*, 1:210–13; Pasquier, *Oeuvres*, 2:89–90 (book 4, letters 12 and 13). See also de Ruble, "L'arrestation de Jean de Hans," pp. 85–94. Some religious violence did occur in the city at this time, though no direct connection to the Jean de Hans affair can be demonstrated. On 20 March 1562, Parlement upheld the conviction of one Jean Fere, known as "Brivelureau," and exiled him from Paris for five years for having killed a shoemaker in the rue Saint-Antoine on 10 December in a quarrel over religious issues. See AN, X^{2a} 129 (20 March 1561/1562).

61. The standard Protestant accounts are given in the *Hist. eccl.*, 1:745–51; Sécousse, ed., *Mémoires de Condé*, 2:541–57; the "Histoire véritable de la mutinerie, tumulte et sédition faicte par les prestres de Sainct-Médard," in *Archives curieuses*, ed. Cimber and

Danjou, 4:51–68 and related documents, pp. 68–102; and *CSP,F*, vol. 4, nos. 783 (4 January 1561/1562) and 789. Catholic accounts include Brulart, *Journal*, pp. 68–69; Grin, "Journal," p. 21; and *Discours sur le saccagement des eglises catholiques par les heretiques anciens & nouveaux Calvinistes en l'an mil cing cens soixante & deux* (n.p., n.d. [1562]), fols. 31–35.

62. Félibien and Lobineau, *Histoire de Paris*, 2:1079.

63. Brulart, *Journal*, pp. 68–69; *Discours sur le saccagement*, fol. 31; Pasquier, *Oeuvres*, 2:89–90 (book 4, letter 13). Indignation over the fact that officers of the watch, who were paid by the Parisian bourgeoisie, were being used to protect the Protestant assemblies is also shown in the *Remonstrances faictes au roy de France par messieurs de la court de Parlement de Paris sur la publication de l'edict du moys de janvier* (Cambrai: [Nicolas Lombard], 1561/1562). See also AN, X^{2a} 129 (29 December 1561). Eventually it was the Protestants who were punished for the tumult of Saint-Médard. See AN, X^{2a} 129 (5, 12, and 20 January; 23 March; 14, 29, and 30 April 1561/1562) and X^{2a} 923 (7 and 16 April 1561/1562); also Brulart, *Journal*, p. 95, regarding pursuits ordered against Huguenots or Huguenot sympathizers accused of having taken part in the affair. In May, when a man nicknamed "Nez d'Argent" was executed for his part in the attack on Saint-Médard, special guards had to be posted to keep order at the execution (La Fosse, *Journal d'un curé ligueur*, p. 49).

64. *Edict du Roy Charles Neufieme . . . sur les moyens les plus propres d'appaiser les troubles & seditions survenus pour le faict de la Religion* (Paris: Robert Estienne, 1562); republished by André Stegmann, ed., *Edits des guerres de religion* (Paris, 1979), pp. 8–14.

65. "Un manifeste parisien contre le premier édit de tolérance (1562)," *BSHPF* 17 (1868): 534–40. City registers (*Reg. BV*, 5:117) make it clear that this was not an official manifesto drawn up by city officials. On the disorders in Paris at this time: Catherine de Medici, *Lettres*, 1:277–78 (letter of 24 February 1561/1562) and AN, X^{2a} 129 (27 February 1561/1562): investigation of incidents occurring on the pont Notre-Dame, in the Cemetery of the Innocents, and other places in Paris.

66. The king sent lettres de jussion ordering registration of the edict on 14 February and again on 1 March. *Remonstrances faictes au roy; CSP,F*, vol. 4, no. 849 (28 January 1562) and 930 (9 March 1562); and Pierre de 'Paschal, *Journal de ce qui s'est passé en France durant l'année 1562, principalement dans Paris et à la cour*, ed. Michel François (Paris, 1950), p. 5.

67. *Reg. BV*, 5:117–18n, citing AN, X^{1a} 1600, fols. 191v and 234v. See also Brulart, *Journal*, p. 73; and Paschal, *Journal de l'année 1562*, p. 6.

68. *CSP,F*, vol. 4, no. 943 (20 March 1562). See also Jacques-Auguste de Thou, *Histoire universelle depuis 1543 jusqu'en 1607*, vol. 4 (London, 1732), p. 172.

69. Paschal, *Journal de l'année 1562*, p. 7. La Fosse, *Journal d'un curé ligueur*, p. 45, gives the date of the event as 15 March.

70. *CSP,F*, vol. 4, no. 943 (20 March 1562). Condé's own explanation for his actions is given in his *Declaration faicte par Monsieur le prince de Condé pour monstrer les raisons qui l'ont contrainct d'entreprendre la defense de l'authorité du roy* (n.p., 1562).

71. Dom Hyacinthe Morice, *Mémoires pour servir de preuves à l'histoire ecclésiastique et civile de Bretagne*. Vol. 3: *Preuves* (Paris, 1746), cols. 1302–3: letters from the Reformed Church of Angers to that of Nantes (22 March 1561/1562) and from the Reformed Church of Paris to that of Angers (10 March 1561/1562). According to La Rivière, writing for the Paris church, "ils font bien leurs efforts de massacrer l'assemblée qui est en ceste ville s'ils la peuvent surpren & si Dieu ne rompoit souvent leurs maudites entreprises. Nous vous prions donc vous tenir prests non seulement pour deffendre vostre Eglise; mais aussi pour secourir celles qui seront les premieres assaillies."

72. Pasquier, *Oeuvres*, 2:95–96 (book 4, letter 14); Paschal, *Journal de l'année 1562*, p. 10. See also La Fosse, *Journal d'un curé ligueur*, p. 46; and *Reg. BV*, 5:117–18n.

73. *Reg. BV*, 5:118–19 (20 March 1562). The cardinal was appointed lieutenant général for Paris because the governor for the Ile-de-France, the maréchal de Montmorency, was reputed to favor the new religion.

74. Condé, *Declaration faicte par Monsieur le prince de Condé*.

75. Pasquier, *Oeuvres*, 2:95–96 (book 4, letter 15). On the other hand, it is hard not to agree with the later judgment of the Huguenot tactician and military leader François de La Noue that Condé was right to withdraw from Paris and thereby to abandon the city to the Catholics, because the Protestants were so badly outnumbered by their enemies in the capital that they could not possibly have held out three days if open fighting had broken out in the city. It would have been, in La Noue's words, "like a little fly up against a big elephant." See La Noue, *Discours politiques et militaires*, pp. 549–53.

76. Ibid., Paschal, *Journal de l'année 1562*, pp. 16–17; Sécousse, *Mémoires de Condé*, 3:198–99; Brulart, *Journal*, pp. 80–81; La Fosse, *Journal d'un curé ligueur*, p. 47.

77. *Declaration du roy sur le faict et police de la religion portant defense de faire presches & conventicules en la ville, faulbours, & banlieue de Paris* (Paris: Vincent Sertenas, 1562).

Chapter 4

1. Paquier, *Oeuvres*, 2:95–96 (book 4, letter 15); Paschal, *Journal de l'année 1562*, p. 15; *Mémoires de Condé*, 3:419–21; *Reg. BV*, 5:119–23.

2. Paschal, *Journal de l'année 1562*, pp. 37–38; also referred to by La Fosse, *Journal d'un curé ligueur*, p. 50. A report in the city records attributes the false alarm to a deliberate testing of the city's defenses by Montmorency, but this report, which was written later, and which makes it appear that the city responded in a prompt and orderly fashion to the alarm, is less credible than the reports that suggest an atmosphere of panic. See *Reg. BV*, 5:164–65.

3. Félibien and Lobineau, *Histoire de Paris*, *Preuves* 1:667: ordonnance du roi de Navarre, 26 May 1562. See also *Reg. BV*, 5:126n.

4. Félibien and Lobineau, *Histoire de Paris*, *Preuves*, 1:667: ordonnance du 27 mai 1562. See also AN, X²ᵇ 34 (7 November 1562); and Paschal, *Journal de l'année 1562*, p. 47.

5. Pasquier, *Oeuvres*, 2:100 (book 4, letter 16); Paschal, *Journal de l'année 1562*, p. 43.

6. Paschal, *Journal de l'année 1562*, p. 43; La Fosse, *Journal d'un curé ligueur*, p. 50.

7. *Reg. BV*, 5:125–26 (14 June 1562); Paschal, *Journal de l'année 1562*, pp. 52–53; Grin, "Journal," pp. 22–24; La Fosse, *Journal d'un curé ligueur*, p. 52.

8. Paschal, *Journal de l'année 1562*, p. 54.

9. *L'arrest de la court de Parlement publié le dernier jour de juin dernier passé, touchant les rebelles & perturbateurs du repos & tranquillité des sujects du roy* (Paris: Guillaume Morel, 1562).

10. Paschal, *Journal de l'année 1562*, pp. 62–63. See also Brulart, *Journal*, pp. 90–91; and La Fosse, *Journal d'un curé ligueur*, p. 52.

11. Paul Guérin, "Délibérations politiques du Parlement et arrêts criminels du milieu de la première guerre de religion (1562)," *MSHParis* 40 (1913): 11.

12. Ibid., pp. 11–14.

13. Ibid., p. 11.

14. Paschal, *Journal de l'année 1562*, p. 93; *Reg. BV*, 5:140–51 and 145n.

15. AN, X^{2b} 34 (19 October 1562); published in *Reg. BV*, 5:147–48; see also Guérin, "Délibérations politiques," pp. 80–81.

16. See AN, X^{2b} 34: many cases from October and November 1562, and X^{2a} 130: many cases from November and December 1562; X^{2a} 1201: list of prisoners in the Conciergerie.

17. AN, X^{2b} 34 (24 October 1562); see also Guérin, "Délibérations politiques," p. 88.

18. AN, X^{2a} 130 (24 November 1562).

19. See, for example, AN, Z^{1h} 59^b, fol. 19 (24 October 1562): case of Ysabeau Le Riche; or X^{2b} 34 (29 October 1562): case of Jehanne Danys.

20. Guérin, "Délibérations politiques," p. 67; Brulart, *Journal*, pp. 94–95.

21. See, for example, AN, X^{2a} 130 (10 December 1562): case of Antoine Poyet (false arrest); X^{2b} 34 (7 November 1562): cases of Guillaume de Hodic and Guillaume François (harassment); X^{2a} 130 (11 December 1562): case of Nicole Richier (imprisoned two months without charges); X^{2a} 130 (23 February 1562/1563): case of Me Jacques de Beauvais (imprisoned five months without trial).

22. See, for example, AN, X^{2a} 130 (13 November 1562): arrest of Nicolas de Lerigny; see also Guérin, "Délibérations politiques," pp. 82–83: report of a crowd throwing two suspects into the Seine.

23. Jacquart, *La crise rurale in Ile-de-France*, pp. 171–72; *Reg. BV*, 5:177–78.

24. Paschal, *Journal de l'année 1562*, p. 100. Guise and Montmorency entered Paris 13 November, the same day the Huguenots took Etampes.

25. Suriano and Barbaro, *Dispatches*, p. 59.

26. Ibid., p. 63; also Paschal, *Journal de l'année 1562*, p. 100; and Brulart, *Journal*, p. 103.

27. *Reg. BV*, 5:179–80.

28. Suriano and Barbaro, *Dispatches*, p. 62 (letters of 22 and 25 November 1562).

29. *Reg. BV* 5:183 and 183n; Paschal, *Journal de l'année 1562*, pp. 109–10.

30. Paschal, *Journal de l'année 1562*, pp. 117–18.

31. *Reg. BV*, 5:184–85 (letter of 5 January 1562/1563).

32. *CSP,F*, 6:49: Smith to the queen, letter of 17 January 1562/1563.

33. Ibid., 6:78: Smith to Privy Council, 26 January 1562/1563; and Pasquier, *Oeuvres*, 2:103–4 (book 4, letter 19).

34. *Reg. BV*, 5:185–86 (arrêt of 16 January 1562/1563); *CSP,F*, 6:78 (Smith to Privy Council, 26 January 1562/1563); Paschal, *Journal de l'année 1562*, p. 122. See also AN, X^{2a} 130 and X^{2a} 1201 (arrests for January and February 1563).

35. AN, X^{2a} 130 (12 February 1562/1563): case of Nicolas Richer. See also Haton, *Mémoires*, 1:276.

36. See, for example, AN, X^{2a} 130 (14 January 1562/1563): case of Jehan Marie; or (26 January 1562/1563): case of Jehan Huet.

37. *CSP,F*, 6:101 (Smith to Cecil, 4 February 1562/1563).

38. *Reg. BV*, 5:188–90; see also La Fosse, *Journal d'un curé ligueur*, p. 60.

39. *CSP,F*, 6:101–4 (Smith to Cecil, letter of 4 February 1562/1563).

40. *Reg. BV*, 5:190–91n.

41. Catherine de Medici, *Lettres*, 1:498–500 (Catherine to Montmorency, letters of 7 and 8 February 1562/1563).

42. La Fosse, *Journal d'un curé ligueur*, p. 62.

43. Suriano and Barbaro, *Dispatches*, p. 81 (letters of 3 and 12 March 1562/1563).

44. *CSP,F*, 6:162–63 ("Occurrences in France," 26 February 1562/1563).

45. AN, X^{2a} 130 (12 March 1562/1563): case of Nicolas du Mont, the husband of the woman in question. This case is crossed out in compliance with a later order to eliminate from the records all cases dealing with the religious troubles, but it is still legible.

46. *Reg. BV*, 5:201 (orders to quarteniers, 12 March 1562/1563); also AN, X^{2a} 130 (15 March 1562/1563): orders for guards to accompany Châtelet officers.

47. AN, X^{2a} 130 (18 March 1562/1563); see also *Reg. BV*, 5:202 and 202n; and Grin, "Journal," pp. 26–27.

48. *Reg. BV*, 5:203–6.

49. La Fosse, *Journal d'un curé ligueur*, p. 62.

50. *Edict de declaration faicte par le roy Charles IX de ce nom sur la pacification des troubles de ce royaume* ([Paris]: Robert Estienne, 1563). The verson published by Stegmann, *Edits des guerres de religion*, pp. 32–36, lacks the clauses pertaining to Paris.

51. *Reg. BV*, 5:213n; Suriano and Barbaro, *Dispatches*, p. 85 (letter of 29 March 1562/1563); *CSP,F*, 6:246 (Middlemore to the queen, 20 March 1562/1563).

52. Haton, *Mémoires*, 1:328.

53. *Reg. BV*, 5:213–14 (letters of 5 April 1562/1563 and 10 April 1562/1563).

54. Ibid., 5:212n, 214–15 (proceedings of 12 April 1563), and 219 (proceedings of 27 April 1563).

55. Ibid., 5:214 (proceedings of 12 April 1563).

56. AN, X^{2a} 130 (7 April 1562/1563).

57. AN, X^{2a} 132 (20 January 1563/1564) and (5 February 1563/1564); *Reg. BV* 5:323 (27 October 1563), 339 (18 December 1563), 401 (19 April 1564), and 420 (12 May 1564).

58. La Fosse, *Journal d'un curé ligueur*, p. 68. The body was that of Nicole Gobelin, the wife of Nicolas Croquet, later one of the victims of the cross of Gastines affair. A journeyman weaver arrested in the riot was sentenced to make a formal admission of guilt and remorse (amende honorable) and was banished from Paris for three years. See AN, X^{2a} 132 (11 April 1564): case of Paul du Four. See also Brulart, *Journal*, pp. 138–39, on the royal edict.

59. See, for example, Brulart, *Journal*, pp. 146–49, and La Fosse, *Journal d'un curé ligueur*, pp. 68–71. See also "La situation politique et religieuse de la France en octobre 1564, d'après un catholique sincère. Lettres de Simon Renard à la duchesse de Parme," *BSHPF* 36 (1887): 641 and 644 (letters of 6 and 10 October 1564).

60. Ruble, "François de Montmorency," pp. 255 and 256, citing letters of Montmorency and of a Spanish envoy.

61. Ibid., pp. 263–64 and 269–71; Brulart, *Journal*, p. 151; La Fosse, *Journal d'un curé ligueur*, p. 72.

62. Haton, *Mémoires*, 1:332–33; Léon Brièle, *Collection de documents pour servir à l'histoire des hôpitaux de Paris* (Paris, 1881–1887), 1:6 and 3:317–18, provides evidence that corroborates Haton's view of the seriousness of the epidemic. See also the comments of Pierre de Paschal, *Journal de l'année 1562*, pp. 71 and 89.

63. Micheline Baulant and Jean Meuvret, *Prix des céréales extraits de la mercuriale de Paris (1520–1698)*, vol. 1: *(1520–1620)* (Paris, 1960), p. 156.

64. Brièle, *Collection de documents*, 1:6 and 3:317.

65. Grin, "Journal," p. 28; Haton, *Mémoires*, 1:391–97.

66. *Reg. BV*, 5:492.

67. Ibid., 5:515–33; Baulant and Meuvret, *Prix des céréales*, 1:51–52 and 170–78.

68. *Reg. BV*, 5:518–20.

69. Ibid., 5:536, 537, and 550n.

70. Baulant and Meuvret, *Prix des céréales*, 1:176 and 177. See also Grin, "Journal," p. 34; and Haton, *Mémoires*, 1:410.

71. *Reg. BV*, 5:564 and 564–65n.

72. Baulant and Meuvret, *Prix des céréales*, 1:52–53.

Chapter 5

1. See, for example, AN, X²ᵃ 132, fol. 190v–191r (5 February 1563/1564): case of Jehan Reculle.

2. Auguste Bernus, "Le ministre Antoine de Chandieu d'après son journal autographe inédit (1534–1591)," *BSHPF* 37 (1888): 133.

3. John Quick, *Synodicon in Gallia Reformata; or The Acts, Decisions, Decrees, and Canons of those Famous National Councils of the Reformed Churches in France* (London, 1692), 1: 56–65. I have consistently used Quick's *Synodicon gallicanorum* as my primary reference where Reformed church synods are concerned because it is more complete, and sometimes also more accurate, than Jean Aymon's *Tous les synodes nationaux des églises réformées de France*, 2 vols. (The Hague, 1710). See also Theodore Beza, *Correspondance*, ed. Hippolyte Aubert, Henri Meylan, Alain Dufour, et al., 14 vols. to date (Geneva, 1960–1990) 6:29–32: Théophile de Banos to Beza (Paris, 16 February 1565) on plans for the synod, which Jean Morély threatened to denounce to the king; and 121: Jean Mallot to Beza (Châtillon-sur-Loing, 8 August 1565).

4. See Bernus, "Antoine de Chandieu," pp. 132–33, in which he cites the "Epitre à l'eglise de Dieu qui est à Paris" with which Chandieu prefaced his *Histoire des persecutions*. Coligny shared this view. See Jules Delaborde, *Gaspard de Coligny, amiral de France* (Paris, 1882), 2:250–52.

5. This was confirmed by another royal declaration in June 1564. See François Isambert, et al., *Recueil général des anciennes lois françaises depuis l'an 42, jusqu'à la Révolution de 1789*, vol. 14, pt. 1 (Paris, 1829): 170–72: "Déclaration qui interdit l'exercice de la Religion réformée dans les lieux de résidence royale" (Lyons, 24 June 1564; registered 13 July 1564).

6. *Declaration & interpretation du roy sur l'edict de la pacification des troubles pour le faict de la religion. Publié en la cour de Parlement à Paris, le XX decembre 1563* (Paris: Robert Estienne, 1563).

7. Catherine de Medici, *Lettres*, 2:21 (letter of 20 April 1564) and 31 (letter of 6 May 1564).

8. Ibid., 2:158 (letters to the maréchal de Montmorency, 28 February and 1 March 1564). *Archives curieuses*, ed. Cimber and Danjou, 5:399–400 (letter of Renée de France to Jean Calvin, 21 March 1563).

9. Beza, *Correspondance*, 6:214–18: Pierre Garnier to Beza (Paris, November 1565).

10. Ibid., 6:179–80: Beza to Bullinger, 23 October 1565.

11. "Affligée et dessous les reliques de la croix": Chandieu, *Histoire des persecutions*, fol. xx.

12. Beza, *Correspondance*, 6:95–98: Letter of Beza to Bullinger (31 May 1564); Brulart, *Journal*, 1:156.

13. "Journal du règne du Roy Henri III," *Recueil de diverses pièces servant à l'histoire de Henry III, roy de France et de Pologne*, new ed., 2 vols. (Cologne, 1699), 1:19–20.

14. Haton, *Mémoires*, 2:1134–36, reproducing placards from BN, Mss. Dupuy 811. Another placard directly equates the presence of Huguenot preachers in the city with a danger of attack ("The enemies of the cross / are ready to cut your throat") and urges the Parisians to strike first: "Think of yourself, Paris; / For if their turbid and thick blood / Isn't spilled by your sanction, / We will never have peace in France."

15. *CSP,F*, 8:158 (Hugh Fitz William to Cecil, 12 December 1566); see also p. 168, a reference in a dispatch of Sir Henry Norris dated 26 January 1566/1567 to the queen of Navarre's having had a preacher in her house in Paris.

16. Beza, *Correspondance*, 8:25–26: Marin Delamare to Beza (La Forest [i.e., Paris], 5 January 1567); see also Ibid., 8:29: Merlin dit l'Espérandière to Beza (Longueville [Paris], 10 January 1567). On Protestant ministers known to be in Paris, see [Simon Vigor], *Les actes de la conference tenue à Paris es moys de juillet et aoust 1566 entre deux docteurs de Sorbonne & deux ministres de Calvin* (Paris: Jean Foucher, 1568), pp 2–3.

17. Catherine de Medici, *Lettres*, 3:20: letter of 22 March 1567.

18. Beza, *Correspondance*, 8:113: Salvard (minister in Lyons) to Beza (19 April 1567).

19. AN, Y 12: Lettres patentes of Charles IX (Paris, 1 June 1567; registered 26 June 1567 and published in the Châtelet 28 June 1567); published by Félibien and Lobineau, *Histoire de Paris, Preuves*, 1:694; see also La Fosse, *Journal d'un curé ligueur*, p. 84.

20. On the Corpus Christi incident, see *CSP,F*, 8:247: dispatch of Norris to Cecil (10 June 1567). In August, Parlement upheld the sentence of the lieutenant criminel condemning a weaver named Simon Le Marchant to be publicly whipped on the quai des Augustins for fomenting riot by throwing stones and encouraging others similarly to attack a group of people suspected of holding an illicit assembly on the "isle du Palais." I have not, however, been able to determine the exact date of the incident. AN, X^{2b} 49 (19 August 1567).

21. Félibien and Lobineau, *Histoire de Paris, Preuves*, 1:701–2 (Lettres patentes, Compiègne, 5 August 1567, registered in Parlement 6 September 1567). See also *Reg. BV*, 5:592–600: articles dated 14 July to 8 August 1567; and Catherine de Medici, *Lettres*, 3:47–50: letters to Villeroy, prévôt des marchands (26 July and 5 and 19 August 1567).

22. See, for example, *CSP,F*, 8:294: Norris to Cecil (23 July 1567). Also see *Memoires des choses advenues sur le traicté de la pacification des troubles qui sont en France. Avec l'exhortation à la paix* (N.p.,1568).

23. Pasquier, *Oeuvres*, 2:117–18: book 5, letter 2, to Monsieur de Querquifinen, seigneur d'Ardivillers. See also Delaborde, *Coligny* 2:474–75.

24. *CSP,F*, 8:340: Norris to Cecil (15 September 1567). See also *Reg. BV*, 5:605–6 (11 September 1567): letter from queen mother and king warning centeniers against violence and urging tranquility.

25. La Noue, *Discours politiques et militaires*, pp. 604–11; see also Delaborde, *Coligny*, 2:480–85.

26. La Noue, *Discours politiques et militaires*, pp. 612–13.

27. Ibid., p. 610.

28. Pasquier, *Oeuvres*, 2:117–18 (book 5, letter 2); Henri Hauser, "Un récit catholique des trois premières guerres de religion. Les *Acta tumultuum gallicanorum*," *Revue historique* 108 (1911): 301–3; Grin, "Journal," p. 41; La Fosse, *Journal d'un curé ligueur*, pp. 85–86. On the rearming of the city: Félibien and Lobineau, *Histoire de Paris, Preuves*, 1:701: lettres patentes of 29 September 1567.

29. The quotation is from Grin, "Journal," p. 41; the rumor from Hauser, *Acta tumultuum*, p. 303.

30. *Reg. BV*, 5:609 (29 and 30 September 1567): orders for search of Protestant houses, which specify a search for weapons but give no indication of a fear of fire.

31. See Catherine de Medici, *Lettres*, 3:60n: letter of Bouchefort to the duchess of Ferrara, written about 29 September 1567. See also Beza, *Correspondance*, 8:198: Zurkinden [a Bernese reformer] to Beza (9 December 1567). Zurkinden's son, who was serving an apprenticeship in Paris, was killed in the riots.

32. Hauser, *Acta tumultuum*, p. 304.

33. Pasquier, *Oeuvres*, 2:117–18 (book 5, letter 2).

34. Hauser, *Acta tumultuum*, pp. 303–4.

35. Ibid., pp. 304–5; Pasquier, *Oeuvres*, 2:119–22 (book 5, letter 4); Grin, "Journal," p. 41.

36. Grin, "Journal," p. 42; Hauser, *Acta tumultuum*, p. 305. See also Brulart, *Journal*, p. 181; and *CSP,F*, 8:365: Norris to Cecil (2 November 1567).

37. De Thou, *Histoire de Monsieur de Thou*, 3:76.

38. Ibid., 3:77.

39. Delaborde, *Coligny*, 2:503, places the renewal of peace talks at the end of November and, in the following pages, includes much of the relevant correspondence.

40. Brulart, *Journal*, p. 187; *CSP,F*, 8:377 (7 December 1567). Also see *Memoires des choses advenues*, for a Protestant view of events.

41. *CSP,F*, 8:381 and 401: Norris to the queen (15 December 1567 and 23 January 1568); see also La Fosse, *Journal d'un curé ligueur*, p. 91.

42. *Advertissement sur le pourparlé qu'on dict de paix entre le roy & ses rebelles* (Paris: Jean Dallier, 1568), fols. Dii–Diii, Ei.

43. Stegmann, *Edits des guerres de religion*, pp. 53–58: Paix de Longjumeau (23 March 1568).

44. Grin, "Journal," p. 46; La Fosse, *Journal d'un curé ligueur*, p. 93. Also see Jean Le Masle, *Brief discours sur les troubles qui depuis douze ans ont continuellement agité et tourmenté le royaume de France; et de la deffaicte d'aucuns chefs plus signalez des mutins & seditieux qui les esmouvoient & mettoyent sus quand bon leur sembloit. Avec une exhortation à iceux mutins de bien tost abjurer leur erreur & heresie* (Lyons: Benoist Rigaud, 1573), fols. 8v–9r.

45. "What does our queen gain from negotiating that peace?" "Hate." Weiss, "Les Protestants parisiens entre 1564 et 1569," *BSHPF*, 50 (1901): 634.

46. Haton, *Mémoires*, 2:527–31.

47. Beza, *Correspondance*, 9:49: Beza to Bullinger (8 April 1568); *CSP,F*, 8:448: Captain Cockburn to Cecil (28 April 1568).

48. La Fosse, *Journal d'un curé ligueur*, pp. 94–95; *CSP,F*, 8:474–75: Norris to the queen (4 June 1568).

49. *Reg. BV*, 6:38–40 (3–16 June 1568); *CSP,F*, 8:516: Norris to the queen (7 August 1568).

50. Pasquier, *Oeuvres*, 2:125–26 (book 5, letter 6).

51. *Reg. BV*, 6:66–67 (9 and 18 November 1568).

52. Ibid., 5:614 (11 October 1567); 622 (25 October 1567); 6:5–7 (22 and 24 January 1568); 76 (11 December 1568); 82 (5 January 1569); and 87 (27 February 1569). See also Félibien and Lobineau, *Histoire de Paris, Preuves*, 1:706–10 (December 1567 and January 1568); and AN, X^{2b} 51 (30 March 1568).

53. *Reg. BV*, 5:610 (2 October 1567); 6:8 (31 January 1568); 8–9n (4 February 1568); 10 (9 February 1568); and 17 (24 March 1568). See also Félibien and Lobineau, *Histoire de Paris, Preuves*, 1:706 (24 December 1567) and 709 (1 February 1568).

54. For orders on public security, see *Reg. BV*, 6:69 (18 November 1568); 76 (11 December 1568); and 78 (18 and 20 December 1568); AN, X^{2a} 137 (11 and 23 December 1568).

55. See, for example, AN, X^{2b} 51 (24 March 1568): Jacques Collin, seigneur de Caze; Nathanaël Weiss, Charles Read, and Henri Bordier, "Poursuites et condemnations à Paris pour hérésie de 1564 à 1572, d'après les registres d'écrou de la Conciergerie du Palais," *BSHPF* 50 (1901): 587 (2 December 1567): Nicolas Beaulmier; 589 (11 February 1568): Roch Du Jardin; and 591 (19 February 1568): Philippes de Gastines and Marie Morendelle.

56. Haton, *Mémoires*, 2:571; Weiss, "Poursuites," 640.

57. Haton, *Mémoires*, 2:570–72.

58. De Thou, *Histoire de Monsieur de Thou*, 3:562. See also La Fosse, *Journal d'un curé ligueur*, p. 107.

59. AN, X^{2b} 56 (30 June 1569). Croquet was also judged guilty of having taken part in iconoclastic acts in the village church of Saint-Pris. La Fosse and Grin accuse the three men of having given financial aid to the rebels, but this is not mentioned in the judgment against them. La Fosse, *Journal d'un curé ligueur*, p. 102; Grin, "Journal," p. 50.

60. Brulart, *Journal*, p. 207 (13 September 1569).

61. Haton, *Mémoires*, 2:565–66. See also La Fosse, *Journal d'un curé ligueur*, p. 110. Coligny was again hung in effigy after Saint Bartholomew's Day. See La Fosse, *Journal d'un curé ligueur*, p. 155.

62. Haton, *Mémoires*, 2:680. See also Jules Gassot, *Sommaire mémorial (souvenirs)*, ed. Pierre Champion (Paris, 1934), p. 105. On the acting out of magisterial roles in religious violence, see Davis, *Society and Culture*, pp. 162–64.

63. *Reg. BV*, 6:178 (17 August 1570) and 189–90 (20 September 1570); La Fosse, *Journal d'un curé ligueur*, pp. 120–21. According to the English envoy, the Parisians had offered to pay for eight months more of war, if the king would only continue to fight. See *CSP,F*, 9:297: Norris to the queen (23 July 1570).

64. Stegmann, *Edits des guerres de religion*, p. 77: Edit de Saint-Germain, paragraph 32.

65. *Reg. BV*, 6:381 (8 October 1571). Also see Haton, *Mémoires*, 2:632; and La Fosse, *Journal d'un curé ligueur*, pp. 132–33.

66. *Reg. BV*, 6:399; "Discours touchant la croix," *Archives curieuses*, ed. Cimber and Danjou, 6:476–78; La Fosse, *Journal d'un curé ligueur*, pp. 134–35. On Catholic sermons, also see AN, X^{1a} 1634, fol. 98 (18 December 1571). See also Simon Vigor, *Sermons catholiques sur les dimanches et festes depuis l'octave de Pasques jusques à l'advent* [hereafter, *SCP*] (Paris: Nicolas du Fossé, 1597), 2:228–44, especially 242–44, for a sermon directed against removal of the cross. This sermon is discussed in Chapter 9 below.

67. *Reg. BV*, 6:398–400; La Fosse, *Journal d'un curé ligueur*, pp. 135–36.

68. *Reg. BV*, 6:401–4.

69. Ibid., 6:406.

70. Ibid., 6:406–14; La Fosse, *Journal d'un curé ligueur*, pp. 135–36. See also AN, X^{2b} 1094, *plumitif* from 10 December 1571, morning session, and draft of letter from the Parlement to the king dated 11 December 1571. I am grateful to Alfred Soman, who provided me with this reference. The X^{2b} 1094 documents cited here and in the following notes have strayed into a carton of miscellaneous criminal proceedings, and it is unlikely that I would have found them had Soman not brought them to my attention. He also furnished copies of those portions of the dossier that he had transcribed, thereby saving me hours of tedious labor deciphering the difficult shorthand of the court reporters.

71. AN, X^{1a} 1634, fols. 98–99 (18 December 1571); *Reg. BV*, 6:414–22 and 421–22n; Catherine de Medici, *Lettres*, 4:84–85: letters to "les eschevins et conseillers de la ville de Paris" (16 December 1571) and to the Parlement (21 December 1571). Also see BN, Mss. Dupuy 775, fol. 26: letter from Charles IX to Claude Marcel, prévôt des marchands, and fol. 27: entry from Marcel's memoirs dated 20 December 1571.

72. *Reg. BV*, 6:423–28; AN, X^{1a} 1634, fols. 102 and 104 (19 and 20 December 1571); X^{2b} 1094, plumitifs of 20 and 22 December 1571, *minutes* of Parlement criminel, 20 and 22 December 1571, minute of a letter sent to the king on 22 December 1571. See also AN, H 2065^2: list of expenses presented to the city by Charles Roger, maître maçon, for expenses incurred 19 December 1571 for putting out a fire in the rue Saint-Denis.

73. Jacques Faye and Charles Faye, *Lettres inédites de Jacques Faye et de Charles Faye*, ed. Eugène Halphen (Paris, 1880), p. 32.

74. "Discours touchant la Croix," in *Archives curieuses*, ed. Cimber and Danjou, 6:477–78.

75. For the attacks on the Le Mercier family (Golden Hammer), see AN, Z^{1h} 71 (3 September 1572) and Q^{1*} 1099^{200}, fols. 69v–70r (28 February 1573). Jacques de Gastines, the son-in-law of Nicolas Le Mercier and a resident, along with his wife, of the Golden Hammer, appears also to have been killed on Saint Bartholomew's Day. See AN, MC, CXXII, 248 (14 February 1571); and Jean Crespin, *Histoire des martyrs persecutez et mis à mort pour la verité de l'evangile, depuis le temps des apostres jusques à present (1619)*, new ed., ed. Daniel Benoît and Mathieu Lelièvre (Toulouse, 1885–1889), 3:677 and 679. On the Dalencourt family (Pearl), see AN, Q^{1*} 1099^{200}, fol. 64 (15 January 1573). Other victims of Saint Bartholomew's Day whose houses had been attacked in 1571 included Mathurin Lussault, the queen's jeweler [AN, MC, LIV, 222 (1 September 1572)]; and Philippe Le Doux, a *passementier* [AN, X^{1h} 70 (22 September 1572) and X^{2b} 74 (27 January 1573)]. Thibault Cressé, also a jeweler, survived the massacres, but his house was again pillaged [AN, X^{2b} 74 (16 January 1573)]. See AN, X^{2b} 1094 for a letter from the king dated 29 December 1571 ordering investigation into reports that the houses of these men were pillaged in the cross of Gastines riots.

76. The wife of "le jeune" Gastines is mentioned in Crespin, *Martyrs*, ed. Benoît and Lelièvre, 3:678. The innkeeper, Loys Brecheux, owner of the Fer de Cheval (ibid., 3:677), had several previous arrests: AN, X^{2b} 1174 interrogation of 1 March 1570; X^{2a} 934 (28 April 1570); and X^{2b} 60 (29 April 1570). The quartenier, Oudin Petit, is mentioned in Crespin, *Histoire des martyrs*, ed. Benoît and Lelièvre, 3:675, and his death is confirmed in AN, Y 113, fol. 231 (21 September 1572) and Y 114, fols. 286–287 (4 September 1573). Petit was arrested 15 March 1568, according to Weiss, "Poursuites," p. 594. Weiss is wrong, however, when he notes, p. 594n, that Petit was killed by July 1572; the date of the relevant donation is *September* 1572, not July. On the clockmaker, Nicolas de Coutancoys, see APP, A^h 3, fols. 98v (18 October 1569) and 293 bis (4 March 1571); AN, X^{2a} 934 (2 December 1569), and Z^{1h} 71 (8 May 1573).

It should be pointed out that the list of massacre victims compiled by Simon Goulart in the *Histoire des martyrs* appears relatively trustworthy. The accuracy of the details given by Goulart is certainly open to question and several names appear twice, but the deaths of many of those he names can be independently confirmed, and it appears that his list is based on accounts given by Parisian Protestants who escaped massacre and took refuge in Geneva. The authors of "La Saint-Barthélemy, le martyrologie de Jean Crespin et Simon Goulart," in *Divers aspects de la réforme aux XVIe et XVIIe siècles: Etudes et documents* (Paris, 1975), pp. 11–36, are only partly correct in saying that Goulart took his account of the massacres from his previously published *Memoires de l'estat de France*. In fact, this only holds true for the murder of Coligny and the other nobles killed those events. The list of ordinary citizens included in the *Memoires de l'estat* is less detailed than in the martyrology.

77. *Reg. BV*, 6:442.

78. AN, X^{2a} 938 (31 December 1571).

79. AN, X^{2b} 1094, plumitif of the Grand'Chambre and minute of the Tournelle, 20 December 1571.

80. AN, X^{2b} 1094 (4 and 11 January and 26 February 1572). Also see AN, X^{2a} 938, plumitifs of the Tournelle (20 and 31 December 1571; 2, 4 and 7 January 1572): prosecutions of Paul Rousselet, Nicolas Lorrain, Guillaume Deschallatz, one named only "Jolly," Estienne David, and Marion Parisy.

81. Gustave Fagniez, ed. "Mémorial juridique et historique de Mc Guillaume Aubert, avocat au Parlement de Paris, avocat général à la Cour des aides (deuxième moitié du XVIe siècle)," *MSHParis* 36 (1909): 66–67.

82. Faye and Faye, *Lettres*, p. 34. Also see La Fosse, *Journal d'un curé ligueur*, p. 139; *CSP,F*, 9:571–72: 7 and 9 December 1571.

83. AN, X²ᵇ 1094, minute of letter sent to the king, 22 December 1571.

84. AN, X²ᵇ 1094, plumitif of the Grand'chambre (22 December 1571).

85. AN, X¹ᵃ 1634, fols. 97–99; Delaborde, *Coligny*, 3:348, citing BN, Mss. fr. 10752, fol. 1289ff. (letter of 26 December 1571): "il est advenue que seulement quelques coquins, comme crocheteurs et autres fainéants, se sont assemblez et tumultuez pour ne voir plus ladite pyramide en son lieu, et se sont voulu servir de ce prétexte pour piller quelques maisons et butiner."

86. See Pierre Champion, *Paris au temps des querres de religion. Fin du règne de Henri II; régence de Catherine de Médicis; Charles IX* (Paris, 1938), pp. 165–70; N. M. Sutherland, *The Huguenot Struggle for Recognition* (New Haven, 1980), p. 193. But also see Charles Hirschauer, *La politique de Sᵗ Pie V en France (1566–1575)* (Paris, 1922), p. 178n, quoting the papal nuncio Frangipani's letter to the pope of 23 November 1571, which casts doubts upon notion that de Alava was caught in a conspiracy against Charles IX.

87. Delaborde, *Coligny*, 3:347–48, citing letter of Charles IX (BN, Mss. fr. 10752, fol. 1207).

88. Champion, *Paris au temps des guerres de religion*, pp. 170–71; Sutherland, *The Huguenot Struggle for Recognition*, p. 193.

89. La Fosse, *Journal d'un curé ligueur*, p. 125.

90. Hirschauer, *La politique de Sᵗ Pie V*, pp. 108–11: Fabio Mirto Frangipani, nuncio to France, to Cardinal Rusticucci (19 August 1570).

91. La Fosse, *Journal d'un curé ligueur*, p. 129.

92. *Reg. BV*, 6:437 (24 January 1572), 445–47 (27 February and 1 March 1572), and 460–61 (13 May 1572).

93. Schnapper, *Les rentes au XVIᵉ siècle. Histoire d'un instrument de crédit* (Paris, 1957), pp. 155–57. Also see Paul Cauwès, "Les commencements du crédit public en France; les rentes sur l'Hôtel de Ville au XVIᵉ siècle," *Revue d'économie politique* 10 (1896): 410–31; *Reg. BV*, 6:371 (21 September 1571) and 458–59 (9–10 May 1572).

94. See, for example, Le Masle, *Brief discours sur les troubles*, fol. 8b, in which Le Masle complains that, because of the king's too great clemency, "ils [the Huguenots] rentroyent en leurs estats / sans qu'on parlast de rendre nos deniers." See also BN, Mss. Dupuy 722, fol. 139 (2 March 1571): "Remonstrances sur l'office de conseiller de la Cour de Mʳ Jean Bonnault, de la Religion pretendue reformée."

95. In February 1568, the leases for eight houses on the pont Notre-Dame were auctioned off to the highest bidder. All fetched premiums of 500 to 725 livres, with the highest price going for the Golden Hammer. These premiums amounted to six to nine times the annual rent of 80 livres and, as such, represented significant sums for the sort of retail merchants who acquired the leases. In principle, the Catholics were compensated with a 325 livre tax levied on returning Protestants, but, as mentioned in the text, it is not clear that these payments ever reached the persons displaced. AN, Q¹ˣ 1099²⁰⁰: Registre des baux, fols. 1–3, 42, 64, 69–71, 89, and 91. See also *Reg. BV*, 6:16 (16 March 1568), 33 (10 May 1568), and 189–90 (20 September 1570). See also the reference to the issue of the return of houses on the pont Notre-Dame in the letter from Henri de Mesmes to Catherine de Medici dated 4 December 1570 in Jean-Denis-Léon Bastard d'Estang, *Vie de Jean de Ferrières, vidame de Chartres, seigneur de Maligny* (Auxerre, 1858), appendix XVI, pp. 248–49.

96. AN, X²ᵇ 1174: "Informations faictes par nous Jacques de Varade et Nicole Favyer, conseillers du Roy en sa court de Parlement et commissaires commis en ceste partie" (17 March 1570).

97. The choice of Pierre de Gondi as bishop was a particularly blatant display of favoritism because in order to name Gondi bishop Charles IX had to violate the reforming edict of Orleans (January 1561), which provided for the election of bishops, and to

insist on a return to terms of the Concordat of Bologna of 1515, which allowed for royal appointments. See *Reg. BV*, 6:32 (6 May 1568), for the order forbidding the city to take part in the election of a new bishop, and Isambert, *Recueil des anciens lois*, vol. 14, pt. 1, p 64: "Ordonnance générale rendue sur les plaintes, doléances et re-montrances des états assemblés à Orléans," (Orleans, 1 January 1560, registered 13 September 1561), article 1.

98. Tommaseo, *Relations des ambassadeurs vénitiens*, 2:143.

99. AN, X^{2b} 1094: plumitif and minute of the Grand'Chambre for 20 June 1572; X^{2b} 71: minute of the Tournelle for 20 June 1572. See also X^{2b} 72: court orders for re-view of trial of Jean Deste, a locksmith, conducted by the Châtelet, for participation in these riots (7 August 1572). Also see *Le tocsain contre les massacreurs et auteurs des confusions en France* (Rheims: Jean Martin, 1577), fol. 55; La Fosse, *Journal d'un curé ligueur*, p. 144.

100. *Tocsain contre les massacreurs*, fol. 55v.

101. *Reg. BV*, 6:455–56 (1 May 1572).

102. La Fosse, *Journal d'un curé ligueur*, pp. 132 and 133. See also Simon Vigor, *Sermons catholiques pour tous les jours de caresme & feriés de Pasques, faits en l'eglise S. Estienne du Mont à Paris* [hereafter *SCC*] (Paris: Gabriel Buon, 1588), fol. 139, in which the admiral is compared to an Arian named Gainas in a sermon delivered during the lenten season of 1572.

103. Sutherland, *The Massacre of St. Bartholomew and the European Conflict, 1559–1572* (London, 1973); see especially p. 316. Also see Sutherland, *The Huguenot Struggle for Recognition*, pp. 178–207, in which she makes it clear that Coligny did not take the initiative but rather had serious reservations about plans for a war with Spain.

104. See La Fosse, *Journal d'un curé ligueur*, p. 132.

105. Ibid., p. 142.

106. Sutherland, *The Massacre of St. Bartholomew*, pp. 223–59 and 306–11.

107. La Fosse, *Journal d'un curé ligueur*, pp. 141 and 142.

108. *Tocsain contre les massacreurs*, fols. 58v–60r and 68v–69r.

109. Edouard Forestié, *Un capitaine gascon du XVIe siècle: Corbeyran de Cardaillac-Sarlabous* (Paris, 1897), p. 137, citing the "Récit véridique de l'assassinat commis en France en 1572" believed to come from Joshua Studer of Vinkelbach, one of the Swiss guards who took part in the murder of Coligny.

110. There may be truth to these reports. Crespin, *Histoire des martyrs*, fol. 781v, reports rather obscurely that Denis Perrot, "estant allé ce jour de Dimanche de bon matin vers la porte de Paris (qui est une place des plus notables de la ville) pour quelque bonne & saincte occasion, selon sa coustume, s'aperceut au retour du bruit estrange qui s'espandoit bien fort de ce qui estoit advenu chez l'Amiral et ailleurs desja." He seems to be hinting that Perrot was returning from some sort of secret religious services. A native Parisian and son of a counselor in Parlement, Denis Perrot was a minister in Geneva until he was dismissed in December 1566 on account of "son indisposition et debilité de sens." He subsequently returned to Paris, where he died in the massacre. See Olivier Fatio and Olivier Labarthe, eds., *Registres de la compagnie des pasteurs de Genève*, vol. 3: *(1565–1574)* (Geneva, 1969), p. 12.

111. Ibid., 7:9–10 (22 August 1571).

112. Henri Dubief, "L'historiographie de la Saint-Barthélemy," in *Actes du colloque l'Amiral de Coligny et son temps* (Paris, 1974), p. 352; more generally on the historiography of Saint Bartholomew's Day, pp. 351–65. See also Sutherland, *The Massacre of Saint Bartholomew*, pp. 312–37; Herbert Butterfield, *Man on his Past. The Study of the History of Historical Scholarship* (Cambridge, 1955), pp. 171–201.

Chapter 6

1. For a summary of contemporary views of Catherine, see Philippe Joutard, et al., *La Saint-Barthélemy, ou les résonances d'un massacre* (Neufchatel, 1976), pp. 61–66.

2. See Gaspard de Saulx de Tavannes, *Mémoires*, ed. Michaud and Poujoulat, Nouvelle collection des mémoires pour servir à l'histoire de France, vol. 8 (Paris, 1838), p. 386; Simon Goulart, "Relation du massacre de la Saint-Barthélemy," in *Archives curieuses*, ed. Cimber and Danjou, 7:82; "Discours sur les causes de l'exécution faicte ès personnes de ceux qui avoient conjuré contre le roy et son estat," ibid., p. 260.

3. Sutherland, *The Massacre of Saint Bartholomew*, pp. 315–16; see also Bourgeon, "Les légendes," pp. 103–8.

4. Bourgeon, "Les légendes," p. 109, discusses these possibilities. See also his more recent article, "Une source sur la Saint-Barthélemy," pp. 515–17, for a thoughtful analysis of why, even if Catherine and Charles were convinced of the Guises' complicity in the attack on Coligny, it would not have served their purposes openly to accuse and punish the Guises for this act.

5. Haton, *Mémoires*, 2:567 and 667; de Thou, *Histoire de Monsieur de Thou*, 3:293–94; see also Sutherland, *The Massacre of Saint Bartholomew*, pp. 104–5. The possibility that Maurevert acted on his own is also supported by the claims made by a Catholic apologist that the man who shot at Coligny was someone whom Coligny "had threatened to have hanged" in order to avenge himself of an unnamed wrong. See BN, Mss. fr. 17309, fols. 66–75: "Discours sur les causes de l'execution faicte ès personnes de ceux qui avoient conjuré contre le roy et son estat." This appears to be the same account as that published in Paris under the same title by Pierre l'Huillier in 1572.

6. Sutherland, *The Massacre of Saint Bartholomew*, pp. 105–8.

7. Tavannes, *Mémoires*, p. 387.

8. *Reg. BV*, 7:10–11.

9. See, for example, "Documents authentiques sur la Saint Barthélemy," *Revue rétrospective*, ser. 2, vol. 5 (1834): 363–64: letter from Charles IX to the Count Palatine, 31 August 1572; and "Lettre écrite par ordre de Charles IX aux cantons Suisses protestants après la Saint-Barthélemy," *BSHPF* 3 (1885): 274–78. See also the discussion of the different variations on this theme of a "Huguenot plot" that were used as royal propaganda in Poland, Switzerland, and Germany in Robert Kingdon, *Myths about the St. Bartholomew's Day Massacres, 1572–1576* (Cambridge, MA, and London, 1988), pp. 88–124. The need to ward off a Huguenot plot is also given as the principal cause of the massacre in the anonymous "Discours" cited above (BN, Mss. fr. 17309, fols. 66–75).

10. Beza denounced this version of events in a private letter written on 10 September 1572, less than two weeks after news of the massacre first arrived in Geneva. He called attention to the fact that the king's very first public statements had placed the blame on the Guises, and that, only when this explanation had failed to prove convincing, had he invented the story of a Huguenot plot. The same arguments were cited by Protestant polemicists, who recognized the need to contradict the king's version of events before it did irreparable harm to their cause. See Beza, *Correspondance*, 13:187–88 (Beza to Thomas van Til, Geneva, 10 September 1572), 192–94 (Beza to Bullinger, Geneva, 24 September 1572), and 203–4 (Bullinger to Beza, Zurich, 10 October 1572).

There is, however, a simple explanation for this contradiction, if indeed it is one. The king may initially have planned to blame the massacre on the Guises, either because he still hoped to avoid war with the Huguenots, or simply to avoid the wrath of the Protestant princes of Europe and diminish their tendency to come to the aid of the Huguenots. It quickly became apparent, however, that war was unavoidable and also that, if the Guises alone were made responsible for the massacre, the powerful Montmorency family would throw its weight in with the Huguenots. Philippe de Mornay, whose escape from the massacre took him to Chantilly, where he spent the night of Tuesday, 26 August, with the maréchal de Montmorency, confirms this for us. When Mornay arrived, the maréchal was "undecided and cool as he could be." He was awaiting news from Paris and "hoping that the king would not admit to the murder of the deceased admiral, resolved in this case to pursue vengeance; but on news to the contrary, he resolved to submit himself to the will of the king." The king's admission of responsibility was thus of great strategic importance in setting the alliances for the war that was to come. See Charlotte d'Arbaleste, *Mémoires de Madame de Mornay sur la vie de son mari*, in Philippe du Plessis-Mornay, *Mémoires et correspondance*, vol. 1 (Geneva, 1969; reprint of Paris edition, 1824–1825), pp. 43–44.

11. La Fosse, *Journal d'un curé ligueur*, p. 148.

12. Haton, *Mémoires*, 2:669–72. The account of events believed to have come from Joshua Studer, a captain of the Swiss guard and eyewitness to Coligny's death, likewise attests to a belief in a Huguenot plot. See Forestié, *Un capitaine gascon*, p. 140.

13. On the historiography of the now discredited view that the assassination attempt was part of a long premeditated plan to annihilate the Huguenot leadership, see Butterfield, *Man on His Past*, pp. 171–201.

14. Joachim Opser, a Swiss monk from Saint Gall studying at the collège de Clermont when the massacres took place, received his account of Coligny's death from a member of the Swiss guard who claimed to have been the third man to strike the admiral. According to this guardsman, the troops were those assigned to the duc d'Anjou. See "Deux lettres de couvent à couvent écrites de Paris pendant le massacre de la Saint-Barthélemy," *BHSPF*, 8 (1859): 288 and 292. Goulart, "Relation du massacre de la Saint-Barthélemy," in *Archives curieuses*, ed. Cimber and Danjou, 7:120, also says the troops that killed Coligny were Anjou's Swiss and adds the detail that they wore black, white, and green—Anjou's colors.

15. *Reg. BV*, 7:10–11. See note 22 below on the reliability of these registers.

16. De Thou, *Histoire de Monsieur de Thou*, 3:658. See also the comments of Bourgeon, "Une source sur la Saint-Barthélemy," pp. 523–28. Besides placing a heavy weight on de Thou's account of orders allegedly given to the prévôt des marchands, Jean Le Charron, and the former prévôt des marchands, Claude Marcel, Bourgeon argues that when de Thou alludes to the Parisians taking up arms, he in fact means the official participation of "la bourgeoisie en armes, de la milice urbaine" (pp. 523–24) and not "la vulgaire populace." Although I find Bourgeon's article a welcome rethinking of many of the historiographical problems of the massacres and I agree entirely with his argument that Jacques-Auguste de Thou is "incontestably among those who have contributed most to the falsification of the story of Saint Bartholomew's Day" (p. 501), I find his choice of what to reject and what to accept as true in de Thou's account somewhat idiosyncratic. How can we dismiss much of what de Thou says took place at the midnight meeting of the king's counselors at the Louvre as specious (p. 509n), and yet accept as true the orders Guise is said to have given the prévôt des marchands? There is no independent evidence to confirm these orders. They are not supported by the account of Jules Gassot, for example, whom Bourgeon considers one of the few "good faith" witnesses to the massacres (p. 513). Moreover, they are directly incompatible with the city's official account of events, which I am inclined to accept as authentic, if somewhat self-serving.

17. Indeed, I tend to agree with Claude Haton here that it would have been dangerous not to give some warning to the municipal officers. Given the rumors that were circulating in the city, there was a grave danger that the townspeople would come bursting out of their houses at the first sound of troops in the streets and attack the king's own soldiers, on the

mistaken belief that they were agents of the Huguenot plot. Haton, *Mémoires*, 2:673. This interpretation also receives support from the account of the death of Pierre Baillet, a merchant dyer living in the rue Saint-Denis, given in Crespin's *Histoire des martyrs*. Simon Goulart, who continued the martyrology after the death of Jean Crespin early in 1572, reports that Baillet, hearing the noise of arms in the street sometime after midnight, sent out one of his servants to find out what was happening. "Comme il vouloit s'avancer, les voisins armez lui commanderent de rentrer et dire à son maistre qu'il se tinst quoi [coi]: que l'on vouloit tuer l'Amiral & qu'ils estoyent en armes pour empescher la sedition." See Crespin, *Histoire des martyrs* (1619 edition), fol. 782v.

18. AN, H 2065²: lists of expenses presented by Jehan Durant, maître de l'artillerye de la ville de Paris (23 and 31 December 1571).

19. *Reg. BV*, 7:11–12 (24 August 1572). By contrast, Goulart, "Relation du massacre de la Saint-Barthélemy," in *Archives curieuses*, ed. Cimber and Danjou, 7:15–16, says the captains and dizainiers met at midnight and places speeches of very dubious authenticity in the mouth of the prevôt des marchands.

20. In principle, the militiamen had to report to the city hall to be issued weapons. It is hard to know, however, how many might already have had weapons at home. As for the timing of the massacre, the sources are contradictory. A student from Strasbourg reported that the streets were peaceful when the Protestant nobles returned to their lodgings from the court sometime after midnight. See Rodolphe Reuss, "Un nouveau récit de la Saint-Barthélemy par un bourgeois de Strasbourg," *BSHPF* 22 (1873): 377–78. On the other hand, Philippe de Mornay, returning very late to his lodgings in the rue Saint-Jacques after spending the evening with the admiral, reported being told that "les armes se remuoient chez quelques bourgeois." Mornay's servant, sent back to check on the admiral, returned around 5 a.m. and warned him "du fracas qui se faisoit." See Arbaleste, *Mémoires*, p. 39.

21. The few unpublished documents in the municipal records that might serve to enlighten us on this point are, on close examination, highly ambiguous. See, for example, the contradictory testimony that emerges in the enquiry into the pillaging of the house of Philippe Le Doux, who was killed in the massacre. AN, Z^{1h} 70 (20 September 1572).

22. *Reg. BV*, 7:12–13 (24 August 1572). The published register of the Bureau de la ville for this period reproduces the manuscript register (AN, H² 1787) exactly, but the manuscript register itself was copied out later from a draft version or minutes that are no longer extant. There is thus no way of determining to what extent the city's official version of events was modified after the fact. Bourgeon ("Pour une histoire, enfin," pp. 113–14) has dismissed these registers as a tardy fabrication and a "veritable tissue of lies," because they do not support his own interpretation of events. I cannot agree, however, with his total dismissal of this source. The narrative of events probably was written somewhat later (though not as late as the reign of Louis XIII—the hand in which the register is written is more characteristic of the sixteenth century), and I certainly agree that it was written in such a way as to place the city's actions in the best possible light. I also think there are certain omissions. I nevertheless find it hard to believe that city officers would some decades later have invented out of whole cloth the royal letters and other documents published in the register, whatever bias may emerge in the narrative that is interspersed with the documents. They might, on royal orders or on their own initiative, simply have erased any trace of these events—as the Parlement did—but I find it hard to imagine this official body collaborating in the deliberate fabrication of official documents in order to rewrite history. And for what purpose? They never expected these registers to be published or placed in public archives and made available to some future generation. Moreover, the few entries in the manuscript *sentences* of the Hôtel de Ville that concern the events of Saint Bartholomew's Day, while incomplete and in many respects puzzling, tend to confirm that orders for the cessation of any attacks on

the Protestants and pillaging of their belongings were issued as early as 24 August and that the militiamen were ordered to protect the Huguenots and their properties. See, for example, AN, Z^{1h} 71 (9 October 1572): request of quartenier Mathurin de Beausse concerning the absence of cinquantenier Claude Delaunay during the troubles and his failure to execute his duties; Z^{1h} 71 (5 September 1572): request of Grandin, as procureur of Rachel de la Personne, concerning the circumstances in which some of her properties were taken; and Z^{1h} 71 (22 September 1572): case between André Pynet, an innkeeper, and Simon Drouyn, huissier et sergent à cheval in the Châtelet, concerning some horses taken by men of the duc d'Anjou.

23. *Reg. BV*, 7:12–13 (24 August 1572).

24. Forestié, *Un capitaine gascon*, pp. 144 and 145; also "Deux lettres de couvent à couvent," pp. 288 and 292.

25. The tocsin is variously said to have sounded in the towers of the Horlogerie and at Saint-Germain-l'Auxerrois. Some claim it sounded twice. Goulart says the original plan was to ring it in the Horlogerie, but that Catherine de Medici got nervous and moved up the start of the massacre by having it rung at Saint-Germain-l'Auxerrois. Other accounts make no mention of it at all. Moreover, in principle an alarm tocsin should have sounded in all parish churches, but none of our sources suggest that this was the case.

26. See the notarial deposition taken from a witness to the massacres, a Strasbourgeois, and intended for Frederick the Pious, the Elector Palatine. The witness testified that "toward daybreak, between three and four o'clock, they sounded the tocsin with two little bells that they call alarm bells, and the word immediately spread that the king had given permission to cut the throats of the Huguenots and pillage their houses." See Reuss, "Un nouveau récit de la Saint-Barthélemy," pp. 377–78. See also the account given by Guillaume de La Faye of the events in which he took part on the night of 24 August (AN, Z^{1h} 70: 22 September 1572), and the testimony of André Pynet (Z^{1h} 71: 22 September 1572), and Noel Thierie (Z^{1h} 71: 22 December 1572).

27. Goulart, "Relation du massacre de la Saint-Barthélemy," *Archives curieuses*, ed. Cimber and Danjou, 7:122.

28. Ibid., 7:136.

29. Crespin, *Histoire des martyrs*, ed. Benoît and Lelièvre, 3:675.

30. AN, MC, LIV, 222 (1 September 1572): inventaire après décès de Mathurin Lussault.

31. Crespin, *Histoire des martyrs*, ed. Benoît and Lelièvre, 3: 676.

32. AN, Z^{1h} 70 (22 September 1572). To my knowledge this document, one of several fragments relating to Saint Bartholomew's Day that are scattered among the much more mundane judiciary proceedings of the Bureau de la ville, has never been published or even mentioned in the literature on Saint Bartholomew's Day.

33. BN, Mss. fr. 11692, fols. 101–2.

34. AN, Z^{1h} 70 (22 September 1572). In January 1573, the guardian of Le Doux's orphaned children appealed to Parlement for the return of properties taken from Le Doux's house at the time of his death. The court ordered their return. AN, X^{2b} 74 (27 January 1573).

35. In addition to the descriptions in the *Histoire des martyrs*, see Reuss, "Un nouveau récit de la Saint-Barthelemy," p. 378.

36. Crespin, *Histoire des martyrs*, ed. Benoît and Lelièvre, 3:678 and 680.

37. Davis, "The Rites of Violence," in her *Society and Culture*, pp. 185–86. See also [Garrisson-]Estèbe, *Tocsin pour un massacre*, pp. 196–97.

38. Crespin, *Histoire des martyrs*, ed. Benoît and Lelièvre, 3:679.

39. Haton, *Mémoires*, 2:680–81; Gassot, *Sommaire mémorial*, p. 105; Crespin, *Histoire des martyrs*, ed. Benoît and Lelièvre, 3:667. See also La Fosse, *Journal d'un curé ligueur*, p. 149, where he likens the dragging of the admiral's corpse through the streets to the punishment the ancient Romans inflicted on tyrants.

40. Crespin, *Histoire des martyrs*, ed. Benoît and Lelièvre, 3:674 and 675.

41. A. Crottet, *Journal du ministre Merlin, pasteur de l'église de La Rochelle au XVIe siècle* (Geneva, 1855), p. 13. She eventually compromised and settled for less.

42. AN, Z^{1h} 71 (22 September 1572). The city claimed that Lat, a tax farmer, owed 46,000 livres in back taxes, and had issued an order for confiscation of his belongings in payment of this sum. Pynet, who was ordered to turn over to the city the horses Lat had left at his inn, claimed that he no longer had the horses in his possession but rather that they had been taken by the duc d'Anjou's men.

43. Arbaleste, *Mémoires*, pp. 63–68.

44. Ibid., p. 39.

45. Ibid., pp. 39–41,

46. "Mémoires de Dlle Renée, fille de Michel Burlamaqui," in Gilles-Denijs-Jacob Schotel, *Jean Diodati* (The Hague, 1844), p. 88.

47. Ibid., pp. 88–89.

48. See Chapter 5, note 14.

49. Denis Crouzet's thesis that the violence of Saint Bartholomew's Day was so horrible to Protestants and Catholics that it forced a retreat to an interiorized, discursive violence is worth noting here. See Crouzet, *Les guerriers de Dieu*, in particular Chapters 13–15.

50. "Deux lettres de couvent à couvent," pp. 288 and 292.

51. Ibid., pp. 293–94.

52. Ibid. See also Haton, *Mémoires*, 2:681–82, from which the quotation about God approving the "Catholic sedition" is taken; Reuss, "Un nouveau récit de la Saint-Barthélemy," p. 380; Goulart, "Relation du massacre de la Saint-Barthélemy," in *Archives curieuses*, ed. Cimber and Danjou, 7:155. The flowering hawthorn is also celebrated in Catholic poetry and song after Saint Bartholomew's Day, for example in the "Chanson nouvelle du miracle advenu à Paris," in the *Complaincte et deploration de l'heresie sur la mort du Prince de Condé, ses alliez & complices* (n.p., n.d.), pp. 29–31.

53. Haton, *Mémoires*, 2:692–93; A. Lynn Martin, "Jesuits and the St. Bartholomew's Day Massacre," *Archivum historicum Societatis Iesu* 43 (1974): 114, reproducing letter of Oliver Manare to Jeronimo Nadal (Paris, 2 September 1572).

Chapter 7

1. *Mémoires de l'estat*, as published in *Archives curieuses*, ed. Cimber and Danjou, "Relation du massacre," 7:137–42. Crespin, *Histoire des martyrs*, ed. Benoît and Lelièvre, 3:670–72. Jean Crespin died early in 1572; Simon Goulart took over the editing of the *Histoire des martyrs* after his death and is consequently responsible for the account of Saint Bartholomew's Day in this book. See "La Saint-Barthélemy, le martyrologie de Jean Crespin et Simon Goulart," in *Divers aspects de la réforme aux XVIe et XVIIe siècles: Etudes et documents* (Paris, 1975), pp. 11–36. Also see Kingdon, *Myths about the Massacres*, pp. 29–50, especially 35–37, on the mythologizing of the victims of Saint Bartholomew's Day in Goulart's *Mémoires de l'estat*.

2. APP, A^b 1 to 4. Every attempt has been made to eliminate duplicate entries, so that persons who were arrested two or more times are counted only once. Extracts of these registers have been published by Weiss, "Poursuites," pp. 575–95 and 639–53, and Weiss, "Huguenots emprisonnés à la Conciergerie du Palais à Paris en mars 1569," *BSHPF* 72 (1923): 86–97.

3. Natalie Zemon Davis, "Printing and the People," in her *Society and Culture*, pp. 209–10.

4. Natalie Zemon Davis, "The Sacred and the Body Social in Sixteenth-Century Lyon,"

Past and Present, no. 90 (1981), pp. 47–48; Benedict, *Rouen during the Wars of Religion*, pp. 71–81; Joan Davies, "Persecution and Protestantism: Toulouse, 1562–1575," *The Historical Journal* 22 (1979): 37–51. See also Emmanuel Le Roy Ladurie, *Les paysans de Languedoc* (Paris, 1966), 1:341–44; Janine Garrisson-Estèbe, *Protestants du Midi, 1559–1598* (Toulouse, 1980), pp. 22–56. Denis Crouzet, *Les guerriers de Dieu*, 1:64–75, offers a perceptive critique of the attempt to define the social bases of Protestantism's appeal.

5. The figures agree well, for example, with estimates that Daniel Roche and others have made about migration to Paris in the eighteenth century. It is not surprising that the percentage of native Parisians (33 percent) corresponds to the level that Roche estimates as the minimal level of residential stability (also 33 percent), rather than his maximal estimate of 60 percent, because the particular hostility directed against outsiders would likely have caused them to be overrepresented in the arrests. See Daniel Roche, *Le peuple de Paris* (Paris, 1981), pp. 23–27. See also Davis, "The Sacred and the Body Social," pp. 48–49. It is difficult to make direct comparisons between Lyons and Paris, however, because of the much larger influx of foreign-born migrants into Lyons.

6. One hundred and two of the 399 suspects (25.6 percent) lived in the quartier Saint-Séverin, of which 69 (17.3 percent of the 399) lived in the faubourg Saint-Germain. Because it was impractical to treat each of the faubourgs as a separate entity, I have counted persons living outside the old walls of the city as part of the nearest quartier. Thus residents of the faubourg Saint-Germain have been counted as part of the quartier Saint-Séverin; residents of the faubourgs Saint-Laurent and Saint-Martin have been counted as part of the quartier Saint-Martin, and so forth. In several cases, these geographical groupings do not match the administrative structures of the city. The single suspect who lived in the faubourg Saint-Jacques and the three suspects who lived in the faubourg Saint-Victor are counted as part of the quartier Sainte-Geneviève, although they were in fact administratively part of the districts of Notre-Dame and Saint-Esprit respectively. These exceptional cases are not important statistically, however. The only faubourg that housed a large number of religious dissidents was the faubourg Saint-Germain.

Furthermore, because the quartiers differed widely in size and population, it was necessary to take into account their relative size in making comparisons among them. Since we have no adequate statistics on the Parisian population in the sixteenth century, the best available measure on which to base this comparison is the tax roll for the special tax levy of 1571, which lists all of the taxable units (households, colleges, and so forth) for each quartier. See BN, Mss. fr. 11692: "Compte du don de trois cents mil livres." I have used here the figures presented by Babelon, *Paris au XVIe siècle*, pp. 511–16, but see also the discussion of this tax list in Descimon, "Paris on the Eve of Saint Bartholomew." I have taken as the basis of my figures only persons who actually had a tax levied on them in 1571. Some argument can be made for counting every entry on each quartier's list. This has the merit of including persons too poor to pay the tax, but it has the disadvantage of also including market stalls whose owners resided elsewhere, properties that were vacant or in ruin, and corporate groups like colleges or monasteries. Furthermore, the very poor, who had to move often in search of a livelihood, were probably the least stable element in the population. Since we know that the new religion found fewest converts among the very poor, it makes sense to diminish the economic variable by examining our religious suspects against a background of the more stable taxpaying population.

7. AN, MC, CXXII, 1394–98 and 247–48: Twenty-eight wills from the registers of Antoine Leal; and CXXII, 38–39: Eight wills from the registers of Eustache Goguier. See also the personal confession of faith that Antoine du Croy, prince de Porcien, had his notaries (who were not Protestants) include as a preface to his will: AN, MC, VIII, 95 (28 April

1567). More generally on sixteenth-century Parisian testaments, see Chaunu, *La mort*, pp. 288–330.

8. See, for example, AN, MC, CXXII, 1396 (24 October 1566): Jacques Brusle; CXXII, 1396 (15 November 1566): Jehan de la Rozere; CXXII, 247 (1 July 1565): Philippes Castille; or CXXII, 1396 (14 July 1566): Jehanne de Pierrebussiere.

9. Gabriel Dupuyherbault, *Deux epistres*, published with Loys de Blois, *Livret elegant et consolable autant que spirituel & propre contre la malice de ce temps* (Paris: Jean de Roigny, 1564), pp. 173–74. A devout Catholic and head of the order of Fontevrault, Dupuyherbault published extracts from this convert's letter (which was sent to him by her niece) in order to refute them. The portions he quotes are nevertheless instructive, and, given the epistolatory conventions of the time, the fact that the letter was not intended for publication by its author suggests that its language and sentiments may be more authentic than if they had been written to be published.

10. Arbaleste, *Mémoires*, p. 46.

11. Ibid., 46–48.

12. Diodati's memoirs are published in Schotel, *Jean Diodati*, pp. 114ff.

13. Ibid., p. 116.

14. Ibid.

15. Arbaleste, *Mémoires*, pp. 50–51.

16. Ibid., pp. 51–52.

17. Nicolas Pithou, "Histoire ecclesiastique de l'eglise de la ville de Troyes, capitale du conté et pays de Champagne. Contenant sa renaissance et accroissance, les troubles, persecutions et autres choses remarcables advenues en la dicte eglise, jusques en l'an mil cing cens quatre vingt et quatorze" (unpublished manuscript: BN, Mss. Dupuy, 698), fols. 131v–132r.

18. Ibid.

19. Ibid., fols. 132v–133r.

20. See Barbara B. Diefendorf, "Les divisions religieuses dans les familles parisiennes avant la Saint-Barthélemy," *Histoire, économie et société* 7 (1988): 55–78. An earlier version of this article has been published as "Houses Divided: Religious Schism in Sixteenth-Century Parisian Families," in *Urban Life in the Renaissance*, ed. Susan Zimmerman and Ronald F. E. Weissman (Newark, DE, 1989), pp. 80–99.

21. Chandieu, *Histoire des persecutions*, p. xviii, described the church at its origins as "qu'une dozeine de personnes contemptibles," but it is impossible to know what literary license was taken with this figure.

22. On the early growth of the Paris church and the need to find a minister to send, see scattered mentions in Beza, *Correspondance*, especially, 2:15–17: Beza to Bullinger (1 January [1556]); 21–27: Beza to Calvin (20 January and 9 February 1556); 28–30: Beza to Bullinger (12 February [1556]); 35–37: Beza to Farel (16 March [1556]), and 57–58: Beza to Bullinger (27 March [1557]). See also *Hist. eccl.*, 1:117–21.

23. Bernus, "Antoine de Chandieu," pp. 8–9.

24. Ibid. See also Coquerel, *Précis*, pp. 178–80 (there are some errors in this list); and Robert M. Kingdon, *Geneva and the Coming of the Wars of Religion in France, 1555–1563* (Geneva, 1956), pp. 61–64.

25. The story of this missionary effort is told by Kingdon, in *The Coming of the Wars of Religion*.

26. Eugène Haag and Emile Haag, eds. *La France protestante, ou vies des protestants français*, 2d ed. (Paris, 1877–1888), vol. 1, col. 175; Coquerel, *Précis*, p. 177, lists D'Amours among Parisian students registered at the Académie de Genève in 1559.

27. Coquerel, *Précis*, pp. xxix: Macar to Calvin (22 February 1558); and lxiii: Macar to Calvin (12 April [1558]). Chandieu was not in Paris in February 1558, but both he and de Lestre were serving as ministers there by April of that year.

28. *C.O.*, vol. 16: cols. 425–26: Calvin à l'église de Paris (15 March 1557); for evidence of La Rivière's continued presence in Paris, see the letters in Coquerel, *Précis*, especially pp. lix: Macar to Calvin (15 October 1558) and ix: Morel to Calvin (15 August 1559).

29. See, for example, Quick, *Synodicon*, 1:45: memorials drawn up at the fourth national synod at Lyons, 1563.

30. A good example of this ambivalence is manifest in the debate that occurred in the Company of Pastors over the invitation for Beza to attend the national synod held at La Rochelle in 1571. At first the Genevan Company refused to let him go, because it was too dangerous—he was too recognizable—and because some people were already saying that Geneva's position was too dominant in the French church, "as if there were not people in France who could advise and give order to church affairs." On the other hand, the French church was, from the Genevan perspective, in a state of crisis, and there seemed no way to guarantee the proper resolution of the issue but for Beza to brave the dangers and travel to La Rochelle, which he did. The next year, the same divisive issue came up again and, once again, after first refusing to allow Beza to attend the national synod of Nîmes, the Company sent him off to France. See Fatio and Labarthe, eds., *Registres de la compagnie des pasteurs de Genève*, 3:27–29, 65–66, and 74–75. See also Robert M. Kingdon, *Geneva and the Consolidation of the French Protestant Movement, 1564–1572* (Geneva, 1967), pp. 43–148, for a complete account of the issues involved.

31. Coquerel, *Précis*, pp. v–vi: Calvin to François de Morel (17 May 1559).

32. On the date of presentation to the king, see Coquerel, *Précis*, pp. xvii–xviii: letter from La Croix [pseudonym for Chandieu] to Calvin (22 July 1561).

33. Quick, *Synodicon*, p. xii, article 27. Translations are taken from Quick; I have, however, modernized spelling and capitalization.

34. Jean Calvin, *Lettres de Jean Calvin. Lettres françaises*, ed. Jules Bonnet (Paris, 1854), 2:156: "Au roi de France" (1557).

35. Quick, *Synodicon*, p. xii, article 27.

36. Ibid., article 28.

37. Ibid., article 26.

38. Quick, *Synodicon*, p. 6: Discipline of 1559, canon 32; but see also p. xxxiv: Discipline of 1571, chapter 5, canon 26. Also see Pithou, "Histoire ecclesiastique de Troyes," fols. 309–10, on the return of the "lost sheep" to the fold of the Troyes church after the first religious war; E. William Monter, "The Consistory of Geneva, 1559–1569," *BHR* 38 (1976): 481–82, on the public repentance required of French immigrants who had, under duress, taken part in Catholic rites before escaping from Lyons in the Catholic takeover of 1567; and Paul Geisendorf, ed., *Livre des habitants de Genève* (Geneva, 1957–1963), vol. 2, in which there are scattered references to refugees after Saint Bartholomew's Day who had attended Catholic mass.

39. Quick, *Synodicon*, p. xlvii: chapter 12, canon 11.

40. On the oath, see ibid., p. 8: "Particular Matters" discussed at the synod of Paris, 1559.

41. See Eugénie Droz, "Calvin et les Nicodemites," in her *Chemins de l'hérésie: Textes et documents* (Geneva, 1974), 1:131–67.

42. See, for example, Arbaleste, *Mémoires*, pp. 63–68; and Schotel, *Jean Diodati*, pp. 88–89: "Mémoires de D^lle Renée fille de Michel Burlamaqui."

43. See, Schotel, *Jean Diodati*, p. 124; Goulart, "Relation du massacre de la Saint-Barthélemy," in *Archives curieuses*, ed. Cimber and Danjou, 7:141.

44. A. Crottet, *Journal du ministre Merlin, pasteur de l'église de La Rochelle au XVIe siècle* (Geneva, 1855), p. 13.

45. Ibid., xxxvi: Discipline of 1571, Chapter 6, canon 2, and xli–xlii: Chapter 9. The churches were represented at these meetings by both clergymen and lay elders or deacons. Both groups had a voice in matters of ecclesiastical governance, but only the clergy in matters of doctrine.

46. Morice, *Mémoires*, vol. 3: *Preuves*, cols. 1302–3. Letter of Le Maçon, dit La Rivière, dated 10 March 1562. See also his letter of 13 March, which asks the churches to determine what "forces" they can provide.

47. Ibid.

48. Bernus, "Antoine de Chandieu," pp. 130–33.

49. *Declaration & interpretation du roy sur l'edict de la pacification* [1563].

50. AN, X^{2b} 1174: Interrogations of Loys Brecheulx and of Marie Creichant, his wife (1 March 1570); Pierre Dumont (30 June 1570); and René Gailloppe (12 July 1570), who also mentions Brie-Comte-Robert.

51. Bernus, "Antoine de Chandieu," p. 135. Bernus claims that Antonio Caraccioli, the former bishop of Troyes, set up a church at Brie-Comte-Robert until 1564, when it was shut down as being too close to the capital. Caraccioli's biographer, Roserot de Melin, disputes this, pointing out that Caraccioli was not on good terms with either religious faction in 1564, but there is a letter from Catherine de Medici that suggests that someone, whether or not it was Caraccioli, was preaching at Brie-Comte-Robert in 1564, and René Gailloppe admitted in 1570 that a child of his had been baptized there. See Joseph Roserot de Melin, *Antonio Caracciolo, évêque de Troyes (1515?–1570)* (Paris, 1923), p. 353n; Catherine de Medici, *Lettres*, 2:179–80: Letter to the prévôt des marchands of Paris, 15 April 1564. On Gailloppe, see previous note. On "La Forest," see Beza, *Correspondance*, 7:238n.

52. Arbaleste, *Mémoires*, p. 48.

53. "Lettres de divers à la duchesse de Ferrare," *BSHPF* 30 (1881): 458–59: letter from Louis Cappel (Chartres, 22 May 1571).

54. Beza, *Correspondance*, 6:437: letter from Pierre Garnier (November 1565); 7:194n, on Jean de L'Espine; 7:235–38: letter from Marin Delamare (25 September 1566); 8:25: letter from Delamare (5 January 1567), in which Théophile de Banos is mentioned; 8:29: letter from Merlin de l'Espérandière (10 January 1567); 8:74: letter from Ducroissant (1 March 1567); 8:213–215: Annex 1B: letter from Jean Morély (Paris, 4 February 1567) countersigned by Guillaume Houbracque, Jean de L'Espine, Arnaud-Guillaume Barbaste [chaplain to Jeanne d'Albret], and Pierre Merlin, dit l'Esperandière; 8:216–17: letter from the Church of Paris to the Church of Geneva (Paris, 12 March 1567), signed by Antoine de la Faye, sieur de la Maisonneuve et de Gournay, and Théophile de Banos "au nom de tous"; 9:114–15: letter from Louis Enoch (Montargis, 9 August [1568]), mentioning Jean de L'Espine in Paris. Coquerel, *Précis*, pp. lxxxi–lxxxiv: letter from Merlin in Paris to Chandieu (2 April 1566), in which he mentions that Capito has gone to Rouen for three months and that La Rivière refuses to leave Anjou. De Lestre appears to be attached to a church in the Vexin. Geisendorf, *Livre des habitants*, 2:35: Mc François de Cherpont, de Paris, "ministre en l'eglise dud. Paris," received as a *habitant* of Geneva 9 October 1572; 77: Roland Capito, ministre de l'église de Paris, received as habitant 19 March 1573 and Gabriel Damonas [sic] received 24 March 1573. See also Bernus, "Antoine de Chandieu," pp. 134–35; Haag and Haag, *La France protestante*, 2d ed., 1:175 (Gabriel D'Amours); and Crottet, *Journal du ministre Merlin*, pp. 11–13.

55. [Jean de L'Espine], *Traitté consolatoire et fort utile contre toutes afflictions qui adviennent ordinairement aux fideles Chrestiens. Composé nouvellement par J. de Spina, ministre de la parolle de Dieu, & adressé à grand seigneur de France* (Lyons: Jean Saugrain,

1565), p. 3. Coquerel, *Précis*, p. lxxxiv: postscript by Merlin to La Mare's letter of 2 April 1566; Beza, *Correspondance*, 7:235–36: letter of 25 September 1566.

56. Charles Pradel, "Un marchand de Paris au XVIe siècle (1560–1588)," *Mémoires de l'Académie des sciences, inscriptions et belles-lettres de Toulouse*, 9th ser., vol. 2 (1890), p. 397.

57. Vigor, *Les actes de la conference tenue à Paris*, preface, fols. 7v–8. The Conciergerie record for Du Rosier's arrest has been published by Weiss, "Poursuites," p. 582. It makes no mention of the charges.

58. Vigor, *Les actes de la conference*, preface, fol. 11v. La Fosse refers to an alleged plot to kill the king to which a prisoner named "May" confessed in July 1566 (*Journal d'un curé ligueur*, p. 79).

59. Bernus, "Antoine de Chandieu," p. 134n.

60. Beza, *Correspondance*, 6:435: letter to Du Pré, ministre à Chalon-sur-Saône (18 November 1565); 7:59–63: letter to Nicolas Pithou and the church of Troyes (24 March 1566); and 7:190–92: letter to Beza from Le Maçon, sieur de la Fontaine [minister at Orleans] (4 August 1566). Nicolas Pithou adds the information that the Troyes church was forced to enact its first excommunication in 1565. The excommunicant was a woman who had abandoned her husband and, despite repeated warnings, refused to return to him. It is significant that the consistory of Troyes did not take this step without first consulting with neighboring churches. See Pithou, "Histoire ecclesiastique de Troyes," fols. 315v–317.

61. On the Morély affair, see Quick, *Synodicon*, pp. 56–57: Paris Synod of 1565: agreement not to deprive Morély of communion if he renounces his book and opinions; Beza, *Correspondance*, 6:29–32 and 227–53; 7:191; 8:29 and 213–15; Fatio and Labarthe, *Registres de la compagnie des pasteurs*, 3:65–67 and 74–75; and Coquerel, *Précis*, pp. lxxxii–lxxxiv: letter to Chandieu from "Merlin, dit l'Esperandieu, au nom de tous" (2 April 1566). See also Kingdon, *The Consolidation of the French Protestant Movement*, pp. 43–137, for a very complete account of this quarrel and its repercussions.

62. In 1565, Morély was angry enough to threaten to betray the time and place of a provincial synod meeting that had been called without the required royal permission. See Beza, *Correspondance*, 6:29–32: Théophile de Banos to Beza (Paris, 16 February [1565]). The church's illegal situation made it all the more difficult to discipline Morély. See ibid., 8:29: Merlin dit l'Espérandière to Beza (Longueville [Paris], 10 January 1567). On the persistence of the conflicts into 1572, see ibid., 13:30–32: Beza to Bullinger (Geneva, 14 January 1572); 91–92: Beza to Bullinger (Geneva, 14 March 1572); 96–99: Jean de Lestre to Beza (Wy-dit-Joli-Village, 19 March [1572]); 135–37: Beza to Bullinger (Geneva, 17 June 1572); and 147–149: Beza to Jean Sturm (Geneva, 1 July 1572).

63. Coquerel, *Précis*, pp. lxv–lxvi: Macar to Calvin (3 September [1558]); and i–iv: "Police et ordre gardez en la distribution des deniers aumosnez aux pauvres de l'Eglise réformée en la ville de Paris" (10 December 1561).

64. AN, MC, CXXII, 1394 (22 March 1564): Catherine Gobelin; 1395 (4 April 1564): Jehan Sergent; 38 (7 November 1565): Claude Marnois and his wife, Michelle Robellet.

65. See AN, X^{2a} 923 (23 June 1569): testimony of Philippe, Richard, François, and Jacques de Gastines. This testimony suggests that the services held in Philippe de Gastines's house in the rue Saint-Denis were intended to be strictly private and completely secret. Jacques de Gastines testified that only about twenty persons attended the illicit ceremony, and he, his brother Richard, and his father all testified that they knew that public ceremonies were illegal but that their private ceremony had created no "scandal" and offended no one. Obviously their judges, who kept insisting on the fact that *all* Protestant ceremonies were forbidden in the city of Paris, did not accept this line of reasoning.

Chapter 8

1. Leal regularly noted the interruptions caused by the religious wars; Goguier passed over them in silence. See MC, CXXII, 1394, 1397, and 1398. Both men were deprived of their offices on account of their religion in 1568 (BN, Mss. fr. 21390, fol. 171v: arrêt of Parlement of 22 December 1568).

2. I have not been able to determine whether Leal or Goguier were killed in the massacres. Neither is listed in the standard martyrologies, but both died sometime between 1571 and 1573, and the possibility that they died as a result of Saint Bartholomew's Day is a strong one. Leal's last register (CXXII, 1399) breaks off the 8 March 1572 in the middle of a contract. An inventory after death that his wife had drawn up on 13 January 1573 establishes that he died sometime between March 1572 and January 1573 but does not allow us to determine the date any more closely (MC, III, 184). Goguier's last contracts date from 1571 (CXXII, 39), but a note appended to one of his contracts informs us that he died sometime before 30 December 1573 (CXXII, 39 [30 December 1573]).

3. AN, MC, CXXII, 248 (24 October 1571).

4. AN, X^{2a} 1201 (8 January 1563): note that Cressé was brought to the Conciergerie from the prisons of the Châtelet and order for him to be put to the question; X^{2a} 131 (13 May 1563): order for his release in accordance with the edict of pacification; X^{2b} 1094: letter from the king dated 29 December 1571, concerning properties pillaged in the cross of Gastines riots; X^{2b} 74 (16 January 1573): request concerning the return of stolen properties.

5. Weiss, "Poursuites," p. 643.

6. Crespin, *Histoire des martyrs*, ed. Benoît and Lelièvre, 3:677; AN, X^{2b} 55 (23 January 1569), and X^{2b} 56 (11 May 1569), which lists Greban as having also been arrested on 29 March.

7. Geisendorf, *Livre des habitants*, 2:71.

8. AN, X^{2b} 56 (30 June 1569); X^{2b} 57 (6, 9, and 29 July 1569).

9. Claude-Stephen Le Paulmier, "Julien Le Paulmier, docteur-régent de la Faculté de médicine de Paris, médecin du roi Henri III et de François, duc d'Anjou," *MHSParis* 21 (1894): 179–80. APP, A^b 4, fol. 96r (27 August 1572); and AN, X^{2b} 73 (21 October 1572). Delor died sometime before 26 October 1570 (BN, P.o., 1291: Gastines, document 2: receipt of 26 October 1570).

10. APP, A^b 3, 29r (3 May 1569): Claude Lenfant, marchant au Palais, living in rue Perpignan, arrested on charge of heresy and released 3 December 1569.

11. AN, MC, CXXII, 247 (29 January 1566): marriage of Pierre Des Friches and Magdaleine de Melays; CXXII, 1397 (29 July 1567): marriage of Michel du Pont and Nicolle Couillard; CXXII, 1398 (5 August 1568): apprenticeship of Thomas Carré, son of Jehan Carré, marchand pourpointier, bourgeois de Paris, to Hector de Fer, marchand drapier and maître chaussetier, bourgeois de Paris. He is probably the same Jean Carré reported absent from the city, having left behind two small children, in April 1563, but I cannot confirm this identification (AN, X^{2a} 130: 27 April 1563).

12. It is possible that he was never sent to the galleys. In October 1569, he was ordered transfered from the Petit Châtelet to the prisons of the bishop of Paris (AN, X^{2b} 58: 26 October 1569).

13. The relationship between Jacques and Philippe de Gastines is established by BN, P.o. 1291, Gastines, document 2: receipt of 26 October 1570; the relationship betwen Jacques de Gastines and the Le Merciers by AN, MC, CXXII, 248 (14 February 1571). See also MC, CXXII, 248 (12 October 1571) and BN, Mss. fr. 11692, fol. 160r, which lists "Nicolas

Mercier'' as owing 60 livres in taxes and ''un nommé de Gastines'' as owing 15 livres. François de Belleforest refers in *Les chroniques et annales de France* (Paris: Gabriel Buon, 1573), fol. 529r, to the properties of ''one of the Gastines'' being burned on the pont Notre-Dame in the cross of Gastines riots. On Saint Bartholomew's Day, see Crespin, *Histoire des martyrs*, ed. Benoît and Lelièvre, 3:677 and 679. The survival of the young daughter Gillette is confirmed by a petition filed in her behalf a week after Saint Bartholomew's Day by Claude Le Mercier, who also survived the massacre. See AN, Z^{1h} 71 (3 September 1572); see also AN, Q^{1*} 1099^{200}, fols., 69v–70r; a petition dated 28 February 1573 and filed on Gillette's behalf, in which she is described as ''a poor little girl unable to speak.'' One must wonder if there was any relation between Gillette's mute state and the frightful experiences she witnessed. See Chapter 6, p. 102 for Crespin's account.

14. AN, Z^{1h} 71 (3 September 1572).

15. See, for example, AN, X^{2a} 125 (14 May 1560): request presented by Jehan Heron, ''pauvre homme colporteur de livres''; X^{2a} 125 (15 April 1560): case of Valleran Judel, ''compagnon libraire et colporteur de livres''; X^{2a} 128 (21 October 1561): case of Mathurin Rotier, colporteur; and X^{2b} 52 (13 July 1568): request by the procureur général referring to sale of books by ''aucuns colporteurs jeunes enffans de douze à quinze ans'' so as to avoid the harsh punishments adults would receive for engaging in such a trade.

16. See, for example, AN, X^{1a} 1625 (23 December 1568), recounting the discovery of three bundles of books addressed to a Paris bookseller hidden in a load of merchandise examined by inspectors for the mercer's corporation. Examined by two Catholic theologians, the books were pronounced heretical and ordered publicly burned. On the importation of clandestine literature, see Francis Higman, ''Le levain de l'évangile,'' in *Histoire de l'édition française*, vol. 1: *Le livre conquérant. Du moyen âge au milieu du XVIIe siècle*, ed. Henri-Jean Martin, Roger Chartier, and Jean-Pierre Vivet (Paris, 1982), pp. 305–23; and H.-L. Schlaepfer, ''Laurent de Normandie,'' in *Aspects de la propagande religieuse* (Travaux d'humanisme et renaissance, 28, Geneva, 1957), pp. 176–230.

17. Philippe Renouard, *Documents sur les imprimeurs, libraires . . . ayant exercé à Paris de 1450 à 1600* (Paris, 1901), pp. 65–66 (3 May 1559).

18. AN, X^{2a} 130 (27 January 1562/1563).

19. AN, X^{2a} 130 (7 April 1562/1563): proceedings for the confiscation of Breton's properties, and Renouard, *Documents*, 28.

20. AN, MC, CXXII, 299 (2 April 1571): inventory after death of Richard Breton. The list of books in the inventory has been published by Georges Wildenstein, ''L'imprimeur-libraire Richard Breton et son inventaire après décès, 1571,'' *BHR* 21 (1959): 364–79.

21. Eugénie Droz, ''Antoine Vincent. La propagande protestante par le psautier,'' in *Aspects de la propagande religieuse* (Travaux d'humanisme et renaissance, 28, Geneva, 1957), pp. 281–82.

22. Pierre Pidoux, *Le psautier huguenot du XVIe siècle* (Basel, 1962), 2:130–33. See also Orentin Douen, *Clément Marot et le psautier huguenot. Etude historique, littéraire, musicale et bibliographique* (Amsterdam, 1967; reprint of Paris edition, 1878), 2:525–27.

23. Droz, ''Antoine Vincent,'' p. 282, gives a list of the nineteen, but her identifications are incomplete. Raoullin La Mothe was arrested along with Martin Lhomme in 1560 for the publication of a pamphlet attacking the cardinal of Lorraine. Lhomme was executed, but the disposition of La Mothe's case is not recorded (AN, X^{2a} 126, 18 July 1560). Richard Breton, Philippes Danfrie, Mathurin Prevost, Gilles Gilles, and Jehan Le Preux were ordered arrested in January 1563 because of the cache of forbidden books found hidden in Breton's house (X^{2a} 130, 27 January 1563). Charles Perier was arrested in 1565 (Weiss, ''Poursuites,'' p. 580: 25 November 1565); 1567 (X^{2a} 928, 21 November 1567); and 1569 (X^{2a} 137, 3 February 1569; and X^{2b} 56, 6 May 1569). Oudin Petit was arrested on religious charges in

1568 (X^{2b} 51, 18 March 1568). There were two Mathurin Prevosts, father and son. It is not clear which was ordered arrested in 1563 or actually was arrested in 1568, but it is the son who was arrested in 1569 (X^{2b} 56, 6 May 1569) and who seems to have had extensive contacts in the Protestant community, MC, CXXII, 247, 26 May 1565: marriage contract of Mathurin Prevost and Claude Jouvenceau, daughter of Claude Girard and the deceased Olivier Jouvenceau; CXXII, 1396, 12 August 1566: marriage between Mathurin's cousin Jean Marnois and Catherine Aulnette, a servant in the house of Nicolas Croquet. Pierre Haultin was arrested and his books were seized in 1567 (AN, X^{2b} 49, 2 and 12 July 1567). His books were again seized in 1570 (AN, L428, pièce no. 9, 20 October 1570).

24. In addition to the cases mentioned in the text and in other notes, Richard Breton appears as a witness to the wedding contract of Pierre des Friches and Madeleine Le Melais (AN, MC, CXXII, 247, 29 January 1565–1566); and Goguier recorded the contract for the remarriage Charles Langellyer's widow Geneviève Landry (who had married the bookseller Girard Tannerie after his death) to Lucian Lartizien in 1571 (AN, MC, CXXII, 39, 1 June 1571; and in Renouard, *Documents*, pp. 148–49).

25. AN, MC, CXXII, 247 (7 and 28 August 1565).

26. Crespin, *Histoire des martyrs*, ed. Benoît and Lelièvre, 3:677 (Perier), and 675 (Petit). Petit's death is confirmed by AN, Y 114 (4 September 1573): contract involving his son Charles Petit, also a Protestant. Perier's son Charles died in the massacre.

27. On Perier's relationship to Wechel, see Parent, *Les métiers du livre*, p. 151. The marriage contract is found in AN, MC, CXXII, 39 (8 June 1571): marriage contract of Marie Perier with Guillaume Aubray.

28. AN, MC, CXXII, 247 (14 November 1565): marriage of Marguerite Ronnet, daughter of Marguerite du Vivier and the deceased Robert Ronnet, with Auguste Gallant; AN, Z^{1h} 71 (18 September 1572): request by Catherine du Vivier, widow of Oudin Petit, for the return of her property on the promise to live as a Catholic and raise her children in this faith. See also AN, MC, CXXII, 248 (24 April 1571): marriage of Oudin Petit's daughter Léonie, by authority of her sister Gabrielle Petit; AN Y114 (4 September 1573): agreement between Charles Petit and his brother-in-law Claude Roussel.

29. Jean Petit's wife, Geneviève de la Pierre, was the stepdaughter of François Pajot, a merchant apothecary. Pajot was charged with aiding in the distribution of clandestine literature in 1563, but he could not be arrested because he had left town on account of the war (AN, X^{2a} 130, 27 January 1562/1563; and X^{2a} 130, 13 November 1562). In 1568 he was charged with bearing arms against the king (X^{2a} 137, 10 December 1568). Catherine de la Pierre, Geneviève's sister was arrested on religious charges in 1570. Interrogated in Parlement, she confessed that she had been brought up in the new faith and that her husband, who was absent on account of the wars, would not have married her had she been a Catholic (X^{2b} 1174, 28 June 1570). She also swore that she had not seen her stepfather since the first troubles began. Whether or not this was true, Pajot did return after the Peace of Saint-Germain. He witnessed a Protestant marriage in June 1571 and helped in the settlement of Jean Petit's estate in January and March 1572 (AN, MC, CXXII, 39, 1 June 1571: marriage of Louise Chevalier, daughter of Jacques Chevalier, with Claude Fevrier; MC, LXXIII, 78, 12 January and 15 March 1572: agreements between Oudin Petit and Geneviève de la Pierre, regarding her dowry rights). Petit's partnership agreement with Le Preux was recorded by Goguier (MC, CXXII, 38, 13 December 1565). The break-up of the partnership after Petit's death was recorded by the notaries Du Boys and Chappelain (MC, LXXIII, 78, 12 January 1572). Le Preux's name figures on the list of clients left by Laurent de Normandie, a French refugee to Geneva who specialized in the publication of religious works for clandestine export to France (see Schlaepfer, "Laurent de Normandie," p. 185).

30. AEG, Ragueau, vol. 7, pp. 164–69, and vol. 9, pp. 407–16, 2 July 1567.

31. François Le Preux was sentenced to be publicly beaten "at the accustomed places near the University" and then banished from the kingdom, but the charges against Perier were dismissed (AN, X^{2b} 41, 7 and 12 December 1565, and X^{2a} 928, 4 December 1565; Weiss, "Poursuites," p. 580).

32. Higman, "Le levain de l'évangile," p. 309, comes to the same conclusion for the sale of Protestant literature in the earlier stages of the French Reformation, but he underestimates the importance of the trade that continued in Paris through the first religious war.

33. On the other hand, there is no evidence linking Pierre du Pre or Oudin Petit to the clandestine book trade. There is nothing to suggest that Oudin Petit was a silent partner in his son Jean's clandestine trade. Indeed, the two men appear to have been estranged between 1567 and Jean's death in about 1571 because of a quarrel over properties that were due Jean and the other children of Oudin's first marriage from the estate of his deceased wife (AN, X^{2a} 135, 11 January 1567; X^{2b} 47, 26 April 1567; MC, LXXIII, 78, 12 January and 13 February 1572). Oudin Petit did not even witness the marriage contract of his daughter Léonie in 1571, presumably because of this same quarrel. She is represented instead by her sister Gabrielle, another party to the lawsuit Jean Petit filed against his father in 1567 (AN, MC, CXXII, 248, 24 April 1571).

34. AN, MC, CXXII, 1397 (21 February 1567): contract between Eustache Jue, maître maçon, and Mathurin Lussault, orfèvre de la reine mère; X^{2a} 130 (18 December 1562): request for release from prison of Eustache Jue, maître maçon, and release on charge of living according to the Catholic faith.

35. AN, MC, CXXII, 1395 (2 August 1564): contract recording sale between Pierre Berthrand and Loys Berthrand, seigneur de Popincourt lez Paris, and Thibault Le Maire, marchand bourgeois de Paris; X^{2a} 137 (10 December 1568): order for confiscation of property of Thibault Le Maire (among others); CXXII, 39 (8 June 1571): marriage contract of Marie Perier, the daughter of Charles Perier, marchand libraire et imprimeur, bourgeois de Paris, and Guillaume Aubray, aussi libraire; CXXII, 39 (21 June 1571): rental contract between Me Claude Tardif, conseiller du roi en son Trésor, and Loys Massicault, doreur sur fer.

36. For an example of a simple loan, see AN, MC, CXXII, 1397 (21 February 1567): Jehan des Margues, former secretary to Monsieur de Cypiere, borrows 260 livres from Nicolas Viarre, marchand, bourgeois de Paris, on the security of two trunks of clothes placed with Me Gilles Du Pre, commissaire et examinateur au Châtelet.

37. AN, MC, CXXII, 247 (16 February 1565/1566). See also CXXII, 247 (7 August 1565): contract in which Pierre Payen, a merchant jeweler, loans his name and serves as a backer for an agreement between Geneviève de Montault and Jehan de Ferrieres, chevalier, sieur de Maligny, and vidame de Chartres.

38. See, for example, AN, MC, CXXII, 247 (28 June and 17 October 1565): contracts in which Thibault Le Maire serves as procureur of "hault & puissant Seigneur Messire Jehan Phelippes, conte sauvaige du Rhein & de Saulne, chevalier de l'ordre du Roi et cappitaine de cinquante hommes d'armes."

39. AN, MC, CXXII, 1397 (25 and 26 January 1567).

40. AN, MC, CXXII, 1396 (26 September 1566): contract involving Symonne Engarde, wife of Jehan Sacre, "maître charpentier de la grand coignée."

41. *Hist. eccl.*, 1:265; Pithou, "Histoire ecclesiastique de Troyes," fol. 140.

42. AN, MC, CXXII, 1395 (7 January 1564/65). Le Melais, who received only 50 livres plus some clothing as his wife's dowry and offered in return a dower of 40 livres, fits at the lower end of the economic scale represented by the Parisian Protestants who made up Leal and Goguier's clientele.

43. AN, MC, CXXII, 1395 (30 July 1564); and CXXII, 1396 (5 August 1566).

44. AN, MC, CXXII, 1396 (16 August 1566). In addition to teaching his young brother-

in-law how to make musical instruments, Verdier promised to teach him music and, for six months, to send him to school one hour a day so that he could learn to read and write.

45. Crespin, *Histoire des martyrs*, ed. Benoît and Lelièvre, 3:677, identifies him as "N. Le Clerc, procureur en Chastelet, fort hais des Catholiques."

46. Although Breton is known to have published his own edition of the Psalms in 1562, none of the psalters listed in his inventory is identified as coming from his own presses and only one is identified as a Parisian imprint, a 1567 edition from the presses of Pierre Haultin. The edition is listed as "Testament et Psalmes, in-seize, Hautin" and identified as a pairing of a New Testament with *Les CL Pseaumes de David avec la prose en marge . . . par M. Augustin Marlorat* (Paris: Haultin, 1567) in Wildenstein, "L'imprimeur-libraire Richard Breton," p. 377n. There were fourteen packets of Psalms among the censured books discovered in Pierre Haultin's house on the rue Saint-Jacques in 1570. See AN, L428, pièce 9 (20 October 1570). This document is reproduced in Louis Desgraves, *Les Haultin, 1571–1623. L'imprimerie à La Rochelle*, vol. 2 (Geneva, 1960), pp. x–xii.

47. Higman, "Le levain de l'évangile," p. 318.

48. Douen, *Clément Marot et le psautier Huguenot*, 2:4–11, cites examples of use of singing of psalms by prisoners and on the field of battle. See also Beza's prefatory epistle to the *Psaumes en vers français*, in which he urges religious prisoners to sing them from their funeral pyres and Crespin, *Histoire des martyrs*, ed. Benoît and Lelièvre, 2:702n, regarding the execution of Anne du Bourg. On the disruption of Catholic services, see La Fosse, *Journal d'un curé ligueur*, p. 41.

49. Aubigné, *Histoire universelle*, book 5, chapter 13, as cited in Jules Bonnet, "Les réfugiés de Montargis et l'exode de 1569," *BSHPF* 38 (1889): 182.

50. Nathanael Weiss, "La Réforme à Bourges au XVIe siècle," *BSHPF* 53 (1904): 350; Goulart, *Memoires de l'estat de France*, 2:10. Psalm 124 also had a special meaning for the Huguenots of Orleans, who believed, until their good fortune deserted them in 1568, that they enjoyed God's special protection and favor. See Daniel Toussain, *L'exercice de l'âme fidèle; assavoir, prières et méditations pour le consoler en toutes sortes d'afflictions. Avec une préface consolatoire aux pauvres résidus de l'église d'Orléans, contenant un brief récit des afflictions qu'a souffert ladite église* (Frankfurt, 1583), unpaginated fol. Avi.

51. Calvin, *Lettres françaises*, 2:122–26 and 140–41: "A l'église de Paris" (15 March and 16 September 1557). The metaphor of taking shelter "under the wings of God" occurs half a dozen times in the Psalms but in only one other place in the Bible. See Louis Jacquet, *Les psaumes et le coeur de l'homme. Etude textuelle, littéraire et doctrinale* (Paris, 1975), pp. 422–23.

52. Calvin, *Lettres françaises*, 2:253-57: "aux prisonniers de Paris," 18 February 1559.

53. Beza, *Correspondance*, 8:29: Merlin de l'Espérandière to Beza (Longueville [Paris], 10 January 1567).

54. AN, MC, VIII, 95 (28 April 1567): testament of Anthoine du Croy, prince de Porcien. The reference is to Psalm 51:2–3.

55. For reference to the Christological meaning, see, for example, the prefatory "arguments" for Psalms 18, 22, and 109.

56. Clément Marot and Theodore Beza, *Les pseaumes en vers français avec leurs mélodies. Fac-similé de l'édition genevoise de Michel Blanchier, 1562*, ed. Pierre Pidoux (Geneva, 1986), p. 89.

57. See, for example, Clément Marot and Theodore Beza, *Les pseaumes de David, mis en rime françoise. Avec une oraison à la fin d'un chacun pseaume faite par M. Augustin Marlorat* (Paris: pour Antoine Vincent, 1566) [BN, Réserve, A.6173].

58. Ibid., see especially pp. 39: Psalm 13; 149: Psalm 42; 304: Psalm 83; and 497–98: Psalm 137. Marlorat was not always given credit for the prayers. See, for example, Clément

Marot and Theodore Beza, *Les cent cinquante pseaumes de David, mis en rime françoise. Avec brieves et sainctes oraisons nouvellement adjoutees en la fin de chacun pseaume pour la consolation de l'église, selon la substance du pseaume* (Paris: Martin le Jeune, pour Antoine Vincent, 1562) [BN, A.10114]. Not all editions that included prayers, however, included those of Marlorat. See, for example, Clément Marot and Theodore Beza, *Les cent et cinquante pseaumes de David, mis en rythme françoise* (N.p., 1562) [BN, Réserve, A.6170]. These prayers are a much closer paraphrase of the Psalms than are Marlorat's.

59. See Calvin, *Lettres françaises*, 2:2–3: letter to the Church of Paris (28 January 1555); 2:122–26: letter to the Church of Paris (15 March 1557); *C.O.*, vol. 16, cols. 726–29: letter to Madame de Rentigny (8 December 1557).

60. The metaphor of God as a shield occurs in Psalm 84, as does the invocation of the "God of armies." The metaphor of God as fortress occurs in Psalms 27, 31, and 144, among others. The "God of vengeance" occurs in the first line of Psalm 94. For examples of the use of these phrases in Huguenot writings, see the letter from Beaumont [Daniel Toussain] to Renée of Ferrara (Orleans, 27 August 1568), in "Lettres de divers à la duchesse de Ferrare," p. 456; and [François Perrot], *Perles d'eslite. Recueillies de l'infini thresor des cent cinquantes pseaumes de David. Traduit de l'italien en françois par l'auteur* ([Geneva]: Jean de Laon, 1577), fol. 3v.

61. Marot and Beza, *Les pseaumes de David* [BN, Réserve, A.6173], pp. 519–20.

62. Pierre Viret, *L'interim fait par dialogues* (Lyons, 1565), fols. Iii–Iiiii.

63. Ibid., fols. Iiiii–Ilii.

64. Chandieu, *Histoire des persecutions*, p. viii.

65. [L'Espine], *Traitté consolatoire*, pp. 6–7.

66. Ibid., pp. 10–12.

67. Daniel Toussain, *Prieres et consolations prises de plusieurs passages de l'Escriture, & des livres des anciens. Le tout accommodé à l'usage des vrai Chrestiens, & au temps auquel nous sommes* (Geneva: pour la veuve de Jean Durant, n.d.). The dedicatory epistle, dated 1 octobre 1366 [sic: 1566], shows the work to have been composed in Orleans between the wars.

68. Ibid., p. 119: prayer on Psalm 34.

69. Jean de L'Espine, *Excellens discours de J. de l'Espine, angevin, touchant le repos & contentement de L'esprit* (Basel, 1587), p. 632.

70. [Jean de L'Espine,] *Traicté des tentations et moyens d'y resister. Composé par un docte et excellent personnage de ce temps* (Lyon: Jean Saugrain, 1566), pp. 59–60.

71. [De L'Espine], *Traicté des tentations*, pp. 56–57; see also p. 58: "aussi la petite foy qui es ès freres infirmes de l'eglise, vit & vivifie aussi bien que la grande qui est plus parfaite."

72. See Pasquier, *Oeuvres*, 2:133–34 (book 5, letter 11, to Monsieur Loysel, advocat); and *Tocsain contre les massacreurs*, fol. 84. See also AN, Z^{1h} 71 (22 December 1572): request by Noel Thierie, captain in the quartier of Pierre Perlan, in which he relates that "one named Taverny" and his servants were beseiged in Taverny's house "tant par les habitans dudict quartier que par la commune de ceste ville de Paris," and tells how several of those attacking the house were injured and even killed by shots from harquebuses before they succeeded in entering the house. Thierie's own interest in the affair seems to be simply to get back the "grande balle de lame" (a kind of shield?) that he had loaned the attackers.

73. Philippe de Gastines was "put to the question," or tortured, in the hope that he would reveal the names of others who attended the services in his house, but those arrested with him do not seem to have shared this fate. See AN, X^{2b} 56: minute of 25 May 1569. One can compare the interrogations of Philippe on 24 May and 23 June 1569 with that of François de Gastines on 23 June (X^{2a} 933). The martyrdom of Richard de Gastines is described

at length in Agrippa d'Aubigné's "Tragiques." Aubigné's purpose, like Crespin's in the *Histoire des martyrs*, is to create the exemplary hero. There is, however, an element of truth behind Aubigné's claim that Richard was preaching the gospel within his prison walls. Five witnesses swore they saw him go up to a fellow prisoner in the chapel of the the the Conciergerie and, laying a hand on his shoulder, tell him he should confess himself to God alone (or to Christ alone; the testimony is not entirely consistent in its terminology). Richard admitted to speaking to the fellow prisoner, who had just been sentenced to death, but he denied the accusation that he was proselytizing. His judges chose not to believe him and sentenced him to a ritual apology (amende honorable) and a 400-livre fine. See AN, X^{2a} 933 (20 January 1569); X^{2b} 56 (16 May 1569); and APP, A^b 3, fol. 45r (4 June 1569).

74. Toussain, *L'exercice de l'âme fidèle*, fol. Biiii. The quotations are taken from a dedicatory letter dated 30 July 1578; the second is a paraphrase of Psalm 89:33–34.

75. See, for example, the anonymous poems by "M.B." ("Complainte et prière des fideles persecutez en la France") and "L.M.S." ("Discours du gouvernement et estat de la vraye eglise," written in 1573) in Goulart, *Memoires de l'estat*, vol. 2, fols 424–31.

76. [Hugues Sureau Du Rosier], *Confession et recognoissance de Hugues Sureau, dict du Rosier, touchant sa cheute en la papauté, & les horribles scandales par luy commis. Servant d'exemple à tout le monde de la fragilité & perversité de l'homme abandonné à soy, & de l'infinie misericorde & ferme verité de Dieu envers ses esleus* (Basel: Martin Cousin, 1574), pp. 7–8. Kingdon, *Myths about the Massacres*, p. 120, also sees Du Rosier's abjuration, though later recanted, as emblematic of a sincere loss of faith that many French Protestants experienced under the pressures of Saint Bartholomew's Day.

77. Du Rosier, *Confession et recognoissance*, p. 22. Du Rosier's return to the Protestant faith was not an easy one. Even after rejecting Catholicism because of the "idolatry" that he continued to find there, he could not bring himself to give up his conviction that the principle of apostolic succession made the Protestant church illegitimate. The Catholic church was one and universal, and it could trace its lineage back to the apostles; the Protestants could make no such claim. Even if errors had crept in, a possibility Du Rosier was willing to admit, did that justify leaving the established church and founding another? In a letter written to Beza on 12 March 1573, Du Rosier discusses these and other problems of faith. It took another year before Du Rosier's view of these questions evolved sufficiently to allow him to compose a statement of faith acceptable to French Protestants. The essential change lay in his eventual rejection of apostolic succession in favor of doctrinal purity as the principle on which the true church must rest. See Hugues Sureau Du Rosier to Beza (12 March 1573) in Beza, *Correspondance*, ed. A. Dufour and B. Nicollier, vol 14 (Geneva, 1990), pp. 41–52. See also the letter from the French Church of Heidelberg to Beza (17 May 1574) in the Musée Historique de la Réformation, Archives Tronchin, vol. 5, fols. 47–48, to be published in Beza, *Correspondance*, vol. 15. I am grateful to Madame Nicollier for sharing these letters with me in advance of publication. Du Rosier's rejection of apostolic succession in favor of the continuity of doctrinal purity is explained in his *Traitté des certaines et inséparables marques de la vraye Eglise de Dieu* (Heidelberg: Jan Mayer, 1574). The dedicatory letter for this volume, addressed to the duchesse de Bouillon, is dated 22 February 1574.

78. See, for example, the *Instruction du devoir de perseverance en la persecution à ceux qui sont tombez. Pour response aux scandales qu'on se propose & confirmation qu'il n'est point permis de dissimuler la profession de l'evangile, & communiquer aux superstitions de la papauté* (n.p., 1573). See also [Jean de L'Espine], *Traicté de l'apostasie faict par M. J. D. L., ministre de la parole de Dieu en l'Eglise d'Angers* (N.p., 1583). See especially his preface, fols. 2 and 3, on the weight of the cross.

79. Fatio and Labarthe, eds., *Registres de la compagnie des pasteurs*, 3:99–100. Du Rosier's own stubbornness (see note 77 above) surely contributed to the situation.

80. Pradel, "Un marchand de Paris," pp. 421–23: letter of 23 September 1572; [de L'Espine], *Traicté de l'apostasie*, fol. Aii.

81. For example, Mathieu Coignet, a maître des requêtes and former ambassador to the Swiss Leagues, along with his wife and children, signed a profession of faith before the official of the bishop of Paris on 7 October 1572. He was registered as a resident of Geneva a year and a half later. See AN, Z^{1h} 71: 13 October 1572; and Geisendorf, *Livre des habitants*, 2:100. See also Fatio and Labarthe, eds., *Registres de la compagnie de pasteurs*, 3:95–96 and 96n, on the reception of the refugees in Geneva. There seems to have been some disagreement between the city magistrates and the pastors about just which acts of "idolatry" required formal acts of repentance. Wearing a cross on one's hat to escape being massacred was one of the acts in dispute.

82. The rebirth of the Reformed Church of Paris after Saint Bartholomew's Day is even more difficult to document than the vicissitudes of the church during the first decade of the religious wars. The first sign I have found of church meetings is in the fall of 1576, when L'Estoile reports that Parisian Catholics harassed Huguenots returning from services in the nearby village of Noisy-le-Sec. See Pierre L'Estoile, *Journal de L'Estoile pour le règne de Henri III (1574–1589)*, ed. Louis-Raymond Lefevre (Paris, 1943), p. 126.

Chapter 9

1. Paschal, *Journal de l'année 1562*, p. 113.

2. Haton, *Mémoires*, 1:214–15.

3. Pasquier, *Oeuvres*, 2:100 (book 4, letter 16).

4. See Chapter 3, note 60.

5. Haton, *Mémoires*, 1:220.

6. Ibid, pp. 220–21. See Chapter 3, note 59, on accusations of seditious preaching in the fall of 1561.

7. Ibid.

8. Once again, Denis Crouzet's new book, *Les guerriers de Dieu*, is an exception here. Arlette Lebigre's recent book on the League, *La révolution des curés: Paris, 1588–1594* (Paris, 1980), appears by its title to promise such an analysis but never in fact delivers it. A more substantial analysis of Catholic preaching in the League apears in Robert Harding, "Revolution and Reform in the Holy League: Angers, Rennes, Nantes," *Journal of Modern History* 53 (1981): 379–416. See note 34 below, however, on Harding's misattribution of Simon Vigor's sermons to his editor Jean Christi. See also the classic but limited study by Charles Labitte, *De la démocratie chez les prédicateurs de la Ligue* (Geneva, 1971; reprint of Paris edition, 1841), and, more broadly, Denis Crouzet, "La représentation du temps à l'époque de la Ligue," *Revue historique* 270 (1984): 297–388.

9. For the Calvinist critique of the Mass, see, for example, Jean Calvin, "Petit traitté de la Saincte Cene de Nostre Seigneur Jesus Christ," in *Recueil des opuscules: C'est à dire, petits traictez de M. Jean Calvin* (Geneva: Baptiste Pinereul, 1566), p. 191. More generally on the effect of this critique, see Theisen, *Mass Liturgy*, p. 17.

10. See Chapter 7, note 9.

11. François Le Picart, *Les sermons et instructions chrestiennes pour tous les dimenches & toutes les festes des saincts depuis Pasques jusques à la Trinité. Avec douze sermons du mesme autheur touchant le sainct sarcrement de l'autel* (Paris: Nicolas Chesneau, 1566), fols. 249ff. See fol. 251 on transubstantiation. In an introductory letter to another volume of Le Picart's sermons, René Benoist describes him as the most "familier & populaire predicateur" Paris has ever had. See François Le Picart, *Les sermons et instructions chres-*

tiennes pour tous les jours de Caresme & feriés de Pasques (Paris: Nicolas Chesneau, 1566), unpaginated letter dated 20 December 1563.

12. Dyvolé, *Dix sermons de la saincte messe.*

13. *SSA*. Among other things, Vigor calls Calvin a "paillard" (pp. 101 and 293) and an imposter (p. 231), and he accuses him of "impieté et athéisme" (p. 283).

14. See, for example, the *Alphabet ou instruction chrestienne pour les petis enfans. Nouvellement reveue & augmentée de plusieurs choses* (Lyons: Pierre Estiard, 1558); Gentian Hervet, *Catechisme ou sommaire du la foy & devoir du vray chrestien, selon la doctrine evangelique & sens de l'eglise & anciens docteurs d'icelle. Recueilly des oeuvres de Guillaume Lindan, eveque alleman* (Paris: Nicolas Chesneau, 1561); or Emond Auger, *La maniere d'ouir la messe.* One might equally cite René Benoist, *Catechisme ou instruction populaire, contenant les principaux poincts de la religion chrestienne, lesquels tous chrestiens sont tenus de sçavoir, & suivant l'expresse parole de Dieu & ordonnance de l'eglise catholique, apostolique & romaine* (Paris: Guillaume de la Noue, 1569). More generally on the new outpouring of theological writings, see F. M. Higman, "Theology in French Religious Pamphlets from the Counter-Reformation," *Renaissance and Modern Studies* 23 (1979): 128–46; see especially p. 130, Table I.

15. To avoid a tedious listing of titles, the reader is referred to the bibliography entries under Benoist. This is not a comprehensive list of Benoist's writings but represents the more important treatises for the period under consideration here. A more complete list is published in Emile Pasquier, *Un curé de Paris pendant les guerres de Religion: René Benoist, le pape des Halles (1521–1608)* (Geneva, 1970; reprint of of Paris and Angers edition, 1913).

16. See, for example, the little treatise entitled "Certaines raisons lesquelles sommairement (si vous voulez bien les gouster & digerer) vous feront apercevoir, & vous persuaderont aisement que vous estes en erreur," published in Benoist's *Advertissement exhortatoire à ceux de la paroisse de S. Eustache à Paris* (Paris: Nicolas Chesneau, 1569).

17. As Simon Vigor explained in one of his sermons on the Mass, this belief is symbolized in the Mass by the mixing of water with the wine of communion, "because this is a sacrament of union, and because the water mixed with the wine signifies to us that we are unified with Jesus Christ our head, and consequently with one another, as all members of the same head" (*SSA*, p. 111).

18. Gabriel Du Preau, *Arrest et condamnation donnée au profit des catholiques, par les propres tesmoignages, confrontations, & sentences de xxiiii des principaux ministres & predicans de la nouvelle doctrine* (Paris: Michel Julian, 1567), fol. 5v.

19. A particularly good exposition of this very common metaphor is found in René Benoist, *Exhortation chrestienne aux fideles et esleus de Dieu, de batailler par tous moyens pour le grand Seigneur contre l'Antechrist* (Paris: Guillaume Chaudiere, 1566), fols. 3–5. See also his *Advertissement exhortatoire*, fol. 3v, and his *Triomphe et excellent victoire de la foy, par le moyen de la veritable & toute-puissante parole de Dieu. Où est monstré le moyen certain & facile de pacifier les troubles presens* (Paris: Nicolas Chesneau, 1568), fol. f; Dupuyherbault, *Deux epistres*, p. 185.

20. Dyvolé, *Dix sermons de la saincte messe*, p. 405.

21. See Chapter 2, note 106.

22. The image of ravishing wolves is used, for example, by Gabriel Du Preau, *Des faux prophetes, seducteurs, & hypochrites, qui viennent à nous en habit de brebis, mais au dedans sont loups ravissans. Et comme il les fault congoistre, & s'il est licite communiquer avec eux sans offenser Dieu* (Paris: Jacques Macé, 1563), and by Benoist, *Exhortation chrestienne*, fol. 5v.

23. René Benoist, *Brieve et facile refutation d'un livret divulgé au nom de J. de l'Espine* (Paris: Guillaume Chaudiere, 1565). See also the prayer for troubled times included in

Benoist's *Catechisme ou instruction populaire*, fols. 16–17, and Antoine Du Val, *Demandes et repliques à Jean Calvin sur son livre de la predestination* (Paris: Nicolas Chesneau, 1561), fol. iii.

24. Desiré, *L'origine et source de tous les maux*, fols. 32–34; Emond Auger, *La maniere d'ouir la messe avec devotion & fruict spirituel* (Paris: Nicolas Chesneau, 1571), fol. Lii; Haton, *Mémoires*, 1:332–33.

25. Benoist, *Exhortation chrestienne*, fol. 12.

26. Ibid., fols. 13–14. See also Benoist's *Certaine resolution et determination des poincts à present controverses touchant la religion chrestienne* (Paris: Guillaume Chaudiere, 1564), fol. Aiii, and Du Preau, *Des faux prophetes*, fol. 8, on the danger of frequenting heretics.

27. "Nous ne sçaurions certes avoir plus evidente demonstrance de l'indignation de Dieu & prochaine ruine, que de voir oster les armes, l'enseigne, & sauvegarde de Jesus Christ, le signe & image de la croix, contre laquelle rien de humaine ne doit prevaloir." René Benoist, *Advertissement ou moyen par lequel aisément tous troubles et différens touchant la croix, de la quelle y a si grande altercation en la ville de Paris, que autres concernans la religion, seront assoupis et ostez* (Paris: Théodore Belot, 1571), fol. 4b.

28. AN, X²ᵇ 1094: Parlement criminel, plumitif of 31 December 1571. The same view is expressed in an anonymous reply to Benoist entitled *Response de la plus saine partie de Messieurs de Paris à l'advertissement à eux envoyé par Maistre René Benoist, docteur en theologie, sur le moyen d'appaiser les troubles advenus pour la croix & autres concernans la religion* (Paris: Estienne des Champs, 1572).

29. Benoist, *Advertissement touchant la croix*, fol. 5a.

30. Ibid., fol. 5b. The implied criticism of the king is reinforced by the statement that God punishes people for their sins by giving them "hypocrites" for kings and by the conclusion that "en temps de punition & fureur de Dieu le peuple est puni & affligé à cause de ses superieurs, & les superieurs à cause du peuple."

31. Benoist, *Le triomphe et excellent victoire de la foy*, unpaginated dedicatory preface.

32. Ibid.

33. Ibid.

34. Vigor's sermons were collected and edited at his request by Jean Christi, theologal of the church of Nantes. Robert Harding's assumption that Vigor's sermons were coauthored rather than merely collected and edited by Christi is totally unwarranted ("Revolution and Reform in the Holy League," p. 399n). It may be true that Christi shared many of the political opinions and religious ideas of his teacher Vigor. It is also possible that a belief that these ideas spoke in some way to the crisis of the League inspired Christi's later editions of Vigor's sermons. The contents of these sermons nevertheless demonstrate that they were composed in Paris during the first decade of the religious wars and not in Nantes at the time of the League. We have, moreover, Christi's own assurance in his introduction to the *Sermons catholiques pour tous les jours de caresme* that he tried hard as editor to reproduce Vigor's sermons as accurately as possible.

35. *SCP*, 1:361; idem, *Oraison funebre prononcée aux obseques de tres-haute, tres-puissante et tres-catholique princesse, ma dame Elizabeth de France, royne des Espagnes* (Paris: Claude Fremy, 1568); *Reg. BV*, 6:146n. See also Pierre Feret, *La Faculté de théologie de Paris et ses docteurs les plus célèbres. Epoque moderne*, vol. 2, *XVIᵉ siècle. Revue Littéraire* (Paris, 1901), pp. 118–19.

36. Vigor, *Les actes de la conference tenue à Paris.*

37. AN, X²ᵇ 1174: interrogation of Claude Grassion (4 September 1569).

38. La Fosse, *Journal d'un curé ligueur*, p. 96.

39. *SCP*, 2:162–63. On this procession, see above, Chapter 2, note 92.

40. Feret, *Faculté de théologie*, 2:119.

41. See, for example, P. Tarbé, *Recueil de poésies calvinistes (1550–1566)*, 2d ed. (Geneva, 1968), pp. 15–16; and BN, Mss. fr. 22560: songs and poems of Ras de Noeux, for mentions of Vigor in satirical verse.

42. Beza, *Correspondance*, 8:25–27 (Delamare to Beza, La Forest [Paris], 5 January 1567).

43. Haton, *Mémoires*, 1:214.

44. Ibid., 2:527–28; *CSP,F*, 8:418–19 (Norris to the queen, 24 February 1568).

45. *CSP,F*, 8:418–19 (Norris to the queen, 24 February 1568).

46. See, for example, *SSA*, p. 111; *SCC*, fols. 161v and 167.

47. *SCP*, 1:361–69; 2:59–61; *SSA*, pp. 7–8.

48. *SCC*, fol. 139.

49. BN, Mss. fr. 454: sermons preached by Claude Despence at Saint-Séverin in 1557; the reference to Ahab occurs fol. 39v. See also Haton, *Mémoires*, 1:210–11, on the common use of this theme in December 1561.

50. *SCP*, 2:195–96. The same three kings are cited in *SCC*, fol. 63.

51. *SCC*, sermon for Ash Wednesday. See especially fols. 6–7.

52. *SCP*, 2:228–44. According to information in the *Reg. BV*, 6:384, this sermon was preached on 4 November 1571.

53. Ibid., 2:243.

54. La Fosse, *Journal d'un curé ligueur*, pp. 134–35.

55. Ibid., pp. 138–39; *Reg. BV*, 6:400n.

56. La Fosse, *Journal d'un curé ligueur*, p. 137.

57. See, for example, René Benoist's defense of the pamphlet he had written about the cross: AN, X^{2b} 1094 (31 December 1571).

58. *SCP*, 1:46.

59. Ibid. 1:47–48, 450, 482, and 660, 2:155–57; *SCC*, fol. 172v.

60. *SCP*, 2:58–61. In a sermon preached in the fall of 1568, Vigor claimed that the Huguenots had promised their soldiers the pillage of the churches of Paris (ibid., fols. 360–61).

61. Ibid., 2:255. This is listed as a sermon for the feast day of Saints Simon and Jude (October 28). Internal evidence allows it to be dated to the fall of 1570.

62. Ibid., 2:162–63. The date of this sermon is identified as 29 September 1568 by François Grin, "Journal," pp. 48–49. See also *Reg. BV*, 6:59–60 and 116–17.

63. *SCC*, fols. 147 and 161v.

64. *SCP*, 1:482; similarly, 2:195–96.

65. Ibid., 1:40; *SCC*, fol. 32r.

66. *SCP*, 1:36–40.

67. Ibid., 1:39–40.

68. Ibid., 2:362.

69. *SCC*, fol. 110v. Vigor goes on to say that there is a king above the law, and that is God. If he commands someone to kill, it must be done. Vigor cites here the example of Abraham being ordered by God to slay his son, but then he immediately tempers this thought by saying that such revelations of God are very rare. We should not go out and follow Abraham's example without God's express commandment. The burden of the message thus falls back on the notion of the king's licit right to order others to wield the sword. The shock value of the proposition "if the king ordered the admiral killed" adds to this emphasis.

70. Ibid., fol. 62v; see also *SCP*, 1:24; 2:92 and 133.

71. *SCP*, 2:367–68.

72. Ibid., 2:26; see also 1:450, on family divisions. In addition, see Benoist, *Advertissement touchant la croix*, fol. 5v.

73. *SCC*, fols. 69v and 6v; *SCP*, 2:376–77.

74. *SCC*, fol. 139. See also, *SCP*, 2:376–80, on the need to reform the church.

75. *SCC*, fol. 126v.

76. *SCP*, 2:88–89.

77. Ibid.

Chapter 10

1. La Fosse, *Journal d'un curé ligueur*, p. 121.

2. BN, Mss. fr. 10304 (Recueils de L'Estoile), pp. 209–14: "Desseins pour la Croix de Gastines, de l'Invention de Jodelle, non imprimez mais donnez et presentez au Roy par led. Jodelle en l'an 1569."

3. "Un manifeste parisien," pp. 534–40; *Remonstrances . . . par Messieurs de la court de Parlement*.

4. Richet, "Conflits religieux à Paris," p. 772.

5. *Reg. BV*, 5:121n.

6. Ibid., pp. 120–21; 121n. This document refers to the creation of one captain for each quartier. Elsewhere, however, it is apparent that the intention was to name one captain for each dizaine, the more local district into which the quartiers were divided.

7. Ibid., p. 122.

8. La Fosse, *Journal d'un curé ligueur*, pp. 50–52; Grin, "Journal," pp. 22–24; Pasquier, *Oeuvres*, 2:100 (book 4, letter 16); Paschal, *Journal de l'année 1562*, p. 43–54.

9. Ordonnances of 25 and 27 May 1562 and order of 17 June 1562, published by Félibien and Lobineau, *Histoire de Paris, Preuves*, 1:667.

10. *Reg. BV*, 5:129–30, 129n.

11. Guérin, "Délibérations politiques," pp. 82–83. See also AN, X^{1a} 1603 (24 July 1563) regarding a brawl between militiamen of two adjoining dizaines.

12. AN, X^{2a} 130 (12 March 1562/1563): case of Nicolas du Mont. This case was ordered erased from the records after one of the treaties of pacification, but it was merely crossed out and is consequently still legible.

13. See, for example, AN, X^{2b} 34 (19 October 1562): order for weekly searches; X^{2b} 34 (29 October 1562): certification of faith for Jehanne Danys; and *Reg. BV*, 6:4–5 (10 January 1568): order for captains to call together four notables from each dizaine to meet with the captain, his lieutenant and ensign to draw up a list of "les notoirement diffamez et suspectz d'heresies en leursdictes dixaines."

14. Guérin, "Délibérations politiques," p. 88; AN, X^{2b} 34 (24 October 1562): request made of the Chambre des vacations by several unnamed prisoners in the Conciergerie.

15. AN, X^{2a} 130 (10 December 1562). See also AN, X^{2b} 34 (13 November 1562): cases of André Cordier and Nicolas de Lebigny.

16. See, for example, AN, X^{2b} 34 (29 October 1562): case of Pierre Croquet, and (7 November 1562): case of Guillaume de Hodic and Guillaume François.

17. APP, A^b 3 and 4. Although suspects were also placed in the Châtelet, Saint-Magloire, and other city prisons, incarceration records have survived only for the Conciergerie, which raises the possibility that existing records do not provide a fair sample of the cases of religious arrest. A close scrutiny of Conciergerie records and a comparison between these records and parlementary interrogations would seem, however, to rule out the likelihood that results are skewed by the reporting techniques. It is clearly *not* the case that just a few men assumed the booking tasks, while many more took charge of the actual arrests.

18. Weiss, "Poursuites," p. 640 (5 January 1569). Croizier also arrested Philippe de Gastines a year earlier (idem, p. 591: 19 February 1568).

19. APP, A^b 3, fol. 23v (22 April 1569).

20. On Simon Le Comte: Archives départmentales de la Haute-Garonne, Hôtel-Dieu B93: "comptes de frais et fournitures ensemble des vaccacions despensés par Simon Le Comte pour les affaires et à la requisition de feu Philippes Le Canaye." See also Pradel, "Un marchand de Paris," p. 332. Le Comte was arrested on 26 March 1569 (Weiss, "Huguenots emprisonnés," p. 95). Pezou is not mentioned in the arrest proceedings. The order for Le Comte's release from the Conciergerie can be found in AN, X^{2a} 137, fol. 399v (27 April 1569).

21. At least four of the sixteen men who held the high office of colonel at the start of the second war were officers of the sovereign courts, yet only one of these men was responsible for any of the known arrests, and he imprisoned only two men. APP, A^b 3 and 4; and *Reg. BV*, 5:161–63: list of militia captains (December 1562), and 6:13: list of colonels (27 February 1568), of whom Masurier and de Vignolles were counselors in Parlement, Grandrue was a maître des comptes, and Michon an auditeur des comptes. De Thou suggests that Croizier was a jeweler (see below, note 63), but I have found no evidence to confirm this. Neither his nor Pezou's occupation is ever mentioned in the records—itself a suggestion that they were men of mediocre professional standing.

22. *Reg. BV*, 5:262 (20 July 1563).

23. AN, X^{1a} 1604 (27 November 1562). The captains' complaint had little direct result. They were ordered to present a further report, with evidence to back up their denunciations, but before action could be taken, a change in the military balance of the war with the battle of Dreux in December 1562 brought Catherine de Medici to negotiate with the prince of Condé for peace. Linda Taber has identified BN, Mss. fr. 4047, fols. 8v–10, as the report the capitains produced. See "Royal Policy and Religious Dissent within the Parlement of Paris, 1559–1563" (unpublished Ph.D. dissertation, Stanford University, 1982).

24. AN, Z^{1h} 59^b, fol. 66r (23 March 1562/1563) makes reference to the "chapelle des Hacquebusiers de lad. ville." The militia's participation in the processions for Corpus Christi and for the reconsecration of Saint-Médard is mentioned in Paschal, *Journal de l'année 1562*, pp. 43 and 52–53. The presence of its members in the 11 July procession from Saint-Germain-l'Auxerrois to the porte Saint-Honoré on account of a sacrilege is the subject of a song included in Christophe de Bordeaux, *Recueil de plusieurs belles chansons spirituelles, avec ceux des huguenots heretics & ennemis de Dieu & de nostre mere saincte eglise* (Paris: Magdaleine Berthelin, n.d.), pp. 5–8: "Chanson nouvelle de l'ymage nostre dame qui a esté remise à la porte Sainct Honoré."

25. La Fosse, *Journal*, pp. 55 and 59–60.

26. Pinet, *Le culte Sainte-Geneviève*, p. 245. Quartenier Guillaume Guerrier was also made a member in 1568.

27. *CSP,F*, 6:408–9; Catherine de Medici, *Lettres*, 2:57; La Fosse, *Journal d'un curé ligueur*, pp. 64–65; and *Reg. BV*, 5:226–27n.

28. *Reg. BV*, 5:226–27 (12 June 1563).

29. Ibid., pp. 236–37 (26 June 1563); also AN, X^{2a} 131 (28 June 1563).

30. *Reg. BV*, 5:239–44 and 240n (28 June–3 July 1563); Brulart, *Journal*, 1:130; La Fosse, *Journal d'un curé ligueur*, pp. 64–65.

31. *Reg. BV*, 5:243 (2 July 1563).

32. AN, Z^{1h} 59^b (10 July 1563); also X^{2a} 131 (11 August and 30 October 1563). Louis du Tartre, the captain whose men were involved in this incident, was one of the most active participants in the militia's search for Huguenots during the first war.

33. The force of feeling within the militia is well demonstrated by the case of Nicolas Presse, who killed a fellow guardsman in July 1563 in a quarrel that broke out over the question of whether or not the guards would soon be ordered to lay down arms (AN, X^{1a} 131: 10 November 1563).

34. *Reg. BV*, 5:259 (18 July 1563) and 261 (19 July 1563).

35. Ibid., pp. 264–65 (23 July 1563).

36. Ibid., pp. 265–66 (26 July 1563) and 272–76 (5–10 August 1563).

37. Ibid., pp. 277 (13 August 1563).

38. Ibid., pp. 280–82 (13 and 14 August 1563).

39. Ibid., pp. 289–90 (letter of Charles IX, 22 August 1563).

40. Ibid., pp. 287–90, 295, 299–303, 309, and 314–15 (21 August–7 October 1563).

41. Ibid., pp. 310–17 (1, 7, 10, 13, and 18 October 1563).

42. Ibid., pp. 592–93 (14 July 1567) and 595–98 (22 and 29 July 1567).

43. Ibid., pp. 607 (29 September 1567) and 618 (18 October 1567).

44. AN, X^{1a} 1624, fol. 29 (28 August 1568); see also *Reg. BV*, 6:58–59 (28 August 1568).

45. AN, X^{1a} 1625 (13 November 1568).

46. *CSP,F*, 9:6–7 (Norris to the queen).

47. AN, X^{2a} 137, fol. 127 (22 January 1569); see also the clarification issued 31 January 1569.

48. See Chapter 8, note 39. On the arrest of the Canayes and their kin, see AN, X^{2a} 137, fols. 147–56 (1–3 February 1569). See also Pradel, ''Un marchand de Paris,'' p. 332.

49. BN, Mss. Dupuy 801, fol. 7: letter from the king written at Joinville, 3 February 1569; *CSP,F* 9:6–7 (Norris to the queen).

50. AN, H 2065^2: list of expenses presented by François Poncet, clerc des capitaines, for meetings held 16 June 1568–31 December 1569. For the arrests, see APP, A^b 3 and 4 passim.

51. La Fosse, *Journal d'un curé ligueur*, p. 108.

52. Ibid., p. 107. See also de Thou, *Histoire universelle*, 6:272–73.

53. *Reg. BV*, 6:111, 130, and 131 (23 June, 2 and 8 August 1569); *CSP,F*, 9:108–9 (Norris to Cecil, 5 August 1569). The English ambassador suggests that the queen mother and the cardinal of Lorraine also had a hand in restoring the captain, whose name was Jean Du Perrier, to his functions. During the weeks prior to his suspension, Du Perrier made a number of politically sensitive arrests—including André Guillart, president of the Parlement of Bretagne and a member of a prominent Parisian family, and Anne Seguier, wife of Jehan Payot, a trésorier de l'extraordinaire des guerres, and well-connected to the families of the Parisian elite (APP, A^b 3, fols. 43v and 44r, 1 June 1569). Although no direct connection can be shown, these arrests may have been the reason for Du Perrier's suspension and almost certainly would have served to increase tensions between the parlementaires and the militia.

54. *Reg. BV*, 6:213 (4 February 1571).

55. Ibid., pp. 407, 410, and 413 (9–11 December 1571). Also, AN, X^{2b} 1094: plumitif du matin, 10 December 1571; and H 2065^2: orders for payment to Jean Ragueneau, Pierre du Ru, and Guichard Grandremy, capitaines des arbalestriers, archers, et harquebuziers de la ville, 12 December 1571.

56. Ibid., p. 429 (20 December 1571).

57. *Reg. BV*, 7:11 (23 and 24 August 1572).

58. See the testimony of Guillaume de La Faye in the case against militia sergent Pierre Coullon heard by the prévôt des marchands on 22 September 1572 (AN, Z^{1h} 70). La Faye's testimony is inconsistent with that given by other witnesses and inconsistent within itself; it

thus seems to me better evidence of the state of confusion reigning in the city on the night of 23 August 1572 than of any particular orders that may have been given to the militia.

59. Arbaleste, *Mémoires*, pp. 58–60.

60. "Choquart, mercier du palais, cruel bourreau & capitaine de son quartier," according to Crespin, *Histoire des martyrs* (1619 edition), fol. 783r.

61. *Reg. BV*, 6:95 (31 March 1569) identifies "Du Perier" as a lawyer in Parlement and captain colonel of the city. On his suspension in 1569, see above, note 53. On the 1578 arrest, see L'Estoile, *Journal de L'Estoile*, p. 197–98.

62. The account Goulart gives of La Place's death in the *Histoire des martyrs*, which he continued after Crespin's death, is directly taken from that which he had already published in his *Mémoires de l'état*. See Goulart, "Relation du massacre," *Archives curieuses*, ed. Cimber and Danjou, 7:140–41, and Crespin, *Histoire des martyrs* (1619 edition), fol. 781r. De Thou's account appears to derive from the same source, and so the direct accusation may be simply the author's interpretation of the events described therein (*Histoire de Monsieur de Thou*, 3:672). Except for the accusation that he stabbed La Place, Aubigné's account would also appear to derive from the same source as Goulart's (*Histoire universelle*, 2:21).

63. Goulart, "Relation du massacre" (*Archives curieuses*, ed. Cimber and Danjou, 7:149), does not actually name Croizier, but calls him the "tireur d'or," a nickname that the *Histoire des martyrs*, in a similar passage obviously derived from the same source, explicitly attaches to Thomas Croizier (*Histoire des martyrs*, 1619 edition, fol. 784r). Aubigné appears to repeat these accounts, but he adds the curious and macabre twist that the scene of these killings was the Vallée de misère, where, behind a red door that led out to some of the mills on the Seine, the men slit the throats of their victims and tossed them into the river. According to Aubigné, more than six hundred persons were killed in this way (*Histoire universelle*, 2:22).

64. De Thou, *Histoire de Monsieur de Thou*, 3:669.

65. Goulart, "Relation du massacre," *Archives curieuses*, ed. Cimber and Danjou, 7:148; de Thou, *Histoire de Monsieur de Thou*, 3:669.

66. None of the other narrative sources I have found—neither Catholic source like Haton and La Fosse, nor Protestant escape accounts, like those written by Charlotte d'Arbaleste, Jacques Merlin, or Renée Burlamaqui (in Schotel, *Jean Diodati*, p. 88)—name militia officers in their accounts of the massacre. Nor are city records any help here. The *audiences* of the Bureau de la ville contain several cases of pillaging but none of murder, which would not in any event have been in the competence of the prévôt des marchands. The few parlementary records that have survived for these events also relate to incidents of pillaging and not accusations of murder.

67. Goulart, "Relation du massacre," *Archives curieuses*, ed. Cimber and Danjou, 7:140.

68. For accusations against Claude Marcel in recent historical literature, see Janine Garrisson, "Le massacre de la Saint-Barthélemy: Qui est responsable?" *L'Histoire*, no. 126 (October 1989), p. 53; and more extensively Ilja Mieck, "Die Bartholomäusnacht als Forschungsproblem: Kritische Bestandsaufnahme und neue Aspekte," *Historische Zeitschrift*, 216 (1973): 86–104. The same implication can be found in Bourgeon, "Une source," pp. 526–27, 533, and 536.

The notion that Marcel was the leader of a group of Parisian bourgeois who profited financially from the massacre seems to be based on a misconstrual of his role in 1570, when, as prévôt des marchands, he was the spokesman for the Catholic tenants of the pont Notre-Dame who refused to give up their leases in favor of the Huguenots who demanded their return. See Chapter 5, note 95; the letter cited there from Henri de Mesmes offers precious insights into Marcel's relations with Huguenot leaders in this key period following the Peace of Saint-Germain.

69. Goulart, "Relation du massacre," in *Archives curieuses*, ed. Cimber and Danjou, 7:149.

70. Mieck, "Die Bartholomäusnacht," pp. 103–4.

71. De Thou, *Histoire de Monsieur de Thou*, 3:646.

72. Ibid. Crespin, *Histoire des martyrs* (1619 edition), fol. 783r.

73. APP, A^h 4, fols. 95–99. Neither Croizier nor Pezou is mentioned among the captains delivering prisoners to the Conciergerie in the immediate aftermath of the massacre.

74. De Thou, *Histoire de Monsieur de Thou*, 3:668.

75. Ibid., pp. 658–59. Goulart also says that Marcel's troops were not ready. Goulart, "Relation du massacre," *Archives curieuses*, ed. Cimber and Danjou, 7:129.

76. Pierre de Bourdeille, seigneur de Brantôme, *Oeuvres complètes*, edited by Ludovic Lalanne, vol. 5 (Paris, 1869), pp. 119–20.

77. Bourgeon, "Une source sur la Saint-Barthélemy," pp. 502–9, gives a good analysis of the personal and political considerations that influenced de Thou's account of Saint Bartholomew's Day.

78. Guérin, "Délibérations politiques," p. 11.

79. *Reg. BV*, 5:518–20 (13 September 1565).

80. See Chapter 5, note 72.

81. *Reg. BV*, 7:13–19 (24–30 August 1572). Bourgeon, "Pour une histoire, enfin," gives a very different view of the role of the Parisian magistrates in Saint Bartholomew's Day.

82. Jacques-Auguste de Thou makes a revealing admission when, trying to explain away his father's apparent approval of the massacres in the reply he delivered to the king's announcement that he had personally ordered the events of Saint Bartholomew's Day, he suggests that Christophe de Thou was dissimulating his real feelings and that in truth he deplored the massacres, "because he feared the example [they gave] and the peril that could result from it." De Thou, *Histoire de Monsieur de Thou*, 3:676.

83. The problem of the attitude of the magistrates of the Parlement of Paris toward heresy is too complex to treat here in any detail. Fortunately, two major studies are nearing completion that will serve to enlighten us on this question. We can look forward to the publication of the revised and extended version of Linda Taber's dissertation, "Royal Policy and Religious Dissent within the Parlement of Paris, 1559–1563," and also to Nancy L. Roelker's broader study of attitudes towards heresy and religious dissent within the Parlement of Paris between 1528 and 1598. In the meantime, see Linda L. Taber, "Religious Dissent within the Parlement of Paris in the Mid-Sixteenth Century: A Reassessment," *French Historical Studies* 16 (1990), pp. 684–99.

84. John H. M. Salmon, *Society in Crisis: France in the Sixteenth Century* (New York, 1975), p. 126, makes some perceptive comments on the difficulties the Edict of Romorantin posed for the magistrates.

85. AN, X^{2a} 128 (23 August 1561): case of Jehan Huot.

86. AN, X^{2a} 130 (6 March 1562/1563): case of Clement Petit, called "Cabroth." The case is identified as one of heresy in X^{2a} 1201 (5 March 1562/1563), but neither document gives any details. X^{2a} 130 (10 February 1562/1563): case of Jehan Bouguier, sentenced despite letters of pardon to be executed "pour les villains et execrables blasphemes, actes seditieux, et autres cas a plain contenuz et declarez aud. proces." X^{2a} 134 (18 August 1564): case of Jehan du Casse, otherwise known as Bernard du Boys, sentenced to be hanged and strangled for having stolen a silver box containing three consecrated hosts from the church of Saint-Jacques de la Boucherie. In fact, Parlement moderated the original punishment handed down by the prévôt of Paris, which called for Du Casse first to have his right hand cut off as punishment for his sacrilege.

87. APP, A^b 3 passim. The most complete interrogations are those preserved in AN, X^{2b} 1094.

88. Given the angry tenor of Paris in the spring of 1569, it would appear that public opinion had something to do with the execution of Lambert Marais in April 1569, as it did with the execution of Croquet and the Gastines. Marais was charged with indoctrinating children into the Huguenot faith. (AN, X^{2b} 56, 15 April 1569; La Fosse, *Journal d'un curé ligueur*, p. 105).

89. Henri Drouot, *Mayenne et la Bourgogne: Etude sur la Ligue (1587–1596)*, 2 vols. (Paris, 1937). A similar theme is developed by Elie Barnavi, *Le parti de Dieu: Etude sociale et politique des chefs de la Ligue parisienne (1585–1594)* (Brussels and Louvain, 1980), p. 51. This argument is effectively criticized by Robert Descimon, *Qui étaient les Seize? Mythes et réalités de la Ligue parisienne* (Paris, 1983), pp. 20–26 and 295.

90. Chevalier, *Les bonnes villes*, p. 308.

91. Ibid.

Conclusion

1. *Reg. BV*, 7:22–23 (3 and 4 September 1572); Pinet, *Le culte de Sainte Geneviève*, p. 114. There may also have been earlier processions—de Thou, for example, refers to one held two days after the king's appearance in Parlement—but it is difficult to reconstruct their exact chronology. De Thou, *Histoire de Monsieur de Thou*, 3:677.

2. La Fosse, *Journal d'un curé ligueur*, p. 151.

3. BN, Mss. fr. 10304: Recueil de L'Estoile, pp. 318–320: "Louange des Parisiens à Dieu et au Roy Charles IX sur la mort de l'Admiral".

> Du prophete roial, Sire, la prophetie
> Accomplie est en vous qui maintenez la loy
> Du grand Dieu eternel . . .
> Or vous estes conduit par l'ange du grand Roy
> Lequel conduit les rois, et prolonge leur vie,
> Les maintenans tousjours en leur premiere foy. . . .
> Le peuple de Paris de vostre fait royal
> Or en graces vous rend et prie tout joyeux
> Pour votre bon succes le Gouverneur des Cieux
> d'avoir exterminé ce cruel admiral,
> Qui avoit bigarré de doctrine nouvelle.

See also the "Chanson nouvelle à l'encontre des Huguenots," in the *Complaincte et deploration de l'heresie*, pp. 32–35, especially p. 32 (addressing Coligny): "Vous avez tant offensé / Charles Noble Roy de France / Que Dieu s'en est courroucé / Et en a prins la vengeance."

4. La Fosse, *Journal d'un curé ligueur*, pp. 156–57. See also Faye and Faye, *Lettres*, pp. 26–27.

5. On the particular sets of events and opinions that touched off the massacres that occurred in different provincial cities, see particularly the article of Philip Benedict, "The Saint Bartholomew's Massacres in the Provinces," *The Historical Journal*, 21 (1978): 205–25.

6. It is on this point that my interpretation of the meaning of the massacre is in most complete accord with that of Denis Crouzet, and I would refer the reader here to the chapter he dedicates to the popular massacre. See his *Les guerriers de Dieu*, 2:82–129.

7. Denis Crouzet's new book, *Les guerriers de Dieu*, is an obvious exception here, which is why it is such a welcome rethinking of this period.

8. This tendency owes much to Lucien Romier's *Les origines politiques des guerres de religion*, 2 vols. (Paris, 1913 1914).

9. Recent studies of noble ideals and clientage have also encouraged this emphasis on the political aspects of the religious wars. Arlette Jouanna, for example, has broadened the traditional frame of reference for this period by tracing in the wars the elements of a noble revolt against a crown that was seen to be denying the nobility the rights and respect that were its natural due. Although she explicitly acknowledges the importance of religious apects of the wars, her approach has the effect of subsuming religious grievances to political ones and portraying the religious revolt as but an episode in the larger and more important process of French state building. See Arlette Jouanna, *Le devoir de révolte: La noblesse française et la gestation de l'état modern, 1559–1661* (Paris, 1989), especially Chapters 5–7, and the conclusion, p. 395, where she subsumes the Huguenots' goal of religious liberty to the larger project of political liberties and describes their "combat for religion" as "essentially a battle over the form to give the state."

10. See Louis I de Bourbon, prince de Condé, *Les recusations envoyees à la cour de Parlement de Paris, contre aucuns des presidens & conseillers d'icelle, par Monseigneur le prince de Condé & ses associez* (n.p., 1562), which lists the members of Parlement accused of being under the influence of the Guises or their allies at the start of the first war.

11. The sources are scanty here, and it is possible that these conclusions could be reversed if some future historian finds a cache of documents that escaped me. I expected when I began this project to find more signs of Guise influence in civic affairs and indications that they were backing the radical preachers, but I found no trace of Guise influence in city correspondence and no sign that they were backing the radical preachers in either parish records (foundation of masses or charitable gifts) or book dedications. Nor was there any indication that Guise clients such as the parlementaires named in Condé's 1562 recusation (see the previous note) were serving as conduits to stir up popular opinion on their behalf. Finally, I found no indication in Catholic memoirs that the Guises were manipulating events in Paris during the first decade of the wars. (Protestant sources cannot be trusted on this point, because blaming the Guises for every act of opposition to their cause was part of the Huguenots' attempt to justify their revolt by claiming it was directed not against the king but rather against the tyranny of the Guises.)

BIBLIOGRAPHY

Primary Sources

Abbatia, Bernard. *Prognostication sur le mariage de tres honnoré & tres-aimé Henry, par la grace de Dieu roy de Navarre, & de tres-illustre princesse Marguerite de France.* Paris: Guillaume Nyerd, [1572].

Advertissement sur la faulsete de plusieurs mensonges semez par les rebelles. Paris: Guillaume Morel, 1562.

Advertissement sur le pourparlé qu'on dict de paix entre le roy & ses rebelles. Paris: Jean Dallier, 1568.

Alby, Ernest. "Documents originaux sur la Saint-Barthélemy." *Revue Rétrospective,* 2d series; vol. 3 (1835): 193–97.

Alphabet ou instruction chrestienne pour les petis enfans. Nouvellement reveue & augmentée de plusieurs choses. Lyons: Pierre Estiard, 1558.

Arbaleste, Charlotte d'. *Mémoires de Madame de Mornay sur la vie de son mari.* In Philippe du Plessis-Mornay, *Mémoires et correspondance,* vol. 1. Geneva, 1969; reprint of Paris edition, 1824–1825.

L'arrest de la court de Parlement publié le dernier jour de juin dernier passé, touchant les rebelles & perturbateurs du repos & tranquillité des subjects du roy. Paris: Guillaume Morel, 1562.

Arrest et ordonnance de la court de Parlement, sur la permission aux communes, tant de villes que villages, de prendre les armes contre les pilleurs d'eglises & maisons & faiseurs de conventicules & assemblées illicites. Paris: Jean Bonfons, 1562.

Arrests & proces verbaulx d'execution d'iceux contre Jean Tanquerel, Maistres Artus Desiré, François de Rosieres, & autres. N.p., n.d.

Les articles generaulx presentez au roy par ceulx de la Religion reformée, lesquels ont esté veuz & responduz par sa Majesté, séant en son Conseil privé. Paris: Jean le Sourd, 1571.

Aubert, Fernand. "A propos de l'affaire de la rue Saint-Jacques (4–5 septembre 1557)—un rapport présenté par l'Eglise de Paris à la délégation helvétique." *Bulletin de la Société de l'histoire du protestantisme français* 95 (1947): 96–102.

Aubigné, Théodore-Agrippa d'. *Histoire universelle du sieur d'Aubigné.* 2 vols. in 1. Maille, 1616–1618.

———. *Mémoires.* Choix de chroniques et mémoires sur l'histoire de France, edited by J. A. C. Buchon, vol. 1, pp. 471–522. Paris, 1836.

Auger, Emond. *Bref discours sur la mort de feu Monsieur le Cardinal de Lorrain, extret d'une lettre escripte d'Avignon le vingt-septiesme du moys passé par M. Maistre Emonde Auger de la Compagnée de Jesus envoyée à l'un de ses amys.* Paris: Michel de Roigny, [1574].

———. *Des sacremens, à savoir du baptême et de la confirmation, de l'Eucharistie, et du sacrifice de la Messe.* Paris, 1567.

———. *Formulaires de prieres catholiques avec plusieurs advertissemens pour tous estats et manieres de gens.* Paris, n.d.

———. *La maniere d'ouir la messe avec devotion et fruict spirituel. Ensemble la maniere de bien confesser ses pechez & se disposer à recevoir le corps de nostre Seigneur.* Paris: Nicolas Chesneau, 1571.

————. *Le pedagogue d'armes, pour instruire un prince chrestien à bien entreprendre et heureusement achever une bonne guerre, pour estre victorieux de tous les ennemis de son estat, et de l'eglise catholique.* Paris, 1568.

————. *Sommaire des heresies, abus, impietez et blasphemes qui sont en la Cene des Calvinistes, & nouvelle Religion pretendue reformée. Extraict des oeuvres de M. Emond Auger, touchant la vraye, reale & corporelle presence de Jesus Christ au s. sacrement de l'autel par Antoine du Val.* Paris: Nicolas Chesneau, 1568.

————. *De la vraye, reale et corporelle presence de Jesus Christ au sainct sacrement de l'autel. Contre les fauses opinions & modernes heresies, tant des Lutheriens, Zwing-liens, & Westphaliens, que Calvinistes.* Paris: Pierre l'Huillier, 1566.

Aymon, Jean. *Tous les synodes nationaux des Eglises réformées de France. Auxquels on a joint des mandemens roiaux et plusieurs lettres politiques.* 2 vols. The Hague, 1710.

Beaux-Amis, Thomas. *Remonstrance salutaire aux devoyez, qu'il n'est permis aux subjects, sous quelque pretexte que ce soit, lever les armes contre leur prince & roy, le tout prouvé par l'escriture saincte.* Paris: Guillaume Chaudiere, 1567.

Belleforest, François de. *Les chroniques et annales de France dès l'origine des Françoys et leur venu es Galles. Faictes brievement par Nicole Gilles, secretaire du roy, jusqu'au Roy Charles huictiesme et depuis continué par Denis Sauvage jusqu'au Françoys second.* Paris: Gabriel Buon, 1573.

Benoist, René. *Advertissement charitable aux femmes et filles, enseignant comme elles doivent aller aux stations & lieux ordonnés pour gagner le present jubilé de ceste année 1576 ordonné en ceste ville de Paris.* Paris: Nicolas Chesneau, 1577.

————. *Advertissement exhortatoire à ceux de la paroisse de S. Eustache à Paris, lesquels ayans esté seduicts & trompez sous couleur & pretexte d'une Eglise reformée & plus pure religion, se sont retranchez de la profession de la foy & religion chrestienne, proposée en l'Eglise catholique, hors laquelle il n'y a point de salut.* Paris: Nicolas Chesneau, 1569.

————. *Advertissement ou moyen par lequel aisément tous troubles et différens touchant la croix, de laquelle y a si grande altercation en la ville de Paris, que autres concernans la religion, seront assoupis et ostez.* Paris: Théodore Belot, 1571.

————. *Antithese des bulles du pape pour le jubilé, pardon et remission des pechez, proposée en l'Eglise de Jesus Christ, qui est la catholique, universelle, and romaine, & celle de l'Eglise pretendue reformée; où le tout est prouvé et examiné par la vive touche de la parole de Dieu. Aussi est adjousté un brief discours contenant les choses necessaires à tous Chrestiens pour gaigner le jubilé et tous autres pardons.* Paris: Guillaume Chaudiere, 1567.

————. *Brief discours touchant le fondement du purgatoire apres ceste vie, des indulgences & pardons, & de satisfaction, troisiesme partie de penitence. Auquel est prouvé par l'escriture saincte que Dieu remettant par sa grace la coulpe & deformité du peché, il ne remet tousjours la peine entierement, ains veult que l'homme luy satisface.* Paris: Nicolas Chesneau, 1566.

————. *Brieve et facile réfutation d'un livret divulgé au nom de J. de l'Espine, se disant ministre de la parole de Dieu, auquel violentant & detorquant l'escripture saincte, il blaspheme malheureusement le sainct sacrifice evangelique, dict vulgairement la saincte messe.* Paris: Guillaume Chaudiere, 1565.

————. *Brieve response à quelque remonstrance faicte à la roine mere du roy par ceux qui se disent persecutez pour la parolle de Dieu.* Paris: Guillaume Guillard and Amaulry Warencore, 1561.

————. *Catechese et instruction touchant les ornemens, vestemens & parures des femmes chrestiennes*. Paris: Nicolas Chesneau, 1573.

————. *Catecheses ou instructions touchant les poincts à present controverses en la religion, accommodées aux evangiles d'un chacun jour de caresme; proposées en sermons en l'eglise S. Eustache à Paris, l'an 1573, pour l'instruction de ceux qui ont esté mal instruicts & catechisez par les heretiques*. Paris: Nicolas Chesneau, 1573.

————. *Catechisme ou instruction populaire, contenant les principaux poincts de la religion chrestienne, lesquels tous Chrestiens sont tenus de sçavoir & suivant l'expresse parole de Dieu & ordonnance de l'Eglise catholique, apostolique & romaine*. Paris: Guillaume de la Noue, 1569.

————. *Certaine resolution et determination des poincts à present controverses touchant la religion chrestienne, faicte par les trois excellentes & celebres facultez de Theologie à Paris, à Louvain, & à Cologne. Ensemble un bref & parfaict catechisme, avec quelques autres petits traictez*. Paris: Guillaume Chaudiere, 1564.

————. *Claire probation de la necessaire manducation de la substantielle & reale humanité de Jesus Christ, vray Dieu & vray homme, au s. sacrement de l'autel*. Paris: Nicolas Chesneau, 1561.

————. *Discours de l'histoire du miracle des Ardents, gueris par Dieu, par les prieres & merites de saincte Geneviefve à Paris, du temps du regne de Louys le Magnanime, fils de Philippes Roy de France. Avec un petit traicté des processions des Chrestiens*. Paris: Thomas Belot, 1568.

————. *Du sacrifice evangelique, où manifestement est prouvé que la saincte messe est le sacrifice eternelle de la nouvelle loy, que Jesus Christ le premier l'a celebrée & commandé aux ministeres de son eglise. Avec un petit traité de la maniere de celebrer la saincte messe en la primitive eglise*. Paris: Nicolas Chesneau, 1564.

————. *Epistre consolatoire à Messieurs les paroissiens de S. Eustache à Paris, contre le present epouventement causé et provenant des guerres civiles, seditions et miseres de ce siecle et temps present*. Paris: Nicolas Chesneau and J. Poupy, 1575.

————. *Exhortation chrestienne aux fideles et esleuz de Dieu, de batailler par tous moyens pour le grand Seigneur contre l'Antechrist*. Paris: Guillaume Chaudiere, 1566.

————. *De l'institution et de l'abus survenu és confrairies populaires, avec la réformation nécessaire en icelles*. Paris: Nicolas Chesneau, 1578.

————. *La manière de cognoistre salutairement Jesus-Christ, en laquelle ouvertement par l'expresse parolle de Dieu le masque des hypocrites, pharisiens, abuseurs, haeretiques, atheistes & libertins & tous autres faulcement soy vendicans la cognoissance de l'eternelle, salutaire & coeleste verité avec le vain & presomptueus espoir qu'ils ont de la vie aeternelle est decelé & rabbatu*. Paris: Guillaume Guillard and Thomas Belot, 1564.

————. *Manifeste et necessaire probation de l'adoration de Jesus Christ, Dieu & homme en l'hostie sacrée, tant en la messe que en tout autre lieu auquel elle est presentée aux Chrestiens*. Paris: Nicolas Chesneau, 1562.

————. *Refutation des vains pretendus fondemens de certains lieux de l'escriture saincte, desquels ordinairement les heretiques abusent pour corrompre la foy des simples & impugner la presence reale du corps de Jesus Christ en l'hostie sacrée*. Paris: Nicolas Chesneau, 1569.

————. *Response à ceux qui appellent idolatres les Chrestiens & vray adoratuers. En laquelle est familierement monstré ce que c'est qu'adoration, à qui est deue adoration, & quelle difference il y a entre l'adoration des creatures, & la vraye & souveraine, laquelle est deue à Dieu seulement*. Paris: Nicolas Chesneau, 1564.

————. *Sermon sur le cantique O Salutaris Hostia, recité en une procession de S. Eustache au couvent des filles religieuses de Saincte Claire, dit l'Ave Maria, à Paris, l'an 1577, apres Pasques. Plus un traitté de l'exercise de la vraye religion, qu'on doit tenir estant au sacrifice de la divine messe, proposé en un sermon à Paris l'an 1561* [sic, 1571?] & *puis redigé par escript, par venerable pere Christofle Cheffontaines, General de l'ordre des Cordeliers.* Paris: Nicolas Chesneau, 1577.

————. *Traicté catholique des images et du vray usage d'icelles, extraict de la saincte escriture & anciens docteurs de l'eglise.* Paris: Nicolas Chesneau, 1564.

————. *Traicté des processions des Chrestiens, auquel il est discouru pour quoy la croix y est eslevée & portée; premierement pourquoy les Chrestiens la portent pour marque & signe.* Paris: Michel de Roigny, 1589.

————. *Traicté du sainct jeusne de caresme, où il est monstré iceluy estre de l'institution de Jesus Christ & commandement de Dieu. Avec la troisiesme epistre à Jean Calvin, Besze, & tous autres partizans de sa secte.* Paris: Guillaume Chaudiere, 1566.

————. *Le triomphe et excellent victoire de la foy, par le moyen de la veritable & toute-puissante parole de Dieu. Où est monstré le moyen certain & facile de pacifier les troubles presens.* Paris: Nicolas Chesneau, 1568.

Beza, Theodore. *Correspondance.* Edited by Hippolyte Aubert, Henri Meylan, Alain Dufour, et al. 14 vols. to date. Geneva, 1960–1990.

————. *Histoire ecclésiastique des Eglises réformées au royaume de France.* Edited by G. Baum and E. Cunitz. 3 vols. Nieuwkoop, 1974; reprint of Paris edition, 1883–1889.

————. *Le passavent de Théodore de Bèze. Epître de Maître Benoît Passavant à Messire Pierre Lizet, où il rend compte de sa mission à Genève, . . . avec la complainte de P. Lizet sur le trepas de son feu nez.* Paris, 1875.

————. *Psaumes mis en vers français (1551–1562).* Edited by Pierre Pidoux. Travaux d'humanisme et renaissance, vol. 199. Geneva, 1984.

Bonnardot, François, et al. *Registres des délibérations du Bureau de la ville de Paris.* Histoire générale de Paris. Vols. 1–7. Paris, 1883–1893.

Bordeaux, Christophe de. *Déploration sur la mort et trespas de deffunct de bonne mémoire frere Jehan de Ham, religieulx de l'ordre des Minimes.* Paris: Claude Blihar, 1562.

————. *Recueil de plusieurs belles chansons spirituelles, avec ceux des huguenots heretiques & ennemis de Dieu, & de nostre mere saincte eglise; faictes et composées par maistre Christofle de Bordeaux.* Paris: Magdaleine Berthelin, n.d.

Bouquet, Simon. *La joyeuse entrée de Charles IX Roy de France en Paris, 1572.* Introduction by Frances A. Yates. Amsterdam and New York, n.d.; facsimile of Paris edition, 1572.

Bournon, Fernand, ed. "Chronique parisienne de Pierre Driart, chambrier de Saint-Victor (1522–1535)." *Mémoires de la Société de l'histoire de Paris et de l'Ile-de-France* 22 (1895): 67–178.

Brantôme, Pierre de Bourdeille, seigneur de. *Oeuvres complètes.* Edited by Ludovic Lalanne. 11 vols. Paris, 1864–1882.

Brièle, Léon. *Collection de documents pour servir à l'histoire des hôpitaux de Paris.* 4 vols. Paris, 1881–1887.

————. *Inventaire sommaire des archives hospitalières antérieures à 1790.* Paris, 1882–1889.

Brulart, Nicolas. *Journal des choses plus remarquables (1559–1569).* In *Mémoires de Condé.* Edited by Denis-François Sécousse. Vol. 1: 2–211. London and Paris, 1743–1745.

Buisseret, David, and Bernard Barbiche, eds. *Les oeconomies royales de Sully.* Vol. 1: *1572–1594.* Paris, 1970.

Calvin, Jean. *Ioannis Calvini Opera quae supersunt omnia*. Edited by W. Baum, E. Cunitz, and E. Reuss. 59 vols. Braunschweig, 1863–1900.

———. *Lettres de Jean Calvin. Lettres françaises*. Edited by Jules Bonnet. Vol 2. Paris, 1854.

———. *Recueil des opuscules. C'est à dire, petits traictez de M. Jean Calvin*. Geneva: Baptiste Pinereul, 1566.

Catherine de Medici. *Lettres*. Edited by Hector de la Ferriere et Baguenault de Puchesse. 11 vols. Paris, 1880–1943.

Chandieu, Antoine de la Roche. *La confirmation de la discipline ecclesiastique, observée es Esglises reformées du royaume de France*. n.p., 1566.

———. *Histoire des persecutions et martyrs de l'Eglise de Paris, depuis l'an 1557 jusques au temps du roy Charles neufviesme*. Lyon, 1563.

Cheffonteines, Christofle. *Le premier livre de la deffense de la foy de nos ancestres, auquel on declare les strategemes & ruses des heretiques de nostre temps*. Paris: Claude Fremy, 1572.

Chocquart, Charles. *Epistre ou discours à Monsieur de Montpensier, touchant l'estat de la religion chrestienne & mauvaise intention pour laquelle plusieurs s'en sont separez*. Paris: Nicolas Chesneau, 1571.

Cimber, L. [pseud. of Louis Lafaist], and Félix Danjou. *Archives curieuses de l'histoire de la France depuis Louis XI jusqu'à Louis XVIII*. 30 vols. Paris and Beauvais, 1834–1841.

Complaincte et deploration de l'heresie sur la mort du Prince de Condé, ses alliez & complices. N.p., n.d. [after 1572].

Complainte des papaux, contenant une sommaire description de la cruauté qui a esté faicte à ceux de la Religion reformée durant la guerre. Ensemble merveilleux exemples de la vengeance de Dieu contre ses ennemis. N.p., 1564.

Condé, Louis I de Bourbon, prince de. *Declaration faicte par Monsieur le prince de Condé pour monstrer les raisons qui l'ont contrainct d'entreprendre la defense de l'authorité du roy*. N.p., 1562.

———. *Le moyen de pacifier le trouble qui est en ce royaume, envoyé à la royne*. N.p., 1562.

———. *Les recusations envoyées à la cour de Parlement de Paris, contre aucuns des presidens & conseillers d'icelle, par Monseigneur le prince de Condé & ses associez*. N.p., 1562.

La consommation de l'idole de Paris, suivant la parole du prophete Jeremie. Lyon, 1562.

Corlieu, François de. *Instruction pour tous estats*. Paris: Philippe Danfrie and Richard Breton, 1559.

Covelle, Alfred L. *Le livre des bourgeois de l'ancienne république de Genève*. Geneva, 1897.

Crespin, Jean. *Histoire des martyrs persecutez et mis à mort pour la verité de l'evangile*. Geneva, 1564.

———. *Histoire des martyrs persecutez et mis à mort pour la verité de l'evangile, depuis le temps des apostres jusques à present*. Geneva: Pierre Aubert, 1619.

Crottet, A. *Journal du Ministre Merlin, pasteur de l'église de La Rochelle au XVIᵉ siècle*. Geneva, 1855.

Declaration du roy sur le faict et police de la religion, portant defense de faire presches & conventicules en la ville, faulbours, & banlieuë de Paris. Paris: Vincent Sertenas, 1562.

Declaration du roy, par laquelle il deffend de ne faire presche, assemblees, ny administrations de sacrementz de la nouvelle Religion pretendue reformée en sa court ne suitte, ne es maisons de sa majesté. Paris: Jean Dallier, 1563.

Declaration & interpretation du roy sur l'edict de la pacification des troubles pour le faict de la religion. Publié en la cour de Parlement à Paris, le XX decembre 1563. Paris: Robert Estienne, 1563.

Declaration faicte par le roy de ceux qui ont à cognoistre des proces des heretiques. Paris: Vincent Sertenas, Jean Dallier, and Jean Bonfons, 1560.

Desautelz, Guillaume. *Harangue au peuple françois contre la rebellion.* Paris: Vincent Sertenas, 1560.

[Des Gallars, Nicolas.] *Seconde apologie ou defense des vrais chrestiens contre les calomnies impudentes des ennemis de l'eglise catholique. Où il est respondu aux diffames redoublez par un nommé Demochares docteur de la Sorbonne.* [Geneva], 1559.

Desiré, Artus. *Les batailles et victoires du chevalier Celeste contre le chevalier Terrestre.* Paris: Jean Ruelle, 1564.

———. *Le contrepoison des cinquante-deux chansons de Clement Marot.* Paris: Pierre Gaultier, 1560.

———. *L'origine et source de tous les maux de ce monde par l'incorrection des peres & meres envers leurs enfants, & de l'inobedience d'iceux. Ensemble de la trop grande familiarité & liberté donnée aux servans & servantes, avec un petit discours de la visitation de Dieu envers son peuple chrestien par afflictions de guerre, peste & famine.* Paris: Jean Dallier, 1571.

———. *Passavent parisien respondant à Pasquin romain, de la vie de ceux qui sont allez demourer à Genève et se disent vivre selon la réformation de l'evangile. Faict en forme de dialogue.* 3d ed. Paris, 1975; reprint of Paris edition, 1556.

Desjardins, Abel, ed. *Négotiations diplomatiques de la France avec la Toscane.* Compiled by Giuseppe Canestrini. 5 vols. Collection de documents inédits sur l'histoire de France, ser. 1. Paris, 1859–1875.

Despence, Claude. *Continuation de la tierce conference avec les ministres extraordinaires de la Religion pretendue reformée.* Paris: Michel Soumies, 1570.

———. *Deux sermons. L'un de l'absolution des pieds, preparatif à la saincte communion; au clergé & peuple de Paris. L'autre, synodal, de l'office des pasteurs; au clergé & peuple de Beauvais.* Paris: Nicolas Chesneau, 1569.

———. *Traicté contre l'erreur vieil et renouvellé des predestinez.* Lyons, [1549].

"Deux lettres de couvent à couvent; écrits de Paris pendant le massacre de la Saint-Barthélemy par Joachim Opser de Wyl, Jésuite, sous-proviseur du collège de Clermont à Paris." *Bulletin de la Société de l'histoire du protestantisme français* 8 (1859): 284–94.

"La diplomatie française et la Saint-Barthélemy: Deux lettres de M. de Schomberg, ambassadeur de France en Allemagne (9 et 10 octobre 1572)." *Bulletin de la Société de l'histoire du protestantisme français* 16 (1867): 546–51.

Discours sur la liberté ou captivité du roy. N.p., 1562.

Discours sur le saccagement des eglises catholiques par les heretiques anciens & nouveaux Calvinistes en l'an mil cinq cens soixante & deux. N.p., n.d. [1562].

"Documents authentiques sur la Saint-Barthélemy." *Revue rétrospective*, ser. 1, vol. 5 (1834): 358–72.

Du Boulay, César Egasse. *Historia Universitatis parisiensis.* 6 vols. Paris, 1665–1673.

Du Breul, Jacques. *Le théâtre des antiquitez de Paris.* Paris, 1612.

Duchesne, Léger. *Exhortation au roy, pour verteusement poursuivre ce que sagement il a commencé contre les huguenots, avec les epitaphes de Gaspar de Colligny, . . . et de Pierre Ramus.* Paris: Gabriel Buon, 1572.

Du Plessis, Toussaint. *Histoire de l'église de Meaux.* Vol. 2: *Pièces justificatives.* Paris, 1731.

Du Preau, Gabriel. *Arrest et condamnation donnée au profit des catholiques, par les propres tesmoignages, confrontations, & sentences de xxiiii des principaux ministres & predicans de la nouvelle doctrine & opinion en la religion, sur le different de xxxii articles de la foy, meu & ajeté entre eux & lesdits catholiques, depuis cinquante ans en ça, & plus.* Paris: Michel Julian, 1567.

———. *L'enchiridion, ou abregé et sommaire de l'instruction en la science de Dieu du fidele chrestien. Qui est une familiere exposition des principaulx poincts & articles de toute nostre foy & religion chrestienne, en forme de dialogue & divisé en huict livres. Avec le formulaire que doivent tenir tous curez & vicaires, pour l'administration des s. sacremens, en ce qui concerne le devoir de leur charge.* Paris: Michel de Roigny, 1567.

———. *Des faux prophetes, seducteurs, & hypochrites, qui viennent à nous en habit de brebis, mais au dedans sont loups ravissans. Et comme il les fault cognoistre, & s'il est licite de communiquer avec eux sans offenser Dieu.* Paris: Jacques Macé, 1563.

———. *Harangue sur les causes de la guerre entreprise contre les rebelles & seditieux, qui en forme d'hostilité ont pris les armes contre le roy en son royaume, & mesme des causes d'où proviennent toutes autres calamitez & miseres qui journellement nous surviennent.* Paris: Nicolas Chesneau, 1562.

Dupuyherbault, Gabriel. *La consolation chrestienne pour fortifier les bons catholiques qui sont affligez & persecutez par la tyrannie des sectaires et desvoyez heretiques de nostre temps.* Paris: Michel de Roigny, 1568.

———. *Deux epistres.* Published with Loys de Blois, *Livret, elegant & consolable, autant que spirituel & propre contre la malice de ce temps.* Paris: Jehan de Roigny, 1564.

———. *Psalmes de David, traduicts au plus pres de leur sens propre & naturel. En faveur de tous fideles; specialement dediez à louer continuellement Dieu en ses sainctes eglises.* 2d ed. Paris: Jean de Roigny, 1563.

[Du Rosier, Hugues Sureau.] *Confession de foy faicte par H. S. Du Rosier avec abjuration & detestation de la profession huguenotique. Faicte tant par devant prelats de l'eglise catholique & romaine, que princes du sang royal de France & autres. Ensemble la refutation de plusieurs poincts mis en avant par Calvin & Beze contre la foy & eglise apostolique. Le tout que dessus confirmé & signé d'iceluy, ainsi qu'il appert par la copie qu'il a baillée.* Paris: Sebastien Nivelle, 1573.

[———.] *Confession et recognoissance de Hugues Sureau, dict du Rosier, touchant sa cheute en la papauté & les horribles scandales par luy commis. Servant d'exemple à tout le monde de la fragilité & perversité de l'homme abandonné à soy, & de l'infinie misericorde & ferme verité de Dieu envers ses esleus.* Basle: Martin Cousin, 1574.

———. *Traité des certaines et inséparables marques de la vraye eglise de Dieu.* Heidelberg: Jan Mayer, 1574.

Du Val, Antoine. *Les contrarietez et contredicts qui se trouvent en la doctrine de Jean Calvin, de Luter, & autres nouveaux evangelistes de nostre temps.* Paris: Nicolas Chesneau, 1561.

———. *Demandes et repliques à Jean Calvin sur son livre de la predestination. Recuellies des oeuvres d'un auteur incogneu.* Paris: Nicolas Chesneau, 1561.

———. *Mirouer des calvinistes et armure des chrestiens, pour rembarrer les lutheriens & nouveaux evangelistes de Genève.* 2d ed. Paris: Nicolas Chesneau, 1562.

———. *Sommaire des heresies, abus, impietez et blasphemes qui sont en la cene des Calvinistes & nouvelle Religion pretendue reformée.* Paris: Nicolas Chesneau, 1568.

Dyvolé, Pierre. *Dix sermons de la saincte Messe & ceremonies d'icelle.* Paris: Guillaume de la Noue, 1596.

Edict de declaration faicte par le roy Charles IX de ce nom sur la pacification des troubles de ce royaume, le xix jour de mars, mil cinq cens soixante deux. Publié en la cour de Parlement à Paris, le vingt-septiesme jour dudict mois. [Paris]: Robert Estienne, 1563.

Edict du Roy Charles Neufieme . . . sur les moyens les plus propres d'appaiser les troubles & seditions survenus pour le faict de la religion. Paris: Robert Estienne, 1562.

Edict du roy, contenant la grace et pardon pour ceux qui cy devant ont mal senty de la foy. Paris: Vincent Sertenas and Jean Dallier, [1560].

Edict du roy sur le faict de la religion, publié en la cour de Parlement à Paris, le dernier jour de juilliet, 1561. Paris: Jean Dallier, [1561].

"L'entrée du duc de Guise à Paris et le presche des Huguenots en cette ville. Lettre inédite de M. François Chastaigner à M. de la Pocheposay son père." *Bulletin de la Société de l'histoire du protestantisme français* 13 (1864): 15–16.

Estienne, Henri. *Apologie pour Hérodote.* Geneva, 1566.

———. *Apologie pour Hérodote. Satire de la société au XVIᵉ siècle.* New ed. Edited by P. Ristelhuber. 2 vols. Paris, 1879.

"Etat nominatif des Protestants de la vicomté de Coutances en 1588." *Bulletin de la Société de l'histoire du protestantisme français* 36 (1887): 246–58.

Exhortation et remonstrance aux princes du sang et seigneurs du privé conseil du roy, pour obvier aux seditions qui occultement semblent menacer les fideles pour le faict de la religion. Oeuvre concluant qu'il est expedient & necessaire pour la gloire de Dieu, illustration du royaume, & repos public, avoir en France une eglise pour les fideles. N.p., 1561.

Factum. M. Jean Poille, conseiller en Parlement, accusé, contre Monsieur Rouillié, aussi conseiller en ladite cour, son accusateur. N.p., n.d.

Fagniez, Gustave, ed. "Livre de raison de Mᶜ Nicolas Versoris, avocat au Parlement de Paris (1514–1530)." *Mémoires de la Société de l'histoire de Paris et de l'Ile-de-France* 12 (1885): 99–222.

———, ed. "Mémorial juridique et historique de Mᶜ Guillaume Aubert, avocat au Parlement de Paris, avocat général à la Cour des aides (deuxième moitié du XVIᵉ siècle)." *Mémoires de la Société de l'histoire de Paris et de l'Ile-de-France* 36 (1909): 47–82.

Fatio, Olivier, and Olivier Labarthe, eds. *Registres de la compagnie des pasteurs de Genéve.* Vol. 3: *(1565–1574).* Geneva, 1969.

Favyer, Nicolas. *Figure et exposition des pourtraictz et dictions contenus es medailles de la conspiration des rebelles.* Paris: Jean Dallier, 1572.

Faye, Jacques, and Faye, Charles. *Lettres inédites de Jacques Faye et de Charles Faye.* Edited by Eugène Halphen. Paris, 1880.

Félibien, Michel. *Histoire de l'abbaye-royale de Saint-Denys en France.* Paris, 1706.

———, and Guy-Alexis Lobineau. *Histoire de la ville de Paris.* 5 vols. Paris, 1725.

Flavin, Melchior. *Remonstrance de la vraye religion au roi tres chrestien.* Paris: Nicolas Chesneau, 1562.

[Floriot, Pierre.] *Traité de la messe de paroisse. Où l'on découvre les grands mysteres cachez sous le voile des ceremonies de la messe publique et solomnelle; & les instructions admirables que Jesus-Christ nous y donne par l'unité de son sacrifice.* Paris 1679.

Gassot, Jules. *Sommaire mémorial (souvenirs).* Edited by Pierre Champion. Paris, 1934.

Geisendorf, Paul, ed. *Livre des habitants de Genève.* 2 vols. Geneva, 1957–1963.

Godefroy, Théodore, and Denys Godefroy. *Le ceremonial françoys.* 2 vols. Paris, 1649.

[Goulart, Simon.] *Memoires de l'estat de France sous Charles IX.* Middleburg, 1578.

[———.] "Relation du massacre de la Saint-Barthélemy," [from the *Mémoires de l'état de France sous Charles IX*]. In *Archives curieuses de l'histoire de France*, ed. L. Cimber and Félix Danjou, ser. 1, vol. 7. Paris, 1835.

La grande trahison et volerie du Roy Guillot, prince & seigneur de tous les larrons bandolliers, sacrileges, voleurs & brigans du royaume de France. N.p., 1567.

Great Britain, Public Record Office. *Calendar of State Papers (Foreign Series) of the Reign of Elizabeth.* Edited by Joseph Stevenson et al. 28 vols. London, 1863–1950.

Grin, François. "Journal de François Grin, religieux de Saint-Victor (1554–1570)." Edited by Baron Alphonse de Ruble. *Mémoires de la Société de l'histoire de Paris et de l'Ile-de-France* 21 (1894): 1–52.

Gringoire, Pierre. *Heures de Nostre Dame.* Paris: Jehan Petit, 1527.

Guérin, Paul. "Délibérations politiques du Parlement et arrêts criminels du milieu de la première guerre de religion (1562)." *Mémoires de la Société de l'histoire de Paris et de l'Ile-de-France* 40 (1913): 1–116.

Guiffrey, Georges, ed. *Chronique du Roy Françoys Premier.* Paris, 1860.

Haton, Claude. *Mémoires contenant le récit des événements accomplis de 1553 à 1582.* Edited by Félix Bourquelot. 2 vols. Paris, 1857.

Hauser, Henri. "Un récit catholique des trois premières guerres de religion. Les *Acta tumultuum gallicanorum*." *Revue historique* 108 (1911): 59–74 and 294–318; 109 (1912): 75–84.

Hervet, Gentian. *Apologie ou defense, contre une reponse des ministres de la nouvelle eglise d'Orléans.* Paris: Nicolas Chesneau, 1562.

———. *Catechisme ou sommaire de la foy & devoir du vray chrestien, selon la doctrine evangelique & sens de l'eglise & anciens docteurs d'icelle. Recueilly des oeuvres de Guillaume Lindan, eveque alleman.* Paris: Nicolas Chesneau, 1561.

———. *Confutation d'un livre pestilent et plein d'erreurs, nommé par son auteur: Les signes sacrez, &c. En laquelle sont clairemont monstrées les impietez & execrables blasphemes, absurditez, & mensonges des Calvinistes & Sacramentaires. Aussi amplement y est traité du sacrifice de la s. messe.* Rheims: Jean de Foigny, 1565; sold in Paris by Nicolas Chesneau.

———. *Discours sur ce que les pilleurs, voleurs, & brusleurs d'eglises disent qu'ilz n'en veulent qu'aux moynes et aux prestres. Au peuple d'Orleans.* Rheims, 1563.

———. *Epistre envoyée à un quidam fauteur des nouveaux evangeliques. En laquelle est clairement monstré que hors l'eglise catholique n'y a nul salut.* Paris: Guillaume de Nyerd, [1561].

———. *Epistre ou advertissement au peuple fidele de l'eglise catholique, touchant les differens qui sont aujourd'huy en la religion.* Paris: Nicolas Chesneau, 1561.

———. *Recueil d'aucuns mensonges de Calvin, Melanchthon, Bucere, & autres nouveaux evangelistes de ce temps, par lesquelles seduisans & donnans faulx à entendre aux simples.* Paris: Nicolas Chesneau, 1561.

———. *Traicté du purgatoire et des prieres pour les trespassez.* Paris: Guillaume Morel, 1562.

Heures de Notre-Dame à l'usaige de Rome. Paris: Magdaleine Boursette, [1550].

Hotman, François. *"Le Tigre" de 1560. Reproduit pour la première fois en fac-similé.* Edited by Charles Read. Geneva, 1970; reprint of Paris edition, 1875.

Instruction du devoir de perseverance en la persecution à ceux qui sont tombez. Pour reponse aux scandales qu'on se propose & confirmation qu'il n'est point permis de dissimuler la profession de l'evangile & communiquer aux superstitions de la papauté. n.p., 1573.

Isambert, François-André, et al. *Recueil général des anciennes lois françaises depuis l'an 420, jusqu'à la Révolution de 1789.* Vol. 14, pt. 1: *(Juillet 1559–Mai 1574).* Paris, 1829.

Jourdain, Charles. *Index chronologicus chartarum pertinentium ad historiam Universitatis parisiensis ab ejus originibus ad finem decimi sexti saeculi.* Brussels, 1966; reprint of Paris edition, 1862.

Journal d'un bourgeois de Paris sous le règne de François Premier (1515–1536). Edited by Ludovic Lalanne. Paris, 1854.

"Journal du règne du Roy Henri III": *Recueil de diverses pièces servant à l'histoire de Henry III, roy de France et de Pologne.* New ed. 2 vols. Cologne, 1699.

Knobelsdorf, Eustache. *Lutetiae descriptio [1543].* Edited and translated by O. Sauvage. Grenoble, 1978.

La Fosse, Jean de. *Journal d'un curé ligueur de Paris sous les trois derniers Valois.* Edited by Edouard de Barthélemy. Paris, 1866.

La Mare, Nicolas de. *Traité de la police.* 2 vols. Paris, 1705–1710.

La Noue, François de. *Discours politiques et militaires du Seigneur de La Noue. Nouvellement recueillis et mis en lumière.* Geneva: François Forest, 1587.

[La Place, Pierre de.] *Commentaire de l'estat de la religion & republique soubs les rois Henry & François seconds, & Charles neufieme.* N.p., 1565.

———. *Traitté de la vocation et maniere de vivre à laquelle chacun est appellé.* Paris: Frederic Morel, 1561.

La Planche, Louis Régnier, sieur de. *Histoire de l'estat de France tant de la république que de la religion sous le règne de François II.* Choix de chroniques et mémoires sur l'histoire de France, edited by J. A. C. Buchon, vol. 1, pp. 202–417. Paris, 1836.

La Vacquerie, Jean de. *Catholique remonstrance aux roys et princes chrestiens, à tous magistrats & gouverneurs de republique, touchant l'abolition des heresies, troubles & scismes que regnent aujourd'huy en la chrestienté.* Paris: Nicolas Chesneau, 1560.

Le Comte, Michel. *Invective contre la mort du seigneur duc de Guyse, et du souldat à Paris executé.* Paris: Guillaume de Niverd, [1562].

Le Hongre, Jacques. *Sermon funebre proclamé par frere Jacques le Hongre, docteur en theologie de l'ordre des freres prescheurs en l'eglise cathedrale de nostre Dame de Paris, le XX mars 1562, aux obseques et enterrement du coeur du feu tres hault et tres puissant prince, François de Lorraine, duc de Guyse.* Paris: Gilles Corrozet and Jean Dallier, 1563.

Le Masle, Jean. *Brief discours sur les troubles qui depuis douze ans ont continuellement agité et tourmenté le royaume de France, et de la deffaicte d'aucuns chefs plus signalez des mutins & seditieux qui les esmouvoient & mettoyent sus quand bon leur sembloit. Avec une exhortation à iceux mutins de bien tost abjurer leur erreur & heresie.* Lyons: Benoist Rigaud, 1573.

———. *Chant d'allegresse sur la mort de Gaspar de Colligny, jadis admiral de France.* Paris: Nicolas Chesneau, 1572.

Le Picart, François. *Epistre contenant un traicté auquel est monstré combien est grande la charité de Jesus Christ en l'institution de la saincte communion de son precieux corps & sang, au s. sacrement de l'autel.* Paris: Nicolas Chesneau, 1564.

———. *Les sermons et instructions chrestiennes pour tous les dimenches & toutes les festes des saincts, depuis la Trinité jusques à l'advent.* Paris: Nicolas Chesneau, 1565.

———. *Les sermons et instructions chrestiennes pour tous les dimenches & toutes les festes des saincts, depuis Pasques jusques à la Trinité. Avec douze sermons du mesme autheur, touchant le sainct sacrement de l'autel.* Paris: Nicolas Chesneau, 1566.

————. *Les sermons et instructions chrestiennes pour tous les jours de caresme & feriés de Pāsques.* Paris: Nicolas Chesneau, 1566.

————. *Les sermons et instructions chrestiennes pour tous les jours de l'Advent jusques à Noel, & tous les dimenches & festes depuis Noel jusques à caresme.* Paris: Nicolas Chesneau, 1566.

Le Primaudaye, Pierre de. *L'Académie françoise; en laquelle est traicté de l'institution des moeurs et de ce qui concerne de bien et heureusement vivre.* 3 vol. in 4. Geneva, 1972; reprint of Paris editions, 1580, 1581, and 1590.

Le Roux de Lincy, Antoine-Jean-Victor. *Recueil de chants historiques français depuis le XIIᵉ jusqu'au XVIIIᵉ siècle,* vol. 2. Geneva, 1969; reprint of Paris edition, 1841–1842.

Le Roy, Louis. *Des differens et troubles advenans entre les hommes par la diversité des opinions en la religion.* Paris: Frederic Morel, 1562.

Lespinasse, René de. *Les métiers et corporations de la ville de Paris.* 3 vols. Paris, 1886–1897.

L'Espine, Jean de. *Dialogue de la cene.* N.p., n. d.

————. *Discours du vray sacrifice, et du vray sacrificateur.* Lyons: Jean Saugrain, 1563.

————. *Excellens discours de J. de L'Espine, angevin, touchant le repos & contentement de l'esprit.* Basle, 1587.

[————.] *Traicté de l'apostasie faict par M. J. D. L., ministre de la parole de Dieu en l'eglise d'Angers.* N.p., 1583.

[————.] *Traicté des tentations et moyens d'y resister. Composé par un docte et excellent personnage de ce temps.* Lyons: Jean Saugrain, 1566.

[————.] *Traitté consolatoire et fort utile contre toutes afflictions qui adviennent ordinairement aux fideles Chrestiens. Composé nouvellement par J. de Spina, ministre de la parolle de Dieu, & adressé à un grand seigneur de France.* Lyons: Jean Saugrain, 1565.

————, and Jean Le Mercier. *Lettres à l'eglise d'Angers.* N.p., [1586].

L'Estoile, Pierre de. *Journal des choses mémorables advenuës durant tout le règne de Henry III.* N.p., 1621.

————. *Journal de L'Estoile pour le règne de Henri III (1574–1589).* Edited by Louis-Raymond Lefèvre. Paris, 1943.

"Lettre écrite par ordre de Charles IX aux cantons suisses protestants après la Saint-Barthélemy." *Bulletin de la Société de l'histoire du protestantisme français* 3 (1855): 274–78.

"Lettres de divers à la duchesse de Ferrare (1564–1572)." *Bulletin de la Société de l'histoire du protestantisme français* 30 (1881): 450–59.

Lettres patentes en forme d'edict sur la diligente inquisition & justice de ceux qui fond conventicules & assemblées illicites & punition des juges negligens de ce faire. Paris: Vincent Sertenas and Jean Bonfons, 1559/1560.

Lindsay, Robert O., and John New. *French Political Pamphlets, 1547–1648: A Catalogue of Major Collections in American Libraries.* Madison, 1969.

Luc, Gemin Théobule. *Pleinte et priere de la France à Dieu; avec le tombeau de monseigneur monsieur le duc de Guise.* Paris: Thomas Richard, 1563.

Maillard, Olivier. *L'histoire de la passion.* Paris: Jean Lambert, 1493.

"Un manifeste parisien contre le premier édit de tolérance." *Bulletin de la Société de l'histoire du protestantisme français* 17 (1868): 534–40.

Le manuel de la grand phrairie des bourgeoys et bourgeoyses de Paris. [Paris, 1534.]

[Marlorat, Augustin.] *Le nouveau testament. Avec annotations reveues et augmentées par*

M. Augustin Marlorat. Published with *Les pseaumes de David, avec la prose en marge & une oraison à la fin d'un chacun pseaume.* Lyons: Henry Hylaire and Loys Cloquemin, 1564.

[————.] *Remonstrance à la royne mere du roy par ceux qui sont persecutés pour la parole de Dieu. En laquelle ils rendent raison des principaux articles de la religion & qui sont aujourd'huy en dispute.* N.p., 1561.

Marot, Clément, and Theodore Beza. *Les cent et cinquante psaumes de David, mis en rythme françoise.* N.p.,1562. [BN, Réserve A. 6170]

————. *Les cent cinquante pseaumes de David, mis en rime françoise. Avec brieves et sainctes oraisons nouvellement adjoutées en la fin de chacun pseaume pour la consolation de l'Eglise, selon la substance du pseaume.* Paris: Martin le Jeune, pour Antoine Vincent, 1562. [BN, A. 10114]

————. *Les pseaumes de David, mis en rime françoise. Avec une oraison à la fin d'un chacun pseaume faite par M. Augustin Marlorat.* Paris: Pour Antoine Vincent, 1566. [BN, Réserve A. 6173]

————. *Les pseaumes mis en rime françoise.* Lyon: Jean de Tournes pour Antoine Vincent, 1563. [Houghton, TYP 515.63.210]

Martin, William, editor and translator. *La Saint-Barthélemy devant le Sénat de Venise. Relations des ambassadeurs Giovanni Michiel et Sigismondo Cavali.* Paris, 1872.

Mémoires des choses advenues sur le traicté de la pacification des troubles qui sont en France. Avec l'exhortation à la paix. N.p., 1568.

"Mémoires sur la cour de Henri II (1547–1559)." *Revue rétrospective*, ser. 1, vol 4 (1834): 5–33.

Merlin, Pierre. *Discours theologique de la tranquillité et vray repos de l'ame.* La Rochelle: Jean Brenovzet, 1604.

Morice, Dom Hyacinthe. *Mémoires pour servir de preuves à l'histoire ecclésiastique et civile de Bretagne.* Vol. 3: *Preuves.* Paris, 1746.

Mort prodigieuse de Gaspart de Coligny, qui fut admiral de France & de ses adherens les noms d'iceux; ensemble des plus signalez Huguenotz morts le jour Sainct Barthelemy, vingt quatriesme jour d'aoust 1572 & aultres jours subsequens. Paris: Germain Fourbet, n.d. [1572?].

Mouchy, Antoine de. *Response à quelque apologie que les heretiques ces jours passés ont mis en avant.* Paris: Claude Fremy, 1560.

L'ordinaire des Chrestiens. Paris: Antoine Vincent, 1495.

"Paris en 1596 vu par un Italien (Récit de Fr. Greg. d'Ierni)." *Bulletin de la Société de l'histoire de Paris et de l'Ile-de-France* 12 (1885): 164–70.

Paschal, Pierre de. *Journal de ce qui s'est passé en France durant l'année 1562, principalement dans Paris et à la cour.* Edited by Michel François. Paris, 1950.

Pasquier, Etienne. *Lettres historiques pour les années 1556–1594.* Edited by Dorothy Thickett. Geneva, 1966.

————. *Les oeuvres.* 2 vols. Amsterdam, 1723.

Passerat, Jean. *Hymne de la paix.* Paris: Gabriel Buon, 1563.

[Perrot, François.] *Perles d'eslite. Recueillies de l'infini thresor des cent cinquantes pseaumes de David. Traduit de l'italien en françois par l'auteur.* [Geneva:] Jean de Laon, 1577.

Petit, Guillaume. *La formation de l'homme et son excellence, et ce qu'il doibt accomplir pour avoir paradis.* Paris: Galliot du Pre, 1536.

Pithou, Nicolas. "Histoire ecclesiastique de l'eglise de la ville de Troyes, capitale du conté et pays de Champagne. Contenant sa renaissance et accroissance, les troubles, persecutions et autres choses remarcables advenues en la dicte eglise, jusques en l'an mil cinq cent quatre vingt et quatorze.'' (Unpublished manuscript: BN, Mss. Dupuy, 698.)

Platter, Thomas. *Description de Paris (1599)*. Translated by L. Sieber and M. Weibel. Paris, 1896.

Poncet, Maurice. *Remonstrance à la noblesse de France de l'utilité et repos que le roy apporte à son peuple, & de l'instruction qu'il doibt avoir pour le bien gouverner*. Paris: Michel Sonnius, 1572.

Quentin, Jean. *L'oreloge de devocion*. Paris, n.d. [ca. 1500].

Quick, John. *Synodicon in Gallia Reformata; or the Acts, Decisions, Decrees, and Canons of those Famous National Councils of the Reformed Churches in France*. 2 vols. London, 1692.

"La Réforme sous Henri II, 1557: Deux lettres de Th. de Bèze et des cantons évangéliques de Suisse, en faveur des réformés français, avec la réponse du roi et du cardinal de Guise." *Bulletin de la Société de l'histoire du protestantisme français* 17 (1868): 162–67.

Remond [Raemond], Florimond de. *L'histoire de la naissance, progrez, et decadence de l'heresie de ce siècle*. Rouen, 1629.

Remonstrances faictes au roy de France par messieurs de la court de Parlement de Paris, sur la publication de l'edict du moys de janvier. Cambrai: [Nicolas Lombard], 1561/1562.

Renouard, Philippe. *Documents sur les imprimeurs, libraires . . . ayant exercé à Paris de 1450 à 1600*. Paris, 1901.

Réponse de la plus saine partie de messieurs de Paris à l'advertissement à eux envoyé par Maistre René Benoist, docteur en theologie, sur le moyen d'appaiser les troubles advenus pour la croix & autres concernans la religion. Paris: Estienne des Champs, 1572.

Requeste presentée au roy et à la royne par le Triumvirat; avec la response faicte par monseigneur le Prince de Condé. N.p., 1562.

Reuss, Rodolphe. "Un nouveau récit de la Saint-Barthélemy par un bourgeois de Strasbourg." *Bulletin de la Société de l'histoire du protestantisme français* 22 (1873): 374–81.

Robin, Paschal, seigneur du Faux [pseud.]. *Monodie sur le trespas de tres vertueux prince François de Lorraine, duc de Guise*. Paris: Thomas Richard, 1563.

Sainctes, Claude de. *Declaration d'aucuns atheismes de la doctrine de Calvin & Beze contre les premiers fondemens de la chrestienté*. Paris: Claude Fremy, 1572.

———. *Discours sur les moyens anciennement practiquez par les princes catholiques contre les sectes*. Paris: Claude Fremy, 1563.

Sauval, Henri. *Histoire et recherches des antiquités de la ville de Paris*. 3 vols. Paris, 1724.

Sécousse, Denis-François, ed. *Mémoires de Condé, servant d'éclaircissement et de preuves à l'Histoire de M. de Thou*. 6 vols. London and Paris, 1743–1745.

"La situation politique et religieuse de la France en octobre 1564, d'après un catholique sincère. Lettres de Simon Renard à la duchesse de Parme." *Bulletin de la Société de l'histoire du protestantisme français* 36 (1887): 638–46.

Les songes drolatiques de Pantagruel, où sont contenus plusieurs figures de l'invention de maistre Francoys Rabelais. Paris: Richard Breton, 1565.

Sorbin, Arnaud. *Allegresse de la France pour l'heureuse victoire obtenue entre Coignac & Chasteauneuf, le 13. de mars 1569, contre les rebelles calvinistes*. Paris: Guillaume Chaudiere, 1569.

————. *Traitté d'oraison chrestienne, contenant la vraye disposition d'icelle, & decision des controverses de la priere intelligible & de la priere des saints, avec un formulaire d'oraisons, pour dire en toutes actions.* Paris: Guillaume Chaudiere, 1567.

————. *Le vray resveille-matin des calvinistes, et publicains françois; où est amplement discouru de l'auctorité des princes, & du devoir des sujets envers iceux.* Paris: Guillaume Chaudiere, 1576.

Stegmann, André. *Edits des guerres de religion.* Paris, 1979.

Stein, Henri. "Nouveaux documents sur les Estienne, imprimeurs parisiens (1517–1665)." *Mémoires de la Société de l'histoire de Paris et de l'Ile-de-France* 22 (1895): 249–95.

Suriano, Michele, and Marc Antonio Barbaro. *Dispatches of Michele Suriano and Marc Antonio Barbaro.* Publications of the Huguenot Society of London, vol. 6. Lymington, 1891.

Tarbé, P. *Recueil de poésies calvinistes (1550–1566).* 2d ed. Geneva, 1968.

Tavannes, Gaspard de Saulx de. *Mémoires.* Nouvelle collection des mémoires pour servir à l'histoire de France, ser. 1, vol. 8. Edited by Joseph-François Michaud and Jean-Joseph-François Poujoulat. Paris, 1838.

Thou, Jacques-Auguste de. *Histoire de Monsieur de Thou des choses arrivées en son temps.* Translated by P. Du Ryer. 3 vols. Paris, 1659.

————. *Histoire universelle depuis 1543 jusqu'en 1607.* Vols. 4–6. London, 1732–1734.

————. *Mémoires depuis 1553 jusqu'en 1601.* Nouvelle collection des mémoires pour servir à l'histoire de France, ser. 1, vol. 11. Edited by Joseph-François Michaud and Jean-Joseph-François Poujoulat. Paris, 1838.

Thou, Nicolas de. *Manière d'administrer les saincts sacremens de l'eglise, y faire prosne et benedictions, avec instructions convenables pour leur intelligence.* Paris: Jacques Kerver, 1580.

Le tocsain contre les massacreurs et auteurs des confusions en France. Rheims: Jean Martin, 1577.

Tommaseo, Niccolo. *Relations des ambassadeurs vénitiens sur les affaires de France au XVIe s.* 2 vols. Documents inédits sur l'histoire de France. Paris, 1838.

Toussain, Daniel. *L'exercice de l'âme fidèle; assavoir, prières et méditations pour le consoler en toutes sortes d'afflictions. Avec une préface consolatoire aux pauvres résidus de l'eglise d'Orléans, contenant un brief récit des afflictions qu'a souffert ladite eglise.* [Frankfurt, 1583.]

————. *Prieres et consolations prises de plusieurs passages de l'escriture & livres des anciens. Le tout accommodé à l'usage des vrais chrestiens & au temps auquel nous sommes.* Geneva: pour la veuve de Jean Durant, n.d. [preface dated 1566].

Van Langeraad, L. A., and A. Vidier. "Description de Paris par Arnold Van Buchel [1585–1586]." *Mémoires de la Société de l'histoire de Paris et de l'Ile-de-France* 26 (1899): 59–195.

Vigor, Simon. *Les actes de la conference tenue à Paris és moys de juillet et aoust 1566 entre deux docteurs de Sorbonne & deux ministres de Calvin.* Paris: Jean Foucher, 1568.

————. *Oraison funebre prononcée aux obseques de tres-haute, tres-puissante et tres-catholique princesse, ma dame Elizabeth de France, royne des Espagnes.* Paris: Claude Fremy, 1568.

————. *Sermons catholiques pour tous les jours de caresme & feriés de Pasques, faits en l'eglise S. Estienne du Mont à Paris.* Paris: Gabriel Buon, 1588.

————. *Sermons catholiques sur les dimanches et festes depuis l'octave de Pasques jusques à l'advent.* 2 vols. Paris: Nicolas du Fossé, 1597.

———. *Sermons et predications chrestiennes et catholiques du s. sacrement de l'autel, accommodées pour tous les jours des octaves de la feste Dieu*. Paris: Nicolas Chesneau, 1577.

Viret, Pierre. *Epistres aux fideles pour les instruire & les admonester & exhorter touchant leur office, & pour les consoler en leurs tribulations*. N.p.: Jean Rivery, 1559.

———. *L'Interim fait par dialogues*. Lyons, 1565.

Weiss, Charles, ed. *Papiers d'état du cardinal de Granvelle*. Vol. 7. Paris, 1849.

Weiss, Nathanaël, Charles Read, and Henri Bordier. "Poursuites et condemnations à Paris pour hérésie de 1564 à 1572, d'après les registres d'écrou de la Conciergerie du Palais." *Bulletin de la Société de l'histoire du protestantisme français* 50 (1901): 575–95 and 639–53.

———. "Huguenots emprisonnés à la Conciergerie du Palais à Paris en mars 1569 (Jean Bodin, Toussaint Berchet, Jacques Budé, etc.)." *Bulletin de la Société de l'histoire du protestantisme français* 72 (1923): 86–97.

———. "Une semaine de la Chambre ardente du Parlement de Paris sous Henri II." *Bulletin de la Société de l'histoire du protestantisme français* 48 (1899): 573–602.

Secondary Works

Babelon, Jean-Pierre. *Nouvelle histoire de Paris: Paris au XVIe siècle*. Paris, 1986.

Barnavi, Elie. *Le parti de Dieu. Etude sociale et politique des chefs de la Ligue parisienne, 1585–1594*. Louvain, 1980.

———, and Robert Descimon. *La sainte Ligue, le juge et la potence. L'assassinat du président Brisson (15 novembre 1591)*. Paris, 1985.

Bastard d'Estang, Jean-Denis-Léon de. *Vie de Jean de Ferrières, vidame de Chartres, seigneur de Maligny*. Auxerre, 1858.

Baulant, Micheline. "Prix et salaires à Paris au XVIe siècle. Source et résultats." *Annales, économies, sociétés, civilisations* 31 (1976): 954–95.

———. "Le salaire des ouvriers du bâtiment à Paris de 1400 à 1726." *Annales, économies, sociétés, civilisations* 26 (1971): 463–83.

———, and Meuvret, Jean. *Prix des céréales extraits de la mercuriale de Paris (1520–1698)*. Vol. 1: *(1520–1620)*. Paris, 1960.

Baumgartner, Frederic J. *Change and Continuity in the French Episcopate: The Bishops and the Wars of Religion, 1547–1610*. Durham, NC, and London, 1986.

———. *Henry II: King of France, 1547–1559*. Durham, NC, and London, 1988.

———. *Radical Revolutionaries: The Political Thought of the French Catholic League*. Geneva, 1976.

Beech, Beatrice. "Charlotte Guillard: A Sixteenth-Century Business Woman." *Renaissance Quarterly* 26 (1983): 345–67.

Benedict, Philip. "The Catholic Response to Protestantism: Church Activity and Popular Piety in Rouen, 1580–1600." In *Religion and the People*, ed. J. Obelkevich. Chapel Hill, 1979.

———. *Rouen during the Wars of Religion*. Cambridge, 1980.

———. "The Saint Bartholomew's Massacres in the Provinces." *Historical Journal* 21 (1978): 205–25.

Bercé, Yves-Marie. *Fête et révolte: Des mentalités populaires du XVIe au XVIIIe siècle*. Paris, 1976.

Bernus, Auguste. "Le ministre Antoine de Chandieu d'après son journal autographe inédit (1534–1591)." *Bulletin de la Société de l'histoire du protestantisme français* 37 (1888): 2–13, 57–69, 124–36, 169–91, 393–415, 449–63, 561–77, and 617–35.

Beutler, Corinne. "Etude de la consommation dans une communauté parisienne entre 1500 et 1640 d'après les registres de comptabilité de l'Hostel des Quinze-Vingts." *Paris et Ile-de-France* 26–27 (1975–1976): 73–122.

Bézard, Yvonne. *La vie rurale dans le sud de la région parisienne de 1450 à 1560*. Paris, 1929.

Biéler, André. *L'homme et la femme dans la morale calviniste*. Geneva, 1963.

Bimbinet-Privat, Michèle. "Le commerce de l'orfèvrerie à Paris sous les derniers Valois (1547–1589)." *Bulletin de la Société de l'histoire de Paris et de l'Ile-de-France* 110 (1983): 17–96.

Biraben, Jean-Noël. "Le mouvement natural de la population en France avant 1670. Présentation d'une enquête par sondage." *Population* (1982): 1099–1132.

Boinet, Amédée. *Les églises parisiennes*. Vol. 1: *Moyen âge et Renaissance*. Paris, 1958.

Bonnardot, François. "La Vierge de la rue des Juifs." *Bulletin de la Société de l'histoire de Paris et de l'Ile-de-France* (1875): 26–29.

Bonnet, Jules. "Jean Macard: Un an de ministère à Paris sous Henri II." *Bulletin de la Société de l'histoire du protestantisme français* 26 (1877): 52–61 and 97–112.

———. "L'Eglise réformée de Paris sous Henri II. Ministère de François Morel (1558–1559)." *Bulletin de la Société de l'histoire du protestantisme français* 27 (1878): 97–107 and 435–50; 28 (1879): 241–54.

———. "Les réfugiés de Montargis et l'exode de 1569." *Bulletin de la Société de l'histoire du protestantisme français* 38 (1889): 3–17 and 169–84.

Bordier, Henri. "La confrérie des pèlerins de Saint-Jacques et ses archives." *Mémoires de la Société de l'histoire de Paris et de l'Ile-de-France* 1 (1875): 186–228.

Bossy, John. *Christianity in the West, 1400–1700*. Oxford and New York, 1985.

———. "The Counter-Reformation and the People of Catholic Europe." *Past and Present*, no. 47 (1970): 51–70.

———. "The Mass as a Social Institution, 1200–1700." *Past and Present*, no. 100 (1983): 29–61.

———. "The Social History of Confession in the Age of the Reformation." *Transactions of the Royal Historical Society*, ser. 5, vol. 25 (1975): 21–38.

Bouillart, Jacques. *Histoire de l'abbaye royale de Saint Germain des Prez*. Paris, 1724.

Bourgeon, Jean-Louis. "Les légendes ont la vie dure: A propos de la Saint-Barthélemy et de quelques livres récents." *Revue d'histoire moderne et contemporaine* 34 (1987): 102–16.

———. "Pour une histoire, enfin, de la Saint-Barthélemy." *Revue historique* 282 (1989): 83–142.

———. "Une source sur la Saint-Barthélemy: l'"Histoire de Monsieur de Thou,' relue et décryptée." *Bulletin de la Société de l'histoire du protestantisme français* 134 (1988): 499–537.

Bourilly, Victor-Louis, and Nathanaël Weiss. "Jean Du Bellay, les Protestants, et la Sorbonne (1529–1535)." *Bulletin de la Société de l'histoire du protestantisme français* 52 (1903): 97–127 and 193–231; 53 (1904): 97–143.

Bouwsma, William J. *John Calvin: A Sixteenth-Century Portrait*. New York and Oxford, 1988.

Braudel, Fernand, and Ernest Labrousse, eds. *Histoire économique et sociale de la France*. Vol. 1: *De 1450 à 1660: L'état et la ville*. Vol. 2: *De 1450 à 1660: Paysannerie et croissance*. Paris, 1977.

Bremme, Hans Joachim. *Buchdrucker und Buchhändler zur Zeit der Glaubenskämpfe: Studien zur Genfer Druckgeschichte, 1565–1580*. Geneva, 1969.

Britnell, Jennifer. "Jean Bouchet's Prayers in French for the Laity." *Bibliothèque d'humanisme et renaissance* 38 (1976): 421–36.

Brochard, Louis. *Saint Gervais: Histoire de la paroisse.* Paris, 1950.

Bryant, Lawrence M. *The King and the City in the Parisian Royal Entry Ceremony: Politics, Ritual, and Art in the Renaissance.* Travaux d'humanisme et renaissance, vol. 216. Geneva, 1986.

Butterfield, Herbert. *Man on His Past: The Study of the History of Historical Scholarship.* Cambridge, 1955.

Carrière, Victor, ed. *Introduction aux études d'histoire ecclésiastique locale.* Vol. 3. Paris 1936.

Cauwès, Paul. "Les commencements du crédit public en France; les rentes sur l'Hôtel de Ville au XVIᵉ siècle." *Revue d'économie politique* 9 (1895): 97–123 and 825–65; 10 (1896): 411–79.

Cazelles, Raymond. *Nouvelle histoire de Paris: Paris de la fin du règne de Philippe Auguste à la mort de Charles V, 1223–1380.* Paris, 1972.

Chaix, Paul, Alain Dufour, and Gustave Moeckli. *Les livres imprimés à Genève de 1550 à 1600.* New ed. Geneva, 1966.

Champion, Pierre. *Paris au temps des guerres de religion. Fin du règne de Henri II; régence de Catherine de Médicis; Charles IX.* Paris, 1938.

"Charles IX a-t-il tiré sur les Huguenots?" *Bulletin de la Société de l'histoire du protestantisme français* 5 (1857): 332–40.

Charon-Parent, Annie. "Le monde de l'imprimerie humaniste: Paris." In *Histoire de l'édition française.* Vol. 1: *Le livre conquérant. Du moyen âge au milieu du XVIIᵉ siècle,* ed. Henri-Jean Martin, Roger Chartier, and Jean Pierre Vivet, pp. 237–53. Paris, 1982.

Chaunu, Pierre. *La mort à Paris. XVIᵉ, XVIIᵉ et XVIIIᵉ siècles.* Paris, 1978.

Chevalier, Bernard. *Les bonnes villes de France du XIVᵉ au XVIᵉ siècle.* Paris, 1982.

Chrisman, Miriam Usher. *Lay Culture, Learned Culture: Books and Social Change in Strasbourg, 1480–1599.* New Haven and London, 1982.

Coornaert, Emile. *Les corporations en France avant 1789.* Paris, 1941.

———. *Les Français et le commerce international à Anvers. Fin du XVᵉ, XVIᵉ siècle.* 2 vols. Paris, 1961.

Coquerel, Athanase. *Précis de l'histoire de l'Eglise réformée de Paris.* Vol. 1: *Première époque: 1512–1594.* Paris, 1862.

Crew, Phyllis Mack. *Calvinist Preaching and Iconoclasm in the Netherlands, 1544–1569.* Cambridge and New York, 1978.

Crouzet, Denis. *Les guerriers de Dieu. La violence au temps des troubles de religion.* 2 vols. Paris, 1990.

———. "Recherches sur les processions blanches, 1583–1584." *Histoire, économie et société* 1 (1982): 511–63.

———. "La représentation du temps à l'époque de la Ligue." *Revue historique* 270 (1984): 297–388.

Csecsy, Madeleine. "Poésie populaire de Paris avant la Saint-Barthélemy." *Bulletin de la Société de l'histoire du protestantisme français* 118 (1972): 697–709.

Dagens, Jean. *Bibliographie chronologigue de la littérature de spiritualité et de ses sources (1501–1610).* Paris, 1952.

Davies, Joan. "Persecution and Protestantism: Toulouse, 1562–1575." *Historical Journal* 22 (1979): 31–51.

Davis, Natalie Zemon. "Ghosts, Kin, and Progeny: Some Features of Family Life in Early Modern France." *Daedalus* 106 (1977): 87–114.

————. "The Sacred and the Body Social in Sixteenth-Century Lyon." *Past and Present*, no. 90 (1981): 40–70.

————. *Society and Culture in Early Modern France*. Stanford, 1976.

Delaborde, Jules. *Gaspard de Coligny, amiral de France*. 3 vols. Paris, 1882.

Delmas, André. "Le procès et la mort de Jacques Spifame." *Bibliothèque d'humanisme et renaissance* 5 (1944): 105–37.

Delteil, Frank. "Sondages à travers le Minutier central des Archives nationales." *Colloque l'amiral de Coligny et son temps. Paris, 1972*, pp. 527–48 and 633–36. Paris, 1974.

Delumeau, Jean. *Le catholicisme entre Luther et Voltaire*. Paris, 1971.

————. *La mort des pays de Cocagne. Comportements collectifs de la renaissance à l'âge classique*. Paris, 1976.

————. *La peur en Occident (XIVe–XVIIIe siècles)*. Paris, 1978.

————. *Rassurer et protéger. Le sentiment de sécurité dans l'Occident d'autrefois*. Paris, 1989.

Denière, Georges. *La juridiction consulaire de Paris: 1563–1792. Sa création, ses luttes, son administration intérieure, ses usages, et ses moeurs*. Paris, 1872.

Depauw, Jacques. "Pratique religieuse et pauvreté à la fin du XVIème siècle." *Histoire, économie et société* 7 (1988): 23–40.

Descimon, Robert. "La Ligue à Paris (1585–1594): une révision" and "La Ligue: des divergences fondamentales." *Annales, économies, sociétés, civilisations* 37 (1982): 72–111 and 122–28.

————. "Paris on the Eve of Saint Bartholomew: Taxation, Privilege, and Social Geography." In *Urban Society in Ancien Regime France*, edited by Philip Benedict, pp. 69–104. London, 1989.

————. *Qui étaient les Seize? Mythes et réalités de la Ligue parisienne (1585–1594)*. Paris, 1983.

————. "Structures d'un marché de draperie dans la Languedoc au milieu du XVIe siècle," *Annales, économies, sociétés, civilisations* 30 (1975): 1414–46.

————, and Jean Nagle. "Les quartiers de Paris du moyen âge au XVIIIe siècle: évolution d'un espace plurifonctionnel." *Annales, économies, sociétés, civilisations* 34 (1979): 956–83.

Desgraves, Louis. *Les Haultin, 1571–1623. L'imprimerie à La Rochelle*, vol. 2. Geneva, 1960.

Deyon, Pierre. "Sur certaines formes de la propagande religieuse au XVIe siècle." *Annales, économies, sociétés, civilisations* 36 (1981): 16–25.

Dhotel, Jean-Claude. *Les origines du catéchisme moderne d'après les premiers manuels imprimés en France*. Paris, 1967.

Diefendorf, Barbara B. "The Catholic League: Social Crisis or Apocalypse Now?" *French Historical Studies* 15 (1987): 332–44.

————. "Les divisions religieuses dans les familles parisiennes avant la Saint-Barthélemy." *Histoire, économie et société* 7 (1988): 55–78.

————. "Houses Divided: Religious Schism in Sixteenth-Century Parisian Families." In *Urban Life in the Renaissance*, edited by Susan Zimmerman and Ronald F. E. Weissman, pp. 80–99. Newark, DE, 1989.

————. *Paris City Councillors in the Sixteenth Century: The Politics of Patrimony*. Princeton, 1983.

————. "Prologue to a Massacre: Popular Unrest in Paris, 1557–1572." *American Historical Review* 90 (1985): 1067–91.

————. "Recent Literature on the Religious Conflicts in Sixteenth-Century France." *Religious Studies Review* 10 (1984): 362–67.

————. "Simon Vigor: A Radical Preacher in Sixteenth-Century Paris." *The Sixteenth Century Journal* 18 (1987): 399–410.

Dieterlen, H. *Le Synode général de Paris, 1559. Etude historique sur la naissance et le développement intérieur des Eglises réformées de France*. Paris, 1873.

Doucet, Roger. *Les bibliothèques parisiennes au XVIᵉ*. Paris, 1956.

————. "Les de Laran, marchands drapiers à Toulouse au XVIᵉ siècle." *Annales du Midi* 54–55 (1942–43): 42–87.

Douen, Orentin. *Clément Marot et le psautier huguenot. Etude historique, littéraire, musicale, et bibliographique*. 2 vols. Amsterdam, 1967; reprint of Paris edition, 1878.

Drouot, Henri. *Mayenne et la Bougogne, 1587–1596*. 2 vols. Paris, 1937.

Droz, Eugénie. "Antoine Vincent. La propagande protestante par le psautier." In *Aspects de la propagande religieuse*. Travaux d'humanisme et renaissance, vol. 28, pp. 276–93. Geneva, 1957.

————. "Bibles françaises après le Concile de Trente." *Journal of the Warburg and Courtauld Institutes* 28 (1965): 209–22.

————. *Chemins de l'hérésie: Textes et documents*. 4 vols. Geneva, 1974.

Dubief, Henri. "L'historiographie de la Saint-Barthélemy." In *Actes du colloque l'amiral de Coligny et son temps*, p. 351–66. Paris, 1974.

Dubois, Jacques, and Laure Beaumont-Maillet. *Sainte Geneviève de Paris. La vie; le culte; l'art*. Paris, 1982.

Duby, Georges, editor. *Histoire de la France urbaine*. 2 vols. Paris, 1981.

Durand, Yves, editor. *Hommage à Roland Mousnier. Clientèles et fidélités en Europe à l'époque moderne*. Paris, 1981.

Ehrmann, Jean. "Tableaux de massacres au XVIᵉ siècle." *Bulletin de la Société de l'histoire du protestantisme français* 118 (1972): 445–55.

Estèbe, Janine [Garrisson]. "Debate: The Rites of Violence: Religious Riot in Sixteenth-Century France. A Comment," and Natalie Zemon Davis, "Rejoinder." *Past and Present*, no. 67 (1975): 127–35.

————. *Tocsin pour un massacre. La saison des Saint-Barthélemy*. Paris, 1968.

Evenett, H. Outram. *The Cardinal of Lorraine and the Council of Trent: A Study in the Counter-Reformation*. Cambridge, 1930.

Fagniez, Gustave. *L'économie sociale de la France sous Henri IV (1589–1610)*. Geneva, 1975; reprint of Paris edition, 1897.

Farge, James K. *Orthodoxy and Reform in Early Reformation France: The Faculty of Theology of Paris, 1500–1543*. Studies in Medieval and Reformation Thought, vol. 32. Leiden, 1985.

Farr, James R. *Hands of Honor: Artisans and Their World in Dijon, 1550–1650*. Ithaca and London, 1988.

————. "Popular Religious Solidarity in Sixteenth-Century Dijon." *French Historical Studies* 14 (1985): 192–214.

Feret, Pierre. *La faculté de théologie de Paris et ses docteurs les plus célèbres. Epoque moderne*. 5 vols. Paris, 1900–1907. Vol. 1: *XVIᵉ siècle. Phases historiques* (1900). Vol. 2: *XVIᵉ siècle. Revue littéraire* (1901).

Forestié, Edouard. *Un capitaine gascon du XVIᵉ siècle: Corbeyran de Cardaillac-Sarlabous*. Paris, 1897.

Fosseyeux, Marcel. "L'assistance parisienne au milieu du XVIᵉ siècle." *Mémoires de la Société de l'histoire de Paris et de l'Ile-de-France* 43 (1916): 83–128.

————. "Processions et pèlerinages parisiens sous l'ancien régime." *Bulletin de la Société de l'histoire de Paris et de l'Ile-de-France* 71–72 (1944–1945): 19–43.

Franklin, Alfred. *Dictionnaire historique des arts, métiers, et professions exercés dans Paris depuis le treizième siècle*. Paris, 1906.

Fritsch-Pinaud, Laurence. "La vie paroissiale à Saint-Jacques-de-la-Boucherie au XVᵉ siècle." *Paris et Ile-de-France* 33 (1982): 7–99.

Galpern, A. N. *The Religions of the People in Sixteenth-Century Champagne*. Cambridge MA, 1976.

Garrisson[-Estèbe], Janine. *La Saint-Barthélemy*. Brussels, 1987.

———. "Le massacre de la Saint-Barthélemy: Qui est responsable?" *L'histoire*, no. 126 (1989): 50–55.

———. *Protestants du Midi, 1559–1598*. Toulouse, 1980.

———, and Bernhard Vogler. "La génèse d'une société protestante: Etude comparée de quelques registres consistoriaux languedociens et palatins vers 1600." *Annales, économies, sociétés, civilisations* 31 (1976): 362–88.

Gascon, Richard. "Economie et pauvreté au XVIᵉ et XVIIᵉ siècles. Lyon, ville exemplaire et prophétique." In *Etudes sur l'histoire de la pauvreté*, edited by Michel Mollat. 2 vols. Paris, 1974. 2:747–60.

———. *Grand commerce et vie urbaine au XVIᵉ siècle. Lyon et ses marchands (environs de 1520–environs de 1580)*. 2 vols. Paris, 1971.

Gennep, Arnold van. *Manuel de folklore français contemporain*. Vol. 1, parts 1–3. Paris, 1937–1949.

Geremek, Bronislaw. *Les marginaux parisiens aux XIVᵉ et XVᵉ siècles*. Paris, 1976.

———. *Le salariat dans l'artisanat parisien au XIIIᵉ-XVᵉ siècles. Etude sur le marché de la main-d'oeuvre au moyen âge*. Translated by Anna Posner and Christiane Klapisch-Zuber. Industrie et Artisanat, vol. 5. Paris, 1982.

Giese, Frank S. *Artus Desiré: Priest and Pamphleteer of the Sixteenth Century*. Chapel Hill, 1973.

Giesey, Ralph E. "Models of Rulership in French Royal Ceremonial." In *Rites of Power*, ed. Sean Wilentz, pp. 41–64. Philadelphia, 1985.

———. "The Presidents of Parlement at the Royal Funeral." *Sixteenth-Century Journal* 7 (1976): 25–34.

Gilmont, Jean-François. *Jean Crespin: Un éditeur réformé du XVIᵉ siècle*. Geneva, 1981.

Girard, Albert. *Le commerce français à Seville et Cadix au temps des Habsbourg: Contribution à l'étude du commerce étranger en Espagne au XVIᵉ et XVIIᵉ siècles*. Paris and Bordeaux, 1932.

Gourmelon, Roger. "Etude sur le rayonnement commercial des marchands drapiers parisiens au XVIᵉ siècle." *Bulletin philologique et historique (jusqu'à 1610) du Comité des travaux historiques et scientifiques (1961)* (1963): 265–75.

Graham, Victor E., and W. McAllister Johnson. *The Paris Entries of Charles IX and Elisabeth of Austria, 1571*. Toronto, 1974.

Greengrass, Mark. "The Anatomy of a Religious Revolt in Toulouse in May 1562." *Journal of Ecclesiastical History* 30–34 (1983): 367–91.

———. *The French Reformation*. Oxford and New York, 1987.

———. "Noble Affinities in Early Modern France: The Case of Henri I de Montmorency, Constable of France." *European History Quarterly* 16 (1986): 275–311.

Guggenheim, Ann H. "The Calvinist Notables of Nîmes during the Era of the Religious Wars." *Sixteenth-Century Journal* 3 (1972): 80–96.

Guiffrey, Jules-Joseph. "Les Gobelin, teinturiers en écarlate au faubourg Saint-Marcel." *Mémoires de la Société de l'histoire de Paris et de l'Ile-de-France* 31 (1904): 1–92.

———. "Les Mays de Notre-Dame de Paris, d'après un manuscrit conservé aux Archives nationales." *Mémoires de la Société de l'histoire de Paris et de l'Ile-de-France* 13 (1886): 289–316.

Haag, Eugène, and Emile Haag. *La France protestante, ou vies des Protestants français.* 1st ed., 10 vols. Paris, 1846–1854. Partial 2d ed., 6 vols. Paris, 1877–1888.

Halphen, Eugène. "Lettres de Jacques Faye à Monseigneur de Bellièvre." *Bulletin de la Société de l'histoire de Paris et de l'Ile-de-France* 8 (1881): 121–23.

Hamel, Charles. *Histoire de l'église Saint-Sulpice.* Paris, 1900.

Harding, Robert. *Anatomy of a Power Elite: The Provincial Governors of Early Modern France.* New Haven and London, 1978.

———. "The Mobilization of Confraternities against the Reformation in France." *Sixteenth-Century Journal* 11 (1980): 85–109.

———. "Revolution and Reform in the Holy League: Angers, Rennes, Nantes." *Journal of Modern History* 53 (1981): 379–416.

Hauser, Henri. *Etudes sur la réforme française.* Paris, 1909.

———. *Travailleurs et marchands dans l'ancienne France.* Paris, 1920.

Heller, Henry. "The Briçonnet Case Reconsidered." *Journal of Medieval and Renaissance Studies* 2 (1972): 223–58.

———. *The Conquest of Poverty: The Calvinist Revolt in Sixteenth Century France.* Studies in Medieval and Reformation Thought, vol. 35. Leiden, 1986.

———. "The Evangelicism of Lefevre d'Etaples: 1525." *Studies in the Renaissance* 19 (1972): 42–77.

———. "Famine, Revolt and Heresy at Meaux: 1521–1525." *Archiv für Reformations Geschichte* 68 (1977): 133–57.

Higman, Francis. *Censorship and the Sorbonne.* Geneva, 1979.

———. "Le levain de l'évangile." In *Histoire de l'édition française.* Vol. 1: *Le livre conquérant. Du moyen âge au milieu du XVIIe siècle,* edited by Henri-Jean Martin, Roger Chartier, and Jean-Pierre Vivet, pp. 305–23. Paris, 1982.

———. "Theology in French Religious Pamphlets from the Counter-Reformation." *Renaissance and Modern Studies* 23 (1979): 128–46.

Hirschauer, Charles. *La politique de St-Pie V en France (1566–1575).* Paris, 1922.

Hogu, Louis. *Jean de l'Espine, moraliste et théologien (1505?–1597).* Paris, 1913.

Imbart de la Tour, Pierre. *Les origines de la Réforme.* 4 vols. Geneva, 1978; reprint of Paris edition, 1905–1935.

Jacquart, Jean. *La crise rurale en Ile-de-France, 1550–1670.* Paris, 1974.

———. "Le poids démographique de Paris et de l'Ile-de-France au XVIe siècle." *Annales de démographie historique* (1980): 87–96.

Jacquet, Louis. *Les psaumes et le coeur de l'homme. Etude textuelle, littéraire et doctrinale.* Paris, 1975.

James, Mervyn. "Ritual, Drama and Social Body in the Late Medieval English Town." *Past and Present,* no. 98 (1983): 3–29.

Jeanneret, Michel. *Poésie et tradition biblique au XVIe siècle. Recherches stylistiques sur les paraphrases des psaumes de Marot à Malherbe.* Paris, 1969.

Jensen, De Lamar. *Diplomacy and Dogmatism: Bernardino de Mendoza and the Ligue.* Cambridge, MA, 1964.

Jouanna, Arlette. *Le devoir de révolte. La noblesse française et la gestation de l'état moderne, 1559–1661.* Paris, 1989.

Joutard, Philippe, Janine Estèbe, Elisabeth Labrousse and Jean Lecuir. *La Saint Barthélemy, ou les resonances d'un massacre.* Neufchatel, 1976.

Jungmann, Joseph Andreas. *The Mass of the Roman Rite: Its Origins and Development.* Translated by Francis A. Brunner. New ed. New York, 1961.

Kaiser, Colin. "Les cours souveraines au XVIe siècle: morale et Contre-Réforme." *Annales, économies, sociétés, civilisations* 37 (1982): 15–31.

Kantorowicz, Ernst H. *The King's Two Bodies: A Study in Medieval Political Theology.* Princeton, 1957.

Kelley, Donald R. *The Beginning of Ideology: Consciousness and Society in the French Reformation.* Cambridge, 1981.

———. *François Hotman: A Revolutionary's Ordeal.* Princeton, 1973.

Kingdon, Robert M. "The Business Activities of Printers Henri and François Estienne." *Aspects de la propagande religieuse.* Travaux d'humanisme et renaissance, vol. 28 pp. 258–75. Geneva, 1957.

———. *Geneva and the Coming of the Wars of Religion in France, 1555–1563.* Geneva, 1956.

———. *Geneva and the Consolidation of the French Protestant Movement, 1564–1572.* Geneva, 1967.

———. *Myths about the St. Bartholomew's Day Massacres, 1572–1576.* Cambridge, MA, and London, 1988.

———. "Patronage, Piety and Printing in the Sixteenth Century." In *A Festschrift for Frederick B. Artz*, edited by David H. Pinkney and Theodore Rapp, pp. 19–36. Durham, NC, 1964.

Klauser, Theodor. *A Short History of the Western Liturgy: An Account and Some Reflections.* Translated by John Halliburton. London, 1969.

Koenigsberger, Hans G. "The Organization of Revolutionary Parties in France and the Netherlands during the Sixteenth Century." In H. G. Koenigsberger, *Estates and Revolutions: Essays in Early Modern European History*, pp. 224–52. Ithaca, 1971.

Konnert, Mark. "Urban Values versus Religious Passion: Châlons-sur-Marne during the Wars of Religion." *Sixteenth Century Journal* 20 (1989): 387–406.

Labitte, Charles. *De la démocratie chez les prédicateurs de la Ligue.* Geneva, 1971; reprint of Paris edition, 1841.

Lamet, Maryélise Suffern. "French Protestants in a Position of Strength. The Early Years of the Reformation at Caen, 1558–1568." *Sixteenth Century Journal* 9 (1978): 35–56.

Lapeyre, Henri. *Une famille de marchands: Les Ruiz.* Paris and Bordeaux, 1955.

Larmour, Ronda. "A Merchant Guild of Sixteenth-Century France: The Grocers of Paris." *Economic History Review* 20 (1967): 467–81.

Lebeuf, l'Abbé. *Histoire de la ville et de tout le diocèse de Paris.* 7 vols. Vol. 6: *Rectifications et additions*, edited by Fernand Bournon (1890). Paris, 1883–1891.

Lebigre, Arlette. *La révolution des curés. Paris, 1588–1594.* Paris, 1980.

Le Bras, Gabriel. *Etudes de sociologie religieuse.* 2 vols. New York, 1975.

Lecaron, Frédéric. "Les origines de la municipalité parisienne." *Mémoires de la Société de l'histoire de Paris et de l'Ile-de-France* 7 (1880): 79–174, and 8 (1881): 161–272.

Le Maresquier, Yvonne-Hélène. "Une confrérie parisienne au XVe siècle: La Confrérie de la Conception Notre-Dame aux marchands et vendeurs de vins de Paris." *Actes du 109e Congrès national des sociétés savantes. Dijon, 1984. Section d'histoire médiévale et de philologie*, vol. 1: *L'encadrement religieux des fidèles au moyen-âge et jusqu'au concile de Trente*, pp. 539–56. Paris, 1985.

Lemaître, Nicole. "L'éducation de la foi dans les paroisses du XVIe siècle," *Actes du 109e Congrès national des sociétés savantes. Dijon, 1984. Section d'histoire médievale et de philologie*, vol. 1: *L'encadrement religieux des fidèles au moyen-âge et jusqu'au concile de Trente*, pp. 429–40. Paris, 1985.

Le Paulmier, Claude-Stephen. *Ambroise Paré, d'après de nouveaux documents découverts aux Archives nationales et des papiers de famille.* Paris, 1887.

――――. "Julien Le Paulmier, docteur-regent de la Faculté de médicine de Paris, médecin du roi Henri III et de François, duc d'Anjou." *Mémoires de la Société de l'histoire de Paris et de l'Ile-de-France* 21 (1894): 177–216.

Le Roy Ladurie, Emmanuel, *Les paysans de Languedoc.* Paris, 1966.

――――, and Pierre Couperie. "Les loyers parisiens (1400–1700)." *Annales, économies, sociétés, civilisations* 25 (1970).

Levasseur, Emile. *Histoire des classes ouvrières et de l'industrie en France avant 1789.* 2 vols. Paris, 1901.

Lombard-Jourdan, Anne. "La bataille de Saint-Denis (10 novembre 1567)." *Paris et Ile-de-France* 29 (1978): 7–54.

――――. "The Birth of a Parisian Legend: The Miracle of Le Lendit." In *Ritual, Religion and the Sacred: Selections from the Annales: Economies, Sociétés, Civilisations,* edited by Robert Forster and Orest Ranum, pp. 128–45. Baltimore and London, 1982. Translated from *Annales, économies, sociétés, civilisations* 28 (1973): 981–96.

――――. "Les confréries parisiennes des peintres." *Bulletin de la Société de l'histoire de Paris et de l'Ile-de-France* 107 (1980): 87–103.

Lottin, Alain. *Lille: Citadelle de la Contre-Réforme? (1598–1668).* Dunkerque, 1984.

McFarlane, I. D. *The Entry of Henry II into Paris, 16 June 1549.* Medieval and Renaissance Texts and Studies. Binghamton, NY, 1982.

Mandrou, Robert. "Les Protestants français réfugiés à Genève après la Saint-Berthélemy." *Revue suisse d'histoire/Schweizerische Zeitschrift für Geschichte* 16 (1966): 243–49.

Manning, Bernard Lord. *The People's Faith in the Time of Wyclif.* The Thirwell Essay, 1917. 2d ed. Totowa, NJ, 1975.

Mariéjol, Jean-H. *La Réforme, la Ligue, l'Edit de Nantes (1559–1598).* Paris, 1983. Originally published in 1904 as Vol. 6, pt. 1 of *L'histoire de France des origines à la Révolution,* edited by Ernest Lavisse.

Martin, A. Lynn. *Henri III and the Jesuit Politicians.* Geneva, 1973.

――――. *The Jesuit Mind: The Mentality of an Elite in Early Modern France.* Ithaca and New York, 1988.

――――. "Jesuits and the St. Bartholomew's Day Massacre." *Archivum historicum Societatis Iesu* 43 (1974): 103–32.

Martin, Henri-Jean. *Livre, pouvoirs et société à Paris au XVIIᵉ siècle (1598–1701).* 2 vols. Geneva, 1969.

Martin-Saint-Léon, Etienne. *Histoire des corporations de métiers depuis leurs origines jusqu'à leur suppression en 1791.* Geneva, 1976; reprint of Paris edition, 1922.

Martineau, Jean. *Les Halles de Paris des origines à 1789. Evolution matérielle, juridique et économique.* Paris, 1960.

Maugis, Edouard. *Histoire du Parlement de Paris.* Vol. 2. Paris, 1914.

"Médailles en l'honneur de la Saint-Barthélemy." *Bulletin de la Société de l'histoire du protestantisme français* 3 (1855): 137–143.

Mentzer, Raymond A. "Calvinist Propaganda and the Parlement of Toulouse." *Archiv für Reformationsgeschichte* 68 (1977): 268–82.

Meurgey, Jacques. *Histoire de la paroisse Saint-Jacques de la Boucherie.* Paris, 1926.

Meuvret, Jean. "Circulation monétaire et utilisation économiqiue de la monnaie dans la France du XVIᵉ et du XVIIᵉ siècle." In Jean Meuvret, *Etudes d'histoire économique: Recueil d'articles,* pp. 127–50. Paris, 1971.

Meylan, Henri. "En dépit des édit royaux." In *Mélanges d'histoire économique et sociale en hommage au professeur Antony Babel*. 2 vols. Vol. 1, pp. 291–302. Geneva, 1963.

Michaud, Claude. "Claude Marcel, prévôt des marchands et receveur du clergé de France (1520–1590)." In *Etudes européennes: Mélanges offerts à Victor L. Tapié*, pp. 295–320. Paris, 1973.

Michel, Marie-Edmée. "Recherches sur la 'compagnie française' au XVIᵉ siècle d'après le commerce vinicole parisien." *Paris et Ile-de-France* 15 (1964): 43–73.

Michon, Louis-Marie. "A propos des grèves d'imprimeurs de Paris et de Lyon au XVIᵉ siècle." *Paris et Ile-de-France* 3 (1951): 103–16.

Mieck, Ilja. "Die Bartholomäusnacht als Forschungsproblem: Kritische Bestandaufnahme und neue Aspekte." *Historische Zeitschrift* 216 (1973): 73–110.

———. "Die Bartholomäusnacht als sozialer Konflikt." In *Soziale und Politische Konflikte im Frankreich des Ancien Régime*, edited by Klaus Malettke. Vol. 2, pp. 1–23. Berlin, 1982.

———. *Die Entstehung des modernen Frankreich 1450–1610: Strukturen, Institutionen, Entwicklungen*. Stuttgart, 1982.

Mollat, Michel. *Le commerce maritime normand à la fin du moyen âge. Etude d'histoire économique et sociale*. Paris, 1952.

Monter, E. William. "The Consistory of Geneva, 1559–1569." *Bibliothèque d'humanisme et renaissance* 38 (1976): 467–84.

Montesquiou-Fezensac, Blaise de. *Le trésor de Saint-Denis: Inventaire de 1634*. Paris, 1973.

Moreau, G. "Un colporteur calviniste en 1563." *Bulletin de la Société de l'histoire du protestantisme français* (1972): 3–31.

Mousnier, Roland. *Les hiérarchies sociales de 1450 à nos jours*. Paris, 1969.

———. *Les institutions de France sous la monarchie absolue, 1598–1789*. Vol. 1: *Etat et société*. Paris, 1974.

Mousseaux, Maurice. *Aux sources françaises de la Réforme. Textes et faits. La Brie protestante*. Paris, 1968.

Mouton, Léo. "L'affaire de la croix de Gastine." *Bulletin de la Société de l'histoire de Paris et de l'Ile-de-France* 56 (1929): 102–13.

Neuschel, Kristen B. *Word of Honor. Interpreting Noble Culture in Sixteenth-Century France*. Ithaca, 1989.

Nicholls, David. "Social Change and Early Protestantism in France: Normandy, 1520–1562." *European Studies Review* 10 (1980): 279–308.

———. "The Social History of the French Reformation: Ideology, Confession and Culture." *Social History* 9 (1984): 25–43.

Nugent, Donald. *Ecumenism in the Age of the Reformation: The Colloguy of Poissy*. Cambridge, 1974.

Olivier-Martin, François. *L'organisation corporative de la France d'ancien régime*. Paris, 1938.

Omont, Henri. "Visite de Jeanne d'Albret à l'imprimerie de Robert Estienne." *Bulletin de la Société de l'histoire de Paris et de l'Ile-de-France* 24 (1897): 165–66.

Pallier, Denis. *Recherches sur l'imprimerie à Paris pendant la Ligue (1585–1594)*. Geneva, 1976.

———. "Les réponses catholiques." In *Histoire de l'édition française*. Vol. 1: *Le livre conquérant. Du moyen âge au milieu du XVIIᵉ siècle*, edited by Henri-Jean Martin, Roger Chartier, and Jean-Pierre Vivet, pp. 327–47. Paris, 1982.

Pannier, Jacques. "L'abbaye de Notre-Dame et les Budé, seigneurs d'Yerres aux XVIᵉ et XVIIᵉ siècles." *Bulletin de la Société de l'histoire du protestantisme français* 48 (1899): 386–88.

————. *L'eglise réformée de Paris sous Henri IV. Rapports de l'église et de l'etat; vie publique et privée des protestants.* Geneva, 1977.

Parent, Annie. *Les métiers du livre à Paris au XVIᵉ siècle (1535–1560).* Geneva, 1974.

Pasquier, Emile. *Un curé de Paris pendant les guerres de religion: René Benoist, le pape des Halles (1521–1608).* Geneva, 1970; reprint of Paris and Angers edition, 1913.

Pecquet, Marguerite. "Des compagnies de pénitents à la compagnie du Saint-Sacrement." *XVIIᵉ siècle* 69 (1965): 3–36.

Pétavel, Emmanuel. *La Bible en France, ou les traductions françaises des saintes écritures. Etude historique et littéraire.* Geneva, 1970; reprint of Paris edition, 1864.

Petit de Julleville, Louis. *Histoire du théâtre en France. Les mystères.* 2 vols. Paris, 1890.

Piaget, Arthur. *Notes sur le Livre des martyrs de Jean Crespin.* Neuchâtel, 1930.

Pidoux, Pierre. *Le psautier huguenot du XVIᵉ siècle.* 2 vols. Basel, 1962.

Pineaux, Jacques. *La poésie des Protestants de langue française du premier synode national jusqu'à la proclamation de l'édit de Nantes (1559–1598).* Paris, 1971.

Pinet, Edouard. *Le culte de Sainte Geneviève à travers les siècles. La compagnie des porteurs de la chasse de Sainte Geneviève, 1525–1902.* Paris, 1903.

Pommeray, Léon. *L'officialité archidiaconale de Paris aux XVᵉ–XVIᵉ siècles.* Paris, 1933.

Pradel, Charles. "Un marchand de Paris au XVIᵉ siècle (1560–1588)." *Mémoires de l'Académie des sciences, inscriptions et belles-lettres de Toulouse,* ser. 9, vol. 1 (Toulouse, 1888): 327–51; vol. 2 (1890): 390–427.

Pythian-Adams, Charles. "Ceremony and the Citizen: The Communal Year at Coventry, 1450–1550." In *Crisis and Order in English Towns, 1500–1700. Essays in Urban History,* edited by Peter Clark and Paul Slack, pp. 57–85. London, 1972.

Réau, Louis. *Iconographie de l'art chrétien.* Vol. 3, pt. 2: *Iconographie des saints.* Paris, 1958.

Reinburg, Virginia. "Popular Prayers in Late Medieval and Reformation France." Unpublished Ph.D. dissertation, Princeton University, 1985.

Renouard, Antoine-Auguste. *Annales de l'imprimerie des Estienne, ou histoire de la famille des Estienne et de ses éditions.* Paris, 1843.

Renouard, Philippe. "Quelques documents sur les Petit, libraires parisiens, et leur famille." *Bulletin de la Société de l'histoire de Paris et de l'Ile-de-France* 23 (1894): 133–53.

Rézeau, Pierre. *Répertoire d'incipit des prières françaises à la fin du moyen âge: Addenda et corrigenda aux répertoires de Sonet et Sinclair. Nouveaux incipit.* Geneva, 1986.

Richet, Denis. "Aspects socio-culturels des conflits religieux à Paris dans la seconde moitié du XVIᵉ siècle." *Annales, économies, sociétés, civilisations* 32 (1977): 764–89.

————. "Politique et religion: Les processions à Paris en 1589." In *La France d'ancien régime. Etudes réunies en l'honneur de Pierre Goubert,* edited by Alain Croix, Jean Jacquart, and François Lebrun. 2 vols. Vol. 2, pp. 623–32. Toulouse, 1984.

Robiquet, Paul. *Histoire municipale de Paris.* Vol. 1: *Depuis les origines jusqu'à l'avènement de Henri III.* Vol. 2: *Règne de Henri III.* Vol. 3: *Règne de Henri IV.* Paris, 1880–1904.

Roche, Daniel. *Le peuple de Paris.* Paris, 1981.

Roelker, Nancy Lyman. "Family, Faith, and *Fortuna*: the Châtillon Brothers in the French Reformation." In *Leaders of the Reformation,* edited by Richard L. DeMolen, pp. 247–77. London and Toronto, 1984.

————. *Queen of Navarre: Jeanne d'Albret, 1528–1572.* Cambridge, MA, 1968.

Romier, Lucien. *Catholiques et huguenots à la cour de Charles IX.* 3d ed. Paris, 1924.

————. *Les origines politiques des guerres de religion.* 2 vols. Paris, 1913–1914.

Roserot de Melin, Joseph. *Antonio Caracciolo. Evêque de Troyes (1515?–1570).* Paris, 1923.

Roulland, Léon. "La foire Saint-Germain sous les règnes de Charles IX, de Henri III et de Henri IV." *Mémoires de la Société de l'histoire de Paris et de l'Ile-de-France* 3 (1876): 192–218.

Ruble, Baron Alphonse de. "L'arrestation de Jean de Hans et le tumulte de Saint-Médard." *Bulletin de la Société de l'histoire de Paris et de l'Ile-de-France* 13 (1886): 85–94.

———. "François de Montmorency, gouverneur de Paris et de l'Ile-de-France." *Mémoires de la Société de l'histoire de Paris et de l'Ile-de-France* 6 (1897): 200–89.

"La Saint-Barthélemy, le martyrologie de Jean Crespin et Simon Goulart." *Divers aspects de la réforme aux XVIe et XVIIe siècles: Etudes et documents*, pp. 11–36. Paris, 1975.

Salmon, John H. M. "French Satire in the Late Sixteenth Century." *Sixteenth Century Journal* 3 (1975): 57–88.

———. "The Paris Sixteen, 1584–94: The Social Analysis of a Revolutionary Movement." *Journal of Modern History* 44 (1972): 540–76.

———. *Society in Crisis: France in the Sixteenth Century.* New York, 1975.

Schlaepfer, H.-L. "Laurent de Normandie." In *Aspects de la propagande religieuse.* Travaux d'humanisme et renaissance, vol. 28, pp. 176–230. Geneva, 1957.

Schnapper, Bernard. "Justice criminelle rendue par le Parlement de Paris sous le règne de François Ier." *Revue historique de droit français et étranger* 52 (1974): 252–84.

———. *Les rentes au XVIe siècle. Histoire d'un instrument de crédit.* Paris, 1957.

Schotel, Gilles-Denijs-Jacob. *Jean Diodati.* The Hague, 1844.

Schutz, Alexander Herman. *Vernacular Books in Parisian Private Libraries of the Sixteenth Century.* Geneva, 1955.

Scribner, Robert W. "Interpreting Religion in Early Modern Europe." *European Studies Review* 13 (1983): 90–105.

———. "Ritual and Popular Religion in Catholic Germany at the Time of the Reformation." *Journal of Ecclesiastical History* 35 (1984): 47–77.

Sealy, R. J. "The Palace Academy of Henry III." *Bibliothèque d' humanisme et renaissance* 40 (1978): 61–83.

Shimizu, Junko. *Conflict of Loyalties: Politics and Religion in the Career of Gaspard de Coligny, Admiral of France, 1519–1572.* Travaux d'humanisme et renaissance, vol. 114. Geneva, 1970.

Skinner, Quentin. *The Foundations of Modern Political Thought.* 2 vols. Cambridge, 1978.

Soman, Alfred. "La justice criminelle aux XVIe–XVIIe siècles: Le Parlement de Paris et les sièges subalternes." *107e Congrés national des sociétés savantes, Brest, 1982. Philologie et histoire jusqu'à 1610.* 2 vols. Paris, 1984. 1:15–52.

———, editor. *The Massacres of St. Bartholomew: Reappraisals and Documents.* The Hague, 1974.

———, and Elisabeth Labrousse. "Le registre consistorial de Coutras, 1582–1584." *Bulletin de la Société de l'histoire du protestantisme français* 126 (1980): 195–228.

Sonet, Jean. *Répertoire d'incipit de prières en ancien français.* Geneva, 1956.

Soulié, Marguerite. *L'inspiration biblique dans la poésie religieuse d'Agrippa d'Aubigné.* Paris, 1977.

———. "La Saint-Barthélemy et la réflexion sur le pouvoir." In *Culture et politique en France à l'époque de l'humanisme et de la Renaissance.* Turin, 1974.

Stein, Henri. "Une saisie de livres protestants en 1570." *Mélanges de bibliographie,* ser. 1. Paris, 1893, pp. 10–13. Reproduced in *L'imprimerie à La Rochelle.* Vol. 2: *Les Haultins,* ed. L. Desgraves. Travaux d'humanisme et renaissance, vol. 34.2. Geneva: Droz, 1960, pp. x–xii.

Stocker, Christopher. "The Calvinist Officers of Orléans, 1560–1572." *Proceedings of the Western Society for French Historical Studies* 6 (1978, published 1979): 21–33.

Strayer, Joseph. "France: The Holy Land, the Chosen People, and the Most Christian King." In *Action and Conviction in Early Modern Europe: Essays in Memory of E. H. Harbison*, ed. Theodore K. Rabb and Jerrold E. Seigel, pp. 3–16. Princeton, 1969.

Sutherland, Nicola Mary. "The Assassination of François duc de Guise, February 1563." *The Historical Journal* 24 (1981): 279–95.

———. *The Huguenot Struggle for Recognition*. New Haven, 1980.

———. *The Massacre of Saint Bartholomew and the European Conflict, 1559–1572*. London, 1973.

Sypher, G. Wylie. " 'Faisant ce qu'il leur vient à plaisir': The Image of Protestantism in French Catholic Polemic on the Eve of the Religious Wars." *Sixteenth Century Journal* 11 (1980): 59–84.

Taber, Linda. "Religious Dissent within the Parlement of Paris in the Mid-Sixteenth Century: A Reassessment." *French Historical Studies* 16 (1990): 684–99.

———. "Royal Policy and Religious Dissent within the Parlement of Paris, 1559–1563." Unpublished Ph.D. dissertation. Stanford University, 1982.

Theisen, Reinhold. *Mass Liturgy and the Council of Trent*. Collegeville, MN, 1965.

Thomson, David. *Renaissance Paris: Architecture and Growth, 1475–1600*. Berkeley and Los Angeles, 1984.

Trexler, Richard C. *Public Life in Renaissance Florence*. New York, 1980.

Valois, Noël. "Les essais de conciliation religieuse au début du règne de Charles IX." *Revue d'histoire de l'église de France* 31 (1945): 237–76.

Vaurigaud, Benjamin. *Essai sur l'histoire des Eglises réformées de Bretagne, 1535–1808*. 3 vols. Paris, 1870.

Venard, Marc. *L'église d'Avignon au XVIe siècle*. 4 vols. Lille, 1980.

"Les victimes de la Saint-Barthélemy à Paris: Essai d'une typographie et d'une nomenclature des massacrés d'après les documents contemporains." *Bulletin de la Société de l'histoire du protestantisme français* 9 (1860): 34–44.

Viénot, John. *Histoire de la Réforme française des origines à l'édit de Nantes*. 1926.

Vimont, Maurice. *Histoire de la rue Saint-Denis*. 3 vols. in 2. Paris, 1936.

Vondrus-Reissner, Jean-Georges. "Présence réelle et juridiction ecclésiastique dans le diocèse de Paris (fin XVème–1530)." *Histoire, économie et société* 7 (1988): 41–54.

Weiss, Nathanaël. "L'assemblée de la rue Saint-Jacques, 4–5 septembre 1557." *Bulletin de la Société de l'histoire du protestantisme français* 65 (1916): 195–235.

———. "Lieux d'assemblées huguenotes à Paris avant l'édit de Nantes (1524–1598)." *Bulletin de la Société de l'histoire du protestantisme français* 48 (1899): 138–71.

———. "Les protestants parisiens entre 1564 et 1569." *Bulletin de la Société de l'histoire du protestantisme français* 50 (1901): 617–38.

———. "La Réforme à Bourges au XVIe siècle." *Bulletin de la Société de l'histoire du protestantisme français* 53 (1904): 307–59.

Wildenstein, Georges. "L'imprimeur-libraire Richard Breton et son inventaire après décès, 1571." *Bibliothèque d'humanisme et renaissance* 21 (1959): 364–79.

Yardeni, Miriam. *La conscience nationale en France pendant les guerres de Religion (1559–1598)*. Louvain, 1971.

———. "Le mythe de Paris comme élément de propagande à l'époque de la Ligue." *Paris et Ile-de-France* 20 (1969): 49–63.

Yates, Frances Amelia. "Dramatic Religious Processions in Paris in the Late Sixteenth Century." *Annales musicologiques* 2 (1954): 215–70.

———. *The French Academies of the Sixteenth Century*. London, 1947.

INDEX